Advance Praise

Journalism is reinventing itself today; more profoundly, all citizens in contemporary democracies need to rediscover the rationale for why journalism should be supported and funded. India as the world's largest democracy is a hugely important site for such rethinking. This vital new book draws together a wide range of experts and thinkers to address the challenges of journalism in the digital age. I urge you to read it!

—**Dr Nick Couldry,**
Professor of Media, Communications and Social Theory,
London School of Economics and Political Science

It will inspire young journalists with the sense of mission that goes with empowering readers with the facts needed for informed decisions. Its emphasis on the Editor's role maintaining standards is timely. Industry's rush to monetise every page, channel and digital feed is perilously short-sighted. Journalism's currency, as the authors point out, rests on accuracy, deep reporting and a keen grasp of the storyteller's art. Marketing teams can't supply that; the Editor does.

—**Dr Brian Patrick O'Donoghue,**
Professor of Communication and Journalism,
University of Alaska Fairbanks, USA

It is a creative conversation between the practitioners and academia in journalism studies. Journalism teaching in India is obsessed with 'training' rather than a 'studies' orientation. Distinguished practitioners and academia rarely reflect on their experiences and introspect on their profession. Much has changed in journalism because of its nature, increasing competition and the rent-seeking behaviour. It would be an interesting book for students of journalism and communication studies.

—**Dr Biswajit Das,**
Director, Centre for Culture, Media and Governance,
Jamia Millia Islamia, New Delhi

Media in the digital age is rapidly evolving, but many of the challenges that journalism faces are not very well understood by the wider public or by media professionals themselves. Given the breadth of topics it seeks to address, this handbook will be a valuable addition to existing literature on the subject.

—Siddharth Varadarajan,
Founding Editor, *The Wire*, and former Editor, *The Hindu*

Any attempt at making sense of the proliferation of media in the digital era is welcome. Print still retains its primacy despite social media and other offshoots. Principles of good journalism remain the same: integrity and competence.

—S. Nihal Singh,
former Editor,
The Statesman and *The Indian Express*, and
Distinguished Columnist

A HANDBOOK OF
JOURNALISM

A HANDBOOK OF
JOURNALISM

MEDIA IN THE
INFORMATION AGE

EDITED BY

V. ESHWAR ANAND • K. JAYANTHI

SAGE

Los Angeles | London | New Delhi
Singapore | Washington DC | Melbourne

First published in 2018 by

SAGE Publications India Pvt Ltd
B1/I-1 Mohan Cooperative Industrial Area
Mathura Road, New Delhi 110 044, India
www.sagepub.in

SAGE Publications Inc
2455 Teller Road
Thousand Oaks, California 91320, USA

SAGE Publications Ltd
1 Oliver's Yard, 55 City Road
London EC1Y 1SP, United Kingdom

SAGE Publications Asia-Pacific Pte Ltd
3 Church Street
#10-04 Samsung Hub
Singapore 049483

Published by Vivek Mehra for SAGE Publications India Pvt Ltd, typeset in 10/12 pts Berkeley by Zaza Eunice, Hosur, Tamil Nadu, India and printed at Chaman Enterprises, New Delhi.

Library of Congress Cataloging-in-Publication Data

Names: Anand, V. Eshwar (Ventrapragada Eshwar), editor. | Jayanthi, K.
  (Krishnamachary), editor.
Title: A handbook of journalism: media in the information age/edited by
  V. Eshwar Anand and K. Jayanthi.
Description: New Delhi, India; Thousand Oaks, California: SAGE Publications
  India Pvt. Ltd., 2018. | Includes bibliographical references and index.
Identifiers: LCCN 2018000711 | ISBN 9789352806287 (print (hb)) | ISBN
  9789352806294 (e-pub) | ISBN 9789352806300 (e-book)
Subjects: LCSH: Journalism. | Mass media.
Classification: LCC PN4731 .H285 2018 | DDC 070.4—dc23 LC record available at https://lccn.loc.
gov/2018000711

ISBN: 978-93-528-0628-7 (HB)

SAGE Team: Rajesh Dey, Alekha Chandra Jena, Megha Dabral and Ritu Chopra

To the craft of journalism which has inspired generations of Editors

Thank you for choosing a SAGE product!
If you have any comment, observation or feedback,
I would like to personally hear from you.

Please write to me at **contactceo@sagepub.in**

Vivek Mehra, Managing Director and CEO, SAGE India.

Bulk Sales

SAGE India offers special discounts
for purchase of books in bulk.
We also make available special imprints
and excerpts from our books on demand.

For orders and enquiries, write to us at

Marketing Department
SAGE Publications India Pvt Ltd
B1/I-1, Mohan Cooperative Industrial Area
Mathura Road, Post Bag 7
New Delhi 110044, India

E-mail us at **marketing@sagepub.in**

Get to know more about SAGE

Be invited to SAGE events, get on our mailing list.
Write today to **marketing@sagepub.in**

This book is also available as an e-book.

Contents

List of Tables

List of Figures

List of Abbreviations

AAAI	Advertising Agencies Association of India
ABC	Audit Bureau of Circulations
ADAG	Anil Dhirubhai Ambani Group
ADR	Association for Democratic Reforms
AICTE	All India Council for Technical Education
AIIMS	All India Institute of Medical Sciences
ATM	automated teller machine
BARC	Broadcast Audience Research Council
BBC	British Broadcasting Corporation
BCCL	Bennett Coleman and Co. Ltd
BJP	Bharatiya Janata Party
BRGF	Backward Region Grant Fund
CAG	Comptroller and Auditor General of India
CBI	Central Bureau of Investigation
CEE	Centre for Environmental Education
CPIL	Centre for Public Interest Litigation
CSIR	Council of Scientific and Industrial Research
DAS	Digital Addressable Systems
DMK	Dravida Munnetra Kazhagam
DNA	Daily News and Analysis
DRDO	Defence Research and Development Organisation
DVR	digital video recorder
D2H	Direct to Home
ECI	Election Commission of India
EIA	environmental impact assessment
ETV	Eenadu Television
FDI	foreign direct investment
FICCI	Federation of Indian Chamber of Commerce and Industry
FTA	free-to-air
GAP	Ganga Action Plan
GDP	gross domestic product

GECs	general entertainment channels
GIPE	Gokhale Institute of Politics and Economics
GST	Goods and Services Tax
GSTN	GST Network
HOPCOMS	Horticultural Producers' Cooperative Marketing and Processing Society
HR	human resource
HT	*Hindustan Times*
IBF	Indian Broadcasting Federation
ICICI	Industrial Credit and Investment Corporation of India
ICT	information and communication technology
IFJ	International Federation of Journalists
IFSC	Indian Financial System Code
IIT	Indian Institute of Technology
IPL	Indian Premier League
ISA	Indian Society of Advertisers
JSTOR	Journal Storage
KBK	Koraput-Bolangir-Kalahandi
KPMG	Klynveld Peat Marwick Goerdeler
LCO	local cable operator
LED	light-emitting diode
MGNREGA	Mahatma Gandhi National Rural Employment Guarantee Act
MISA	Maintenance of Internal Security Act
MLA	Member of Legislative Assembly
MP	Member of Parliament
MPLADS	MP's Local Area Development Scheme
MSO	multisystem operator
MSP	minimum support price
MSW	municipal solid waste
NBA	National Broadcasting Authority
NBSA	News Broadcasting Standards Authority
NEW	National Election Watch
NGOs	non-governmental organisations
NITI	National Institution for Transforming India
NRHM	National Rural Health Mission
NRI	non-resident Indian
OTP	one-time password
PCI	Press Council of India
PCK	Plantation Corporation of Kerala
PMC	Pune Municipal Corporation
PMJDY	Pradhan Mantri Jan Dhan Yojana

PPP	public–private partnership
PURA	Provision of Urban Amenities in Rural Areas
RFID	radio-frequency identification
RO	reverse osmosis
RPA	Representation of the People Act
RTI	Right to Information
R&R	rehabilitation and resettlement
SAGY	Sansad Adarsh Gram Yojana
SBA	Swachh Bharat Abhiyan
SCWMS	Symbiosis Centre for Waste Management and Sustainability
SIA	social impact assessment
SIMC	Symbiosis Institute of Media and Communication
SIOM	Symbiosis Institute of Operations Management
SIU	Symbiosis International University
SPV	special purpose vehicle
SRB	sex ratio at birth
TAM	television audience measurement
TRAI	Telecom Regulatory Authority of India
TRPs	television rating points
UGC	University Grants Commission
ULB	urban local bodies
UNI	United News of India
UPA	United Progressive Alliance
UPI	United Payments Interface
USSD	Unstructured Supplementary Service Data
VOD	video on demand
WAT	Writing Ability Test
YMCA	Young Men's Christian Association

Foreword

Journalism in India has been transformed in the past two decades by a combination of political, economic, technological and cultural changes, triggered by processes associated with globalisation. Television news has grown exponentially in this period, from drab and dull limited bulletins on state monopoly Doordarshan until 1991, to more than 400 dedicated news channels today.

This makes India the world's most competitive news arena, catering to a huge national and regional audience, as well as to the vast Indian diaspora around the world. Indian newspapers—especially the vernacular variety—have also expanded massively at a time when newspapers elsewhere are losing circulation or even closing down.

Following the privatisation and deregulation of the media and communication sector, news media have become a commodity to be bought and sold in an increasingly crowded market. The trend towards a concentration of media power is evident across the country, as media ownership rules are relaxed and many non-media groups invest in media, expanding their presence across various segments of the media and entertainment world, including news. The takeover of news providers by huge media corporations, whose primary interest is in the entertainment business, has altered news agendas and priorities.

Celebrities from the world of entertainment and sport receive prominent coverage on news bulletins and in newspapers. Digitisation and the resultant availability of content from all around the world have contributed to a fragmentation of the audience into separate linguistic, class, age and gender categories, forcing news providers to produce content which will translate into ratings and circulation growth and acquire new programming to ensure a regular stream of advertising revenue.

There is a tendency to make news entertaining, which often means drawing on Bollywood or Bollywoodised content. A flashier presentation style has been routinised in news studios, where often 'fake' debates are more akin to shouting matches than reasoned argumentation. Revenue-delivering programmes—sports, entertainment and lifestyle—have increased, while sober news and analysis have shown a corresponding decline. The popularisation of celebrity-driven and sensationalist news may have made it a more marketable commodity and democratised communication, but this has also lowered the standards of public discourse, which appears to stoop to the lowest common denominator.

With a few honourable exceptions, much of television news has almost negligible reporting on developmental issues. This is a sad commentary on the state of journalism in a country where, despite impressive economic performance, nearly 300 million people live in extreme poverty. Most major media networks in India do not have dedicated rural affairs Editors or even industrial or agricultural correspondents. As a result, coverage rarely translates into ratings to attract advertisers, on whose support the edifice of a commodified news system is ultimately based.

Such trends in the Indian news media landscape have significant and negative implications for the quality of journalism and more broadly for India's vigorous democracy, in which media have traditionally played a significant role. However, excessive marketisation and the changing nature of the profession of journalism itself in the age of user-generated content, 'fake news' and primacy of public relations have contributed to an ethical deficiency, most notably visible in such phenomenon as 'paid' news and partisan news—in terms of unabashed affiliation with political parties or corporate interests, undermining professional standards.

Despite the extraordinary growth of news media in India, it remains perhaps the only major nation without any significant presence within the global news space. With dozens of round-the-clock dedicated news channels—many of these in the English language, the language of global communication of commerce—and a strong tradition of English-language journalism, India should have been an early adopter for global journalism. However, DD News is one of the few major state news networks not available in global media centres such as London where I live and work: this at a time when global television news in English has expanded to include channels from countries where English is not widely used, including France, Germany, Turkey, China, Japan and Iran. Although a committee headed by Sam Pitroda recommended in 2014 that Prasar Bharati, India's public sector broadcaster, should have a 'global outreach', nothing seems to have been done to promote Indian journalism abroad.

Will the Internet succeed where television has failed? The growth of the Internet in India has been remarkable: it took a decade for the number of Internet users to grow from 10 million to 100 million, but just three years to double that number to 200 million. Compared with international standards, Internet penetration remains low—by 2017, below 40 per cent of India's 1.2 billion population.

However, in terms of the absolute number of users, India has the world's largest 'open' Internet, second only to China. According to industry estimates, the number of Internet users in India is expected to cross 900 million by 2021, increasingly driven by wireless connections. With 3G phones becoming affordable and 4G accessible, this will accelerate, paralleled with the affordability of other digital delivery mechanisms as telecom companies achieve economies of scale, and more and more Internet users will be mobile-only subscribers using Internet-enabled devices.

Such connectivity will ensure that Indian journalism will go global, using various digital platforms. As elsewhere, young people in India are the biggest consumers, as well as producers, of mobile digital content. Already, online English-language newspapers from India, notably the *Times of India* (the world's largest-circulated English-language quality daily), are widely accessed across the world, while such portals as the *Wire* and *Scroll.in* have created a niche for a globalised audience.

Against this background, this book is a very valuable contribution to understanding journalism practices and policies in India. The Editors V. Eshwar Anand and K. Jayanthi, have been able to gather a group of eminent Editors, journalism scholars and practitioners, as well as legal luminaries, such as Soli Sorabjee and former Chief Election Commissioner S.Y. Quraishi, to give a comprehensive overview of the main problems facing journalism in the world's largest democracy.

The contributors provide professional and pedagogical insights into issues in journalism in India, including media ethics and law, challenges and opportunities offered by digitisation, political interference in journalism and the shrinking role of Editors, as marketing managers set the news agenda.

As India marks its 70th year of Independence, such a volume is a welcome addition to the literature on journalism in one of the world's most complex, multilingual, multilayered and multimedia systems.

Dr Daya Kishan Thussu
Professor of International Communication and
Co-Director of India Media Centre
University of Westminster, London

Preface

When there is already a large body of work on specific areas of journalism and the mass media, where does another work on the subject fit in? How can it make a difference to the understanding of a very important activity, performed purely in the public interest, in a large democracy? Will it help reinforce the need for continuity of journalistic practice, which is facing challenges on various fronts? These and several such thoughts kept popping up time and again at different stages of the project.

Initially, the plan was to put together a collection of essays on various aspects of editing and reporting. Considering the importance of these two functions in maintaining the credibility of the news industry, and in order to make the book more relevant and give it an identity of its own in the realm of journalistic essays, it was decided to open the anthology with the experiences of Editors who edited mainstream English newspapers at crucial periods of independent India's political, economic and social transformation. The Editor's role and the Editor–publisher relationship brought out in these first-person narratives, it seems, have provided the right setting for the broader canvas.

Digital technology has created a huge opportunity for people who wanted to express themselves but never found the right platform to share their thoughts and views. It has made journalists of everybody with access to the digital format. Although the print media has been quick to provide serious bloggers column space, abundant online writing has its flip side—unregulated, this media platform has tended to become a veritable storehouse of biased and unauthentic news. This huge consumption of bandwidth space for sharing information has made the traditional media's role daunting. Journalists have been forced to re-establish the core mandate of journalism to tell the story using new techniques and tools, striving by the hour to make their story the choice of the algorithm's viral news feed. The idea of introducing the section on 'Digital Media' was an outcome of this paradox of plenty.

The times are such that the media have to strive very hard to maintain two of the core values of journalism: truth and impartiality. The reader has a right to know, a right to be informed about governance and the decision-making process. It is the duty of the media to inform, give column and byte space to multiple voices and broaden the discourse on matters that concern the people in order to help them make informed choices. The essay on freedom of expression seeks to reinforce this critical function of the media in a democracy.

Paid news, sting operations to obtain a story and advertisements as news have raised concerns about violation of journalistic ethics. News coverage during elections can be tricky as it is the season for publicity push. A reporter who does not succumb to pressure can be said to have maintained his/her professional pride. The section on 'Media Laws' is relevant in this context.

The off-the-cuff journalism in digital, broadcast and even in the print media makes the need to gain expertise in various areas of journalistic writing important: More so, if one is going to comment on a piece of news. It was decided to include various areas that need specialised coverage to help journalism students understand the range and scope of journalistic writing.

The craft of 'Editing and Reporting', the original seed for the book, was naturally overtaken by expertise. Good copyediting can lift the worth of a news item and the writing. This section has included instances of humorous pitfalls at the desk. Reporting can be an adventurous experience for those who go out in the field, maintain sources and stay updated. This aspect has been underlined in a matter-of-fact style.

This collection of articles re-emphasises the core responsibility of journalism in a digitised and globalised world village.

Acknowledgements

As co-editors, we have drawn inspiration from several people who have been in the business of news. We were clear that a book consisting of articles by a diverse set of people—Editors, practising journalists, academics, experts and research scholars—would be appropriate for journalism education and the profession itself.

However, when we drew up a list of writers whom we could approach, we grew nervous. When we approached some senior Editors to request their contributions for the book, these misgivings vanished. Dr V. Eshwar Anand met Dr Dileep Padgaonkar and requested him personally to contribute an article for the book project. Dr Padgaonkar not only readily agreed to write, he even offered to read the entire manuscript when it was ready. That took a load off our minds. He kept his promise. But sadly, his untimely demise on 25 November 2016 took away a well-wisher.

The Editors are grateful to Dr Daya Kishan Thussu, Professor of International Communication, University of Westminster, London, for writing the Foreword. His gesture shows his unflinching commitment to promoting research and excellence in journalism.

Suggestions came from friends in academia to include articles pertaining to several other aspects of journalism. We thank them for their encouragement.

Special thanks to Dr Neela Rayavarapu for formatting the manuscript, giving valuable suggestions on the content and, more importantly, serving delicious meals when we were racing against time to complete the work.

V. Sundar Raju was a consistent source of support and encouragement right from the inception of the project. Sunandiny Raghavan's gentle prodding was of immense help in meeting the deadline.

We thank all the contributors for believing in us.

It is unfortunate that Dr V. Eshwar Anand passed away on 30 December 30 2017, before the manuscript saw light of day. With single-minded determination, he had approached several people in the field of media and communication to participate in the project and 'write a chapter'. It was his organisational and interpersonal skills that were responsible for the immediate response from eminent Editors, the former Attorney General of India Soli J. Sorabjee, the former Election Commissioner of India S.Y. Quraishi, and Eshwar Anand's colleagues in the media and academia.

Introduction:
New Challenges, New Roles

V. Eshwar Anand

The advent of digital media has changed the way readers consume news, and the control of news content by market forces has changed the way column and screen space is used. With the critical function of the media becoming increasingly compromised, there is an urgent need for responsible journalism.

Journalism's vital function in a democracy needs no elaboration. It is the builder of public opinion, which in its turn helps influence the decision-making process at the top level. It is called the Fourth Estate for the simple reason that it stands next to the three magnificent pillars of democracy—the legislature, the executive and the judiciary. In modern parlance, it is called the Second Government in view of its unique and stupendous role in shaping the destiny of the country. Journalism has been passing through a period of stress and strain. It is buffeted by new challenges that demand a clear understanding of the current media environment as also the essential functions of journalism in the technology-driven age. It is facing a three-pronged challenge—the proliferation of social media, the heightened commercial competition in the mainstream media and the emergence of the media as a powerful actor in public policy and governance. A fourth facet can be added to these—the functioning of the media in a celebrity-driven, entertainment mode.

Indisputably, the quartet of factors calls for fresh thinking about the teaching and practice of journalism. It must take into account the need for both a sound grounding in subjects such as political science, economics and sociology as well as some degree of specialisation in disciplines of one's choice. The former will provide the intellectual wherewithal required to grasp the trends and processes that shape individuals and events. These will include the interplay of political, economic, social, cultural and technological forces in India and abroad.

At no point of time in independent India has the need for informed journalism been as crucial as it is today. The advent of digital media has changed the way readers consume news, and the control of news content by market forces has changed the way column and screen space is used. With the critical function of the media becoming increasingly compromised, there is an urgent need for responsible journalism. Clearly, serious journalism has become the worst casualty today because of a plethora of 24×7 television channels and online news sources competing to break news and give opinion in a tearing hurry.

Though the role of the press in the freedom struggle and after Independence is beyond the scope of this project, this writer would like to place on record the effective use of the print media by illustrious national leaders such as Bal Gangadhar Tilak, Gopal Krishna Gokhale, Mahatma Gandhi and Jawaharlal Nehru. They not only created tremendous public awareness about the freedom movement but also championed the cause of a casteless society and a society free from superstition, exploitation and communalism. They stood for progressive journalism and demonstrated their indomitable courage and spirit of sacrifice in fighting against the injustices in the system.

Newspapers have played an important role in protecting the fundamental rights and civil liberties of the people and safeguarding their interests against state oppression and arbitrariness. They have also been upholding moral values, institutional integrity and probity and rectitude in governance. Their contribution to the movement for social advocacy is no less important. In tune with the constitutional goal for a welfare state, the print media has covered extensively the plight of the marginalised and weaker sections of society and brought their problems, sufferings and difficulties to the attention of the government—at the Centre and in the states—for redressal. Their contribution to sensitising the people on important issues confronting the country and, more important, stressing the need for speedy dispensation of justice by the courts of law, especially the Supreme Court of India, is no less. Surely, over the last 70 years since Independence, the print media has been playing a dominant role in safeguarding the fundamental rights and civil liberties of the citizens. In all fairness, in addition to the print medium, the Supreme Court and High Courts, too, have emerged as strong pillars of liberty, equality and justice and effective watchdogs of the Constitution.

Editor Short-circuited

Undoubtedly, it is market forces and revenues that seem to decide the running of a newspaper. One cannot overlook the influence and role of corporatisation in the print media. Big newspapers defend it on the grounds that they have to keep pace with the changing times. A publication will simply lose the race if it does not see the ground realities. The flip side is the seeming dilution of ethical standards and professional integrity.

The marginalisation of the Editor is cause for major concern. If market teams dictate terms to the Editor even on matters pertaining to treatment and presentation of news, why is there an Editor and what is his/her relevance and role in journalism? Today, the Editor seems to have lost the authority to decide how much space should be given to news, say, on Page 1, on any given day. The advertisement manager or the marketing manager decides the page layout. There is no denying that advertisements are bread and butter to a newspaper.

Disturbingly, even on matters pertaining to appointments to editorial positions, the Editor has no say. In many newspapers, he/she has to merely communicate the vacancy position(s) in the editorial department to the Human Resource (HR) Manager or, in some cases, the Marketing Manager from time to time. All requests for appointments are directed to HR and/or Marketing Managers for appropriate follow-up. Interviews for senior editorial or reporting positions are conducted by HR and Marketing Managers and not the Editor anymore. Interestingly, in tune with the management's policy thrust on markets, the designation of the *Times of India*'s Editors carries the 'market' tag—Editor (Bengaluru Market), Editor (Pune Market), etc.

This writer came in for a shock when the Resident Editor of a prominent national newspaper in Mumbai told him over phone that he was not the deciding authority for internships and that I would have to get in touch with the newspaper's HR Manager based in New Delhi! Of course, it is a different matter that the Delhi HR boss was convinced of our student's CV and offered internship to him in the Mumbai office. The bottom line is clear: The Editor has no say even in the matter of internship, leave alone appointments to various positions. In other words, even if the Editor is convinced of a person's academic credentials, competence and experience, he cannot offer a position to an applicant unless the HR boss is pleased or deems him/her fit. This also speaks volumes about the centralisation of authority in national newspapers having multiple editions. The regional editions merely function as branch offices with the bosses sitting in Delhi and taking decisions.

There was an interesting development in the *Tribune*, Chandigarh, a few years ago. The Editor had always been the custodian of the files and records of the editorial staff, including those of senior Editors. This is the way it should be and journalists do feel comfortable if the Editor directly supervises their work and day-to-day functioning. However, for some reason, the Editor-in-Chief one day directed his secretary to shift all files of the editorial staff to the HR Manager as he had 'no business' with them. This reflects the changing mindset of the new-age Editors. These are hard realities the journalists will have to cope with.

Political interference in the working of newspapers is common knowledge. The manner in which independent and conscientious Editors were treated by the Indira Gandhi government, especially during the 19 months of the Emergency, is well known. Newspapers such as the *Indian Express* and the *Statesman* stood firm and refused to buckle under political pressure. In protest against press censorship, Editors left editorial columns blank whenever the censors objected to a news item or applied their scissors on it. One is often reminded of veteran Bharatiya Janata Party (BJP) leader L.K. Advani's comment, 'When they were asked to bend, they crawled.' Editors who refused to kowtow to the political establishment were peremptorily dismissed. The shabby treatment meted out to media mogul, Ramnath Goenka, by Indira Gandhi and Rajiv Gandhi for opposing the Congress government's authoritarian rule and policies is well known.

This book seeks to inform aspiring journalists about the role played by some eminent Editors in modern India in shaping policy decisions by voicing their strong views on important issues in their hard-hitting editorials; instruct them in reporting and writing without compromising the values of credibility, fair play and journalistic ethics; and explain the invaluable craft of subediting. It is time the Editor's pre-eminent position was restored in the newspaper organisation. If a newspaper should uphold highest professional standards, the Editor has to reassert his primary position in the hierarchy. Eminent Editors such as the late B.G. Verghese, the late Dileep Padgaonkar, Raj Chengappa, Hiranmay Karlekar, H.K. Dua and Hari Jaisingh have emphasised this point in their respective articles in Section I dealing with Editors' experiences. In his article, Verghese dwells on the diminishing role of the Editor and says that he always had the final say on editorial matters. As the Editor of

Hindustan Times, he used to pull out advertisements which, in his opinion, were 'offensive and in bad taste', notwithstanding the management's objections that it would lead to 'revenue loss'. Decrying the interference of the management in the functioning of the newspapers he edited, he writes that for the survival of democracy, the Editor's 'legal and moral position' will have to be restored at any cost.

An Editor needs to be bold and courageous in dealing with the powers that be. Otherwise, it will become difficult to uphold the professional standards in journalism, says Hiranmay Karlekar. In his article 'Playing little games', he says he always held 'four qualities to be most important in life—courage, wisdom, compassion and truth.' 'Courage is the most important of them all because without it one may not be able to act as one should,' he says.

Equally important for a newspaper or magazine is credibility. It can be described as the soul of a free and fair publication. In his article 'Credibility is the key', H.K. Dua feels that an Editor needs to be upright always so that he can 'sleep better'. Maintaining that journalism is not for the 'chicken-hearted', he says that readers will trust a newspaper only if they are convinced that the Editor is committed to 'uphold truth' and the 'basic values' of the journalistic profession.

The late Dileep Padgaonkar was very much for strengthening the skill set of journalists. He was for imparting quality training to journalists in several areas. In his article, 'Coping with the times', he wrote:

> The instinct for curiosity needs to be nurtured much like the flair for story-telling. Care must be taken about the use of language for effective communication. There can be no end to learning in any and every area of one's interest. The reading habit must be revived. And the habit to ask tough questions.

Challenge of Digital Media

The entry of digital media has changed the face of the media significantly. Clearly, the Internet has revolutionised the pace of dissemination of information. It has led to the democratisation of news and the way the news is presented—swiftly and decisively. But then, democratisation has also given rise to problems, the foremost being the absence of filters. For an online or web edition, there is a general impression that anyone can write anything, and therein lies the danger. It is common knowledge how reporting without responsibility has invited trouble for some. But this is not the case with the print media. The principles of gatekeeping are fully in force in the print media which prevent one from resorting to irresponsible reporting—a fact which the electronic media or television channels cannot boast about.

Indeed, in some newspapers, especially big papers, there is a unique convergence of the digital and print media. Correspondents of these papers are first required to submit reports for their online or web edition in the morning for use. Subsequently, they update stories/reports and file copy as and when necessary. Moreover, there is a subtle distinction between the copy submitted for online and traditional or print media. While the online copy (depending upon the occurrence of an event and the time of submission) is preliminary in nature, the copy meant for the print medium, especially for the late city edition, is expected to be comprehensive in its nature, extent and scope—complete in all respects in terms of content, style, presentation, details, infographics and visuals. More to the point, in some newspapers like the *Times of India*, a correspondent's annual increment and perks would depend upon the number of stories he/she had shared via WhatsApp and Photoshop during the period under review.

Indeed, the challenge from digital media to the print media has become serious. The latter will have to wake up and reorient itself suitably to face the challenge from the former. This writer does not feel that digital media will ever sound the death knell for the print media. Though people are able to read the day's papers in their mobile phones as early as 1 or 2 AM, the print media will continue to hold its sway in the market. However, some problems remain which the print media will have to take cognisance of and act accordingly with a sense of urgency.

The first is the need to improve research content in the newspapers and magazines. Today, press release journalism is passé and people look beyond the news, for which, journalists need to do a lot of legwork. Data for development stories or corruption in high places, for instance, cannot be obtained from the reporters' air-conditioned cabins. One has to go out hunting for data. Smartphones, WhatsApp, iPads, Skype, etc., may have helped journalists in bridging the distance and obtaining information fast. But one cannot wholly depend on these devices for a comprehensive story or report. One must speak to individuals/people face-to-face for a full-fledged story. This cannot be done otherwise. Those who see Skype as the ultimate answer seem to be missing the wood for the trees. No doubt, Skype will help the correspondent in interviewing the person(s) in question or relevant to the story. However, one will miss the mood, visual effects and other relevant details if he/she is lazy to travel to ground zero.

At the same time, as one has to accept the increasing role of the new media; young journalists joining the print, television or even online-specific organisations need to be social media savvy. In fact, the managements expect journalists to be adept in using these digital devices and social media platforms. However, in the absence of formal training in the use of digital media technology, they frequently remain ill-equipped to use the potential of the digital platforms to augment their print and broadcast stories.

Many news organisations in India, including some of the big names in the business, remain unprepared for some of the basic challenges journalism presents in the online age. They still think of themselves in the print or television binary, a description that robs them of opportunities the online medium offers. It also blinds them to the challenges they face, often leaving them cocooned in pointless arguments. The readership of India's leading English dailies may have grown during 2009–2014—a period when Internet penetration exploded. However, the print and electronic media have not reoriented themselves adequately to face the advent of digital technology.

The digital medium has its own set of unique challenges. These include an absence of a clear code of ethics and ambiguities over the application of media laws to the medium. In his paper on online journalism in Section II (Digital Media), Charu Sudan Kasturi maintains that none of these challenges have easy answers, but there is enough evidence to show that the digital media will emerge and shape the way journalism is consumed in the years and decades ahead. How journalists respond to these challenges will shape them, their careers and Indian journalism.

Equally noteworthy is the series of changes in the business of print and electronic media following the advent of digital media in recent years. The change is not only in the way people consume media or the technology with which it is disseminated but also the way business is done and the way the media and entertainment industry functions. While newspapers are now often read as e-editions, television content is increasingly viewed on laptops, smartphones and other screens.

Clearly, the business of television in India has undergone a metamorphosis in the last few years. In her article on the TV–print–digital businesses, Professor Pooja Valecha points out three major changes in this context. The first major development in the country has been the change in the audience measurement service provider that is now also giving services in TV ratings for the rural region. It is bringing to light a hitherto unknown area and a number of probable changes to the way advertisers and marketers plan their campaigns. The second big change has been the government making digital access of television compulsory through the initiative of Digital Addressable Systems (DAS) for cable TV in four phases from 2012 to 2016–2017. This is bringing in addressability on the consumer end and increased subscription revenues for the broadcasters, which may lead to a revolution in the programming content. And the third phenomenon affecting television is 'multi-screening' which allows viewers to access television content through devices other than the TV (e.g., laptops and smartphones). This has obviously led to a change in the TV consumption behaviour with broadcasters and programmers looking at ways to ensure that the audience stayed with them across media and, more importantly, ways to monetise this consumer attention.

While the television business in India is behaving almost similar to its counterpart in most other countries, the business of print is behaving differently. This business is in dire straits across large markets due to the digital advent and e-editions taking away the share of physical copies, though in India the print industry is flourishing and growing at a healthy rate. Professor Pooja feels that it is not that digital has not affected the market here, but for now that is mostly limited to the affluent sections in bigger cities and the major growth is coming from the smaller cities and rural regions. The growth of the Indian economy is leading to increased purchasing power and the government's initiatives towards literacy are leading to increased readership providing an impetus both for subscription revenue as well as increased advertising revenue due to the increased purchasing power. Consequently, according to her, while the growth of English publications may be limited, it is the Hindi and vernacular publications that are providing the major growth impetus to the industry.

All in all, this is an evolutionary phase in the Indian media industry. Since the speed of digital penetration is comparatively slow in India, it is giving the businesses an interval to plan their strategies and evolve for the digital age, learning from the experiences in other major countries and perhaps also developing unique India-specific business models.

In his piece, 'Multimedia mosaic', Professor Sushobhan Patankar examines the strengths and weaknesses of the print media vis-à-vis the television and the Internet. How to survive in today's competitive media environment is a 'tough challenge' for the print media, he says, arguing that the print media will have to 'adapt to changes'. Ranjona Banerji, in her piece, 'The talking point', says Twitter, an integral part of a journalist's work, is steadily replacing the traditional ways of newsgathering. This, however, has placed an enormous responsibility on journalists. Calling it the 'dial-a-quote' brand of journalism, she says that any responsible journalist will first check the authenticity of a story before he/she uses Twitter as the 'sole source.'

No Threat to Print

This writer is fully convinced that television or web editions are no threat to the print media. First we will discuss web editions. Some of them—scroll.in, thewire.in, thequint.com, firstpost.com and www.dailyo.in and the web editions of various international, national and regional newspapers—are popular. However, to maintain that the print media is 'dead' because of the web editions is to put the cart before the horse. Successive reports of the Audit Bureau of Circulations (ABC) have been maintaining that the print media in India has been growing year after year. According to the ABC's June 2017 report, the print media saw a growth of 61 per cent in 10 years. The reputed watchdog, which certifies circulation figures of publications every six months, has said that the average sale of copies per day has risen from 3.91 crore in 2006 to 6.28 crore in 2016 (*New Indian Express*, 2017).

The less said the better about television channels. Honestly speaking, the mushrooming of news channels, though a healthy sign for the world's largest democracy, is not indicative of a fall in print readership. Most news channels simply do not bother about accuracy and indulge in attention grabbing most of the time. In order to be one up in the mad race for television rating points (TRPs), their only aim seems to be to hit the bull's eye even at the cost of factual accuracy. Breaking News, whether it merits that description or not, has become the monopoly and raison d'être of all news channels. Every channel claims exclusivity of a piece of news even while all of them telecast the same news simultaneously! On 5 August 2017, for instance, when the counting for election of the Vice President was in progress, Republic TV repeatedly flashed the message that it was the 'only channel' giving the latest figures on M. Venkaiah Naidu's lead over Gopalkrishna Gandhi! When every channel was covering the lead in this election, whom was Republic TV trying to fool? Same was the case with the Income Tax Department sleuths' raids on Karnataka Energy Minister D.K. Shivakumar's residences and properties in Delhi, Bengaluru and other parts of the country in 2–4 August 2017. All channels were reporting the raids, but Republic TV was claiming 'exclusive' reporting. Indeed, after Nitish Kumar announced his resignation as Chief Minister of Bihar on 26 July 2017, the TV channels' claim of breaking the news 'first' was amusing. Republic TV was claiming that it was 'half an hour early' in breaking the news though facts spoke otherwise. Do these channels think that they can fool the people all the time with such false claims? Rajdeep Sardesai, Consulting Editor, India Today Television, does not mince words in admitting the compulsions of news channels to rush through Breaking News most of the time.

Unfortunately, hard news has become the worst casualty in television journalism. What we find in the so-called 'Prime News' at 9 PM on weekdays is just hectoring, shouting and pontification and no news. News is virtually dead during Prime News. Even otherwise, Union Finance Minister Arun Jaitley says that these channels are only interested in bytes, that too, for Prime Time News. Senior Television Editors admit that while competition among various channels is increasing day by day, it has become difficult for channels to sustain news 24×7. There are very few television journalists who are known for their investigative skills and breaking stories. This is not the case with newspapers, most of which have senior journalists and Editors on their staff with wide contacts and rich experience.

It goes to the credit of the print media that most of the time television channels follow scoops by newspaper. Two examples will suffice: the *Indian Express* scoop on controversial visitors to the Central Bureau of Investigation (CBI) Director's residence (4 September 2014); another in the same newspaper on how the Manmohan Singh government had vetted the coal scam report (13 April 2013), which revealed how former Union Law Minister Ashwani Kumar had summoned former CBI Director Ranjit Sinha to make some changes in the report to be submitted to the Supreme Court and how it was 'toned down' after the meeting. Again, it was the same newspaper which broke the kickbacks in the AgustaWestland helicopter deal (14 February 2013). Similarly, while the *Hindu* played a leading role in exposing Robert Vadra's land deals in New Delhi, Haryana and Rajasthan, the role played by the *Pioneer* in breaking the 2G spectrum scam during the United Progressive Alliance (UPA) dispensation is well known.

Both print and television have been playing an important role in disseminating information on issues such as the unrest in Jammu and Kashmir and the continued tension on the Indo-Pakistan border. Remarkably, the media, especially all major national newspapers and television news channels, had reported the late Tamil Nadu Chief Minister Jayalalithaa's treatment in Chennai's Apollo Hospital without resorting to gossip and speculation. However, a few television channels, without confirmation from the authorities, jumped the gun by announcing Jayalalithaa's death on 4 December 2016 only to retract later. (Her death was officially announced only at 11.50 PM on 5 December 2016.) The media gave front-page coverage to the Centre's arguments in the Supreme Court against the practice of triple *talaq* on the grounds that it was repugnant to the right to equality under Article 14 of the Indian Constitution. Subsequently, all the newspapers gave good coverage to the three important judgements of the Supreme Court: one, the ruling declaring instant talaq as unconstitutional and *null* and *void*; two, Col. Purohit's release on bail after almost nine years of incarceration without investigation and even a charge sheet being filed; and three, the historic nine-member Bench judgement declaring the right to privacy as a fundamental right subject to reasonable restrictions and equating it to the right to life under Article 21 of the Constitution. Significantly, a few newspapers carried excerpts of the 547-page judgement on the right to privacy, which is expected to have a bearing on Aadhar, Section 377 of the Indian Penal Code, the Right to Information and the overall question of cyber security (Supreme Court of India, 2017).[1]

The print and the electronic media have also given due coverage to the disturbing trend of terrorists burning government schools in Jammu and Kashmir. As many as 30 government schools were reduced to ashes in the state, affecting the interest of over 12 lakh students. However, the main point of the State government's failure to check this trend was not covered properly and adequately.

Apparently, the administration seems to be slipping out of the hands of the Mehbooba Mufti government ever since the Burhan Wani killing on 8 July 2016. For several months, schools were open only on Saturdays and Sundays. The schools could conduct examinations only after the separatists decided to suspend their agitation.

Television channels collect data from their own sources and the quantum of coverage depends upon the material they obtain in the shortest possible time. However, one has to examine whether a channel should do carpet-bombing day in and day out for weeks on end as if the world has no other matter to discuss. Sometimes the coverage of an issue by a channel is so huge that it is disproportionate to the seriousness of the issue. Certainly, one does not see this kind of carpet-bombing in newspapers unless, of course, developments like the Uri massacre and surgical strikes, which deserve prominence and special treatment.

More important, some television anchors are so abrasive and arrogant that they are not prepared to accept or cover a contrarian view in any debate or discussion.

---

[1] For the text of the 547-page judgement on the right to privacy, see http://www.thehindubusinessline.com/multimedia/archive/03195/Right_to_Privacy 3195287a.pdf (accessed on 5 September 2017).

Indeed, what we notice in television today is incomplete, off-the-cuff and half-hearted ramblings, frequently interrupted by anchors. True, it is always interesting for one to watch a live debate between Arun Jaitley and Kapil Sibal or between Soli Sorabjee and Markandey Katju on television. But it would be disgusting and intellectually defeating for people if the anchors, with no expertise on the subject of the debate in question, frequently interrupt luminaries and impose their own views and comments on the subject. According to N. Ram, Chairman, The Hindu Group Publishing Private Limited, this is 'journalism at its worst'.

This is not the case with newspaper editorials or articles. A lot of effort goes into making of either the news or opinion pages. The principles of gate-keeping are in full force and the filters at various levels take due care in checking and cross-checking facts and figures before they go into print.

A 24×7 news channel is supposed to have an edge over a daily newspaper for the simple reason that television news is news as it happens, and visuals, said to be more powerful than write-ups, leave a lasting impression on viewers' minds. But then, when it comes to serious study and follow-up of a debate on an important issue, there is no substitute for a newspaper report or article. An article (or even a news item) is deemed a document and has greater legitimacy and credibility than a television report. The reason is: Editors judiciously organise articles from experts. For instance, an article on police reforms by a retired Director General of Police will have greater value and credibility than an article by a layman having no exposure in police administration. Even otherwise, in a situation where both articles are relevant, analytical and well-written with two different perspectives on a crucial theme, the Editors organise a debate on the issue by carrying both the pieces either in the Edit or Oped Page and leave them to the discretion of the readers to form a final opinion on the subject.

Media and Demonetisation

In recent times, the media's responsibility in administration and governance has increased by leaps and bounds. As the true friend of the people—and of the government at the Centre and in the states—the media should report developments in a fair and objective manner. The media can take sides only at the cost of their credibility.

Considering the scope and nature of the Narendra Modi government's demonetisation decision in November 2016 and its impact on transparency, clean administration and good governance, demonetisation definitely forms a crucial part of good journalism. Indeed, this is one decision of the government which has affected the day-to-day life of every citizen in the country. Consequently, the media faced challenges in covering issues concerning demonetisation.

Ideally, journalists should cover developments relating to demonetisation from a non-political and humane angle. It would be fair if politics is kept off any discussion on the subject. As there are many issues involved, any reference to the political dimension of demonetisation will tend to overlook or sidetrack the larger vision of the Modi government to usher in a cashless and digital economy. Surely, India cannot become Sweden (the world's only cashless country) overnight.

Many studies have examined the issue of cashless economy in the past few years. The Tuft University's 2014 study entitled *The Cost of Cash in India* and the 2015 report of the PricewaterhouseCoopers are noteworthy. While the former estimated that the cash operations cost the Reserve Bank of India and commercial banks about ₹21,000 crore annually (not an encouraging development for a country that aspires to be a developed and progressive power), the latter puts the country's unbanked population at 233 million. Experts, including former Prime Minister Dr Manmohan Singh and Dr Amartya Sen, may have underlined the impracticability of India's transition to a cashless society, particularly because a whopping 86 per cent of transactions in the country are cash-based.

The mobile Internet penetration for the whole country is only 23 per cent, according to the World Bank Report (2015), and 47 per cent people have no bank accounts. If the inclusion drive has to succeed, the Centre and the states should, in close cooperation with each other, enlarge and expand the reach so that the benefits of Digital India are reaped by one and all.

Encouragingly, e-wallet services in the country started catching up since 8 November. In addition to e-wallets of commercial banks, many firms have been providing this service to the people. Suffice to mention, it is not altogether a new concept. Industrial Credit and Investment Corporation of India (ICICI) launched 'pockets'—India's first digital bank on a mobile phone—as far back as February 2015. In fact, each bank has its own e-wallet application.

In August 2016, the National Payments Corporation of India had launched United Payments Interface (UPI). The objective of UPI is to make digital transactions as simple as sending a text message. It has an edge over other digital payment platforms for the simple reason that it facilitates a customer to pay directly from a bank account to different merchants, online and offline, without the need for typing credit card details, Indian Financial System Code (IFSC) code or net banking/wallet passwords. It is also said to be safe as customers only share a virtual address and provide no other information. The government is also trying to popularise Aadhar-enabled payment systems.

In a study in July 2016, three months before demonetisation, the Boston Consulting Group and Google came up with two important findings: that e-wallet users had outnumbered the number of mobile banking users; and that they were three times the number of credit card users. Against this background, it should not be difficult for the government to popularise the use of e-wallets when the people have begun to realise that they must reduce their dependence on cash.

The NITI Aayog's estimate that 53 per cent of urban areas in the country have mobile Internet connectivity does not present a dismal picture. Surely, the situation can be improved by bold and pragmatic policies. Worthy of mention in this context is the Union Government's decision to launch sarkari e-wallet service at the grass-roots. While the NITI Aayog is the nodal authority for monitoring and governance of this project, three Union Ministries are together implementing the service— Finance, Telecommunications and Information Technology. Having realised the absence of adequate number of smartphones in most rural households—a prerequisite for the success of the e-wallet service—the government has decided to sell them in villages at subsidised rates. It is the duty of the media to study this project carefully and report on its implementation. The media's focus should be more on popularising the programme among the people rather than discouraging it through a negative campaign.

As part of its avowed objective to enhance mobile banking for greater financial inclusion, the Telecom Regulatory Authority of India (TRAI) has reduced tariffs for Unstructured Supplementary Service Data (USSD)-based mobile banking transaction to a maximum of 50 paise per transaction, from the earlier rate of ₹1.50 per session. It has also increased the number of stages from five to eight per USSD session (*Business Standard*, 2016). Obviously, the TRAI has taken the decision with the hope that demonetisation will have a profound impact on customer priorities and overall economic growth (Kale, 2016).

The media's mission should not be restricted to reporting the day-to-day events alone but to provide timely feedback to the nation and introduce necessary course corrections. Needless to say, the media must give adequate coverage to innovative methods and practices of tackling cash crunch and digital payments.

Interestingly, during the critical period of cash crunch soon after demonetisation, amid the gloomy picture painted by some newspapers, magazines and television channels, a few fascinating stories came from the countryside which deserve attention. Dharavi village, 70 kilometres from Mumbai, was perhaps India's first village to get hundred per cent e-wallet coverage. Bank of Baroda, under a special project, distributed 70 special swipe machines in this village, which not only put an end to cash-based transactions but also expedited the use of digital payment platforms for all kinds of transaction. The people of Dharavi bought vegetables, essential commodities and other goods through Paytm and other platforms.

Not to be left behind, Andhra Pradesh Chief Minister N. Chandrababu Naidu, known for his proactive approach towards e-governance and information technology, launched 'AP Purse' for cashless transactions. AP Purse was a mobile wallet which, certainly, was a refreshing change as against dissenting voices from a few Opposition-ruled Chief Ministers like Mamata Banerjee and Arvind Kejriwal. Going a step further, the Telangana government started a novel experiment to face the cash crunch. Having taken stock of the situation in the fruit and vegetable markets, the government's Marketing Department replaced cash with tokens for ₹5, ₹10 and ₹20 (Janyala, 2016). The State's Industrial Development Financial Corporation issued these tokens at various locations. While the Rythu Bazars (farmers' markets) made good business, people lauded this user-friendly move.

In Karnataka, the Horticultural Producers' Cooperative Marketing and Processing Society (HOPCOMS), which directly sells fruits and vegetables to consumers, started accepting cards after 8 November. In addition, Bengaluru's K.R. Market traders obtained many swipe machines to tide over the cash crunch.

Critics have sprung into action and reiterated their opposition to demonetisation and sought to present a gloomy picture on the Indian economy, particularly after the gross domestic product (GDP) figures dropped to 5.7 per cent in the first quarter, April–June 2017. However, there is no need to press the panic button. The Modi government seems to have taken it as a challenge as reflected in Arun Jaitley's observation that the Centre would need to redouble its efforts on policy and investment in the next few quarters (*Indian Express*, 2017). It remains to be seen how the Centre will tackle the spectre of loss of jobs and revive demand and investment. The recent Union Cabinet reshuffle is a pointer to the Modi government's resolve to give a push to skill development and employment generation in the next one-and-a-half years before the nation goes for Lok Sabha elections in May 2019. Clearly, the new Union Skill Development Minister, Dharmendra Pradhan, has a big task at hand.

Black Money

The Centre has been taking various measures to recover black money. Through the voluntary disclosure scheme, the Income Tax Department has recovered black money in the form of undisclosed income to the tune of a whopping ₹65,250 crore from 64,275 declarations. This implies that the Centre got ₹30,000 crore on the basis of 45 per cent tax requirement. The Union Finance Ministry is claimed to have unearthed ₹71,000 crore of black money in two years—₹50,000 crore of indirect tax evasion and ₹21,000 crore of undisclosed income (*Economic Times*, 2016). Black money of the past had been tackled to some extent by demonetisation. What about black money in the future? As company donations to political parties constitute over 87 per cent of their funds, electoral reforms have become imperative. Company donations will have to be through cheques and the collection process should be made transparent and foolproof. Figure I.1 shows the balance sheet of all national parties in the 2014 Lok Sabha elections. State funding of elections to all political parties recognised by the Election Commission of India merits a fair trial (Anand, 2011; also see Anand, 1987; Panda, 2016). Tax evasion can also be tackled. With the Goods and Services Tax (GST) Act architecture coming into effect on 1 July 2017, evasion of direct and indirect tax will become difficult. A look at the balance sheet of national parties in the 2014 Lok Sabha elections, prepared by the Association for Democratic Reforms (ADR), suggests that while the BJP collected ₹588.5 crore, its expenditure was ₹712.5 crore. The Indian National Congress' collection was ₹350.4 crore and its expenditure ₹486.2 crore.

The Modi government followed up its commitment and determination to ensure transparency in the collection of funds by political parties with a slew of measures in the Union Budget for 2017–2018. Union Finance Minister Arun Jaitley, for instance, accepted the Election Commission's recommendation to prohibit 'anonymous' contributions exceeding ₹2,000 and proposed, in the Union Budget, to bring down 'anonymous' or 'unnamed' cash donations by individuals to political parties from the current ₹20,000 to ₹2,000. He also proposed the electoral bonds scheme under which political parties may purchase electoral bonds from authorised banks after making due amendments to the Reserve Bank of India Act. This decision expectedly evoked criticism in the media. It is common knowledge that political parties have been violating the rule on the donation-limit of ₹20,000. Donors could adopt the same tactic of dividing the money in small amounts to circumvent the new donation-limit of ₹2,000. If the government is committed to transparency in election expenditure, it would be eminently desirable to make donations of

Figure I.1

Balance sheet of national parties in 2014 LS polls (in crores)

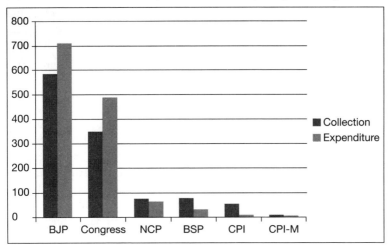

Source: ADR, New Delhi.

every rupee accountable. As regards bonds, it is feared that unscrupulous political parties could print bogus electoral bonds like Abdul Karim Telgi's counterfeit stamp paper racket. The government needs to tread with caution on this issue (Mahtab, 2017).

Covering Parliament

An issue that has been engaging the nation's attention is the steady decline of Parliament as a lawmaking body (Anand, 1986; see also Anand, 1985, 1994). During the two stints of the UPA at the Centre (2004–2009 and 2009–2014), the main Opposition BJP did not allow parliamentary proceedings most of the time. The Congress, following in the footsteps of the BJP, virtually paralysed the winter session, which started on 16 November 2016.

On the face of it, the Opposition had no justification for disruption. If it had an issue, including the demand for the Prime Minister's presence in Parliament during the debate on demonetisation, it should have placed it properly, including in the Business Advisory Committee or any other suitable forum rather than holding Parliament to ransom. Even otherwise, experience suggests that the Prime Minister's presence is not mandatory in each and every debate. Moreover, the presiding officers of both Houses of Parliament have been reiterating that Finance Minister Arun Jaitley was readily available not only to listen to the members but also to reply to the debate at the end of the discussion in both Houses. Figure I.2 shows the poor productivity of Parliament in the first two weeks of its winter session on 16–30 November 2016, due to disruption by the Opposition on the issue of demonetisation.

Under Rule 56, members can table a motion for an adjournment of the business of the House for purposes of discussing a 'definite matter of urgent public importance' with the consent of the Lok Sabha Speaker.

Same is the case with the demand for a short-duration discussion under Rule 193 of the Lok Sabha (equivalent of Rule 178 of the Rajya Sabha) or Rule 184 of the Lok Sabha (equivalent of Rule 167 of the Rajya Sabha). In the case of the former, discussion can take place which does not entail voting. However, in the case of the latter, voting follows the discussion which virtually implies a censure of the government. In a parliamentary democracy like ours, the single largest party which commands majority support in either house of Parliament always sets the agenda for any discussion or debate and no country will ever allow the Opposition to call the shots in this important parliamentary business even though the Opposition has its due place of honour.

Figure I.2

Productivity of Parliament's winter session, 16–30 November 2016 (in %)

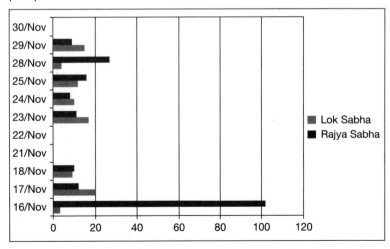

Source: PRS Legislative Research, New Delhi.

Parliament's image and performance has seen a steady decline over the years. According to data analysed by PRS Legislative Research, while the Lok Sabha worked for 98 per cent of the winter session in 2014, the Rajya Sabha worked for only 59 per cent of the time. In 15 of the 22 days, less than three minutes were spent in responding to members' questions. There was no problem in the Lok Sabha, where the BJP has got majority. However, this is not the case with the Rajya Sabha where the BJP has no numbers (*Times of India*, 2014).

During the UPA regime, disruptions affected the legislative business and Bills worth crores of rupees were passed without debate in Parliament. The Andhra Pradesh (Reorganisation) Bill, 2013, was rushed through by the government without proper debate and discussion and with almost all the Congress members from Andhra Pradesh, including Union Ministers from that state, protesting against the bifurcation of the state. This showed that the government was in no mood to understand and appreciate the sense and concern of Parliament and that it was solely guided by narrow political considerations to reap political harvest in the Lok Sabha and Assembly elections. The manner in which the Congress was decimated at the hustings demonstrated the strong public mood in the undivided state against bifurcation.

Of what purpose is Parliament when members cannot or do not discuss major issues concerning people? This is against all canons of parliamentary democracy. According to PRS Legislative Research, the productivity of the 15th Lok Sabha (2009–2014) was the 'worst'. The Lok Sabha worked for only 61 per cent of its scheduled time and passed 179 Bills—a dismal performance compared with the earlier periods. The winter session of the 15th Lok Sabha was a complete washout on the issue of the 2G spectrum scam; the Rajya Sabha spent only 2 per cent of the allotted time (Sen, 2014). See Figure I.3 for Parliament's record during the winter session, 26 November–23 December 2015.

The conduct of Members of Parliament (MPs)—as also the members of the state legislatures—during the sessions leaves much to be desired. The pepper spray incident in the Lok Sabha during the debate on the Andhra Pradesh (Reorganisation) Bill, 2013, is fresh in memory. The misconduct of Congress and All India Trinamool Congress MPs during former Prime Minister Manmohan Singh's speech on the Bill in the Lok Sabha was totally unacceptable. Sadly, these incidents were not highlighted properly and adequately in the media. In the monsoon session of Parliament, the Modi government stepped up its efforts to tame a defiant Congress party and coaxed it to support the GST Bill, 2016. In a major political initiative, it not only isolated the Congress in its larger game plan

Figure I.3
Winter session of Parliament (26 November–23 December 2015)

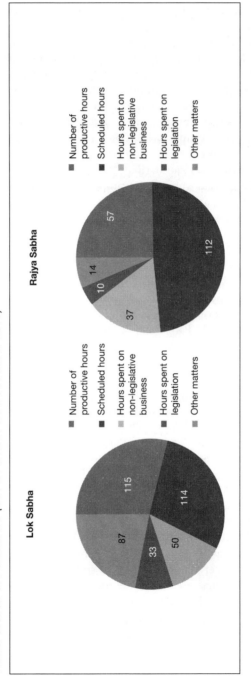

Lok Sabha

Rajya Sabha

- Number of productive hours
- Scheduled hours
- Hours spent on non-legislative business
- Hours spent on legislation
- Other matters

Source: PRS Legislative Research, New Delhi.

to rope in the maximum number of parties to support the Bill but also continued to talk to the Congress. Clearly, it created a situation which made the Congress look like the only stumbling block in the passage of the Bill in Parliament. The Congress, on its part, was forced to feel guilty in the whole exercise. The result: The Modi government succeeded in enlisting the support of the main Opposition. All this resulted in a good turnout of members in both Houses of Parliament. Encouragingly, in the monsoon session, the productivity in the Lok Sabha was as high as 97 per cent while in the Rajya Sabha it was a record 88 per cent, as is illustrated in Figure I.4.

Creditably, the monsoon session of Parliament in 2017 was better than the earlier sessions in terms of productivity. While the Rajya Sabha achieved 79.95 per cent productivity, it was 77.94 per cent for the Lok Sabha (*Times of India*, 2017). The flip side of this session was the suspension of six Congress members (Lok Sabha) for five days. They were suspended for hurling papers at the Lok Sabha Speaker (*Times of India*, 2017).

People have the right to know how their MPs and Members of Legislative Assembly (MLAs) are behaving and conducting themselves. The media cannot shirk their responsibility of assessing the performance of elected representatives. Facts speak for themselves. Sadly, in the past

Figure I.4

Record productivity in monsoon session of Parliament, 2016

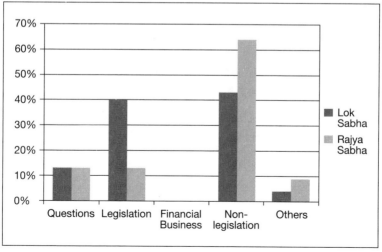

Source: PRS Legislative Research, New Delhi.

two decades, Indian Parliament never sat for more than 100 days in a year. These sittings, too, were marked by frequent disruptions and adjournments on trivial issues. This is in sharp contrast to the practice that obtains in the United Kingdom whose Westminster model of governance we have imbibed. The British Parliament sits for at least 160 days every year and does productive and qualitative lawmaking. The Communist Party of India (Marxist) stalwart, Sitaram Yechury, has aptly suggested a constitutional amendment making 100 sittings a year mandatory for Parliament.

Parliament symbolises the aims and aspiration of the people and every MP has the right to express his dissent on any issue that concerns his constituency, state or the nation as a whole. However, there is a way of expressing one's opinion and drawing the attention of the government through Parliament. Nobody has the right to hold Parliament or the state legislature to ransom. Those who thought that the days of disruption were over because of the BJP's majority support in the current Lok Sabha (this is the first time that a single party is enjoying a majority in the Lower House since 1984) were proved wrong when the first day of its Budget session was disrupted on the issue of price rise. And the leader of the disrupters who rushed to the well of the House was none other than Congress Vicepresident Rahul Gandhi.

While addressing the Platinum Jubilee celebrations of the West Bengal Assembly on 6 December 2013, President Pranab Mukherjee aptly said: 'Opposition should oppose and expose, but cannot disrupt. Disposition and exposition should go on, but not disruption' (*Times of India*, 2013; also see *Times of India*, 2014a, 2014b). Going a step further, in a lighter vein though, Omar Abdullah (who was Chief Minister of Jammu and Kashmir) said: 'Earmark a particular day for disruption, but Parliament work must go on' (*Economic Times*, 2013).

It is also time India emulated the Salisbury Convention. Keeping in view the propensity of the Opposition to create hurdles in the enactment of legislations such as the GST Act, India needs to replicate the Salisbury Convention. Under the Salisbury Convention, a constitutional convention in the United Kingdom, the House of Lords (equivalent of India's Rajya Sabha or the Council of states) will not oppose the second or third reading of any government legislation promised in its election manifesto.

If MPs should behave and deliver, the media should take up the responsibility of monitoring and evaluating their activities. Watch the post-lunch session of Parliament on any day of the session. Empty benches would greet the visitors and the media. Worse, most of the members do not raise questions at all, let alone participate in discussions. Ministers are absent when they are expected to respond to questions, starred or non-starred. Rajya Sabha Chairman Hamid Ansari had pulled up the Manmohan Singh government for the cavalier attitude of its Ministers towards the conduct of parliamentary business. It is the duty of the media to expose such conduct and call for corrective measures.

Another cause for concern is weak expenditure control by Parliament. We have three important parliamentary committees—the Public Accounts Committee, the Estimates Committee and the Committee on Public Undertakings. Of late, they do not seem to be doing good work. Moreover, the mandated role and functions of the first two committees often overlap. Why cannot we learn from the United Kingdom? There, the Public Accounts Committee and the Estimates Committee have been merged into a single committee, called the Public Expenditure Committee. This was done with an avowed objective: to focus attention on public expenditure rather than on supply estimates and to examine a wider selection of issues arising in this field (Godbole, 2003).

It is imperative that the media give wider coverage to Parliament, especially when it deliberates on issues of major national and international importance. Even if the sessions are telecast live, this should not be an excuse for the print media to neglect or downgrade its coverage. In fact, the present coverage falls short of expectations and leaves much to be desired. While presenting the Ramnath Goenka Award for Excellence in Journalism to journalists in New Delhi in September 2014, Lok Sabha Speaker Sumitra Mahajan lamented that the media were not doing their job properly and said they should cover Parliament sessions adequately and comprehensively (Ghose, 2014).

This writer is of the opinion that the media should concentrate on the inter-session period as well. For, it is during the inter-session period that parliamentary committees work actively. It would be in the fitness of things if the media are given access to the proceedings of all the committees, including department-related standing committees. These meetings need to be telecast live by both the television channels of Parliament—the Lok Sabha channel and the Rajya Sabha channel. The then Lok Sabha Speaker Somnath Chatterjee did try to see this through, but he could not meet the long-standing demand from the media and the general public because of resistance from some members (Chatterjee, 2010, p. 208). If India is the world's largest democracy, every effort to strengthen the parliamentary democracy and its glorious institutions needs to be pursued to its logical conclusion.

RS Poll: All for One Seat

Rajya Sabha elections normally do not cause any excitement. These elections are considered a pale affair with newspapers and television channels hardly attaching any importance to them. The results are taken for granted for the simple reason that the candidates win seats on the basis of the numerical strength of the legislators of political parties in their respective state Assemblies. This being the case, the manner in which the BJP and the Congress fought for one Rajya Sabha seat in Gujarat in August 2017 raised eyebrows. It was a cliff-hanger, a nail-biting finish and an election down to the wire till the last minute! Naturally, it was one of those momentous events which the media made full use of in terms of coverage. It was a feast especially for news channels which rolled out moment-to-moment developments from no less than the precincts of New Delhi's Nirvachan Sadan—the seat of the Election Commission of India—in the evening of 8 August 2017. There was no end to delegations from both the Congress and BJP camps to the Election Commission that forcefully presented their views on whether the votes cast by two MLAs should be disqualified or not. The results, which were expected to be announced at about 6 PM, were finally out only around midnight after a series of confabulations between the Chief Election Commissioner Achal Kumar Joti, Election Commissioner Om Prakash Rawat and Gujarat's Chief Electoral Officer B.B. Swain (who was based in Ahmedabad).

Clearly, the focus was on one candidate—Congress' five-time candidate for the Rajya Sabha and party supremo Sonia Gandhi's Political Secretary Ahmed Patel—which subsequently made the election of two other candidates—BJP President Amit Shah and Union Information and Broadcasting Minister Smriti Irani—pale into insignificance. Indisputably, with a view to denying a fifth term for Ahmed Patel, the BJP top brass left no stone unturned to defeat him. Not to be left behind, the Congress, too, was up in the game. Having faced the brunt of defections in its camp, the party airlifted 44 MLAs to Bengaluru's Eagleton Resort to prevent 'poaching' by the BJP. Though resort politics is nothing new in the country (one is reminded of the 1984 episode when the N.T. Rama Rao government in Andhra Pradesh airlifted its Telugu Desam Party MLAs to Bengaluru's Nandi Hills to prevent 'poaching' by the Congress), the controversies surrounding the Eagleton Resort together with the purported involvement of Karnataka Power Minister D.K. Shivakumar and the massive income tax raids on his properties only added spice to the Gujarat drama.

Undoubtedly, the Election Commission, with its late-night verdict, which ultimately tilted the scales in favour of Ahmed Patel, once again restored people's faith and confidence in the fairness of the electoral process and the impartiality of the Commission itself (Quraishi, 2017). Contrary to meaningless apprehensions in some sections that the Chief Election Commissioner Achal Kumar Joti, who was Chief Secretary of Gujarat when Modi was Chief Minister, might bail out the BJP candidate, strictly went by the rulebook to invalidate the votes cast by two rebel Congress legislators. Having watched the video clip, the Election Commission was convinced that the two MLAs, by showing their votes to an unauthorised representative of the party, had violated Rule 39 of the Code of Election Rules, 1961, and consequently declared their votes as invalid. It was also guided by precedents in Haryana and Rajasthan (Chauhan, 2017). Commendably, it was not impressed by the BJP delegations' claim that the Congress should have raised objections at about 9.30 AM itself when the legislators in question had exercised their franchise and that the votes could not be identified for the simple reason that they had already been inserted in the ballot box.

The Gujarat episode holds out three important lessons for the media—one, do not be carried away by the trappings of power and underestimate the strength of the rival camp; two, attach utmost importance to established norms and values of the Constitution and past precedents; and three, repose trust and confidence in the Election Commission of India.

Freedom of Speech and Expression

Significantly, freedom of speech and expression is one of the most important rights in media laws. Every journalist, especially those in the Legal Bureau, should have a proper background on media laws. Newspapers or television channels have no special or exclusive provision in the Constitution to exercise their fundamental right to speech and expression. They draw and exercise this right directly from Article 19(1) of the Constitution. This is the most cherished right that a citizen in a functional democracy such as ours can be proud of. Indeed, the media have the right to exercise it to their fullest potential. However, what most media professionals do not seem to appreciate is the fact that it is not an unfettered or absolute right. Every citizen, including the media—print, electronic or digital—will have to exercise it with utmost caution and circumspection. Not surprisingly, Article 19(1) is circumscribed by Article 19(2) of the Constitution, which deals with reasonable restrictions.

There are eight clauses under which reasonable restrictions apply. These are sovereignty and territorial integrity of India, security of the state, friendly relations with foreign states, public order, decency and morality, contempt of court, defamation and incitement to an offence. Any responsible media organisation, agency or a citizen is expected to know this fundamental distinction between the freedom of speech and expression and reasonable restrictions. In essence, this right is an important right and hence needs to be exercised in a responsible manner.

Since the Indian Constitution does not comprehensively and adequately define the term, 'reasonable restrictions', the test of reasonableness has to be applied to each individual statute impugned and no abstract standard or general pattern of reasonableness can be laid down as applicable to all cases. In *V.G. Row vs. The State of Madras*, All India Reporter 1952, the Supreme Court ruled that the definition of reasonable restrictions would include several factors such as 'the manner of restrictions imposed by the impugned law; the underlying purposes of the restrictions imposed; the extent and urgency of the evils sought to be remedied thereby; the disproportion of the imposition; the prevailing conditions at that time and the duration of the restrictions'. Consequently, the standard is not only an elastic one but also varies with time, space and condition. Worthy of mention in this context is the slew of essential principles which the Supreme Court has affirmed in determining the reasonableness of restrictions in some leading cases. These are the principle of proper balancing, the principle of objectivity, the principle of reasonableness involving substantive as well as procedural aspects, the principle of the reasonableness of the restriction and not of law and the principle of reasonable restrictions distinguished from the principle of due process of law.

In Section III on Media Laws, Mr Soli J. Sorabjee, distinguished jurist and former Attorney General of India, examines this most important right from the constitutional perspective. He emphasises the importance of freedom of speech and expression in a functioning democracy like ours and maintains that it is only through the citizen's right to know that the government of the day can be made accountable for its actions. 'When in doubt, tilt the balance in favour of expression rather than its suppression,' he says.

Menace of Paid News

A malaise affecting journalism in the recent past is the menace of paid news. This has the potential of subverting democracy (Anand, 2010; see also Pande, 2010; Sainath, 2011; Thakurta, 2012; Viswanathan, 2010). It has become a big threat to journalism as news, features and even photographs have price tags, especially during elections. In the 2014 Lok Sabha elections, the Election Commission served notices in 3,053 cases of suspected paid news and found 694 cases to be 'genuine' (DNA, 2014), raising questions about the moral and ethical foundation of journalism. The problem was endemic in the Assembly elections in Tamil Nadu and Kerala. While some pay for positive coverage to boost their electoral prospects, many others pay to prevent negative coverage. The phenomenon of paid news strikes at the very edifice of the noble profession.

In the 2010 Bihar Assembly elections, S.Y. Quraishi, who was then the Chief Election Commissioner, set up an elaborate institutional mechanism at the national, state and district level to check paid news—the Election Expenditure Monitoring Mechanism and a Media Certification and Monitoring Mechanism in each district at the level of the Returning Officer for certification of advertisements in the media. In the absence of quantifiable data, it is not clear how this system works. The Election Commission's observation that media houses or publications are beyond its purview and it is forwarding the cases to the Press Council of India (PCI) and the News Broadcasting Standards Association are indicative of its helplessness in tackling the problem (DNA, 2014). The PCI, on the other hand, maintains that it has not received any information from the Election Commission. In any case, the PCI has no control over the electronic media and even otherwise, it lacks teeth (DNA, 2014).

There is a need for effective legislation to combat this malady. The government should try to build an all-party consensus on ending paid news. The Election Commission's disqualification of two legislators— Narottam Mishra, Madhya Pradesh's Water Resources, Public Health and Legislative Affairs Minister; and Umlesh Yadav, Uttar Pradesh MLA—for a period of three years for submitting incorrect accounts of expenditure is a good beginning. While Mishra's case pertains to his election from Datia in Madhya Pradesh in 2008, Umlesh's case dates back to 2007 from Bisauli in Uttar Pradesh. Unfortunately, our lawmakers try every tactic to hoodwink justice. Mishra has obtained a stay from the Supreme Court, which in turn has asked the Delhi High Court to dispose of his petition. He was earlier barred from exercising his franchise in the presidential election. It would be interesting to see how the courts will treat his disqualification because earlier both the Madhya Pradesh High Court and the Delhi High Court refused to stay his disqualification.

The media are bound to have doubts on the final course of justice against the backdrop of the Ashok Chavan case. The former Maharashtra Chief Minister tried every stratagem to delay speedy adjudication of a case of paid news against him for his role in the October 2009 Maharashtra Assembly elections. He won the Bhokar seat in Nanded district. The Supreme Court cleared all legal hurdles challenging the constitutional legitimacy of the Election Commission to hear the petition against him. It directed the Commission to decide the case within a time frame of 45 days and serve him a show-cause notice. Yet Chavan sprang a surprise. He appealed in the Delhi High Court, obtained a stay and won the case. The court has upheld Chavan's appeal and quashed the Election Commission's show-cause notice. In view of the immense interest the case has generated in the media, it may be worth recalling why the Delhi High Court gave a clean chit to Chavan.

Lawyers Kapil Sibal and Rajiv Nayar, who appeared for Chavan, argued that the Election Commission should have given him an opportunity to file revised election expenses instead of serving him a show-cause notice. The lawyer Jayant Bhushan, who appeared for Madhavrao Kinhalkar, petitioner and independent candidate who lost the 2009 election against Chavan from the Bhokar Assembly constituency, argued that the petition was just a 'ploy' to stall the proceedings before the Election Commission (*Mint*, 2014).

Significantly, the court relied on affidavits filed by Maharashtra Congress leaders who claimed that they had published advertisements on Chavan's behalf without him being aware of them. This was the reason why Chavan did not account for the expenditure in his account of election spending, they maintained. The court made three important observations. One, there was no evidence before the Election Commission that Chavan had provided inputs for the advertisements. Two, there was no 'express authorisation' in any form given by the petitioner to any advertiser. And three, no inducements in cash or kind was paid or even promised as a consideration against the alleged publication by the petitioner or his election agent (*Mint*, 2014). Notwithstanding the Delhi High Court order, the problem remains. The Narendra Modi government should bring in legislation to tackle the menace.

In his article on media and elections, Quraishi has not only emphasised the need to check the menace of paid news but has also stressed the need for some genuine electoral reforms to protect and strengthen democracy. Referring to the symbiotic relationship between the media and the Election Commission, he spells out the terms of engagement between the two important pillars of the world's largest democracy. He also examines the problem of opinion polls, hate speech and a few grey areas in the Representation of the People Act (RPA), 1951, and writes how political parties are taking advantage of the loopholes in the law.

To rectify the situation, for instance, Quraishi suggests an amendment to the RPA.

Sting operation is yet another issue that has been engaging the attention of the media for some years. The practitioners of good journalism are especially concerned about it. Is it ethical on the part of the media to indulge in such an exercise? Can the media use sting operation for any issue in the public interest? In her article, Dr Shashikala Gurpur examines the mission of the media to ferret out the truth and the ethico-legal dimension of sting operations.

Question of Ethics

The issue of journalistic ethics and propriety comes to the fore whenever a journalist is under a cloud and arrested. The arrest of a senior journalist for his alleged involvement in the corporate espionage racket is disturbing. True, some journalists, in the course of their work, develop a corporate face over a period of time in the media industry. However, the tragedy is that some of them, compromising their professional standards, willingly submit themselves to be on the payrolls of industrialists or corporates. There are rotten apples in every basket. The issue in question, however, is: How serious is the breach of ethics and morality in the espionage case involving the Government of India's three important departments—Petroleum and Natural Gas, Power and Coal? The claim of Santanu Saikia, the arrested journalist when he was being taken away by the police to a Delhi court, that he was only doing a 'cover up' of a whopping ₹10,000-crore scam' seems to be the tip of a very large iceberg (*Economic Times*, 2015). Saikia not only let down the profession of journalism but also some important processes and institutions. Clearly, paid news had become a menace.

One needs to refer to the experience of Mohan Guruswamy, who was the Adviser to the then Union Finance Minister Yashwant Sinha, and currently Chairman, New Delhi's Centre for Policy Alternatives. If Guruswamy is to be believed, the note he had written on Maruti's disinvestment and saved in his word processor and sent to the Minister for his signature, appeared in the *Financial Express* the very next morning. One does not know how the note was leaked to Santanu Saikia, who was on the staff of the *Financial Express* then, notwithstanding the precautions taken by Guruswamy (*Hindu*, 2015). And yet when he reveals this with all authority and sense of responsibility, one cannot help but believe him. Far more serious is the response of the Expenditure Secretary to the Government of India to Guruswamy's suggestion to restrict Saikia's access to the Ministry. The bureaucrat reportedly told him that it was simply not done and no curbs could be imposed on the journalist's entry into the Ministry.

Guruswamy also refers to another incident in which the top management of Boeing returned to the Government of India important documents setting up standards and requirements for India's biggest defence contract. He says the documents had surprisingly landed at the company's headquarters.

It is said that when S. Jaipal Reddy was Union Minister for Petroleum and Natural Gas, he had instructed his Secretary to limit the access of sensitive documents in the Ministry to only three to four officials. One does not know to what extent this fiat helped maintain the documents' confidentiality.

Clearly, the Saikia episode has opened a can of worms. The stain or blemish will remain even if the journalist in question is acquitted of the charge of espionage. It goes without saying that journalists need access to official documents for doing special/exclusive stories. But, in the process, if they get paid, it would be a serious breach of ethics and a gross violation of journalistic standards. Even if a newspaper organisation, television channel or a news portal is desperately in need of a sensitive document to buttress an argument in a given story in today's age of cut-throat competition and Breaking News, it will have to be obtained through fair means and, more important, this should not be misused. Journalists, in pursuit of exclusive stories, would do well to justify the means to the end.

It is high time for a clean-up. The PCI is toothless and can hardly deliver the goods. Moreover, it has no control over the electronic media. Even if its scope is expanded by bringing television channels within its ambit, it is doubtful whether it can measure up to expectations, given its shoddy record in rejecting the paid news report submitted to it by a two-member sub-committee comprising Paranjoy Guha Thakurtha and K. Srinivasa Reddy in July 2010. If the government comes forward with any regulatory institutional mechanism, the media will jump in and, in one voice, cry foul maintaining that it was an attack on the freedom of press. Self-regulation is best, but it should be stringent and bite the offenders sometimes to act as a strong deterrent.

Meanwhile, the arrest of an aide to a Samajwadi Party MP (Rajya Sabha) in the Pakistan spy ring is a major cause for concern. According to the Crime Branch of the Delhi Police, Farhat, the aide of Munavvar Saleem, the MP, played an 'integral role' in espionage and provided documents to Pakistan mission staffers, including Mehmood Akhtar, an official of the Pakistan High Commission in New Delhi, who was declared persona non grata and sent back to Pakistan. The Delhi Police and the Government of India are quite capable of handling the issue and ferret out the truth. However, what is of particular concern is Farhat's association with the MP. The MPs do receive important documents and other sensitive information from various government departments and agencies from time to time for information. It is not clear whether Farhat took advantage of his official position and leaked any confidential information to Pakistan mission staffers.

On his part, the MP may have claimed innocence and ignorance of the matter, especially the misconduct of his aide. In fact, the MP in question has gone a step further by saying that he will 'commit suicide' if he is held guilty. However, in view of the sensitive nature of the issue and the MPs' regular access to confidential and privileged information, a thorough investigation at the highest level brooks no delay. The media should step in and conduct their own survey to pinpoint similar leakages. True, no MP can be blamed for lapses, if any, without proper investigation and evidence. This, however, does not prevent the government from ordering a thorough survey of all aides to MPs and ministers. Our people's representatives may be considered patriotic and committed to national welfare and development. But their offices cannot be allowed to become porous, leaking sensitive information to the staffers of foreign embassies and missions. A close look of the antecedents of all aides of our MPs and a drastic overhaul of the system of recruitment or appointment of these aides and other personal staff will be in order.

Tainted Ministers, MPs, MLAs

The issue of criminalisation of politics and tainted ministers has been bothering the media for a long time. The *Tribune* launched a sustained campaign against this through news reports, editorials and articles (Anand, 2005). The Manmohan Singh-led Congress government adopted double standards by initially passing the Representation of the People (Second Amendment and Validation) Bill, 2013, to protect convicted politicians such as Lalu Prasad in exchange for their support to the Congress-led UPA government and then withdrawing it following Congress Vice-president Rahul Gandhi's *tantrums* in the Delhi Press Club. The Supreme Court has left the issue of tainted ministers to the Prime Minister's discretion. It recognised the importance of the Prime Minister in the parliamentary system of governance based on the Westminster model and wisely left the matter of Cabinet formation and inclusion of Ministers to his wisdom and discretion. At the same time, the five-judge Constitution Bench headed by former Chief Justice R.M. Lodha said:

> It can always be legitimately expected ... the Prime Minister, while living up to the trust reposed in him, would consider not choosing a person with criminal antecedents against whom charges have been framed for heinous or serious criminal offences or charges of corruption to become a Minister of the Council of Ministers. This is what the Constitution suggests and that is the constitutional expectation from the Prime Minister. Rest has to be left to the wisdom of the Prime Minister. We say nothing more, nothing less. (Sinha, 2014)

According to the ADR, 12 of the 45 Union Ministers in the Narendra Modi government have been charged with criminal offences. While Water Resources and Ganga Rejuvenation Minister Uma Bharti has 13 cases registered against her, Transport and Shipping Minister Nitin Gadkari has four cases (Sinha, 2014). It is indeed a challenge for Modi and the BJP-led National Democratic Alliance government he heads to come clean on the matter. Sadly, there has been no change in this election after election.

Figure I.5 shows no improvement in the elections in Tamil Nadu, West Bengal, Assam, Kerala and Puducherry. Disturbingly, 294 elected MLAs in the four states and Union Territory of Puducherry have pending criminal cases against them. Among them, Kerala tops the list with 62 per cent of MLAs elected with criminal antecedents followed by West Bengal (37 per cent), Tamil Nadu (37 per cent), Puducherry (37 per cent) and Assam (11 per cent) (Avienaash, 2016). In the Rajya Sabha elections held on 11 June 2016, Bihar's BJP candidate had as many as 28 criminal cases against him (Kumar, 2016).

Close on the heels of the Supreme Court's stand on tainted ministers, the Centre's communique to the Chief Ministers of all states and chief justices of High Courts to fix the responsibility on district administrations to expedite probe and trial of MPs and MLAs facing charges for serious crimes is a good beginning. The Centre would do well to step up pressure on the states. The communiqué is crystal clear inasmuch as it has made the district administrations responsible for speedy disposal of cases (Thakur, 2014). However, in the absence of any follow-up, one does not know the status of these cases as on date. Moreover, this is a violation of the one-year time frame fixed by the Supreme Court to dispose pending cases.

Criminalisation of politics has been haunting the nation for quite some time. The media should pick up the threads and monitor the progress of the cases regularly to stem the rot. There should be no problem

Figure I.5
MLAs with criminal records (in %)

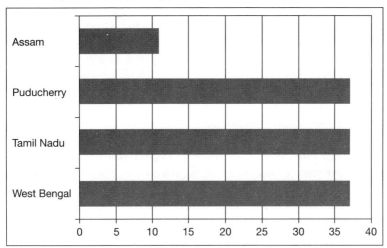

Source: Avienaash (2016).

regarding availability of data. On the basis of the particulars provided by candidates in their respective affidavits submitted to the returning officers during elections, the ADR and the National Election Watch (NEW) have been compiling data on tainted candidates and releasing them to the media from time to time. The data are credible enough to merit attention. The Election Commission's figures on this are also available on its website. However, in the context of the Centre's directive to states as also to fix accountability on the district administration for disposal of all pending cases in a year, the media should revert to the problem and monitor the progress of investigation and disposal of individual cases in all districts.

As for giving the party ticket to tainted candidates in the Lok Sabha, Rajya Sabha and Assembly elections, the onus lies squarely on political parties themselves. The solution to this problem should necessarily begin at the entry level itself. Criminals, with their muscle power and money power, get elected to representative institutions, become MPs, MLAs and even ministers and pollute the system. The issue in question is: How can a tainted person become a lawmaker and minister? If the quality of governance has to change, political parties should resolve not to nominate persons with criminal antecedents (Anand, 2012).

In a significant order, a Supreme Court Bench comprising Justice Dipak Misra and Justice P.C. Pant ruled that candidates who concealed their criminal antecedents while filing nomination papers would run the risk of disqualification. It said that the candidates will have to give details, especially those relating to heinous crimes or serious offences like corruption (*Mint*, 2015).

In a 97-page ruling, the apex court said that a candidate's non-disclosure of criminal antecedents would amount to a 'corrupt practice' under Section 123 of the RPA, 1951. Such a corrupt practice would make the candidate liable for disqualification under Section 8(A) of the same Act.

Tamil Nadu Chief Minister Jayalalithaa passed away on 5 December 2016, after a 75-day hospitalisation. The award of a four-year jail term to her together with a fine of ₹100 crore is a benchmark in the Disproportionate Assets case. The Supreme Court released her on bail, giving her an opportunity to appeal against the trial court verdict. She fought the case, got the judgement delivered by Special Judge John Michael D'Cunha of the Bangalore Special Court reversed. She returned to the post of Chief Minister after a brief spell. The Karnataka High Court gave her a clean chit, but the Karnataka government challenged her acquittal, maintaining that the court had 'committed error in calculating her assets' (*Times of India*, 2016). The Supreme Court judgement upholding the trial court ruling and convicting Sasikala, her confidante, and two others in the Disproportionate Assets case with a four-year sentence and a fine of ₹10 crore each has reinforced people's faith in the judiciary. The fact that the Supreme Court has imposed a fine of ₹100 on the deceased Jayalalithaa of ₹100 crore together with attachment of her properties doubly proves the commitment of the judiciary to stem the rot of corruption.

Interestingly, during the hearing, the Supreme Court Bench consisting of Justice P.C. Ghose and Justice Amitava Ray ruled that the court could declare a person guilty only because he/she had assets disproportionate to his/her known sources of income. It observed that he/she could be held guilty only if it was proved that the person acquired these assets through 'illegal means' (*Times of India*, 2016). The speed with which the Supreme Court expedited this ruling is in line with two of its earlier guidelines: that cases of corruption in high places should be adjudicated within a specific time frame; and that the courts should not show any leniency towards those punished under the Prevention of Corruption Act.

The media have a crucial role to play in informing and educating the people on the day-to-day events in the country. In a functioning democracy such as ours, the duties and responsibilities of the media are enormous. It has to protect all institutions and help strengthen them.

It cannot close its eyes and ears to any development that may have the potential of bringing public institutions to disrepute.

Attack on CAG

While the media need to examine the ways and means to strengthen parliamentary institutions, they cannot afford to lose sight of any development that may have the potential of bringing institutions to disrepute. One remembers the blistering attack on the then Comptroller and Auditor General (CAG) of India Vinod Rai by former Union Law Minister Kapil Sibal and other Congress leaders for his report on the 2G spectrum. When the CAG cited ₹1.76 lakh crore as the notional loss to the national exchequer in the 2G deal in his report, Sibal debunked it and maintained that there was 'zero loss'. The CAG, like the Chief Election Commissioner of India and the Chairman of the Union Public Service Commission, is a constitutional functionary who deserves all respect and attention. Where will the scales of justice meet if the Union Law Minister himself leads the attack on a constitutional authority?

If a constitutional functionary questions another authority, the delicate constitutional balance would be disturbed, and hence, such friction should be avoided. Rai, known for his unimpeachable character and high professional integrity, was only performing his duty as mandated by the Constitution and crying foul against financial malfeasance in the government's issuance of telecommunication licenses or allocation of coal blocks to private individuals. Indeed, his stand has been vindicated in letter and spirit after the Supreme Court quashed issuance of the telecommunication licenses as well as the allocation of coal blocks.

In his memoirs, *Not Just an Accountant*, Rai has stuck to his stand and the CAG's report on the 2G scam (Rai, 2014). Of particular concern is his revelation in both television and newspaper interviews that a lot of pressure was put on him to keep Manmohan Singh's name out of the 2G episode. He said he refused to buckle under pressure even though Congress leaders such as Sanjay Nirupam tried to convince him to bail out Manmohan Singh.

CBI on the Mat

Encouragingly, newspapers such as the *Indian Express* have created a name for themselves in investigative journalism. The *Indian Express'* scoop on the number of controversial visitors calling on former CBI Director Ranjit Sinha at his official residence is commendable. People have the right to know why these people had been flocking around Sinha. In view of his sensitive position, Sinha's meeting with the visitors at his residence was grossly inappropriate. What prevented him from meeting them in his office? His explanation that his meeting with the Reliance Anil Dhirubhai Ambani Group (ADAG) officials was routine and that he did not grant any 'favours' to them was unconvincing. If this and other reports that Moin Qureshi, accused of money laundering, visited Sinha as many as '90 times in 15 months' were to bear scrutiny, these were a fit case for investigation. The media needed to probe this, including whether Sinha had granted any favours to the officials.

The Supreme Court had turned down Sinha's plea to stop the media from disclosing the identity of his visitors at his official residence, 2, Janpath, New Delhi. At the same time, on the court's directive, Sinha filed an affidavit on the guests' visits. Though the court directed Prashant Bhushan to disclose the source of information regarding the visitors, he refused to do so.

Newspapers have the responsibility of investigating the malaise affecting the country's premier investigating agency. Herein lies the media's responsibility towards society and the nation as a whole.

It is widely believed that the CBI does not seem to be independent and that it acts as the handmaiden of the government. The Supreme Court, not so long ago, said that it was a 'caged parrot'. According to Fali S. Nariman, noted jurist and constitutional expert, the CBI has been functioning under successive governments 'not by notes on files but on nods and winks of the minister or senior officers in charge of the administrative ministry' (Sen, 2013; see also Anand, 2010, 2005).

Though the CBI Director is not a constitutional functionary, he holds an important official position. Thus, it is expected that he should be above suspicion and should not give room for any speculation about his conduct. As he is an important functionary holding a public office, his stand that his right to privacy is violated by the media coverage is unconvincing and does not stand the test of legal scrutiny. Students of political science and journalism are always told that the right to privacy is a deemed right and a limited right. The scope and extent of this right can be appreciated properly if one understands the fact that public interest always overrides the right to privacy of public functionaries. A government official or a politician cannot take shelter under the right to privacy for the simple reason that the people have a right to know his/her acts of omission and commission and that public interest is greater than individual interest.

The Supreme Court's directive to Sinha to keep off the 2G spectrum probe, a fortnight before his superannuation, speaks volumes about the credibility of the CBI. The bench comprising Chief Justice H.L. Dattu, Justice Madan B. Lokur and Justice A.K. Sikri accepted the contention of the Centre for Public Interest Litigation (CPIL) that Sinha had a series of meetings with executives from companies being investigated by the CBI in connection with the 2G scam. The CPIL had accused Sinha of trying to influence the findings of the probe. Sinha's denial of the charge did not help matters for the simple reason that the apex court had ruled that the information supplied by the CPIL (relating to the guest register showing the names of visitors to Sinha's official residence) was 'prima facie credible' and that 'a reasoned and lengthy order would affect the CBI's reputation'.

Even as the Supreme Court Bench consisting of Justice Madan B. Lokur, Justice Kurien Joseph and Justice A.K. Sikri were adjudicating the case, on 12 July 2016, the Supreme Court-appointed panel headed by former Special Director of CBI M.L. Sharma held that there was an attempt to influence the coal block allocation. The issue in question is whether it was proper on the part of Sinha to entertain questionable visitors at his official residence. The media rightly supported the Supreme Court ruling and called upon Sinha to quit office and protect the image and reputation of the high office. However, he refused to see reason and decided to cling on to his position like a limpet. It augurs well that the apex court allowed the CBI Director Anil Sinha to go ahead with the 2G spectrum probe. It is hoped that the leadership will learn lessons from the Sinha episode and strive to restore the credibility of the CBI.

Focus on Development

Development is one area where the media will have to play an important role today. In the light of the Narendra Modi government's special focus on development, the media would do well to concentrate on development journalism. The Planning Commission has been scrapped and replaced by NITI Aayog. As the government is going ahead with its agenda, there is a bonanza of information for journalists to study and analyse the contours of the new planning machinery and developmental plan programmes.

The Prime Minister's call, while replying to the Motion of Thanks on President Pranab Mukherjee's speech to the joint session of Parliament on 11 June 2014, to make development the 'war cry' and a 'mass movement' should be taken in the right spirit and pursued to its logical conclusion (*Times of India*, 2014). On the face of it, there is nothing wrong in what Modi said regarding making states the fulcrum of development. For long, the Centre has neglected the states. The late Jyoti Basu had lamented how the states had been relegated to a 'mendicant status' by an overbearing Centre. Things will, certainly, improve if the government, with sincerity and earnestness, stepped up efforts to make development a 'mass movement' similar to the freedom struggle.

At the tail end of its second term in office, the UPA government launched many big-ticket programmes such as the Direct Benefit Transfers or cash transfer scheme, the National Food Security Act and the Land Acquisition Act. The Manmohan Singh government may have lost the elections, but the conceptualisation, structural design and utility of these schemes are appreciable. Initially, the Modi government wanted to implement the Land Acquisition Act, albeit with some changes here and there. The UPA government rechristened the Land Acquisition Act as the Right to Fair Compensation, Resettlement, Rehabilitation and Transparency in Land Acquisition Act, 2013. Following the Modi government's consultation with the states on the Act, on 29 December 2014, the President promulgated an Ordinance to amend the Act to 'strike a balance between the farmers' interests and industrial growth'. Though the Centre was keen on pursuing the legislation to its logical conclusion, it failed to do so because of the Congress' obstruction tactics in the Rajya Sabha. The Modi government has the numbers in the Lok Sabha and passage of any Bill in the Lower House has never been a problem. But this is not so in the Rajya Sabha, the Upper House. After repeatedly failing to ensure its passage in the Rajya Sabha, the Centre abandoned the idea of trying the Ordinance route and finally left it to the states' discretion to enact a legislation on this.

The Modi government has renamed the Provision of Urban Amenities in Rural Areas (PURA), a centrally sponsored scheme, as the Shyama Prasad Mukherji Rurban Mission. The Rurban (rural–urban) mission will be implemented on the Gujarat model. As a pilot project, the Modi government has launched the programme in three districts: Sangli and Buldhana in Maharashtra and Warangal in Telangana. These schemes are expected to usher in new forces in rural India. The media has a duty to monitor the implementation of these schemes in the villages and towns and bring to light the functional problems for the common good.

In his chapter on 'Partner in Development', this writer has examined the pitfalls of planning, the contours of the NITI Aayog and the media's role. Now that Dr Arvind Panagariya has left the NITI Aayog and returned to academics in the United States, there is a new chief at the helm—Dr Rajiv Kumar. It would be interesting to see how he will carry the mission forward. While examining the Centre–state relations over the years, the writer has stressed the need to pursue the Goods and Services Act to its logical conclusion as it will be a game-changer in the Centre's efforts to promote cooperative federalism in letter and spirit. He has also highlighted how students of journalism have been trained on development through the Rural Survey Project and the Right to Information at the Symbiosis Institute of Media and Communication under the guidance of the late Dr Dileep Padgaonkar, R.K. Laxman Chair Professor of Symbiosis International University.

Degrees for Journos

This brings to the fore the importance of having knowledgeable, well-educated and qualified journalists in the print media. This writer does not want to enter into a debate on former PCI Chairman Justice Markandey Katju's suggestion for a basic qualification for journalists. While one does not know the fate of the three-member committee appointed by Justice Katju on the issue, it would suffice to say that journalism is a profession which cannot be confined to only those having the basic graduate and postgraduate degrees in journalism.

Justice Katju's argument that doctors, engineers, lawyers and chartered accountants will have to complete their respective professional degrees first before becoming eligible to do their respective jobs may have merit and be relevant to these technical professions. However, this argument is unconvincing and does not hold water in the case of journalists. The very nature and scope of the journalistic profession is such that one can make a mark in journalism only if he/she has a flair for writing and reporting irrespective of whether he/she is a student of political science, literature, philosophy, engineering or architecture. It is precisely for this reason that the Symbiosis Institute of Media and Communication holds a Writing Ability Test (WAT) for admission to Master of Arts (Mass Communication) programme, in addition to the national aptitude test, every year irrespective of the undergraduate candidates' discipline. If a professional body like the Editors' Guild of India (or even the PCI) commissions a random survey on journalists in major newspapers and news agencies such as the Press Trust of India and the United News of India, it would be interesting to see how many of them have the requisite journalism degrees—graduation or post-graduation. Be that as it may, there is no second opinion on the need for attracting bright and young minds to journalism.

Wide Array of Issues

This project, perhaps first of its kind in the field of journalism in the country in terms of its professional approach, content, expertise and intellectual worth, comprises five sections—Editors' Experiences, Digital Media, Media Laws, Special Areas, and Reporting and Editing. Section I consists of six articles by distinguished Editors, known for their impeccable credentials and proven track record—the late B.G. Verghese, the late Dileep Padgaonkar, H.K. Dua, Hiranmay Karlekar, Hari Jaisingh and Raj Chengappa.

Section II on digital media consists of four pieces, each one dealing with a specific area: Internet, smartphone journalism, TV–print–digital businesses and television.

Section III deals with media laws. It has three pieces: one on freedom of speech and expression by the eminent jurist and constitutional expert Soli J. Sorabjee; the second on elections and the media by S.Y. Quraishi, former Chief Election Commissioner of India; and the third on sting operations by Dr Shashikala Gurpur, Dean, Faculty of Law, Symbiosis International University and former Member, Law Commission of India.

Section IV on special areas consists of 10 articles. These cover a wide array of issues—Edit Page specialisation, journalistic ethics, development issues, research in journalism, investigative journalism and environment. The writers are known for their expertise in these areas. While some of them are recipients of national awards for excellence in journalism, others have demonstrated their leadership in their chosen areas of specialisation over the years. Section V has five articles, dealing with the dynamics of reporting and editing.

These articles seek to present a comprehensive picture of the media to students, academics, industry professionals and the general public. Peers should treat the book as a primer on journalism. The book seeks to inform and educate not only students and journalists but also the general public on some of the major contemporary trends, issues and processes in governance, institutions, administration and development, among others, and the role of the media, including the new media. This is perhaps for the first time in the history of Indian journalism that many eminent Editors, experts and academics have been brought together on one forum to discuss a critical discipline, which is at the crossroads. The efforts of the Editors would fructify if this project helps stimulate good journalistic practices and contributes to the existing body of knowledge.

References

Anand, V. Eshwar. (1985, 10 February). Parliamentary work: Need to reform procedures. *The Statesman.*

———. (1986, 25 February). Parliament at work: Some ideas for reform. *The Statesman.*

———. (1987, 11 September). State funding for elections. *Hindustan Times,* New Delhi.

———. (1994, 2 February). The need for parliamentary reforms. *The Indian Express.*

———. (2002, 1 September). Will ordinance check criminalisation of politics? When politicians betray people's trust. *The Tribune.*

———. (2005, 17 January). Criminals in Bihar elections: Patna High Court cracks the whip. *The Tribune.*

———. (2005, 21 February). Directive is undemocratic: Top bureaucrats not above rule of law. *The Tribune.*

———. (2007, 14 September). Polity under strain: Making political parties accountable. *The Tribune.*

———. (2010, 16 March). Power to order CBI probe: SC settles the law. *The Tribune.*

———. (2010, 23 April). Subversion of democracy: Time to root out the menace of paid news. *The Tribune,* Chandigarh.

———. (2011, 13 April). State funding: An overdue reform. *The Tribune.*

———. (2012, 22 May). Why recall? Elect carefully. *The Tribune.*

Avienaash. (2016, 27 May). Assembly elections 2016: One in three MLAs have criminal record. *The Hindu,* Chennai.

Business Standard. (2016, 22 November). TRAI slashes ceiling tariffs for USSD-based mobile banking. *Business Standard.*

Chatterjee, Somnath. (2010). *Keeping the Faith: Memoirs of a Parliamentarian.* NOIDA: HarperCollins.

Chauhan, Chetan. (2017, 10 August). Poll panel's order to disqualify two votes in Gujarat is extraordinary. *Hindustan Times.*

Daily News and Analysis (DNA). (2014, 18 May). Almost 700 paid news cases detected in 2014 Lok Sabha elections. DNA.

Ghose, Dipankar. (2014, 10 September). Free, fearless press is in interest of society and nation: Speaker. *The Indian Express.*

Godbole, Madhav. (2003). Parliament and democratic governance. In Ajay K. Mehra and Gert W. Kueck (Eds.), *The Indian Parliament: A comparative perspective* (p. 152). Delhi: Konark Publishers.

The Indian Express. (2017, 2 September). Slowing down. *The Indian Express,* editorial.

Janyala, Sreenivas. (2016, 22 November). At Telangana's vegetable market, new currency is tokens for ₹5, ₹10 or ₹20. *The Indian Express.*

Kale, Sumita. (2016, 29 November). Payments banks in unchartered territory. *Mint.*

Kumar, Manish. (2016, 1 June). ndtv.com.

Mahtab, Bhartruhari. (2017, 24 February). Throttle the insatiable vice of corruption. *Mint*.

Mint. (2014, 12 September). Court sets aside EC order on Ashok Chavan's poll spending. *Mint*.

———. (2015, 6 February). Supreme Court Draws the Line On Criminal Records. *Mint*.

ndtv.com. (2016, 8 December). For God's sake, do your job: President Pranab Mukherjee's rebuke amid Parliament chaos. Retrieved 22 November 2017, from https://www.ndtv.com/india-news/for-gods-sake-do-your-job-president-pranab-mukherjees-rebuke-amid-parliament-chaos-1635540

New Indian Express. (2017, 24 June). *New Indian Express*, Bengaluru.

Panda, Baijayant 'Jay'. (2016, 23 November). Now reform political funding: If we have the will, here is how to make a lasting impact on black money. *The Times of India*.

Pande, Mrinal. (2010, 27 August). The classified truth. *The Indian Express*, New Delhi.

Quraishi, S.Y. (2017, 10 August). And the winner is EC. *The Indian Express*.

Rai, Vinod. (2014). *Not just an accountant: The diary of the nation's conscience keeper*. New Delhi: Rupa.

Sainath, P. (2011, 4 February). Censorship by pay-to-print. *The Hindu*, Chennai.

Sen, Sankar. (2013, 16 May). Liberating the CBI. *The Telegraph*.

Sen, Ronojoy. (2014, 8 July). Disruptions will remain plentiful. *The Times of India*.

Sinha, Bhadra. (2014, 27 August). Onus of disqualifying tainted ministers on PM: SC. *Hindustan Times*.

Supreme Court of India. (2017). Writ Petition (Civil) No. 494 of 2012.

Thakur, Pradeep. (2014, 7 September). Centre asks states to speed up trial against tainted politicians. *The Times of India*.

Thakurta, Paranjoy Guha. (2012). Paid news: Corruption in the Indian media. In *Media Ethics* (pp. 212–257). Oxford: Oxford University Press.

The Economic Times. (2013, 9 December). *The Economic Times*.

———. (2015, 22 February). It's ₹10000-crore scam, says Santanu Saikia. *The Economic Times*.

———. (2016, 11 May). *The Economic Times*.

The Hindu. (2015, 22 February). Saikia sold info, says ex-official. *The Hindu*.

The Indian Express. (2016, 12 July). *The Indian Express*.

The Indian Express. (2017, 2 September). Slowing down. *The Indian Express*, editorial.

The Times of India. (2013, 7 December). *The Times of India*.

———. (2014a, 12 June). *The Times of India*.

———. (2014b, 24 December). *The Times of India*.

The Times of India. (2016, 2 June). Possessing disproportionate assets not a crime in itself: SC. *The Times of India*.

———. (2017, 12 August). Record productivity in monsoon session. *The Times of India*.

Viswanathan, S. (2010, 4 October). Ending paid news: It's time to act. *The Hindu*.

SECTION I

Editors' Experiences

1

The Last Word

B.G. Verghese

The newspaper Editor's role as the ultimate gatekeeper of everything published must be restored.

The Editor is the kingpin of any newspaper or journal. This is not merely a truism but a legal truth as confirmed by the Supreme Court in a case concerning *Sandesh*, a leading Gujarati journal, in respect of a news item published in the Vadodara edition of its state-wide chain in 1999. The Mamlatdar had filed a case against the paper's Chief Editor, Falgunni Chimanbhai Patel, alleging that the item in question had defamed him. The Editor argued that since he was in Ahmedabad, the Resident Editor of the Vadodara edition must be held responsible.

The High Court upheld this contention. However, on appeal, the Supreme Court ruled in March 2013 that wherever he be, the Chief Editor, whose name appears on the imprint line of the paper, as required under Section 7 of the Press and Registration of Books Act, 1867, was liable for the entire printed content of his paper 'as the PRB Act does not recognise any other legal entity'. He is the watchdog and ultimate gatekeeper for everything published, including advertisements, 'advertorials', columns, letters to the Editor, cartoons, graphics, photographs and captions.

This is well established. As Editor of *Hindustan Times* (HT; 1969–1975), I had on occasion pulled out advertisements and other material from the paper before printing, on the grounds that the matter was offensive or in bad taste or propagated superstition or magic remedies. The management did not take kindly to this intervention and would plead revenue loss and contractual obligations. But I always had the last word as Editor.

My relations with the proprietor of HT, K.K. Birla, were cordial. While he would critique the paper and offer a variety of suggestions, I followed an independent line consistent with the liberal policy framework I was contracted to observe when appointed. If the proprietor differed or had a change of heart, it was open to him to sack his Editor and not dictate to him, unless the Editor was pliable, not principled and succumbed.

Differences did develop in 1974–1975 in the run-up to the Emergency. Birla told me he had three complaints regarding the HT's coverage. Sanjay Gandhi felt HT had been unfair in reporting the affairs of his Maruti project. The owners of Modi Flour Mills believed they were being targeted since we had persevered in covering a case involving the company despite requests to desist from doing so. And Birla felt we were gunning for L.N. Mishra (who was later assassinated) for his role in Bihar's troubled politics. I had no difficulty in countering all three complaints but was firm in stating that while we had no desire to pillory anybody, corruption was eating into the vitals of the country and we could not, therefore, be muzzled, and would continue to report all matters of public interest fairly and objectively.

The hapless Birla had come under the influence of the political powers that be, especially Sanjay Gandhi. I said I was ready to quit as Editor if I had lost the confidence of the proprietor but owed HT readers an explanation. Birla, however, decided to 'retire' me despite expressing full confidence in me at the same time! The matter went to the Press Council of India and subsequently to the Delhi High Court. The matter became a cause célèbre and resulted in the abolition of the Press Council in 1975. The government feared the stingingly adverse verdict the Council was known to have formulated.

I had earlier written to Birla as follows:

> The ultimate test of freedom of the press is the right of dissent. This cannot mean irresponsibility. It does mean, however, that we must have the courage to state our views openly and frankly. We must be prepared to stand up and be counted. We must have the courage of our convictions. And if we are shown to be wrong, we must have the integrity to correct ourselves and apologise. This we have done and shall always strive to do. We certainly shall not be dictated to by a bunch of faceless men, those contemptible creatures be they politicians, howsoever powerful, or others who dare not face the Editor but would stab him in the back.

I closed with Tagore's 'Where the mind is without fear, and the head is held high …' and said these words eloquently conveyed what I was talking about. I was sacked. I had been Information Adviser to the Prime

Minister from 1966 to 1968. A contemporary cartoon commented: 'Indira admired, Verghese hired. Indira tired, Verghese fired'!

The Delhi High Court, however, continued its hearing and delivered its judgement on 22 September 1975. One of my counsels, R.P.K. Shankardass, wrote in *Seminar*, then edited by Romesh Thapar (excerpted from *First Draft* by B.G. Verghese, 2010):

> The most important question before the court was the scope and content of 'freedom of the press' and, in particular, whether it extended to the Editor as a separate entity. HT had submitted that the Editor has no fundamental right to freedom of the press under Article 19 as against the proprietor of a newspaper.
>
> Proprietors had a right to lay down the policy of their newspapers and were entitled to select the Editor. In other words, it was contended by the HT that the expression 'newspaper' in Section 12 of the Press Council Act, whose independence was sought to be protected by the Council, implied the proprietor but not the Editor, who was a limb of the newspaper.
>
> The court differed. It held that the concept of freedom of the press could not be put in a straitjacket. It was a living concept and liable to grow. The court observed that the Editor is the living, articulate voice of the press and speaks through the paper. The value of the newspaper lies in its content, the selection of which is the sole and undivided responsibility of the Editor. The court agreed that the proprietors had the right to lay down the policy of the paper. But the selection of news, its truthful, objective and comprehensive presentation from all corners of the world was the Editor's responsibility. Once the policy was laid down, the Editor must be left to work independently within that framework.

Birla's writ was dismissed.

That was 1975. It was so in 1986 when I demitted office as Editor of the *Indian Express*. The rot started in the mid-1990s with economic reform, market liberalisation, an end to the licence-permit raj and a proliferation of the print and broadcast media, with chains and satellite editions and a fierce competition for television rating points (TRPs) and circulation.

The *Times of India* led the pack. Editors were abolished and managers took over. The bottom line mattered more than the news line. 'Publish and be damned' became the unspoken motto. Paid news, private treaties, advertorials and the like became widespread. Salaries soared and mission was overtaken by commerce. The media having now become the First Estate the world over in the wake of the communications revolution, power all too often exceeds responsibility. Anything goes: sensation, trivia, gossip.

The *Times of India*'s new philosophy was cogently outlined by Vineet Jain, Managing Director, Bennett Coleman and Co. Ltd (BCCL), in an interview published in the *New Yorker* in October 2012 under the heading 'Citizen Jain'.

'We are not in the newspaper business. We are in the advertising business,' said Mr Jain. With newspapers priced so low, little revenue comes from circulation. Therefore, if 90 per cent of your revenue comes from advertisements then you are in the advertising business. 'Both Samir Jain (the Vice-Chairman of BCCL) and I think out of the box. We don't go by the traditional way of doing business.'

There are honourable exceptions. Younger journalists, fired with idealism, are restive. But in the absence of regulation—the Press Council is a broken reed; there is no formal, statutory broadcast complaints commission, and the public service broadcaster has been emasculated—the reader and the viewer have little choice.

Congeries of Individual Views

Social media is growingly popular but is not mediated and at best represents a congeries of individual views that do not add up to the voice of the people. It can be manipulated and that can be as dangerous as mistaken notions of direct democracy with total transparency, advocated by some. That is the road to anarchy.

Everything said, the Editor, not just as a person but as a collective, must be restored to the legal and moral position he/she once enjoyed and that the law has always enjoined. The mainline media constitute a public trust entrusted with the people's right to know and be informed of all sides of all matters of public interest. That role, that freedom, cannot be bartered away and must not be jeopardised for political or personal aggrandisement if democracy is to survive.

2

Playing Little Games

Hiranmay Karlekar

Reflections on being an Editor during the Emergency and gaining access to information in the times of censorship.

I was in two minds when the editorship of *Hindustan Times* was offered to me in October 1975. The Indira Gandhi government had declared a state of Emergency, and the paper's management was said to be close to the government at the Centre. A close family friend, whose advice I had sought, said that he would check with Ramnath Goenka, Chairman of the Indian Express group, and a dear friend of his, and let me know.

He called me up a few days later and told me when we met that Goenka wanted me to take the job, use it to get as close to Indira Gandhi and her inner circle as possible, find out what was going on and keep him briefed about her political plans and moves. Specifically, I should find out whether the Emergency was going to be permanent or temporary and, if temporary, when was it likely to be lifted, and whether she would hold elections and when. Was she going to make herself dictator permanently? Also did she plan to oust the Tamil Nadu and Gujarat governments and, if so, when?

On my pointing out that this could be 'risky,' he had countered, 'I would have never thought you would shy away from risks. You certainly never did that when you were in politics in Kolkata.' I told him that things had changed. I now had a wife and a son (my daughter was not yet born) and an aged mother-in-law to look after.

The family friend, a distinguished retired civil servant, had replied smilingly, that Goenka had anticipated my problem and had promised that if I was jailed, he would ensure that for the entire period of my incarceration, my family would enjoy the kind of life they were used to. This arrangement would stay for as long as my wife wanted if I was killed. And, of course, he would give me a job with roughly the same kind of perks I enjoyed as the Editor of *Hindustan Times* if I was sacked.

I had yet another misgiving: Would I not be risking my reputation as a journalist if I became Editor of *Hindustan Times* during the Emergency? He said that it was a legitimate question and that he would consult Goenka and let me know.

Risking Reputation

The next day he said:

> Here is your answer from Goenka. George Fernandes is fighting the Emergency from the underground and risking his life every moment. You are being asked to risk your reputation temporarily. Goenka will make everything clear once Indira Gandhi is out of power and the Emergency regime is thrown out.

Knowing Ramnathji to be a man who kept his word, there was hardly a way I could say 'no' after that. In the event, he not only kept his part of the bargain but also took me into the *Indian Express* after the contract for my editorship of *Hindustan Times* was prematurely terminated with effect from 1 May 1980.

I took up my new assignment on 1 November 1975, fully prepared for a bumpy ride. Fortunately, the general manager of the Hindustan Times group at that time was Santosh Nath, a thorough gentleman and a professional. He, in turn, had excellent support from Naresh Mohan, a senior executive, who, besides being most helpful, knew his job inside out. He has since carved out a distinguished place for himself in the Indian newspaper industry.

Having people like them in the management was a major advantage, as was the presence of men like Prithvis Chakravarti on the editorial side. A Radical Humanist and a great believer in human freedom, he was a fierce opponent of the Emergency. He had, as secretary-general of the National Union of Journalists of India, protested strongly against press censorship. I never told him in so many words about what I was up to. But I guess he had some idea from his own sources from the underground, and, besides repeatedly telling me to be careful, was solid as a rock in his support.

Obnoxious and Intolerable

As an Editor and journalist committed to freedom of the press, I found censorship the most obnoxious and intolerable part of the Emergency. The most one could do, however, was to play little games with the censors and publish items the government would later frown upon. Ramnathji had advised against this early on as he feared it might draw the government's attention and lead to investigation that might expose my role. He suggested that I should think of ways to get close to Indira Gandhi. I had met her a couple of times earlier, but did know her well. She knew my father-in-law, the late Asok Kumar Chanda (chairman of the committee that drafted the Chanda Committee Report advocating autonomy for radio and television), as well as my uncle-in-law, the late Anil Kumar Chanda, principal of Vishwa Bharati, secretary to Rabindranath Tagore and a Deputy Minister in the Union Council of Ministers.

Ramnathji had a bright idea (which, as in the case of all our exchanges, was conveyed through the family friend), that I should interview Indira Gandhi and make the piece as flattering as possible! I balked at the suggestion. But he insisted, as did another stalwart from the underground who knew what I was up to. I interviewed the Prime Minister as directed. She liked it. The interview was in the nature of an insurance policy. After it was published, officials who wielded the sledgehammer during the Emergency never turned their magnifying glasses on me. The freedom this gave me enabled me to gather as much information as I could.

I, however, took great pains to keep my distance from the bureaucrats and politicians who actually ran the Emergency. This was for two reasons. First, I thoroughly disliked almost all of them and the authoritarian dispensation they served with zeal. Second, I was afraid that being a free-speaking and loquacious journalist, I could let slip a casual remark that could arouse their suspicion, land me in trouble and scuttle my mission.

My life outside my home moved in two distinct streams. One was my role as the eyes and ears of the underground. The other was that of an Editor. The first had its stresses and tensions. I was lucky not to have been found out. The second was my role in running *Hindustan Times*. As for the first, I always had my antennae up—during meetings with officials, chance encounters with the authorities, on formal social occasions and so on. My main advantage was that people liked to show off their proximity to the powers that be and boast of being privy to inside information.

An example would be the way I came to know about the timing of the parliamentary elections of March 1977. During a visit to the Birla House in New Delhi in late September, 1976, to meet K.K. Birla, chairman and owner of *Hindustan Times*, I overheard a Kolkata-based industrialist, known to be close to Congress circles, tell someone that the time was March next year and that Sanjay Gandhi was dead against it.

I made a mental note of it but did not tell anyone because I wanted to be doubly sure. Then in the first week of October, I attended a tea party Indira Gandhi had thrown in honour of Michael Foot, the British Labour Party Member of Parliament (MP), known for his fiercely articulated Left-wing views. As I was leaving, I heard Sanjay Gandhi tell an important Congress leader from Punjab that the elections were going to be held in March the following year, his opposition notwithstanding, and that they should all be prepared. I went straight to the residence of my family friend and informed him. He said he would pass on the information. Four days later, he told me that Ramnathji had his doubts but would still ask his friends to get ready for the elections as he did not want to take a chance.

Pressure from the Government

There was, of course, pressure from the government to do this or that. One such was to sack Bhupen Datta-Bhaumik, our correspondent in Tripura, who had been sent to jail under the Maintenance of Internal Security Act (MISA). I sent a note to Santosh Nath saying that his retainership fee of ₹250 should be sent to him every month without fail, irrespective of whether he filed stories or not. Santosh Nath ensured that it was done. Datta-Bhaumik, who was treated as being on duty, resumed work after the March 1977 elections.

The elections were a momentous occasion and censorship was suspended during the period of campaigning. I told my colleagues that they should function as they did when there was no censorship. There was a bit of problem because many of them thought that the Congress might come back to power and penalise them if they offended it. I, however, made sure that, on critical days at least, our coverage was absolutely fair. This led to trouble with the officials on several occasions, such as in early February when Jagjivan Ram and H.N. Bahuguna announced the formation of the Congress for Democracy, Subramanian Swamy dramatically reappeared on the scene and the Janata Party published its manifesto.

There was anger against me in the establishment and veiled threats were held out. But these came to nothing as the Congress was defeated in the elections. As the streets exploded in joy, I felt Indira Gandhi, who held the elections and abided by their outcome, should not suffer vindictive action. I made this clear in my editorial on the results, which also recounted her many achievements. I followed it up by writing in my signed column that there should be no vindictive action or settling of personal scores. My cordial ties with her, however, ended when she found out about my role during the Emergency shortly thereafter. When she returned to power in January 1980, I knew that my tenure at *Hindustan Times* would soon be over.

Meanwhile, the second stream of my life, was flowing routinely—reading the newspapers in the morning, planning editorials and news coverage before coming to office, holding editorial and news conferences after reaching office, writing own editorials and column, meeting people, holding the evening news conference and having a late-night chat with the Night News Editor, if necessary. The routine remained pretty much the same even after the Janata Dal came to power. It was normal journalism again.

As I look back upon this period, I particularly remember the angry signed front-page editorial I wrote in August 1978, on the murder of two brave teen-aged siblings, Sanjay and Geeta Chopra, and the stir it created. I also recall with some satisfaction the campaign I ran against eve-teasing, again kicked off by a signed front-page editorial, in the following month.

Instant Resolve

There are several highlights that I can recall. But I have always wondered whether these have achieved anything lasting and whether little events with their ephemeral ripples add to the critical mass of developments that one day create history. A very different thought, however, occupied my mind as I left the Hindustan Times House at the end of my last day in office on 30 April 1980. Except for rare and brief spells, I had come to this building in the morning and left late in the evening every day. Henceforth, all this would be a part of a past alienated from me. I will carry with me only the impact of the experience on my psyche and memories. The result of this reflection was an instant resolve: Never again will I hold the post of Editor. I would be in journalism, which had become a part of my blood but not at the cost of doing what I always wanted to do—reading, reflecting, writing and taking photographs.

Looking back, as an Editor, I did what I had to; so have I as a journalist before and after my four-and-a-half year stint as Editor. There is, of course, the question of my relationship with K.K. Birla. These had their warm and cold phases. I will not dwell on them as what passes between an Editor and a proprietor belongs to the domain of privileged conversation not to be revealed. During my cold passages with him and, indeed, throughout my life, I have been sustained by my reading of the Bhagavad Gita, particularly the injunction, 'Therefore, without attachment, perform always the work that has to be done, for man attains to the highest by doing work without attachment' (Chapter Three, verse 19; translated by S. Radhakrishnan). I cannot claim that I have always succeeded in doing that. But I have tried, all the time.

Finally, I have always held four qualities to be most important in life— courage, wisdom, compassion and truth. Courage is the most important of them all because without it one may not be able to act as one should.

3

Credibility Is the Key

H.K. Dua

> An Editor can be said to have succeeded when readers begin to have an enduring faith in the content of the newspaper he edits.

'Can I join your paper as a subeditor or a reporter, Sir?'

'Do you have any experience?' the Editor looked up and asked.

'No, Sir, but I have a postgraduate diploma in journalism,' I said handing him my CV.

'We don't have an opening.'

'It's all right, Sir. But how do you get experience without working?' He gave me a look which clearly meant the meeting was over.

Maybe, he was busy writing, or perhaps he was trying to meet a deadline between puffs on his pipe. It was not his job to answer this kind of question. I had asked about the elementary equation between work and experience.

The Editor was the fourth in Delhi I had approached for an entry into journalism, but I had not succeeded beyond evoking a 'No' tinged with varied levels of courtesy.

Maybe the openings in journalism those days were few, and I had no contacts in the profession I was set upon joining. Was I asking for too much?

Bitterness was not the answer to the situation, nor despair. I carried on my search for a sub's job and ultimately found one in United News of India (UNI), a fledgling news agency.

It took 25 years and much hard work, besides curiosity, a questioning spirit, enthusiasm, a relentless chasing of news, late hours at the news agency in the initial years and two decades in the *Indian Express* for me to become the Editor of *Hindustan Times*, and later of the *Indian Express* and the *Tribune* and the Editorial Adviser of the *Times of India*.

It is a privilege to have had the opportunity to provide editorial leadership to four major newspapers of the country.

In the years I was special correspondent, parliamentary correspondent and political correspondent for the *Indian Express*, I learnt something new every day. I learnt even more in the 17 years I was at the top, editing four dailies at different times. Each paper had a different history and background and proprietors of varied persuasion, values and visions.

Three of these newspapers—*Hindustan Times*, the *Indian Express* and the *Times of India*—were owned by corporate groups and one— the *Tribune*—was run by a public trust. I was considered an upcoming journalist determined to take these papers forward and to make a mark as a professional with some concern for values. My experience in those newspapers was varied, but worth the effort, which, I am happy, was welcomed by the profession.

Pursuit of Truth

There are some beliefs that are sacred to journalism, and I tried to uphold them in my reporting days and as an Editor. That facts should always remain sacred and opinions free was more than an adage to me. Adherence to these basics is of importance when an Editor is set upon coming out with a newspaper that is respected for its credible news coverage and for its editorials and opinion articles. An Editor can be said to have succeeded when readers begin to have an enduring faith in the content of the newspaper he edits. This faith, like friendship, has to be kept under constant repair.

A major portion of the content of newspapers in India is political, the inheritance of a long freedom struggle. I myself spent years doing political reporting and later commenting on vital developments, beginning with Jawaharlal Nehru's death, through the brief tenure of Lal Bahadur Shastri, Indira Gandhi's years in power, the Emergency, the Janata Party rule, the return of Indira Gandhi, her assassination, Rajiv Gandhi's ascension to power, the political instability of the 1990s, the six years of Atal Bihari Vajpayee's government and then the years of the United Progressive Alliance-led by Sonia Gandhi and Manmohan Singh. Politics has remained the staple of Indian newspapers, enjoying high readership.

My attempt was certainly to compete with other newspapers by giving the most comprehensive news coverage, what is behind the news and objective analysis to help readers understand what it actually means so that they can form their own opinions on the basis of facts that must take into account all sides of the developments. One-sided news cannot help in the pursuit of truth, and the credibility of the newspaper and its Editor will suffer.

Attention to Unreported India

In whichever newspaper I was working, I was keen to draw—while not underplaying political news and articles—attention to the unreported India that had been neglected by newspapers and television channels. Shining India is not the only India that ought to be the focus of the attention of newspapers and TV news channels. My attempt was to get the neglected people of the north-eastern region, Dalits, tribal people, women and villages and small towns covered in greater detail than before. I sought to bring into focus issues such as job opportunities, health care, education, human rights, malnutrition, housing, drinking water, and the absence of toilets in most parts of the country so that public policymakers did not forget the essential concerns of the people, which are generally sidestepped. A related article titled 'Areas of Neglect: Media and Development' appears in this volume.

Also, no Editor—or journalist—in the present times can neglect issues that have marred the country's political, economic and social scene. It is sad that caste, which still decides the fate of a child through the accident of birth, is no longer fought by newspapers. The grisly phenomenon of the criminalisation of politics has become a major stigma on India's parliamentary democracy. Corruption across the country is wrecking the political system from within.

Are newspapers meant to serve the people or are they run to make profits for the proprietors? This question often crops up in the career of a newspaper Editor, particularly when owners of newspapers happen to be business groups. This question also came up during my days as an Editor and, at times, led to differences with proprietors. Any Editor who believes that journalism is meant to serve society and not the commercial interests of the proprietors is bound to run into unenviable situations that will demand clarity, tact and firmness on the part of the Editor. The basic values of the profession cannot be compromised, nor can truth be allowed to be sacrificed.

Allied is the question of editorial freedom. 'How much freedom a proprietor gives to an Editor?' I have often been asked this question by those wanting to join the media.

My answer is: 'Freedom is never given; it is exercised.'

'Isn't there a risk of losing the job?'

'Journalism is not a profession for the chicken-hearted,' I have said in answer to those who are not sure in their mind whether journalism is a mission or commercial activity. One sleeps better if one adheres to the values that guide every journalist, more so when one is an Editor.

To the question whether an Editor is supposed to serve the public interest or the private interests of the owners, the only answer is he or she has no choice but to serve the public interest—a choice a journalist in a way makes while joining the profession. It is sad, however, that journalism is increasingly becoming more a commercial enterprise than a mission. This, unfortunately, is costing the media its credibility, the maintaining of which ought to remain its creed and primary concern.

Unfortunately, independent-minded Editors are a dying species. In a large number of newspapers, owners are Editors; in many others, managers have become Editors. The *Lakshman Rekha* between Editor and proprietor has got blurred for various reasons. It is a pity that the credibility of newspapers is getting eroded. It requires serious introspection by all those who believe—and rightly so—that a free press enjoying credibility is essential for the survival of democracy in the country.

4

Reaching out to People

Hari Jaisingh

The Editor has to be an honest communicator of people's feelings and problems and keep a constant vigil against the erosion of the public good.

There are theories and sub-theories on editorial writings and how an Editor should conduct himself. In my over 40 years of career as a journalist, I have never been a textbook mediaperson. This was possibly because of the fact that I never went for a diploma or degree course in journalism. This did not handicap me professionally in my stints as Assistant Editor of the *Tribune*, Resident Editor of the *Indian Express* in Ahmedabad and Mumbai and later as a full-fledged Editor of *National Herald* (New Delhi and Lucknow), Acting Editor of *Business & Political Observer* (New Delhi and Mumbai) and nine years at the helm of the Tribune Group of Publications (English, Hindi and Punjabi).

The last stint was the hallmark of my professional career. I bowed out of the reputed Trust-run publication at the zenith of my career for reasons which I may spell out if the flow of this write-up permits me to do so. For the past seven years, I have been running an independent think tank journal called *Power Politics* with the same fervour, zeal, fearlessness and commitment to public causes I had showed when I served as Editor of the national dailies. My only regret is the magazine's limited readership base in contrast to the *Tribune*, which caters to the northern states of Punjab, Haryana, Himachal Pradesh, Jammu and Kashmir and Delhi to some extent.

Sorry for rolling out some elementary personal information. The media today do not suffer from informational, geographical or operational limitations. Information technology and social media have changed the character and reach of the media. Today, it is both personalised and globalised because of the power of the Internet, television news channels and social media platforms such as Twitter and Facebook. I have come to believe that despite occasional nonsensical elements, social media has emerged as the most powerful instrument of change in building public opinion on several sensitive issues by the articulate and assertive new generation that thinks differently and nurses different kinds of expectations from those in power, whether it is in Egypt or in India.

Here my heart goes out to the computer programmer and activist Aaron Swartz who, at 26, fought and committed suicide for wider freedom for the availability of research work via Journal Storage (JSTOR). I fully support Aaron since this will ensure greater transparency and accountability in the public arena of research work done by thinking and not-so-thinking persons.

Coming back to the main theme, I believe that an Editor has to constantly evolve with an open mind and be tuned to the changing needs and expectations of society. An Editor cannot remain in an ivory tower, nor can he be an armchair person. He must reach out to the people in order to understand their hopes and frustrations. He must not allow himself to be used by the powers that be or upmarket manipulators. His job demands that he keep himself abreast of the rights and wrongs in different segments of society.

Social Responsibility

I uphold the principle of social responsibility of the media. The Editor has to conduct himself as a guide, friend and philosopher of members of his editorial team so that each person plays his or her role meaningfully and correctly.

I shall give two examples from my diary since I practise what I believe in as a matter of my personal conviction in this highly sensitive public domain. First of all, I shall talk about a middle class lady from Ludhiana, Punjab. She came to see me at the office of the *Tribune* in Chandigarh and narrated her troubles at the hands of a land mafia.

I asked the *Tribune* Bureau Chief, Prabhjot Singh, to join me as the woman narrated her agonising story involving a property dealer who was harassing her in connivance with the local police with an eye on her property. A widow, she was living with her young daughter.

I gently grilled her about her predicament just to ensure that the newspaper was not being taken for a ride for an unknown reason. What clinched the matter was her frank remark: 'I do not want my young daughter to suffer the sort of harassment I am facing now because of this mafia's evil intentions.'

This settled the matter. I told Prabhjot to speak to her and do a comprehensive story. The story appeared on the front page of the paper the following day.

The advantage of the *Tribune* is the credibility it has established with its readers and the establishment. This credibility was built over hundred years of its existence initially in Lahore, Shimla and Ambala Cantonment, and later in Le Corbusier's modern city of Chandigarh.

A galaxy of eminent journalists, each with their own set of values and convictions, has served as its Editors.

The Ludhiana story had its desired impact in the process of fair play and justice for citizens facing harassment at the hands of the police–mafia nexus. This is the power of the *Tribune* if the Editor plays his public interest role honestly.

I shall recall another case. A young middle class woman of modest means with a postgraduate degree in science was being denied a teaching job in a school because of her inability to pay a big sum as bribe. She wrote a letter to the then Punjab Chief Minister, Parkash Singh Badal, narrating her ordeal. In the letter, she stated: 'I went to see a bank manager in my area to seek a loan on account of bribery amount.' The bank manager told her that 'the bank has no provision for giving a loan on account of bribery'. So she asked the Chief Minister for a loan, which she promised to pay back in instalment out of the salary she would draw as a teacher.

The woman sent a copy of the letter to the *Tribune*. I decided to publish it in the Editor's column. However, having realised that it may not get noticed on the Edit Page, I decided to carry the contents of the letter as a news story on the front page in order to highlight two sickening facets of society: the plight of the educated unemployed and corruption.

As expected, the story created waves in Punjab, which was in election mode. The Chief Minister was defeated. The woman got the job she wanted. The *Tribune* was blamed for a decline in the vote share of the Shiromani Akali Dal–Bharatiya Janata Party combine, which resulted in its defeat and the election of the Congress, led by Captain Amarinder Singh, to power. I was happy about highlighting the plight of an unemployed educated woman.

Public Spiritedness

An Editor should be known for his public spiritedness and not for the literary flavour of his editorials and writing skills alone. The power of the pen has to move in the direction of the people and not as a cover-up for undesirable characters in the establishment. The Editor has to be an honest communicator of people's feelings and problems. Otherwise, he is not worthy of the high chair he happens to occupy.

Similarly, when it comes to questioning the authorities on the grounds of morality and principles, the Editor is expected to take a correct and unbiased stand on men, matters and issues without fear or favour.

Let me give you another story. Young journalists in the *Tribune* reported a molestation case involving the Haryana Director General of Police, S.P.S. Rathore, who was protected by the then Haryana Chief Minister, O.P. Chautala, apparently for certain odd jobs he might have done for him. I decided that powerful individuals should not be allowed to take undue liberties with young girls. At stake were the safety, honour and dignity of these helpless women.

I wrote a signed front-page editorial under the heading, 'It's a question of dharma, Mr. Chautala' (Jaisingh, 2000). It invoked the concept of dharma as spelt out by Krishna in the Bhagavad Gita, and asked the Chief Minster to live up to the high tradition of morality in the holy land of Kurukshetra and take action against the erring police chief of his state.

It is for the Editor to carve out his role within the broad liberal parameters. The *Tribune* is known as a custodian of people's rights and freedom. That is why people look up to the Editor for guidance on critical issues of public policy. If he fails to play that role, the reputation of both the Editor and the institution would suffer.

The editorial had the desired effect not only on Chautala but also on the judiciary. The Sessions Court judge, A.K. Tyagi, was to deliver his judgement in Ambala on the day the editorial appeared.

I was told by the special correspondent, Yoginder Gupta, who covered Haryana, that the judge modified his judgement on admission of the charge sheet against the police chief and delivered his verdict on its admission in the evening instead of the scheduled time in the morning.

I am making this point to underline the importance of a responsible media, which help to keep the instruments of power on the right track. Of course, when it comes to the question of press freedom or any form of censorship, the choice before the Editor is clear and sharp. He has to rise to the occasion and express his views against censorship eloquently. Everything depends on the Editor's craftsmanship and ability to convey his views to the readers.

I was Editor of *National Herald* for three years, from 1980 to 1983, after the post was vacated by the well-known writer and columnist, Khushwant Singh. *National Herald* was founded by Jawaharlal Nehru, India's first Prime Minister. It has been known to be the Congress party's paper. Still, the Editor enjoyed sufficient freedom to write freely and fearlessly on matters of policy. Everything depends on the courage of the Editor.

When we talk of the freedom of the press, it needs to be emphasised that it all depends on the Editor. An Editor will exercise his freedom if he has no axe to grind with and no favours to seek from the powers that be. I wrote against the Bihar Press Bill, which Congress Prime Minister Indira Gandhi was supporting publicly. I wrote an edit against this move since it went against the spirit and nuances of press freedom. I need not say that it required more courage to take a stand against the Prime Minister as Editor of a paper that has close ties with the Congress. I am making this submission not for personal glorification, but to stress the point that the Editor must be honest to the profession and to his readers. It is his job to take a just stand on an issue of public interest if the government or its leaders go on the wrong track.

This is absolutely necessary for the healthy growth of a democratic polity. In a democracy, a newspaper is not only a mirror of the society it serves but also provides an outlet for public feelings and grievances. In fact, the newspaper has to identify itself with the people. It must also be a rich reservoir of varied thoughts and opinions expressed freely but logically and with an open mind and without prejudices. A dynamic democratic society such as India cannot allow its people to be blinded by half-truths and distorted thoughts. Such a situation will lead to 'a defective understanding' of people, which in itself should be a big handicap to cope with new challenges and circumstances. It is the Editor's job to ensure that his publication provides a forum for diversity and richness, which are essential elements for the healthy growth of democracy.

The landmark in my professional career was my front-page edit, 'No, my Lord!' (Jaisingh, 2002), in which I had named three judges of the Punjab and Haryana High Court for the Punjab Public Service Commission scam involving their wards. I will not go into the details of the case. I, however, believe that a wrong act has to be projected in the public domain and treated as a wrong act.

It may be mentioned that I named the three judges in the scam, overlooking the fact that two of the five members of The Tribune Trust were former Chief Justices of the Supreme Court and the Allahabad High Court. They too read the editorial like other readers. No prior permission was sought from them; nor was anything shared with anyone on this count.

Freedom has to be exercised with a sense of responsibility and in the public interest and not to score brownie points. However, one has to be correct with facts and these facts have to be based on credible documentary evidence. This requires tremendous homework. What is more, every fact has to be tested on the touchstone of public interest. In all such high-profile matters, one has to be prepared to pay a price by way of one's job.

I must say that I received the maximum number of telephone calls in my entire professional career on the day the editorial appeared, and that too from all sections of society. Like William Wordsworth's daffodils,

> They flash upon that inward eye
> Which is the bliss of solitude.

This is the only privilege I have enjoyed in my long career as journalist–Editor and author. A credible Editor should have stakes in the success of his colleagues, whether senior or junior. It is his job to see that youngsters are given opportunities according to their aptitude and calibre with a view to helping them move in the right direction. There are no shortcuts or easy ways to achieve professional excellence in journalism. It requires hard work, discipline, dedication and awareness of where public good begins and personal interests end.

Reputations are built on public interest journalism. This reputation can travel faster than light provided one conducts himself/herself honestly and professionally. It is also a fact that an Editor's image is made or unmade by one simple factor: whether one is prone to temptations or pressures from vested interests. This is a difficult task in the changing patterns of the media where moneyed proprietors call the shots. Still, even in this limited range, one can play his role honestly and consciously.

Exposing the Wrongs

Equally important is the exposure of acts of corruption, harassment and injustice. It is our job to inform people correctly and make them realise the wrongs and rights of men, matters and issues.

It is this 'input' to create public awareness that will ultimately make a difference in the quality of publications, democracy and society as a whole. In other words, we have to act as watchdogs not only of democracy but also of the quality of governance and the system.

This will be easier if the Editor works with his editorial team to heighten the understanding of important realities through the presentation of a wide spectrum of thoughts and analyses, which will provide the readers real insights into the social and political process.

My mantra has been: An Editor should neither be saleable nor purchasable. An Editor may not suit the powers that be and vested interests. Herein lies the challenge for an Editor who puts the people's interests before his personal pursuits and interests.

Editors are not born great. They acquire greatness by their karma—the karma for the good of the people—and by upholding high principles and democratic norms. An Editor has to stand for the freedom of expression and dignity and honour of all sections of society.

In his momentous work, *The Age of Reason*, Thomas Paine (1737–1809) has said that the greatest tyranny in the world is to tie the future generation to a set of dogmas and beliefs.

The philosopher of the American Revolution is right. In today's setting, dogmas and beliefs apart, tying youngsters to an unfair system and wrong decisions should also be seen as part of the tyranny syndrome of the twenty-first century.

Buddha once told his principal disciple Ananda: 'Be ye lamps unto yourself.' He did not tie them to dogmas or the tyranny of a wrong system, but left them free to be guided by the 'lamp' within them.

More than anything else, I would like persons occupying key positions in public life to be guided by the 'lamp' within and refrain from inflicting injustice on others.

There is more to life than making lakhs and crores of rupees at the cost of the future of the youth population. The public system has to be clean and fair and has to be seen as such.

I do hope what I have stated is sufficient to prick the conscience of the powers that be who invariably resort to manipulative tactics and dirty means to promote themselves and their patrons. These persons misuse their power and position for their own good or for the benefit of their patrons. It is never too late to correct the wrong course and set things right for the good of society.

It is necessary that an Editor is on constant vigil against erosion of the public good. In this context, it is worth remembering the following words of wisdom.

> Where the subjects are watchful a prince is entirely dependent on them for his status. Where the subjects are overtaken by sleepy indifference, there is every possibility that the prince will cease to function as a protector and become an oppressor instead. They who are not wide awake have no right to blame their prince....

References

Jaisingh, Hari. (2000, 5 December). 'It's a question of dharma, Mr. Chautala.' *The Tribune*, editorial.

———. (2002, 5 May). 'No, my Lord!' *The Sunday Tribune*, special editorial.

5
Coping with the Times

Dileep Padgaonkar

Newspapers must learn to afflict the comfortable and comfort the afflicted with panache: Wit and humour are needed along with sincerity and commitment.

I stepped into the world of journalism in Pune half a century ago. I was all of 17 and had been hired as a feature writer in *Poona Herald*, a new paper launched by Atur Sangtani, a builder and a philanthropist. The Editor, Abel David, had used some of my letters and the occasional article when he edited a paper called *Poona Daily News*.

I had walked out of this latter publication when the owner scrapped my column to accommodate a legal notice. It had arrived after the deadline to receive advertisements but the lawyer agreed to pay twice the normal rate and the owner accepted the offer with alacrity. He reasoned that I could always see my column in print the following day but that an opportunity to make easy money rarely knocked on the door. I had my first taste of the economics of newspapers and decided that it was a bitter pill to swallow.

David no doubt remembered this episode and probably reckoned that I was made of stern professional stuff. I was paid a monthly salary of ₹50, a handsome amount of money in those days. I spent it on second-hand books sold by pavement vendors and *raddiwalas*, on the occasional cigarette and beer and to give my friends in Fergusson College and my family a treat.

My job at *Poona Herald* was to write a daily column on foreign affairs. The subject fascinated me since I was in thrall of foreign correspondents like John Gunther, Edgar Snow and Arthur Koestler. I nursed the ambition to become such a correspondent someday, especially after I saw the film *Roman Holiday*, which featured Gregory Peck as an American correspondent in the Italian capital. Three individuals directed my reading on foreign affairs: Professor S.V. Kogekar, principal of Fergusson College, Dr D.D. Kosambi, the great Marxist scholar, and my political science teacher, and Raosaheb Patwardhan, a freedom fighter and an authority on democratic socialism.

The Profumo Scandal

My other job at the paper was to conduct interviews and provide the paper with special news stories. The first public figure I interviewed was Y.B. Chavan, the then Defence Minister. What he had to tell me hardly made news. But the fact that such a senior politician had spoken to the representative—and that too to a greenhorn—of a recently established paper saw my stock go up in the newsroom.

It rose higher when I gave the paper a scoop. The Profumo scandal was then making headlines in the United Kingdom and indeed in the international media. Profumo, a senior Minister in the British Cabinet, was involved with Christine Keeler, a prostitute. But the damaging part was that Christine Keeler was also involved with a Soviet spy. The go-between was Stephen Ward, a dashing medical doctor whose patients belonged to the country's upper crust.

In the now defunct Manney's bookshop, I spotted a paperback on the scandal. Browsing through it, I came across a passage that said that Dr Ward had spent time in Poona in the armed forces medical corps. He frequented a bar-cum-restaurant run by an Italian on East Street, a stone's throw from the offices of *Poona Herald*. David ran the story across five columns on the front page. That day I walked several inches taller.

Two days later a limousine arrived at the office. Out stepped a moustachioed gentleman. A peon rushed upstairs to say that he was looking for me. He introduced himself as Capt Colobavala, special correspondent of their weekly tabloid, *Blitz*, edited by Russi Karanjia. He said he wished to have a private word with me. Would I like to drive around with him for a few minutes?

Excited, yet nervous, about what lay in store for me, I asked a colleague, Forooq Dhondy, to accompany me. We drove down Main Street. Forooq winked and waved at the girls while I answered the captain's queries about how I had managed to get the scoop. I gave him a cock-and-bull story, which he used with his own concocted details in *Blitz* four days later. My name did not figure in this 'world exclusive' which some British tabloids had picked up. No matter. I was grateful to the swashbuckling captain, not least because he treated Farooq and me to a copious lunch at the Dorabjee restaurant at the end of the drive in the limousine.

My stint in *Poona Herald* did not last long. During the elections, the paper, under instructions from the owner, backed a Congress candidate. My own preference, given my budding interest in Marxism, was for a Left candidate. Defying the paper's policy, I wrote a column listing the reasons for my choice. The very first thing I noticed on my desk the next day was a letter saying I had been fired. This is the second lesson I learnt about journalism: If you are not happy with the paper's policy, better quit before you are shown the door.

When I look back, I am pleased with the way things turned out. The 'setbacks' were a prelude to other, far more rewarding successes, including, first and foremost, my long association with the *Times of India*, first in Paris and later in Mumbai and Delhi.

When I left Pune to pursue higher studies in France, the city had only a few daily newspapers. *Sakal* led the pack in the Marathi segment and the *Times of India* in the English one. Our sole source of news other than print was the 9 PM bulletin on All India Radio—ah!—the mellifluous voice of Melville de Mello—and other foreign radio stations such as the British Broadcasting Corporation (BBC) and the Voice of America.

The media in the city to which I returned for good in 2011, after 47 years, has reached a saturation point: more dailies, TV news channels, Internet, the works. Thanks to economic reforms, competition has grown. The country's demographics have changed and so have the tastes, interests and concerns of audiences. Once, coverage of politics dominated the media. The emphasis is now on entertainment and sports, business, shopping, food and civic affairs. The big ideological debates of times past have yielded place to debates about more mundane, practical matters.

Everything, it would appear, is driven by two factors: celebrity and entertainment. That explains, partially at least, why students in mass communication educational establishments aspire to work in advertising, PR, event management and TV rather than in print. The glamour quotient, and the money that goes with it, matters more than anything else.

Issues That Matter

But none of this makes me either cynical or pessimistic. Journalism is bound to triumph as people have had had enough of froth. The issues that have a bearing on daily life are bound to attract the energies and talents of the best in the fraternity.

And what are these issues? Poverty, energy, water, environment, health, food, security, identity questions, religious extremism and terrorism, corruption, the physical infrastructure in cities, but especially in rural India, gender and caste inequalities, the roadblocks in the path to scientific and technological innovations and entrepreneurship.

All this calls for training of journalists in several areas. The instinct for curiosity needs to be nurtured much like the flair for storytelling. Care must be taken about the use of language for effective communication. There can be no end to learning in any and every area of one's interest. The reading habit must be revived, and so should the habit to ask tough questions.

Moreover, journalists must be aware of the economics of the media much like brand managers must be aware of the potential of good journalism to further business interests. The best newspapers of the future will be the ones that strike the right balance between these imperatives. They must learn to afflict the comfortable and comfort the afflicted with panache: Wit, humour, satire will be needed along with sincerity, sense of purpose, effort and commitment. Money will follow. And so, too, doubtless, will something else that matters more than money: the satisfaction of a job well done.

6

Who Gives a Damn?[1]

Raj Chengappa

Journalism is a constant quest, not just to find out who gives a damn but also why they should.

'If you don't move out of the office and get the story, you're fired!' yelled my Editor, P.N.A. Tharakan. Given the mood that he was in, it was no empty threat. He waved a letter we had received the previous week from a doctor, who said that he had spotted a woman suffering from severe malnutrition at the city railway station and wanted us to do something about her.

I had just finished the course on mass communications from Bangalore University, where Tharakan, till then a veteran news agency journalist, had taught the fundamentals of good reporting. He was amongst our favourite teachers, both for the zest that he brought to his lectures and the narration of his scoops. Soon after we passed out of the course in June 1977, Tharakan said he was giving up his job as Chief of Bureau to launch a weekly city tabloid newspaper, the *City Tab*, with his savings. Four of us, all Tharakan's students, agreed to join, delighted not to have to look for jobs and at the prospect of our first salaries.

Hard-nosed News

Publishing weekly meant we had to hunt for a cover story that would get people to pick up our newspaper from the stands. Tharakan didn't

---

[1] Reprinted with permission from the Prem Bhatia Memorial Trust, New Delhi. This piece was published earlier in Mathur (2005).

want us to do the usual political reports or indulge in sensational tabloid journalism. Instead, the pages had to be filled with good, hard-nosed news that dealt with the triumphs and travails of Bangalore's citizens. It was easier said than done. On many weeks there would be a desperate scramble to find a powerful story; the morning Tharakan threatened me with dire consequences was one such.

When I reached the railway station, I finally located the destitute woman. She was in bad shape; only a torn gunnysack covered her emaciated body. Her unwashed hair was crawling with maggots; too weak to move, she urinated and defecated where she lay. Since I had to do my job as a reporter, I shook her gently to find out how she had come to such a state of despair. She was too feeble to even open her eyes, so I decided to get her a glass of milk. Ignoring the maggots, I lifted her head and fed her the milk. Another footpath dweller, the wife of a cobbler, came to my rescue and got her to drink the milk. Meanwhile, a sizeable crowd of curious onlookers gathered at the scene. Some threw coins at us; others spat and went away.

When some life seemed to return to the woman, I got down to the job of collecting facts for my story. I asked her name. The woman's eyes lit up momentarily and then went blank as if to say that having a name was no longer of any consequence. I shot her other questions: Where did she come from? Did she have a family? Again, only her eyes answered me, flickering with recognition at the import of the questions before their light was snuffed out by the apparent hopelessness of her state.

I decided to get her medical attention. I called the superintendent of the largest government hospital in the city, whom I knew. He said that his ambulances were busy, but if I brought her to the hospital he would ensure that she was treated on priority. The Municipal Corporation, which had ambulances on standby, brushed aside my request to send one across. In desperation, I approached the City Police Commissioner, also a friend, who said that as a special case he would spare an accident relief vehicle.

By then I realised that this was drama in real life and called a photographer to rush to the spot. We photographed the entire sequence: her lying on the footpath; crowds assisting us to lift her into the ambulance; the hospital, where her hair was shaved off to get rid of the maggots before she was put on a clean bed and given treatment. Unfortunately, she was too far gone, and the next day the doctors called up to say that she had died. They only got to know her name: Lakshmi.

We ran the entire episode as our lead story with the banner: 'Woman dies of starvation' and a kicker below: 'Abetted by pass-the-buck rules and an insensitive city'. The impact was instantaneous. The Municipal Corporation Chairman called up to say that he was assigning two new ambulances with telephone numbers for anyone who wanted to help the destitute. Our office was flooded with calls from people who had spotted people in a similar condition, asking how they could go about rescuing them.

Few stories that I have done in my 28 years as a journalist have had such an impact on me as that of Lakshmi's plight. Since then I have reported extensively on a range of subjects whether on environment, science, health, politics, business, international affairs and even India's nuclear tests. Throughout these years of chronicling contemporary events, when I look back, the reports that satisfied me the most were the ones in which I could get the reader to relate to people or events I wrote about with emotion, get them deeply involved in the story and make them believe that, howsoever small they were in the scheme of things, it was still in their power to make the difference.

Around the same time that I wrote the report on Lakshmi, I had a visitor to my office, a deaf-mute who wanted to explain to me how he felt society perceived his handicap. Since I didn't follow sign language, we spent an hour conversing by writing on pieces of paper. So powerful was the way he presented his case that we carried the report in that format. That, too, saw a wave of letters flow in, and his grateful father presented me with a book that I still cherish, *The Art of Creative Interviewing*. It was here that I first got to read about the question that professors in American schools of journalism taught their students to ask whenever they started on a report: Who Gives a Damn?

For me it was a powerful question, one I ask myself even today when I set out to do a story. Journalists tend to get so caught up with the story that they assume an equal level of reader interest in events happening not just around the city but also the country and the world. But why should a reader in Delhi or Bangalore (now Bengaluru) care about people dying of starvation in Darfur in Sudan? Why should we be subjected to daily reports of the shoot-outs in Baghdad instead of more in-depth reports of what is happening in our own cities and towns? How do you get an urban reader involved in the plight of women in villages who have to walk kilometres every day to fetch a bucket of water or collect firewood? Why should the poaching of tigers be of such interest when a majority have not seen the animal in the wild and probably never will?

Never have these questions been more relevant for journalists as they are today. As the world shrinks and the proverbial global village becomes a reality, our readers and viewers are being bombarded by images and reports of the goings-on in the remotest corner of the globe—of people and places they have never seen or never will, of events that have little impact on their daily lives except perhaps to be of limited curiosity value. It may seem blasphemous to ask, but why should Tony Blair's re-election as Prime Minister of UK be banner headlines in Indian newspapers? Why should Vladimir Putin's efforts to retain an iron grip over Russian politics be of any concern to an Indian salesman in Hyderabad? People unconnected with these developments need to be told *why* they should care about them. I believe most of us are failing to do that job.

What Really Interests Readers?

Let's turn the searchlight closer home and ask ourselves the same deep and perhaps troubling questions: Who cares? Why should they? What really interests readers or viewers? Some answers are easy. A woman is raped in Delhi; naturally its citizens want to know the details of the crime and what the city police have done about it. Such an incident directly threatens the security of every family in Delhi. But should someone in Bangalore, who might never visit Delhi, be equally concerned, and if so why? Or why should the news of Indian garment exports growing by 50 per cent involve a reader with no stake in the subject? Why should the victory of the AIADMK in two by-elections in Tamil Nadu be of interest to someone in Punjab and Bihar?

I could go on but perhaps I found the answer to the question about who really gives a damn while covering reports on the environment. When I went to cover the Earth Summit in Rio in 1992, the most significant moment for me was not when 150 world leaders who had assembled there spoke out in one voice to save the environment. The event that moved me the most was when Chief Oren N. Lyons, faith keeper of the Onondagas and head of the Confederation of Native Americans, spoke simply but passionately to a gathering of pressmen about the destruction of the environment. He told us:

> The elders told us almost 500 years ago that there is going to come a time when you will not be able to drink the water. Water will become the enemy. That our great elder brother, the Sun, from whom all life comes, will burn and smoke and now we have global warming. That the thundering voices of the grandfathers that bring the rain will begin to kill the trees, as it happens with acid rain.

Then, talking about the future course of action, Chief Lyons said:

> We were taught that every chief must have skin seven spans thick to withstand the barbs and arrows mostly from his own people and not to hold

counsel only for ourselves, our family or our generation. But every decision should reflect on the welfare of the seventh generation.

There was not a dry-eyed hack present when he finished his speech. And we all gave him a standing ovation. Till then the summit was filled with dense negotiations over the commitment of nations—largely bland statements that typified UN meetings. There was very little of the human touch and it was the Native American chieftain who brought home with such eloquence and feeling the reason why we had all assembled in Rio.

It was while covering the environment that I discovered what I call the thread of life and the fragile but significant connection that links us all. While doing reports on biodiversity we learnt that every habitat from the thick forests in the Western Ghats to the deserts of Rajasthan and the snow-covered mountains of the Himalayas harbours a unique combination of plants and animals that live in a delicate balance. Each plant or animal living there is linked in the food web to only a small part of the other species. But eliminate one species and there is a cascading impact on all other species in the food chain, resulting in an entire ecosystem being eroded or even becoming extinct.

Postulate all this to the environment that we live in, and we begin to see the links between seemingly unconnected news events. We need to know about the struggle of a village woman to fetch water to think about where we get water from in the city and whether we will face the same shortages. We are already experiencing this in most cities, where water supply is restricted to several hours daily, and in some of them to every alternate day during summers. Also, if that woman isn't getting basic amenities in the village where she lives, it could start a chain of migration of rural families to cities and put enormous pressure on the existing urban infrastructure. If there were no jobs available, they would end up as destitute as Lakshmi or turn to begging or, worse, crime. Our families and we could become victims of such neglect.

The Complex Web of Connections

The answer lies in understanding a concept we tend to easily forget—the complex web of connections between a nation and its citizens. There is a compact that exists between all Indians who, after Independence, agreed on certain principles that would guide this nation: we would ensure, while working for our own well-being, that our work is for the benefit of the nation and also the world; we would live together in harmony and be governed by the rule of law; we would ensure that all men and women live with equality, freedom and justice; we would elect representatives who we believe would reflect our collective will and ensure that we are governed well.

Like the millions of cells that populate our body and work quietly to keep us alive, the people of a nation cooperate and contribute to ensure that the whole prospers. An errant cell can turn cancerous and impact the entire body and, therefore, has to be dealt with at an early stage. A cut in the finger, however minor, still hurts and signals are sent to the rest of the body. The nation then is like an organic entity and part of a journalist's job is to make its readers constantly aware of that slender connection that links us all to it so vitally. So the victory in the by-elections in Tamil Nadu is an affirmation that we are living up to our democratic ideals and, in these days of coalition politics, could impact the national government as well. A rise in textile exports could mean jobs across many sectors, so we need to tell the reader where and how. If there is a breakdown in law and order in Delhi then it is a bleeding wound that could spread elsewhere to the body politic and must be treated.

There is also a global compact that we have all entered, which makes events across the world relevant to each of us, even though the connections may be difficult to pin down. When I went to Kuwait in 2003 to cover the Iraq war, I had to ask why an Indian reader should be involved in the battle to evict Saddam Hussein. Was it the rise in oil prices that we should be worried about? Would the large number of Indian expatriates working in the Gulf be impacted? Why shouldn't India be sending troops to assist the US or, conversely, working with other nations to prevent the US from carrying out an unjust war? When I flew to Afghanistan to cover the war against terror post 9/11, I had to again keep in mind the relevance to readers back home: That, by wiping out the rule of the Taliban, it would, in an odd way, be advantageous for India in its fight against terror in Kashmir.

Some of what I am saying is so obvious. But when it comes to the daily grind of news, we quite easily forget to explain the links in the presumption that the reader is aware. The increasing popularity of vacuous city supplements is an example of just how disconnected readers are getting from the main newspapers and how easily distracted by less serious and even frivolous stuff. If there is a rape in Delhi and we are reporting it from Bangalore, we need to question just how safe women are in that city. Then the relevance of the crime hits home rather than leaving the reader with only a voyeuristic view of events. We have to keep revealing to readers the link or the thread of life between them and events as disparate as the re-election of Blair, the war in Iraq or the famine in Darfur. For the degree of interdependence between nations is high, anything that happens anywhere in the world, in some way, small or big, has its impact on our lives. We have to end indifference among readers, or it would ultimately result in a drop of readership and reduce the mass media's place as the main source of information.

Give this a boring tab and call it 'relevant journalism'. But it is the kind of stuff that would make the difference and keep readers coming back to us. It would help them understand better the complex world they live in, and make them feel less impotent in dealing with or comprehending events that always seem to happen in fast forward in the emerging new world order of things. Paradoxically, even as we control the forces of nature, as individuals, we have less and less control over our own surroundings. There is a high degree of compartmentalisation in everything we do, and the thread of life and the connections are rarely visible. We may have learnt to travel faster and with more comfort in a car, but if it broke down in the middle of the road, most of us would not be competent to fix it ourselves. Compare this with the time we only used to have cycles, when everyone knew how to dismantle one and put it together. Technology, which is a great enabler, can also be a source of disempowerment. So it is important that we journalists help our readers interpret the world and understand the connections and empower them with the knowledge to act if they wanted to.

Recording People's Experiences

Most often, while we chase the big story, we forget the little things that are happening around us that probably have more relevance to readers. Journalism is also about recording people's experiences that help us to learn about the world and ourselves. At *India Today*, I was travelling in a train from Delhi to Agra to do a feature on the boom of domestic tourism in the mid-1980s. I noticed a blind couple with two sighted children seated ahead of me. At the Taj Mahal, I was moved to see them walk around the monument, touching its sides to fathom its beauty. On the way back, we were in the same carriage and when we reached our destination, I offered to drop them in my taxi.

I soon discovered Mangalsain Bhalla and his wife, the couple, were better at directions than I was. For when the taxi took a left turn, Bhalla screamed at him and asked him why he was taking the longer route. Surprised, I asked Bhalla how he could make all this out. He replied that he had timed the journey from the station to his house and had memorised every turn so he knew when the driver was playing up. As we kept talking, my respect grew for the couple and how well they had adapted to their handicap. So I requested them to allow me to spend a few days with them trying to chronicle their remarkable life.

In the office, to the credit of my Editor-in-Chief, Arun Purie, he agreed to allow me to work on such an abstract idea. Raghu Rai, India's best-known news photographer, was instantly interested and together we put out a moving photo feature in the magazine that brought us tremendous reader response. We had mentioned that Bhalla needed a Braille thermometer to check whether his children had fever when they fell sick but couldn't get one in India. Offers from all over the world poured in for this simple need. To me, Bhalla's most memorable line was when I asked him if he knew what light was. His reply: 'I don't know what darkness is.'

For me the need to understand the world of a blind man was self-empowering—it had forever changed my notions about the way they lived. Many of our readers who wrote in expressed similar emotions. The litmus test of the effectiveness of any article that I wrote is whether it changed the way that my reader looked at things. While doing a report on the rise in cancer, when I saw patients without one of their lungs, I quit smoking and was in some way gratified that readers wrote in saying they had also done so. When I wrote about depression and alcoholism, I was inspired by the way psychiatrist got people to take one day at a time on the way back to rehabilitation. To do the small tasks first so that it gave them the confidence of taking on bigger responsibilities. It taught me how to tackle my own simple problems of life, as I believe it did to many people who read that article. When I held the hands of orphaned children of Afghanistan and Somalia, I felt they were no different from my own children. I wept at how destructive humans can be of their own societies and wrote about how we should cherish Indian democracy.

No journalist, I believe, can write with conviction unless he or she begins to understand that thread of life, that cord that binds us all, that makes us aware of the oneness of the universe that our ancient philosophy espouses. For me, journalism is a constant quest not just to find out who gives a damn but also why they should. In doing so, we empower people with the knowledge to understand themselves and the complex world around them and bring a certain cosmos to the chaos of information that we constantly bombard them with.

Reference

Mathur, Asha Rani (Ed.). (2005). *The Indian media: Illusion, delusion and reality. Essays in Honour of Prem Bhatia*. New Delhi: Rupa.

SECTION II
Digital Media

7

Online Challenges

Charu Sudan Kasturi

Embracing the digital media will earn traditional media organisations and journalists a valuable friend.

In April 2011, *Miami Herald*, among United States' greatest legacy newspapers and winner of 20 Pulitzer Prizes lost some of the bragging rights that came with the rare, idyllic view it offered senior Editors and executives from their offices.

The newspaper was headquartered on the edge of the Biscayne Bay in Florida, and tiny islands dotted the Atlantic Ocean that stretched out beyond its building's windows.

However, as the newspaper's revenues tanked, it was forced to turn for advertising to the very rival threatening to disrupt its century-old history like never before. That spring, boats and planes surveying the Miami coastline saw a giant hoarding carrying an advertisement for iPad blocking one part of the facade of the Herald headquarters.[1]

In 2013, the Herald sold its waterfront property to a Malaysian developer and shifted to a two-storey building in a Miami suburb. But the Herald was fortunate. It survived. On 27 February 2009, Colorado's oldest newspaper, the *Rocky Mountain News*, wound up its print operations altogether, the first major paper in America to shut down after the 2008 economic recession.

---

[1] Grueskin, Bill, Seaves, Ava, and Graves, Lucas. (2011). Columbia Journalism Review. The story so far: What we know about the business of digital journalism. http://www.cjr.org/the_business_of_digital_journalism/introduction.php (accessed on 21 November 2017).

The *New York Times*, on the other hand, has crossed 2 million online-only paid subscriptions, and its total subscriptions—print and online together—today total over 3.5 million, the highest ever in the history of the newspaper.[2]

More than 12,874 miles away in India, the newspaper industry on the whole continues to grow, fuelled by rising literacy and relatively low Internet penetration—34.8 per cent—nationally.[3] No major Indian newspaper has had to shut down so far following a collapse of its revenue stream because of digital journalism.

However, worrying signs are already visible. Between 2009—when the *Rocky Mountain News* died—and 2014, the readership of India's six largest English dailies—the *Times of India*, *Hindustan Times*, the *Hindu*, the *Telegraph*, the *Economic Times* and *Mumbai Mirror*—cumulatively grew only by 8.4 per cent.[4] This was a period when, despite an economic slowdown, the Indian economy grew by 75 per cent.

Internet penetration has increased sixfold, from 5.1 per cent of India's total population to 34.8 per cent, or 462 million users in this period.

Young journalists entering the workforce in India are today expected by their print or television organisations to be social media savvy. Several credible online-only news organisations have emerged, drawing on young talent.

But in the absence of any formal training in the history and evolution of the digital medium, they remain ill-equipped to use the potential of this platform to augment their print and broadcast stories, strengthen their ties with readers and viewers and prepare for the future.

Many legacy news organisations in India, including some of the biggest names in the business, remain unprepared for some of the basic challenges journalism presents in the online age. They still think of themselves in the print or television binary, a description that robs them of opportunities the online medium offers them.

That, according to John Temple, the last Editor of *Rocky Mountain News*, was precisely what felled the 130-year-old newspaper that was brought out by the Scripps Company, one of America's most venerable publishers. 'You have to know what business you are in. We thought we were in the newspaper business,' Temple said, in a lecture at the

---

[2] The Niemann Lab. http://www.niemanlab.org/reading/the-new-york-times-now-has-more-than-3-5-million-subscribers/ (accessed on 21 November 2017).
[3] Estimated Internet penetration in India. http://www.internetlivestats.com/internet-users/india/ (accessed on 21 November 2017).
[4] Indian Readership Survey statistics, from 2009 to 2014. http://www.mruc.net/ (accessed on 21 November 2017).

University of California Berkeley Technology Summit at the Google complex in Silicon Valley in 2009. 'Well, Scripps is not a newspaper company anymore in what was its biggest market.'[5]

The Economics of the Digital Medium

To be sure, the economics of the digital medium are still evolving, and the debate over financial models that work and those that do not is ongoing. Unlike in the traditional medium, media ethics and law in the digital space also remain largely undefined, particularly in India.

However, to deny that the digital medium will increasingly shape the future of journalism in India as it has in the rest of the world would be akin to arguing that climate change, while a valid concern globally, is not something Indians need to worry about. The good news is that the digital medium need not be bad news if today's journalists grasp the potential and the challenges posed by the online platform. The key to this is to shake off a few popular myths.

First, the growth of the digital medium in no way reduces the importance of the journalist. In fact, trained journalists have an even more important responsibility in the online age because they alone have the skills and understanding to separate the important from the redundant and facts from claims and rumours that flood our information landscape. When everyone with access to the Internet thinks he or she can communicate with the rest of the world, it democratises the information space. But the information overload this can create risks leaving the discerning news consumer lost and confused. It is the job of journalists in the digital age to guide them from that chaos to clarity.

Second, the fundamental skills that are required for quality journalism remain the same across various media platforms. The ability to spot hidden stories, to tap and cultivate sources, to investigate cleverly but doggedly, and to write in a way that grips the reader or produce a news video in a manner that holds the viewer's attention are skills journalists need in the digital sphere, too.

Third, the digital medium can kill traditional news organisations only if they refuse to evolve. If they see the online platform as an opportunity to develop and share content and to reach out to an audience they

---

[5] Speech by John Temple, former Editor of the Rocky Mountain News, on the newspaper's demise. http://www.johntemple.net/2009/09/lessons-from-rocky-mountain-news-text.html (accessed on 21 November 2017).

previously could not, the transition, while bumpy, can prove as exciting as it is challenging.

Over the past two decades, newspaper stories in India have shrunk in length, owing to a combination of growing advertisement pressures and perceptions that the attention span of readers is declining. Many news channels today sell either entertainment or hyperbole as news, carefully avoiding any multiplicity of views or different shades of perspective. Again, this phenomenon is laid at the door of the viewer—who, it is argued, wants such content on his or her television screen.

These arguments can be debated. But even assuming that they have merit, the revival in readership of long-form journalism through online-only platforms such as the Big Roundtable[6]—and of online, app-based publishing houses such Juggernaut Books[7]—also suggests a different, growing market.

Long-form Narratives Online

Nothing stops mainstream newspapers from offering online—apart from their short news stories—occasional long-form narratives that capture the nuances of subjects that may need more in-depth reporting. There is no space constraint in the online medium. Newspapers have a chance to compete for the niche long-form reading audience as well. An example is the *Guardian*, one of the UK's most respected publications, and its *Long Reads* section.[8]

Already, some Indian news organisations are seizing the opportunities the digital platform offers, to try and expand their reach in ways they never could. The *Indian Express*, always influential but with a limited reach because of a small print circulation, is now reaching more readers than ever before, as one of India's fastest growing digital news companies.[9]

---

[6] Big Roundtable. http://www.thebigroundtable.com/about/ (accessed on 21 November 2017).

[7] Juggernaut Publishers. http://www.juggernaut.in/ (accessed on 21 November 2017).

[8] *The Guardian* Longread. http://www.theguardian.com/news/series/the-long-read (accessed on 21 November 2017).

[9] Indian Express Digital Is Now India's Number 2 Digital Media Group. http://indianexpress.com/article/business/companies/indian-express-digital-is-now-indias-no-2-digital-media-group-4533328/ (accessed on 21 November 2017)

Television channels can likewise report and produce videos on subjects that may be of more niche interest, but that no longer need to be ignored because of the limitations of airtime and the priorities of grabbing eyeballs on screen. That can continue, but these more in-depth videos can be made available online. Television channels can broaden their audience base and cater to wider interests. There is no reason why quality broadcast channels cannot move, for instance, videos of science stories online.

Ironically, it is radio, the oldest of broadcast medium that has made some of the best use of the digital media. It does not matter whether you are in New Delhi or New Haven, the National Public Radio site allows you to live-stream its contents. Archives of podcasts enable listeners to look up shows they missed and listen to them at their convenience. All India Radio has started live-streaming four music channels.[10]

User-friendly graphics online can make the navigation of news stories more interactive. As the US Presidential nomination contests wound their way through the spring of 2016, many newspapers and channels online offered visitors the option of graphically visualising the votes the various candidates would need in different states to numerically win them their party's nomination.[11] News organisations can use social media to crowd-source updates and contacts during a crisis that may be unfolding in a remote location where no reporter can be sent immediately.

Journalists and news organisations can now engage readers and viewers in a manner they never could earlier, through chats and conversations, about stories on Facebook, Twitter or on Google Hangout. They can post online links to source documents they have used for stories, enabling readers to verify them, thus enhancing the credibility of the news story.

All of this needs care. For instance, crowdsourced information and videos need vetting before they are published or broadcast, their sources verified and authenticity confirmed.

That is where it becomes critical for young journalists entering the profession to understand the digital medium, its limitless possibilities

---

[10] All India Radio: http://allindiaradio.gov.in/Default.aspx (accessed on 21 November 2017).

[11] A *New York Times* interactive feature that allows users to see how much each US Presidential candidate would need to win to earn his or her party's nomination, http://www.nytimes.com/interactive/2016/03/30/upshot/trump-clinton-delegate-calculator.html?actionclick&contentCollectionPolitics&regionFooter& moduleWhatsNext&versionWhatsNext&contentIDWhatsNext&moduleDetailu ndefined&pgtypeMultimedia (accessed on 21 November 2017).

and unprecedented challenges. The economics of digital journalism, too, are very different from those of print and broadcast. Understanding the best metrics to measure visitor interest, capturing those on the website and successfully marketing those numbers to advertisers are skills that will make online journalists lead the changes needed in their newsrooms.

Organisations, too, need to invest in research, to sharpen these metrics and strive towards a financial model that can keep pace with the digital medium—print advertising is falling much faster, globally, and online advertising revenues are rising.

By embracing the digital medium, traditional media organisations and journalists in India will earn a valuable friend. Shunning it or treating it as an appendage will turn it into an enemy, one that has not found a victor so far. The choice should be easy.

8

The Talking Point

Ranjona Banerji

Twitter, an unbeatable form of communication, has become an integral part of any journalist's working life.

In 2008, sceptical about the digital space and involved in a debate at the time about the dangers of blogs being mistaken for journalism, I joined Twitter and Facebook. My intention was to dismiss their use, and I even wrote an opinion piece about how they served little purpose and how they tried to destroy normal human communication. How wrong I was. For one, I was almost immediately addicted. And secondly, Twitter did not take long to demonstrate how vital it is to the dissemination of news.

Three things happened in quick succession to convince me to rethink my Luddite misconceptions about being sceptical of social media. In all three, I was able to provide information to the news desk at the newspaper I worked in at the time before any other agency had put it out. Two of them demonstrated how fast social media worked and how quick it was to get a response.

In the first example, someone I followed re-tweeted a call for help from people stuck inside a burning building in Bengaluru. We contacted our Bengaluru office, who called the fire brigade, and reporters rushed to the scene. The people were rescued solely on the basis of the message on social media as others who were on Twitter at the time had also contacted the fire brigade.

A friend in Singapore tweeted that his building was shaking. It turned out to be an earthquake. Once again, information was shared with people in Singapore, and the story was 'broken' via Twitter.

The news that Barack Obama, the President of the United States, had won the Nobel Peace prize broke first on Twitter. This personal anecdote is only here to represent how easily we can reject something new only because we cannot understand it. An anti-progress approach to life and work can be counterproductive. The tools with which we practise journalism have changed remarkably over the past three decades, not least with the advent of computers in the newsroom and the upgrading of printing technology. Since then, the mobile phone has become a method of communication un-envisaged except perhaps in sci-fi stories and movies. Journalists have been given a remarkable boon here.

Until the Internet exploded and 'social media' became a phenomenon, news desks and reporters kept a close watch on feeds from news agencies to get instant information on what was going on. Reporters on the field were in constant touch with their sources, both official and unofficial. These were the traditional ways in which journalists collected information.

The Power of Twitter

Less than a decade later, Twitter has become an integral part of any journalist's working life—or it should be. It is used by governments, politicians, news agencies, media houses and journalists themselves to spread the word, share a link, inform and question. One media house has even made it imperative for journalists to open twitter accounts linked to the journal they work for and tweet all news-related information from there. Even more incredible, journalists' increments are linked to the amount of news they break on WhatsApp groups.

To go back in time a bit, however, it was in 2011 and the rise of the Arab Spring that Twitter really emerged as a method of communication that could shake governments. Egyptian Internet executive and now techie, Wael Ghonim, and others like him kept the world and the people of the Arab Spring movements informed of what was happening as agitators clashed with government forces. Although sadly Arab Spring did not have the effect the protesters had hoped for, it helped establish Twitter as an unbeatable form of communication.

In fact, although blogs are still a source of entertainment, discussion and information for many people (over eight million blogs out there being read and commented on), the blog is already old school.

Media houses use the word 'blog' (from weblog) when they mean opinion piece or column. Some journalists have columns which appear in the actual physical newspaper, some only appear on the website.

News television websites also carry opinion pieces. Some media houses do not pay writers but offer them the 'privilege' (I use the word sarcastically because people who write for free and media houses who do not pay are both on the path to destruction) of appearing on their website. The payment model is still experimental—it will survive as long as these writers can continue to work for free while queering the pitch for others who write for a living—and, yet, it is Twitter that is used to promote these blogs and all news stories.

Web Journalism

Several news channels in India carry a constant stream of tweets from well-known people and regular tweeters on their screens. Some news channels announce the 'hashtag', or talking point, for its nightly debates to help it either track traffic or increase traffic to itself. Newspapers regularly do stories based on reactions from people on Twitter. And web journalism—with no printed copy—has become an excellent form of media. India itself has websites such as scroll.in and thewire.in to name a few, which are often of higher quality than traditional media. What was started in India by rediff.com decades ago is now thriving in these days of social media.

The sheer volume of tweets on a subject can influence governments, organisations, corporations and people. Politicians such as Barack Obama and the Indian Prime Minister, Narendra Modi, have successfully used Twitter to win elections and reach out to younger voters. They have employed teams of people to keep their social media presence alive and up-to-date. This gives journalists access to their most recent ideas, which they can report on or editorialise about.

Facebook posts have also become sources for stories or ways for the common person to make his or her views public—and these are often picked up and made into stories by journalists. However, the Twitter story is not all sugary treats for journalists with no consequences. Both reporters and Editors have to be cautious about how far they can take social media as a source.

At the first, most obvious layer, using Twitter alone to create stories is just sheer laziness. It is the equivalent of the 'dial-a-quote' brand of journalism without even having to make the effort of talking to someone. You just scroll through your timeline, string together a few connecting sentences and add your byline to that great effort.

If that does not make enough of a mockery of the craft, there are other inherent problems. You have to be able to sift rumour from fact, which means you have to make an effort, especially if the subject is serious. Verification requires effort, which becomes a problem in the race to be first with everything.

Television news especially suffers from this malaise and we see the results of its jumping the gun all too often. Twitter is not responsible but Twitter certainly exacerbates the condition. Responsible journalism requires that you wait to check whether the earthquake is really an earthquake before you use Twitter as your sole source.

Unfortunately, and this is important for all journalists, the rules of gathering information remain the same, regardless of the source. You have to be certain of the facts before you put them out, you have to be able to verify those facts and you have to be able to stand up and justify your conclusion. Indian media houses do not as a rule employ fact-checkers and, therefore, the onus is on the reporter or the writer.

It is also vital to remember that the whole world is not on social media. There is a larger society out there with other, often serious, problems and issues, which have nothing to do with subjects that interest those on Twitter. If, on a given day, Twitter is obsessed with why someone did not stand up for the national anthem, it means matters like people dying in floods get ignored. As a journalist, you cannot be unaware of the wider reality.

Social Leveller

However, even as one writes this, mobile phone connectivity and access spreads to even remote areas of the world. Smartphones and data packs are not only much cheaper than they were, there is also a wide range available for all sizes of wallets and layers of aspiration. Where once it was shared caller tunes that levelled social snobbery, now it is access to the Internet. A feature such as WhatsApp, which encourages easy and cheap sharing of data, is used by corporate executives and service providers alike.

Even with India's bandwidth problems, the mobile phone explosion continues. Smartphones will replace computers for some and will provide computers for those who cannot afford them. There is no doubt that smartphones—or something similar—are the future. They are also ideal for travelling journalists to send back information and visuals to their newsrooms, and as an endless source of stories.

Regardless of technological advances though, human error will remain and needs to be dealt with. On platforms such as Twitter especially, many journalists mistake parody accounts for real ones, which causes its own sort of confusion not least with attribution. You pick up a joke and take it as real. If your immediate boss is not social media-savvy, together you create a fine mess, to quote Laurel and Hardy.

(This archaic cinematic reference is intentional if only because it underlines the other problematic Internet source for journalists: unflinching trust in Wikipedia.)

Interaction Democratised

Or, a news agency or media house tweets information itself, which is unchecked or sometimes, as the *Times of India* found when its entertainment account discussed film actor Deepika Padukone's cleavage, offensive. Social media has democratised interaction. No longer can the journalist be safe in his or her byline, away from the people who read or watch the media. Deepika Padukone responded immediately, her fans picked up on her anger and what followed was a PR disaster for the newspaper.

It is true that as journalists, we have felt that we deserve to be distant from our readers or viewers. We write a story or an opinion and we move on. 'The ivory tower' is the old cliché for Editors and edit writers. Twitter changes all that. People read your stories and they respond immediately.

A good number will be offensive but no more than those who get into fights with one another on the 'comments' sections on news websites. The anonymity of the Internet is used by some people to have fun at your expense or to rile you for a response or to display their own worst side.

Many such distasteful responses come because of a political viewpoint or a polarised atmosphere. However, it is important to note that offence on the Internet is not limited to politics. More seriously, it can be gender-specific abuse. Most women journalists on Twitter have to face personal attacks and vicious abuse.

There are methods to deal with this, by complaining to Twitter, which can cancel the abusive account, or by blocking the offensive person. Sadly, abuse is a reality that one has to deal with. It may help in some instances to fight back, to not take it personally and to try and develop a thicker skin. Because the converse is also true, there will be people who will support you when you are attacked.

Unlike any other form of communication used so far, Twitter is direct and aimed at you. It is important to be able to deal with this without crumbling. Despite the problems described here, the benefits of using Twitter or being on Twitter far outweigh the negatives. It just has to be used intelligently and with understanding rather than blind faith.

Human behaviour remains what it is, in some ways the Internet just enhances or underlines it.

As I began, I would like to end, with a personal understanding of this form of communication. As a tennis fan, earlier I had to depend on newspapers for additional information on the game. Then the Internet provided the rest. But with Twitter, I can get everything instantly and can communicate with a vast network of tennis fans worldwide. It makes me part of a global family in an unparalleled manner. Imagine the benefit to a sports journalist. Then posit this to any other kind of specialised journalist.

And finally, and this may strike the closest chord of all, being on Twitter as a journalist makes you accessible not only to finding stories, to sources and to celebrities, it also makes you accessible to head-hunters and job offers. Now, that is something to ponder over, a benefit that beats all the others, perhaps?

9

Old Dynamics, New Approaches

Pooja Valecha

Television and print media are competing with one another and with the digital media for the same set of audience.

The business of television and print has been witnessing a multitude of changes in recent years. From dissemination technology to consumption patterns to the entire business ecosystem, all aspects of the print and broadcast media seem to be undergoing a sea change. The common denominator in this is the advent of the digital medium. This new medium has not only changed the way people consume media or interact socially, it has also changed the way business is done and the way the media and the entertainment industry functions. E-editions of newspapers are now more widely read than their physical versions in a lot of cases. TV content is increasingly viewed on laptops, smartphones and other screens. Moreover, even the time of consuming the content is now determined by the viewer/reader. You can now view your favourite TV show at any time at any place using your smartphone. You even record it on your smart TV and view it at your convenience. News is now delivered instantly to mobile phones through apps. You don't have to wait for the morning newspaper anymore.

While these changes may be taking the world by storm, in India, this phenomenon is still relatively new. Nevertheless, it is bringing a lot of change in the way business is done. Most major media houses are looking at ensuring that they do not lose their audience by securing their place in the social media and digital technology spaces through mobile apps, web platforms such as Hotstar and Sony LIV for video content to news apps and web portals for special choices. In all of this, the common attempt is to ensure consumer engagement across media and to monetise this engagement.

TV constitutes nearly half of the media and entertainment industry's revenue, although its share of advertising revenue is 38 per cent with print being the leader with 40 per cent. Of course, in overall terms, it is only 25 per cent of the entire industry. Digital media (advertising) constitutes only 5 per cent of the industry and 13 per cent of the advertisement revenues. However, it has been growing at an incremental rate: It has doubled between 2013 and 2015. (In 2013, it was worth 30.1 billion, and in 2015 it was 60.1 billion, according to Federation of Indian Chamber of Commerce and Industry [FICCI] Klynveld Peat Marwick Goerdeler [KPMG] Report 2016, see Figures 9.1 and 9.2.)

The Business of Television

The television broadcast industry follows a vertical supply chain from television software makers to broadcasters to distributors (see Figure 9.3).

Figure 9.1
Indian M&E industry size (INR billions; 2015)

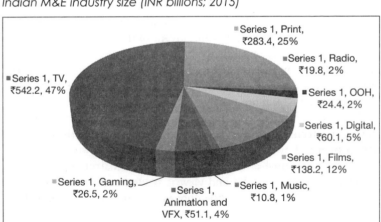

Source: FICCI KPMG Report 2016.

Figure 9.2
Indian M&E industry: Advertising revenue (INR billions; 2015)

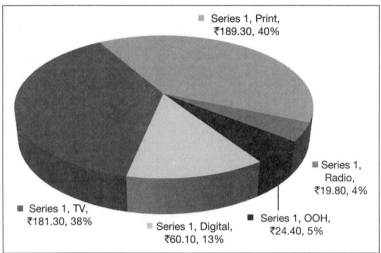

- Series 1, Print, ₹189.30, 40%
- Series 1, Radio, ₹19.80, 4%
- Series 1, TV, ₹181.30, 38%
- Series 1, Digital, ₹60.10, 13%
- Series 1, OOH, ₹24.40, 5%

Source: FICCI KPMG Report 2016.

There are two important arms that affect each of these stages: research or audience measurement firms and advertisers. In the Indian context, software makers would be content producers like Balaji Telefilms, Endemol and Fremantle Media, and film production houses whose movies are shown on television and sports authorities who allow their games to be broadcast. Broadcasters would be Star TV Network, Viacom Network and Sun TV Network, among others. In terms of distribution, the major players are Tata Sky, Videocon Direct to Home (D2H), DD Free Dish, Hathway and SITI Cable, among others.

The other important player in the business of television (or any media business for that matter) is the advertising fraternity. This group provides a major chunk of the revenue to a broadcaster, the other major chunk being subscription money. Advertisers run their ad-spots on TV channels (or branded content or advertiser-funded programmes and other forms) for which they pay a cost to the broadcaster.

To understand the dynamics here, let us turn to the economics of the media. The market for television broadcasting is a dual product market,

Figure 9.3
The virtual cycle of broadcasting

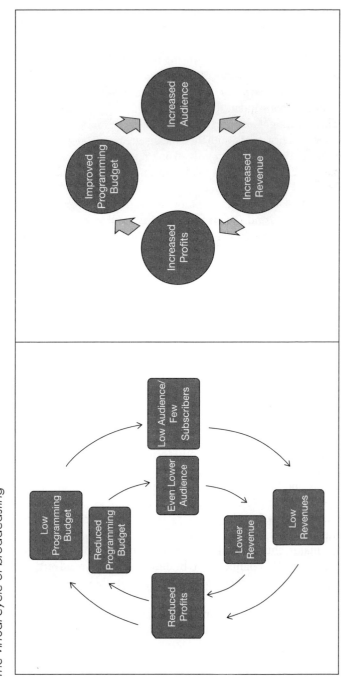

Source: Author.

which is highly pronounced in the Indian market scenario. It is a dual market in the sense that broadcasters produce content, which gets sold to viewers or audiences and, in turn, broadcasters sell this audience attention to marketers as advertising in its various forms. It is interesting in that for the broadcaster, the marginal cost of getting each new audience is minimal. However, each of these audiences adds incrementally to the value of that content for the marketer.

Thus, getting maximum audiences makes a lot of sense to broadcasters: one, because more audience means greater economies of scale; and two, for getting maximum advertising revenue as marketers are willing to pay more for consumers than consumers will pay for content (Doyle, 2004).

Having established that the more the audience a channel has the more revenue it earns and thus is more profitable, the question that arises is, how does one know which channel or which show has how many audiences and if their profile meets the desired target definition of the advertiser? The answer to this is the next important player in the broadcasting business—the audience measurement firms.

Each country usually has a single firm that measures and releases the audience numbers for channels and shows, which the industry uses as the currency to trade for advertising business. In India, the firm that does this job is the Broadcast Audience Research Council (BARC).[1] Though it was established in 2011 to develop a reliable television audience measurement (TAM) system, it started releasing audience data only in 2014.

It is promoted by three industry associations. These are the Indian Broadcasting Federation (IBF)—60 per cent; the Advertising Agencies Association of India (AAAI)—20 per cent; and the Indian Society of Advertisers (ISA)—20 per cent. Before BARC, this job was done by TAM India, but the industry took on TAM in 2012–2013 on multiple issues from lower sample size to unreliable data. This led to the formation of BARC to provide television ratings (in the future, holistic device-agnostic audience measurement) for the country.

Apart from using a more advanced technology, different research methodology and a bigger sample size, BARC data also reports rural India, which until now had no representation in the TV audience measurement space, which is a huge draw considering that almost 69 per cent of the Indian population still resides in rural India (Census of India, 2011).

---

[1] Barcindia.co.in

Distribution

The distribution scenario in India is a bit different from international models. The birth of pay television in India happened in the form of analogue cable, which meant a multisystem operator (MSO) downlinking the broadcasted signal, sending it to a local cable operator (LCO) who, then, passes on the signal to television homes in his region through co-axial cables. The system seemed to work pretty well for a long time despite its multiple flaws, which were felt mostly by broadcasters—a couple of them being fewer channels carried due to low spectrum and hence high carriage and placement fees, no transparency of subscriber count and consequently loss of subscription revenue. As a result, the industry began pushing for accountability, which finally came through in the form of digitisation. The Government of India along with the Telecom Regulatory Authority of India (TRAI) launched DAS (Digital Addressable System) for digitisation of cable TV across India in four phases from 2012 to 2016–2017.

Recent Developments and Outlook for the Near Future

India is currently looking at completing the Phases 3 and 4 of DAS and of monetising the previously executed Phases 1 and 2. Adding to the digitisation of Indian television scenario are newer technologies like Over the Top (OTT) and newer players like Reliance Jio, trying to change the business dynamics. Once completed, digitisation of the Indian television industry is expected to affect all facets of broadcasting. At the macro level, it may mean more revenue from subscription for broadcasters and hence a greater reliance on the subscription side as compared to the current scenario where the major thrust is on advertising revenue, implying that for a broadcaster, content choices of the audience are secondary to the demands of advertisers.

However, when subscription becomes the key revenue driver, content will become the actual king, because the audience will choose to subscribe only to channels that provide them differentiated content attuned to the choices of each consumer. This will eventually lead to more differentiated content, and what is referred to as niche content to cater to individual choices. These effects have been listed in Figure 9.4.

Figure 9.4
Expected effects of digitisation

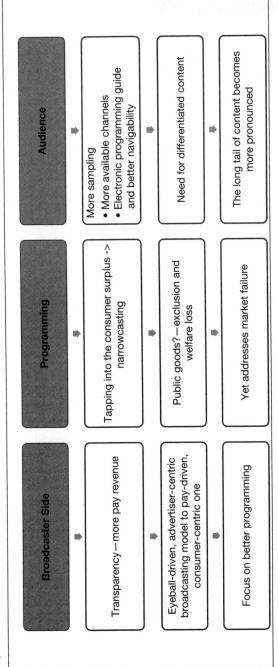

Source: Author.

Programming and Content

As supported by a host of theories such as the programme choice model, the law of central tendency (Dunnett, 1993) and the Hotelling model (Hughes and Vines, 1989), when the broadcasting industry is supported by advertising revenue, there is a high chance of 'competitive duplication', that is, most channels will air similar programmes that cater to the majority taste to maximise their audience size, thus alienating the minority. In an unregulated market, the interests of the minority will be served only when the number of channels is large enough to exhaust the profits from competitive duplication and then target the largest pocket of minority.

These theories have been clearly evident in the Indian scenario, where there was a certain level of variety to programming until there was a single channel monopoly. With the advent of cable television and multiple channels came a group of general entertainment channels (GECs) which were full of saas–bahu dramas and talent shows that copied the format of international shows. All Hindi and regional news channels had similar programmes making it tough to differentiate among them. Even in radio broadcasting, India has witnessed all FM radio channels playing exactly the same type of shows and music. The advent of FM Phase III increased the number of channels in the metro markets to a level that made it viable to cater to varied interests, thus leading to the appearance of radio channels in slightly differentiated genres such as retro.

Improvement in distribution technologies, spurt in the number of channels and growth of pay revenue have led to stress on content (as discussed in the previous section). This content stress implies that the channels now require competitive programming to fill these extra hours leading to what is called the bidding wars. The satellite rights of blockbuster films are sold upwards of ₹500 million and the rights of sporting events are also sold at millions of rupees (Indicine Team, 2011). The rights of Indian Premier League (IPL) were sold for $918 million for 10 years (Krishna, 2008). In 2012, Star group bought the rights for Indian cricket telecast for 2012–2018 for a whopping $750 million (Engineer, 2012).

Another trend this kind of competition leads to is upstream vertical integration because of urgent needs to secure the programme format and software rights. For example, in the kids genre, more than 50 per cent of Nickelodeon's weekly ratings were coming from a licensed show called Oggy and Cockroaches, putting the channel at the Number One spot in the genre. When the show license came up for renewal, competitor,

Cartoon Network bagged the rights to the show and that went on to help them recover from the flagging situation. Additionally, even when Nickelodeon had the rights to the show, it was unable to harness or monetize it in any other way. On the other hand, another channel Pogo relies heavily on the show *Chhota Bheem*. It was smart enough to purchase the production house of that show, thus securing it for the channel and providing it complete rights to the property, including merchandising, in-programme advertising, events and feature films.

The Indian television market is going through a major shift, mainly in three broad areas: Digitisation of TV distribution through DAS, change in audience measurement due to BARC, and technological shifts.

Digitisation of TV Distribution Through DAS

Emphasis on Pay TV and direct charge for each channel subscribed will mean that on the one hand broadcasters tap into the consumer surplus, increasing their subscription revenue hence making it viable to produce content for the minorities, leading to diversity of TV content and what is called niche content, as seen in the spurt of niche channels such as Colors Infinity and Food and Travel. Another thing that it has led to in the specific Indian case is regional monetisation. The Indian audiences now have access to a much greater number of channels in their regional language, and pay revenue makes it a blessing for both viewers and broadcasters (Figure 9.5).

For example, the Viacom network bought five regional channels from the Eenadu Television (ETV) group in 2012, which they have recently rebranded as Colors regional, bringing them all into their flagship Colors brand umbrella and have also improved their production and content quality, thus making these five channels a major revenue generator for the group.

Change in Audience Measurement

The incumbent audience measurement system TAM was measuring only the urban markets with a population greater than one lakh, but BARC measures the entire country, including rural India. This new system has led to some interesting shift in the rankings of channels, bringing in a number of free-to-air (FTA) channels such as Zee Anmol among the top

Figure 9.5
Monetisation through digitisation of television

Source: Facebook.
Disclaimer: This image is for representation purpose only.

most of these channels, all owned by major networks simply run library content and thus have minimal production and content costs. These channels seem to be a major draw in the highly cost-sensitive rural and semi-urban markets, which house almost 70 per cent of the country's population. While this shift in the rankings of channels has not yet made a dent in the revenues of the erstwhile top channels, and it is not even expected that these channels will choose to go FTA anytime soon, the laggard channels may actually go FTA to catch the rural audience. There is also an increased likelihood of major networks launching FTA channels for library of film content.

Technological Shifts

The digital boom has been making broadcasters impatient the world over. A major phenomenon experienced is multi-screening and time and place shifted viewing of television content instead of the traditional linear and appointment viewing. Technologies such as digital video recorder (DVRs) allow for time shifted viewing, while the proliferation of the other screens—computers, laptops, smartphones and tablets—allow for all other types of viewing.

In the current context, this has two major effects; the first being that the current audience measurement measures only the linear, on-television viewership and does not account for any of these time, place or device shifted viewing.

This implies that though the content is consumed, the broadcaster cannot monetise it from the advertiser because it is not accounted for, until either it starts getting measured with TV viewership or the broadcasters figure a way to monetise the content on the digital screen. This has led to a race among major networks to be available across platforms, leading to the birth of smart apps such as Hotstar, Sony LIV and Ditto TV. There are currently hundreds of branded M&E Apps in India but very few among them feature in Top 100 (FICCI KPMG, 2016).

Consequently, these media companies are looking at strategies for tapping mainstream apps and platforms such as major social networks. Further, this technological shift has moved TV viewing from a social activity to a solo activity, and an increase in the digital viewing combined with increasing content consumption on video on demand (VOD) will lead to the generation and production of specialised content, catering to these differentiated audiences, and also production of short duration format content compatible with the mobile phone viewing of content.

This also affects the way broadcasters schedule content on the channel. For example, the newly launched Colors Infinity airs multiple episodes of a series in succession during evening prime time to cater to the habit of binge watching (over the Internet) among their major audience.

It does not imply that the TV screen is slowly becoming redundant. Indeed, it is the opposite. It continues to be the king, becoming larger in size as well as more technologically advanced. From flat screen to home theatres to 4k to smart TVs, they are all prevalent in the market. HD is the new 'it' thing in the Indian TV scene. While it has been present in India for a few years now, it is only with the growth of digitisation that it has taken wings and most major networks and channels are marking their presence in the HD format, leading to a cycle for increased demand for HD set-top boxes, followed by increased viewership and subscription, more revenue, more and improved content and back to greater demand.

After HD, smart TVs and the growth of Internet bandwidth are expected to increase content viewership on the Internet and increased consumption through VOD, opening up those avenues also for monetisation. Further, interactive TV and augmented and virtual reality on TV are the things to look out for.

Advertising and Other Forms of Revenue

As is evident from Table 9.1, advertising constitutes approximately one-third of the Indian TV industry's revenue. While subscription forms a nother major chunk, some of the other sources of revenue are syndication, overseas revenue, mobile and digital. In terms of product categories, FMCG contribute the maximum chunk while auto and telecom form other big chunks, though the growth in the last couple of years has ridden on the back of e-commerce and mobile. Among channel genres, traditionally the Hindi GECs have managed to get the biggest share of the pie though the biggest revenue generating events have been the cricketing events (ICC World Cup and IPL).

The spurt in the number of channels and distribution, as discussed earlier, has had paradoxical effects on advertising. Since no channel, network or genre has a monopoly over a major chunk of audience, it has actually led to a fall in advertising rates and, yet, for the same reason it has become more expensive to reach the same number of audience. In 2013, TRAI had put a limit of 12 minutes of advertising per hour. This had led to a great amount of uproar and discussions in the market, in terms of increased ad-rates versus reduced ad avoidance and hence increased efficiency.

Though the directive continues to be bound by legal proceedings and has not yet had much visible effect, except a few channels experimenting with very short ad breaks to encourage viewers to continue on the

Table 9.1
Indian TV industry size

INR Billion	2014	2015	Growth Rate (%)
Total industry size	474.9	542.2	14.2
Advertising revenue	154.9	181.3	17
Ad as % of total	32.62%	33.44%	2.5

Source: FICCI KPMG Report 2016.

channel. Further, while in-programme integrations have always existed, they seem to be becoming the norm in the current scenario of increasing ad avoidance and multi-screening.

Recent Developments and New Approaches

Advertising on most media (print, OOH, Internet, radio) has always been targeted, except TV, which has mostly been mass and national. But in the current scenario advertising is seeing a major shift the world over, driven by technological advancements, changed content consumption behaviour and global content distribution. Some of the changes in India would be as follows.

Geo-targeted Advertising

This method involves splitting the feed of a channel to deliver different advertising to different regions. It has been seen as a great method to enhance the use of available ad-inventory for broadcasters while maximising impact and reducing costs for advertisers. It is expected to work wonders in a highly heterogeneous and cost-sensitive market like India. It will even allow local and retail players with a smaller budget to advertise on premium national channels due to its lower cost and regional airing.

While it currently forms a very small portion of the total advertising pie, it is expected to grow with major networks like Star India and Zee TV jumping on to the bandwagon in the last couple of years after this was introduced by Amagi Media.

Personalised Targeting

As TV content consumption increases on Internet-connected devices through smart TVs and other devices, the possibility of personally targeted advertising (just like on the Internet) continues to grow. A host of TV networks in India are bringing their content libraries online, as discussed earlier, and expect it to provide increasing advertising revenues. One of the most successful monetisation experiments in this regard has been Star Network's Hotstar. Worldwide there are multiple initiatives to harness this phenomenon and the future could see more and more personalisation of the TV content viewing experience and increased ad-monetisation for networks.

The Business of Print

Interestingly, India is one of the few large economies that continues to see a growth in its print industry when several other markets are facing a serious decline. Questions are raised about its sustainability as a medium in light of the digital revolution. On the other hand, the print business in India is not only sustainable but is growing, both in terms of the monetary size of the business and in the number of publications. There are a number of reasons for this growth, the most prominent among them being the growth of the Indian economy and an overall positive macroeconomic environment. It is also noteworthy that most of this growth is coming from Tier II and Tier III cities and rural areas and from vernacular language publications instead of English.

From Figure 9.6(a, b), two points are clearly observed. First, that advertising contributes almost two-thirds of the revenue of print in India, and it has been steadily growing at close to 8 per cent year on year (although so has circulation revenue), both maintaining the growth of the industry.

Second, it is newspapers that actually constitute a major portion of the print industry in India. The contribution of magazines is just about 5–6 per cent, and this has been decreasing continuously.

Another interesting fact to note, which puts the Indian print business away from that in many countries, is that the number of actual publications has continued to grow. Over 5,000 new publications are registered almost every year with Gujarati and Tamil languages witnessing the highest change between 2014 and 2015 with 23.6 per cent and 23.4 per cent growth, respectively. As on 31 March 2015, the total number of registered publications in India was 105,443 (14,984 newspapers and 90,459 periodicals) of which 40 per cent are in the Hindi language and 47 per cent are in vernacular languages, according to the KPMG Report, 2016.

Factors Leading to a Growing Print Industry

The Indian economy has been growing steadily over the past few years. According to the IMF, India is likely to become the fastest growing large economy in the world in 2016 (IMF, 2016). This economic growth spurs increased consumption and greater educational opportunities

Figure 9.6
Print industry Y-O-Y revenue

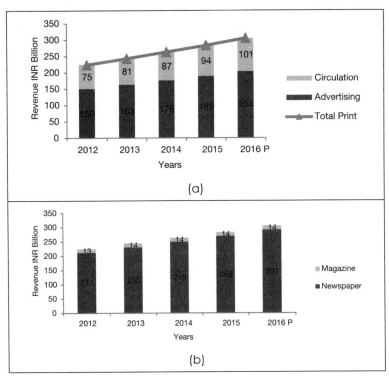

Source: KPMG Report, 2016.

leading to higher advertising and maximal advertising revenue for the media industry, including print. There are several economic theories that link gross domestic product (GDP) growth of an economy to the advertising spends in that market.

Rising Literacy Levels

The ceiling to the reach of the print medium is determined by the literacy rate in the country and that has not been very impressive. Yet the growth of the economy and government initiatives such as the Sarva Shiksha Abhiyan towards universalisation of elementary education 'in a time-bound manner' have led to an incremental increase in literacy levels and, hence, the availability of new readers to spur the growth of the print medium.

Increasing Size of the Middle Class

Again, the growth of the economy has led to the growth in incomes and the spending power of the middle class. It has also spurred literacy and increased consumption in Tier II and III cities. This increased spending power means the middle class is becoming an important target audience for advertisers, leading to increased advertising spends in these markets. Further, since a big chunk of this group reads in vernacular languages, it leads to localised advertising in regional editions of vernacular publications. Also this trend has led to an increased demand for content in the regional language, thus spurring growth in the number of publications in these non-metro markets. These newer publications are either new editions of existing publications or entirely new publications themselves.

Vernacular News on Television

One would ideally think that the availability of TV news channels in regional languages would reduce the readership of print news but in reality the effect has been the opposite. As more and more TV news channels in each language grew, there was a mad race to be the first to report an event without suitable credibility checks, thus hampering their credibility as a news medium. Moreover, all of them eventually started to look and sound almost the same. As a result, when the viewers see a piece of news on the TV, they turn to their newspaper to check its authenticity and read up further since the newspaper still holds its trust value, which is leading to an increase in newspaper readership.

Contribution of Advertising Revenue

As seen in the data above, advertising revenue contributes almost two-thirds of the revenue of the Indian print industry and its numbers have been growing steadily. Yes, the share of print in the overall pie has reduced to 40 per cent from 50 per cent. However, with the growing economy and increasing expenditure on advertising, the absolute revenues for the print industry continue to grow. Further, on the international front, the category of advertising that was hit the maximum by the Internet was classified ads. Since they formed a large part of the industry's advertising revenue, the overall revenue fell with the classifieds moving to the Internet. But then, in India, classifieds form a very small portion of the total advertising pie and so even if it entirely moves off print, it would not hit the bottom line in a very hard manner.

Limited Internet Access

While the digital medium has grown at an exponential rate, it still reaches only 27 per cent of Indians. This implies that more than 70 per cent of India does not have access to the Internet, unlike other markets where the Internet reach is fairly high with close to 87 per cent in the US and 46 per cent in China (KPMG analysis). In such a situation, the cheap newspaper with deep reach and high credibility continues to be the medium of choice.

Thus, digital, as of date, has not impacted the Indian print market too much. In fact, while even in the US, 60 per cent of Internet penetration was the tipping point for the newspaper business, India is still some time away from reaching that level.

Newsprint Prices

With the advent of the digital medium, worldwide the demand for newsprint has reduced, thus putting India in a better position to negotiate on the rate of newsprint. Further, India imports most of its newsprint from Russia and the Indian rupee to rouble rate has also improved, thus reducing newsprint prices. Moreover, since newsprint forms almost 50 per cent of the cost of newspaper companies, this fall in price is highly welcome. The year 2015 saw a 7 per cent drop in newsprint prices, giving the much-needed bottom-line thrust.

As is clear from Figure 9.7(a, b), in terms of revenue, English publications continue to be the leader despite being only 13 per cent of all publications. However, Hindi and vernacular publications are fast catching up, specially in terms of subscription revenue. In this context, it needs to be noted that though English is read by a smaller portion of the population and the actual count of publications as well as its readers would be very small compared with others, it is this small group of people which is ideally the most affluent class and, hence, one of the major target audiences for most advertisers.

This is the reason why these publications charge a premium for advertising space, and hence greater revenue. Furthermore, since this affluent class also has a higher consumer surplus, the cover price of English publications is generally higher than the others, and, hence, the subscription revenue is higher as well despite smaller circulation numbers.

Figure 9.7

The Hindi and vernacular growth story: (a) Subscription vs advertising revenue by language; (b) Language-wise Y-O-Y trends

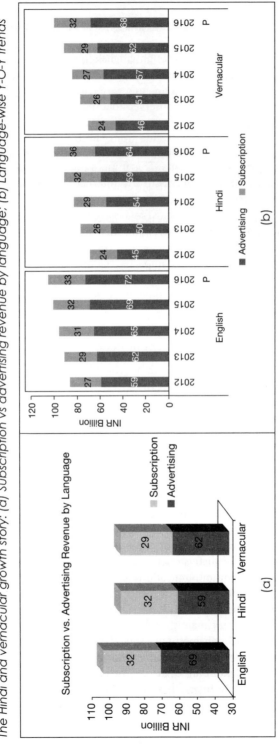

Source: KPMG Report, 2016.

Consequently, it is clear that though English publications drive the value, it is the Hindi and vernacular publications that drive the volume of the business.

From Figure 9.7(a), it can be observed that the ad revenue from vernacular publications has the highest growth rate (for factors discussed earlier) and has outpaced the revenue from Hindi publications and is fast catching up with the English numbers. Given that the ad rates are at a premium in English publications, the rate of growth of vernacular ad revenue goes on to emphasise the sheer increase in the ad volumes in these publications. On the other hand, if we observe the bottom portion of the second chart, we will see that it is actually Hindi publications that are driving the growth of the subscription revenue, having registered a higher than 10 per cent rate of growth over the past three years. This is followed by the growth of vernacular publications, which have seen a sharp rise in 2015, where at the same time the growth in English subscription has almost come to a standstill (perhaps courtesy the digital editions taking away a lot of new English readers; Figure 9.7(b)).

It is thus evident that while English may currently hold the largest chunk in terms of revenue of the print industry because of its value proposition, the growth in the near future is coming from the Hindi and vernacular publications, while English, especially in terms of subscription, may reach a standstill, if not a decline, owing to the advent of digital.

Response to the Digital Challenge

Though the digital media may not have outstaged print, it has made some dents in its armour. True, those in the 35 and above age group continue with their habit of reading the morning newspaper, and Tier II and III cities and rural India may be getting more and more publications. However, the youth in metropolitan cities seem to be moving towards digital. And since they are the most prized audience for most marketers and the mainstay audience for English publications, the print industry has been somewhat affected by this phenomenon.

While the players have mainly worked on stabilising revenues by consolidating the regional non-metro markets, they are working out ways to keep the Gen-Y from migrating to the new medium. One of the ways is by going 'Phygital'—an extension of the physical newspaper into the digital space—by launching web portals and mobile apps and also partnering with the deep-penetrating social media options as well as third party news providers and collectors such as Flipboard and Dailyhunt.

This adaptation to the digital world is not limited to English language publications. Even regional publications such as *Dainik Jagran, Dainik Bhaskar* (both Hindi) and *Malayala Manorama* (Malayalam) are focussing their energies on digitising their publications.

To examine this in detail, let us discuss this in three sections—the changes brought to advertising, to content and to the technology of disseminating the content.

Advertising

Frequency to Impact: Newspaper advertising now has moved from fulfilling the impact objective of marketing instead of bringing frequency to the campaign. To that end, newspapers and magazines have been experimenting with various innovations to catch the readers' attention. These innovations are not only in terms of shape, size and placement; they go far beyond innovations involving 3D graphics, light-emitting diode (LED) lights and perfumed paper, among others.

Advertising to Marketing Solutions: A lot of publication houses have gone multimedia, implying that they now have properties across media. For example, the Bennett Coleman and Co. Ltd that runs the *Times of India* newspaper has newspapers in various languages and genres such as *Navbharat Times* in Hindi, *Maharashtra Times* in Marathi, the *Economic Times* for financial news, and *Mumbai Mirror* as a tabloid. In addition to publications, the company also has TV news channels, Times Now and ET Now, Entertainment TV Channel, Zoom, FM radio station, Radio Mirchi and various online websites such as indiatimes.com, economic-times.com and magicbricks.com.

This horizontal and diagonal expansion, other than economies of scale and scope, helps the group in bundling media offerings, and when its sales executives meet an advertiser, they sell not only ad space in a newspaper but holistic solutions in branding, response and marketing impact that span across media.

Tech-orientation: Ads in newspapers and magazines have now started to include technological 'gimmicks' in their ads. For example, a lot of print ads now have QR codes included in them. QR codes are like bar codes in a square, scanning them through the smartphone leads the user to the intended webpage of the advertiser, thus providing a platform for further information and reader engagement all in the 'phygital' space.

Content

Content-wise, the mantra is hyper-localisation. As seen earlier, the future growth is in the vernacular-speaking non-metro markets and even marketers are increasingly targeting these markets. Thus, from sides of revenue it makes sense for publications to customise the content to meet these hyper-local markets.

This customisation goes even beyond market to genre of content. As in TV consumption, it is now all about individual choices and any publication that has to survive needs to meet the requirements of a sizable chunk of the niche demand along with the mass requirement. This trend is observed even in magazines where while the niche magazines have registered growth, general interest magazines have actually dropped in circulation. So much so that one of the leading general interest news magazines—*India Today*—had to discontinue three of its vernacular editions recently. Hence, it is specific interests and vernacular language content even on the digital medium. Another group that publication houses are targeting with their digital editions is the international audience, specifically non-resident Indians (NRIs). As NRIs like to keep themselves abreast of the happenings back home, the content needs to cater to their specific needs and interests.

Technology

Beyond launching their own web portals and mobile apps, leading publication houses have been using social media as they have realised that while being most engaging they are also among the fastest ways of news dissemination. Further, they have also been dabbling with newer technologies to keep the Gen-Y engaged. For example, the Times of India Group forayed into augmented reality with its app, Times Alive, which seems to be a successful experiment. Another successful example is the Malayala Manorama Group's attempt at Virtual Reality with its 360° app.

International outlook for near future also involves things such as news for smartwatches, which leading international publications such as British Broadcasting Corporation (BBC), the *New York Times*, the *Guardian* and the *Wall Street Journal* are already providing. There is also exploration for opportunities like Foldable e-paper.

While going digital is working well, it will be most critical to ensure that the revenues lost in the physical medium are compensated by digital, and yet monetisation of the e-space, especially in publication, is something that has not yet been mastered.

Conclusion

TV and print had their individual ecosystems, but in the digital age they may be competing not just with one another but also with tech companies, social media, telecom companies, mobile apps and others for the same set of audience and attention. It will perhaps eventually be about content that is media-agnostic and can engage with the audience across media and devices.

Even the so-called advertising will have to change its form to become media-agnostic as it becomes more and more tech-driven and sharply targeted. A fact that works in favour of the Indian industry is that the revolution in the other countries has given India a peek into the future while allowing some time to be able to plan and strategise to cope with the upcoming change rather than rush into a knee-jerk strategy to face the digital phenomenon that has overtaken a lot of other markets.

Eventually, only companies that are able to adapt themselves and their offerings to the changing consumer and their behaviour will be able to survive. While the technology of dissemination of content may change, at least in the near future, no medium, be it TV or print, is going to become extinct though the media may simply change their form and strategy. Eventually, in contrast to Marshall McLuhan's statement 'Medium is the message', perhaps, the message will be the medium, thus maintaining the supremacy of content and its compliance of various media options.

References

Doyle, G. (2004). *Understanding media economics* (1sy ed.). New Delhi: SAGE Publications.

Dunnett, P. (1993). *The World television industry: An economic analysis.* London: Routledge.

Engineer, T. (2012, 2 April). Star TV bags rights for Indian cricket. Retrieved 4 August 2017, from http://www.espncricinfo.com/india/content/story/559538.html

FICCI KPMG. (2016). M&E Report 2016: The future now streaming. Retrieved 11 March 2017, from https://home.kpmg.com/content/dam/kpmg/pdf/2016/04/The-Future-now-streaming.pdf

IMF. (2016, January). *World Economic Outlook update.* Retrieved 4 August 2017, from https://www.imf.org/~/media/.../IMF/imported.../2016/update/.../_weoinfo0116pdf

Indicine Team. (2011). Top 5: Satellite rights prices of Bollywood films. Retrieved 4 August 2017, from http://www.indicine.com/movies/bollywood/
top-5-satellite-rights-prices-of-bollywood-films/

Krishna, S. (2008, June 3). IPL bowls out malls, box office. *The Economic Times*,
p. 4. Retrieved 27 December 2017, from http://epaper.timesofindia.com/De-
fault/Scripting/ArticleWin.asp?From=Archive&Source=Page&Skin=pastissu
es2&BaseHref=ETM/2008/06/03&PageLabel=4&EntityId=Ar00402&View
Mode=GIF

10

Multimedia Mosaic

Sushobhan Patankar

By adapting to social media platforms, print media organisations are catering to the changing consumption patterns of news consumers.

News plays an important role in the daily routine of a person. Based on updates in news, people develop a perspective about events happening around them. They develop an opinion about a person in the news and alter their daily routine as per the updates. Many other things are influenced by news.

The rise of television and the Internet has redefined many aspects relating to the news media. The Web is spreading through wired and wireless connections; more and more people are getting connected through the Internet. Today a news consumer can access and read news anywhere, anytime using smartphones. The growing popularity of television in the late twentieth century and the growth of the Internet in the twenty-first century have posed a challenge to the once-popular medium of news dissemination, that is, newspapers. Globally, newspapers are struggling to stay afloat in the changing media scenario. This article tries to explore how television and the Internet threatened the once dominant position of the print media.

Before the advent of radio, television and the Internet, newspapers were the only trusted source of news. Although a newspaper is published only once a day, it provided news readers content about diverse subjects, provided perspectives and gave daily updates on politics, business, sports and other news topics that made newspapers a very popular medium of news dissemination. The world over levels of literacy rose gradually and that resulted in increase in circulation of newspapers.

Soon newspapers were published in different languages and that further popularised the medium. Later with the invention of radio, audio signal was transmitted and that enabled even uneducated people to access news. The invention of radio did not change the news reading habits of people; people added radio to their consumption routine. The invention of television created competition for newspapers as the only source of news. Television is an audio–visual medium and people adopted this medium gradually.

In the early years of television, the cost of a television set was exorbitant, the production cost of television programmes was high and the equipment required for television production was bulky. This resulted in the slow growth of the television as a medium. In many countries, television was launched as an experiment. In the late twentieth century, technological developments in electronics and satellite communication gave a boost to the development of television as a medium.

Development in satellite communication technologies in the twentieth century has changed human life in many ways. Satellite communication technologies have changed the way we communicate with each other; people have been able to communicate with each other in real time irrespective of the distance separating them. This ability of satellite communication has fundamentally changed the news media globally. Satellite communication has enabled television news stations to transmit the broadcast news content over a large area and reach out to a large population in real time. Over the years, development in satellite communication has evolved further. Now, analogue transmission has replaced digital transmission. Development of digital transmission has reduced costs involved in television broadcast; it has also enhanced the quality of audio-visual signals.

These technological advancements have made television news operations more efficient. The core functions of television news stations such as newsgathering, news processing and news transmission are gaining speed. Television news broadcasters can transmit news stories from any place on the globe on TV sets of audiences situated at any location in the world in real time. Today, large broadcast trucks are being replaced by portable broadcast units, which a cameraperson can carry on his/her shoulder. These units make it possible to incorporate opinion of newsmakers, government authorities and common people in a news bulletin in real time.

Television news graphics are generated in real time and that adds to the value of the television news story. With the advent of the Internet and with faster data transmission, television content can be accessed anytime, anywhere.

Social media has opened a new window of opportunity for television news producers. Social media platforms such as Twitter, Facebook, Instagram, and Vine enable news producers to make a news programme interactive. Using these platforms audience reactions can be incorporated in a television news programme. On the basis of audience response to a news story, News Editors and producers can take editorial decisions and incorporate relevant content in a news story.

Today, audiences are turning into 'producers', which means that they are not just consumers of television content, but by using their mobile phones they can record audio-visual content and become a producer of content. They can share it with the rest of the world using social media platforms, and even television news channels use such user-generated content in their news programmes.

The aforementioned discussion highlights the features of the television and the Internet, which makes these mediums more attractive to news consumers than the print media. News consumption patterns of news consumers are changing. However, the nature of the print medium is such that it cannot change with the changing needs of consumers; it lags behind television and the Internet in the following aspects.

Updates: The print media has benefitted largely by new communication technologies. However, for content to reach the reader, it still has to undergo a process of printing and distribution. These processes create a time gap between newsgathering and actual consumption of a news story. Today news consumers get news as it happens. As a result, the news which appears in a newspaper in the morning is already known to news consumers.

Space: Print media has to accommodate content in limited space. This constraint is applicable to television medium as well, but the Internet has no such constraints. A news consumer can read limited number of news stories in the print medium, whereas on the Internet, one has virtually unlimited access to news content. Lack of space in the print medium leads to compromise in diversity of news. On the Internet, however, a news consumer can read news from any news source. Space also has a different dimension and, if a news consumer wishes to store a news article for future reference, it requires space to store. However, in the case of the Internet, information can be stored on a pen drive.

Interactivity: Though two-way communication is possible in the print media, news consumers' feedback cannot be incorporated in news content immediately. As discussed earlier, space constraint in the print media leads to limited allocation of space to different types of content. In the case of television, through audience-based shows, citizen journalism initiatives, audience calls, television news viewers can interact and participate in television. In the case of the Internet, interactivity is possible at a greater level.

Nature of Content: Television is an audio-visual medium; on the Internet, consumers get multimedia experience. Computer graphics enhance news consumers' experience even further. The print media lags behind television and the Internet on these aspects. Advanced printing technology has enhanced printing quality and added colour to newspapers and magazines. However, the nature of the medium is such that interactive graphics and computer animation is not possible.

For the print media to survive with these inadequacies in today's competitive media environment is a tough challenge. The print media will have to adapt to this change.

Consumers' Changing Needs: Today, apart from regular news coverage, a news consumer needs perspectives on news and analysis of news. The print medium can fill this gap. Television and Internet may have captured large chunks of the news repertoire of a news consumer. However, many of them still rely on the print media for news updates, news analysis, news features and different perspectives.

The print media can cater to these specific needs of news consumers. In television and Internet, the race is against time and the objective is to put the story on air or online as soon as possible. In comparison, the time available for newsgathering and analysis is more for the print media. This can be turned into an advantage and the print media can provide content, which the television and Internet may have missed.

Providing Content in Regional Languages: Globally, the print media is struggling with the advent of the television and the Internet. However, with an increase in the literacy rate, more and more people are reading newspapers. This growth is more evident in the regional space. In the Indian context, the print media can focus more on regional language news space by providing quality news content and analysis.

Adapting to the New Medium: Many print media organisations have adapted to the Internet with several organisations providing multimedia content through their web portals. The prime example is the *Indian*

Express website. Using social media platforms, print media organisations are connecting with many readers.

To sum up, in the twenty-first century, the print media is facing a stiff challenge from the television and the Internet. By adapting to the new medium, print media organisations are trying to stay afloat. However, in the digital age when content is available in abundance and free of cost, only quality content can provide some respite to the print media.

In this era of media convergence, the consumer will go to any medium to fulfil his need for quality content. If the print media can offer that content, it will be able to secure its future in the information technology age.

SECTION III

Media Laws

11

Free Speech

Soli J. Sorabjee

> Freedom of expression embodies the right to know, which is essential for the effective functioning of a democracy.

Freedom of speech and expression are not new-fangled fads. They have been humanity's yearning, in times ancient and modern. Cato's anguished cri de coeur, 'Where a man cannot call his tongue his own, he can scarce call anything else his own', articulates an almost universal sentiment.

Freedom of expression, if it is to be effective and real, must have a capacious content. It cannot be restricted to expression of thoughts and ideas, which are accepted and acceptable but must extend to those that 'offend, shock or disturb' the state or any section of the population.

It must accord an accommodation as hospitable to the thought which we hate as that which it assures to the orthodoxies of the day. It is essential that there should be dissemination of information and ideas from different and antagonistic sources coupled with the right to receive them. Right conclusions are more likely to emerge from a multitude of voices than through one voice preaching the official gospel. In essence, freedom of expression embodies the Right to Know.

The Right to Know has been spelt out by the Supreme Court from the guarantee of free speech in Article 19(1)(a) in its path-breaking judgement in *S.P. Gupta vs Union of India & Ann. [1981 Supp SCC 87]*. The Right to Know is not meant for gratifying idle curiosity or mere inquisitiveness but is essential for the effective functioning of a democracy. Transparency and accountability are the sine qua non of a genuine democracy.

In the memorable words of Justice K.K. Mathew of the Supreme Court: 'The people of this country have a right to know every public act, everything that is done in a public way by their public functionaries. They are entitled to know the particulars of every public transaction in all its bearing.'

This enables citizens to make intelligent and informed decisions amongst a variety of choices and thus play their part in controlling the government and enforcing the accountability of the holders of power. As recent events have shown, informed public opinion is a potent check on maladministration.

The founding fathers of the Indian Constitution attached great importance to freedom of speech and expression. But this freedom, like other fundamental rights enshrined in the Constitution, is not absolute. It can be restricted, provided three distinct and independent prerequisites are satisfied.

1. The restriction imposed must have the authority of law to support it. Freedom of expression cannot be curtailed by executive orders or administrative instructions, which lack the sanction of law.
2. The law must fall squarely within one or more heads of restrictions specified in Article 19(2), namely, (a) security of the state, (b) sovereignty and integrity of India, (c) friendly relations with foreign states, (d) public order, (e) decency or morality, (f) contempt of court, (g) defamation or (h) incitement to an offence. Restriction on freedom of expression cannot be imposed on omnibus grounds as 'in the interest of the general public' as in the case of other fundamental rights.
3. The restriction must be reasonable. In other words, it must not be excessive or disproportionate. The procedure and the manner of imposition of the restriction also must be just, fair and reasonable.

The validity of the restriction is justiciable. Courts in India exercising the power of judicial review have invalidated laws and measures which did not satisfy the aforementioned requirements, and have done so in several cases.

The guarantee of freedom of speech also guarantees the right not to speak. That is the effect of the landmark decision of the Supreme Court of India in *Bijoe Emmanuel vs State of Kerala*. The court upheld the claim made by three students of the Jehovah's Witnesses faith that they were forbidden by their religious beliefs to sing the national anthem of any country. The students were expelled by the educational authorities because of their refusal to sing the national anthem, even though they respectfully stood up in silence when the anthem was sung.

The Supreme Court held that expulsion was violative of their fundamental right of freedom of expression, which embodies the right not to speak and to remain silent. The court concluded with a ringing note: 'Our tradition teaches tolerance; our philosophy preaches tolerance; our Constitution practises tolerance; let us not dilute it.'

The real protection to freedom of expression would lie in creating a temperament of tolerance, mutual understanding of and respect for the beliefs and tenets of others. This requires a sustained effort to change the attitudes of persons and to sensitise them to the value of free speech and freedom of expression and in particular the importance of dissent.

It needs to be emphasised that no group has the monopoly of truth and morality about which there may be genuinely different perceptions. And as in all walks of life, the crux of the problem lies in performing the balancing act, in balancing relevant factors in determining whether expression of a particular kind should or should not be permitted at a particular time and place. There is not and cannot be any universal prototype which is acceptable to everybody and which is workable everywhere. Different countries have different cultures and values, different problems and challenges.

There can be no hard-and-fast rule, except one: When in doubt, tilt the balance in favour of expression rather than its suppression.

And always remember the memorable words of the great American jurist James Madison, endorsed by the Supreme Court of India, that 'it is better to leave a few of its noxious branches to their luxuriant growth, than, by pruning them away, to injure the vigour of those yielding the proper fruits'.

12

Elections and the Media

S.Y. Quraishi

> The media need their own voluntary code of conduct and punitive
> mechanism to check malpractices in covering elections.

Free and fair elections are the bedrock of democracy and well-informed voters, its mainstay. It is, therefore, imperative that the news media disseminate among the electorate accurate and fair reports on the campaigns of the contesting parties and candidates.

In the Election Commission of India's (ECI's) endeavour to ensure free, fair and peaceful elections, the media are its most potent and formidable ally. The collaborative relationship between the media and the ECI goes beyond dissemination of information relating to the announcement of elections, nomination of candidates, scrutiny of nominations, the campaign process, security arrangements, polling, counting and the declaration of results. Violations of the Model Code of Conduct and laws and rules relating to expenditure by candidates and parties often come to the notice of the ECI first through the media. The ECI, on its part, supports the media by not just providing the information but also allowing them full access to polling stations and counting centres.

The relation between the ECI and the media is close and symbiotic. It is, therefore, important that the terms of engagement are clearly spelt out.

Guidelines to Media for Election Coverage

Media are governed by various rules, regulations and guidelines of the ECI as also those stipulated by the Press Council of India (PCI) and the News Broadcasting Standards Authority (NBSA). The Election Commission's regulations are based on the Representation of the People Act (RPA), 1951, the Model Code of Conduct and guidelines issued from time to time for different aspects of elections, including paid news, and opinion and exit polls. Before every election, the ECI issues a press release recapitulating all the aforementioned provisions for convenience and ready reference.

Section 126 of the RPA prohibits displaying any election matter by means of television or similar apparatus during the 48-hour period just prior to the conclusion of the election in a constituency. 'Election matter' has been defined as any matter intended or calculated to influence or affect the result of an election. Violation of the aforesaid provisions is punishable with two years' imprisonment or with fine or both. Surprisingly and unfortunately, the print media is not mentioned in this ban and many political parties regularly exploit this lacuna. In its proposals for electoral reforms, the Election Commission has asked the government for rectification of this omission.

There are allegations of violation of the provisions of this section by TV news channels in the telecast of their panel discussions and debates and other news and current affairs programmes. When elections are held in many phases, this problem becomes very serious.

The guidelines for TV/radio channels and cable networks enjoin them to ensure that the programmes, during the period of 48 hours, do not contain any material, including views and appeals by panelists and participants that may be construed as promoting or prejudicing the prospect of any particular party or candidate or influencing the result of the election. This includes display of result of any opinion poll and analysis.

In 2008, subsection A was added to Section 126, which prohibited both the conduct of exit polls and dissemination of their results from the beginning of the first phase of the elections to the close of the last phase. But even between the many phases of elections, model code restrictions and the programme code laid down by the Ministry of Information and Broadcasting under the Cable Network (Regulation) Act with regard to decency and maintenance of communal harmony apply.

They are also required to stay within the provisions of the ECI's guidelines (dated 27 August 2012) regarding paid news and related matters.

Political advertisements need pre-telecast/broadcast certification by the committees set up at the state/district level (Commission's order No. 509/75//2004/JS-I, dated 15 April 2004).

Press Council of India's Guidelines

Apart from ECI's guidelines, which are omnibus for all media, the PCI has its own set of regulations for the print media. The foremost is that the press should abide by all the laws and rules and regulations of the ECI. The Press is obliged to give objective reports about elections and the candidates and not to indulge in unhealthy election campaigns, exaggerated reports about any candidate/party or incident. Since election campaign along communal or caste lines is banned under election laws and rules, the press should eschew reports that tend to promote feelings of enmity or hatred between people on the grounds of religion, race, caste, community or language. It should also refrain from publishing false or critical statements about the personal character and conduct of any candidate or any unverified allegations against any candidate/party.

The press is prohibited from accepting any kind of inducement, financial or otherwise, to project a candidate/party or to accept any hospitality or other facilities on behalf of any candidate/party. The press must not indulge in canvassing of a particular candidate/party. If it does, it shall allow the right of reply to the other candidate/party.

NBSA Guidelines

Since the writ of the PCI is limited to the press, there are separate guidelines for television channels issued by the NBSA for the election broadcasts (3 March 2014). The NBSA is a voluntary self-regulation mechanism created by the News Broadcasters Association (NBA). It was first headed by Justice J.S. Verma, the legendary former Chief Justice of India. Justice Verma was succeeded by a senior retired judge of the Supreme Court. The nine-member authority is a balanced mix of representatives of broadcasters and eminent independent persons. Being fiercely independent and neutral, it has proved to be a credible instrument. Its drawback, however, is that its writ is limited to the members of the NBA. Non-members refuse to abide by the code.

Since government regulation is not the option, it is important to encourage the self-regulation model that the NBSA has the potential of becoming. The government could make it obligatory for all news channels to come into the ambit of the NBSA, much like the Model Code of Conduct for political parties, which many people agree is a classic case of a voluntary code of conduct that is accepted by all political parties. However, its effectiveness lies in its strict enforcement by a neutral body, the ECI. The media, too, need their own voluntary code of conduct and punitive mechanism for those who transgress the code under the eye of a truly independent regulator.

NBSA guidelines are comprehensive. These require complete objectivity and fairness, for which the news channels must disclose any political affiliations, either towards a party or candidate unless they publicly endorse or support a particular party or candidate. All forms of rumours, baseless speculation and disinformation about specific political parties or candidates must be eschewed. Any candidate or political party, which has been defamed or misrepresented by a broadcast, should be afforded prompt correction and an opportunity of reply. All political and financial pressures, which may affect coverage of elections and election-related matters, must be resisted.

News broadcasters should maintain a clear distinction between editorial and expert opinion carried on their news channels. Those who use video feed from political parties should disclose it. A gross violation of this was visible in the general election of 2014 and later.

Every element of a news/programmes dealing with election-related matters must be accurate on all facts relating to events, dates, places and quotes. If by mistake or inadvertence any inaccurate information is broadcast, the broadcaster must correct it as soon as it comes to its notice with the same prominence as the original broadcast.

In order to ensure integrity and neutrality, broadcasters, their journalists and officials must not accept any money or gifts or any favour that could influence or appear to influence, create a conflict of interest or damage the credibility of the broadcaster or their personnel.

No broadcast must contain any form of 'hate speech' or other obnoxious content that may lead to incitement of violence or promote public unrest or disorder. Reports that tend to promote feelings of enmity or hatred among people, on the grounds of religion, race, caste, community, region or language, must not be carried.

In view of the recent phenomenon of surrogate and paid news, the news broadcasters are required to scrupulously maintain a distinction between news and paid content. All paid content should be clearly marked as 'Paid Advertisement' or 'Paid Content' and paid content must be carried in compliance with the 'Norms and Guidelines on Paid News' (24 November 2011).

The guidelines deal with opinion polls, too, which must be reported accurately and fairly, by disclosing to viewers information such as who commissioned, conducted and paid for the conduct of the opinion polls and the broadcast; the methodology used, the sample size, the margin of error, the fieldwork dates, and data used; and how vote shares are converted into seat shares.

The ECI monitors the broadcasts made by news broadcasters from the time elections are announced until the conclusion and announcement of election results. Any violation by NBA members reported to the NBSA by the ECI will be dealt with by the NBSA.

News broadcasters must not air any final, formal and definite results until such results are formally announced by the returning officer, unless such results are carried with clear disclaimer that they are unofficial or incomplete or projections, which should not be taken as final results.

Besides the dos and don'ts, NBSA guidelines also appeal to broadcasters to carry, to the extent possible, voter education programmes to inform voters about the voting process, the importance of voting, to register to vote, and how, when and where to vote, and the secrecy of the ballot.

Both the ECI and the media have worked in tandem and the partnership has already begun impacting voter apathy, especially in the urban areas and among the middle and upper classes, increased participation by youth and women and contributed to ethical voting and democratic practices—all of which has led to an increase in voter turnout. A great partnership is, however, marred by some major aberrations.

Paid News—A Deadly Cancer

While the media have largely played a crucial role as a watchdog of democracy, in recent years, corruption in the Indian media has gone beyond the corruption of individual journalists and specific media organisations. From 'planting' information and views for favours received in cash or kind, to more institutionalised and organised forms of corruption, wherein newspapers and television channels receive funds for publishing or broadcasting information in favour of particular individuals, corporate entities, film producers and actors, you have it all. Though media had been used in the past to manipulate the stock and the real estate markets, the phenomenon of 'paid news' acquired a new and even more pernicious dimension.

Paid news not only seeks to circumvent election laws relating to ceilings on expenditure that can be incurred by a candidate, but such advertising, masquerading as news, has the potential to exercise undue influence on voters (which is an electoral offence) and adversely affect their right to factually correct information.

This malpractice has become widespread across newspapers and television channels. These illegal operations have become 'organised' and involve advertising agencies and public relations firms, besides journalists, managers and owners of media companies. The so-called 'rate cards' or 'packages' that are distributed often include rates for publication of 'news' items, which in a predetermined manner, not merely praise particular candidates but also criticise their political opponents. Candidates who do not fall for such extortionist practices are blacked out, if not tarnished brutally. *Outlook*, in its February 2012 issue, highlighted this problem in its cover story. If paid news goes unchecked, this writer's fear is that the 'Fourth Pillar' of democracy may degenerate into a 'fifth column'.

What can be done to check the malaise? The answer is not easy. Despite its quasi-judicial status, the PCI has limited powers. It can only admonish, reprimand and pass strictures but cannot penalise the errant journalist. Besides, its mandate is limited to the print medium. A proposal to amend Section 15(4) of the Press Council Act, 1978, to give the PCI more teeth to make its directions binding has been pending for a long time.

A better option would be self-regulation. Media organisations could appoint ombudsmen to check all malpractices, including paid news. Certain publications have indeed drawn up their own codes of ethics that are worthy of emulation. *Mint*, a daily business newspaper published by the Hindustan Times group in New Delhi, has devised a comprehensive code of journalistic conduct that provides its employees with guidelines for appropriate professional conduct.

However, self-regulation, though ideal, never seems to work without a compelling desire on the part of media owners. Some offenders refuse to abide by voluntary codes of conduct and ethical norms that are not legally mandated. Fortunately, the movement against paid news was initiated by some concerned journalists, namely Prabhash Joshi, Kuldip Nayar and Mrinal Pande. P. Sainath, formerly with the *Hindu*, made it a crusade.

On the Election Commission's request, the PCI defined 'paid news' as 'any news or analysis appearing in any media (print and electronic) for a price in cash or kind as consideration'.

On its part, the ECI constituted Media Certification and Monitoring Committees at district level to locate political advertisements and suspected paid news. During the election process, these committees submit daily reports to returning officers and expenditure observers on all expenditure on advertising, including paid news. During the five state Assembly elections in 2011, the ECI noticed that the media were not only polarised along political lines, they were even owned by political parties. It issued fresh guidelines requiring the notional cost as per rate card of the media time and space used to be included as 'expenditure'.

The most decisive action by the ECI was against Umlesh Yadav, a Member of the Uttar Pradesh Legislative Assembly, who became the first Indian politician who was unseated and disqualified for failing to provide a 'true and correct account' of her election expenses by not including what had been spent on advertisements, dressed up as news, that were published in leading newspapers such as *Dainik Jagran* and *Amar Ujala*.

The case arose out of an adjudication by the PCI holding the newspapers 'guilty of ethical violations'. The PCI had asked the ECI to take 'such action as deemed fit'. The ECI made a wider observation that 'by suppressing expenditure on "paid news" and filing an incorrect or false account, the candidate involved is guilty of not merely circumventing the law relating to election expenses but also of resorting to false propaganda by projecting a wrong picture and defrauding the electorate'.[1] The *Hindu* described it as a 'landmark order' that 'deserves the highest praise for functioning without fear or favour as the upstanding institution of Indian democracy that it is'. The Umlesh Yadav case is an outstanding example of the fruit of coordination between the PCI and the ECI.

A Happier Note—Elections and Cartoons

Not everything about elections is serious and strict. Elections are a cartoonist's delight. Their tongue-in-cheek one-liners provide a comic relief in an otherwise surcharged atmosphere. The contents of the cartoons vary from serious to hilarious. One cartoon commented on voter turnout comments: 'I hope Punjab's record voter turnout does not mean that voters want to turn us out.' Another lampooned the freebies offered by a candidate: 'It was not your dream! He actually promised a free house, land, bank balance, son's education, job, daughter's marriage....' One poked fun at the insincere poll promises: 'Oops ... I forgot our promises, find out from that fellow, he must have read our manifesto!'

---

[1] See www.eci.nic.in for the order.

13

Risky Choice

Shashikala Gurpur[1]

> Sting operation to unearth information poses a difficult ethical and legal paradox. It should be implemented judiciously.

> No one shall be subjected to arbitrary interference with his privacy, family, home or correspondence, nor to attack upon his honour and reputation. Everyone has the right to the protection of the law against such interference or attacks.
>
> —Article 12, Universal Declaration of Human Rights, 1949

Truth is elusive on the face of such prized value of privacy and media's mission of truth. Truth is the shared territory of law and ethics. Rights and justice are bound up with truth. The media and journalists march closer to it while the rule of law elements and systems ensure it. Both serve the public interest.

The media and journalists embark on truth as an adventurous mission and embrace it as life breath. Journalistic skills and art involve presentation of the truth through synthesised information. Such information is carefully sifted from illusions and lesser truths dispersed in power shadows. They adopt courageous, unconventional, free engagement in democratic reality. This is because the media can perform a meaningful function in a democracy only if it is conducive to clear the unwelcome climate of asymmetric information dissemination.

---

[1] The author would like to record her special gratitude to Shethin Chacko, LLB student, and Aditya Kedari, Assistant Professor, SLS, Pune, for the research assistance; and Professor V. Eshwar Anand, SIMC, Pune, for constant support and encouragement.

Information is important to hold the government accountable while voting and to ensure democratic participation. Information is an aspect of the right to know, which is the judicial derivative of the fundamental right to freedom of speech and expression. In the words of Justice K.K. Mathew in *State of UP vs Raj Narain*, 'People of India have a right to know every public act' (1975 AIR 865).

This right correlates with the duty of the media to inform. Thus, the role of the media is bound up with protection of human rights and service to justice. It was reiterated in *Express Newspaper and other vs Union of India* (1986 AIR 515) where the freedom was hailed as vital to the realisation of human rights enshrined in the universal declaration of human rights.

The Johannesburg principles and the Camden principles have emphasised the importance of access to information as key to monitoring the government's conduct and societal participation in governance (www.article19.org). In this context, news, as a version of reality in its multifarious forms and with related types of journalistic content and approaches, serve another important democratic catalytic function of informed citizenry.

Origins and Parallels

Although primarily serving such a noble end of information, sting operation, being a new tool in 'new-age journalism', is a dubious theme, recurring in many debates and discourses. A string of sensational cases, with controversial sting operations, have emerged in recent years in India (Srivastava, 2016). Instances of investigative journalism resulting in legal reforms and systemic transformation are seen in the unearthing of sex rackets as well as media corruption, in the context of a legal and constitutional framework (Singh, 2014).

The significance of sting operations lies in the fact that this method has helped unearth information and truth in cases where the right to information avenue had been inadequate or ineffective. In journalism, sting represents a fine line between entrapment and investigative journalism.

Editors walk a tightrope donning the robe of a responsible media as well as a democratic functionary while overseeing such investigative journalism. Every act of such tightrope walking is embedded in sting operations while exposing the painful dysfunction of under-performance or deviation from the rule of law and democratic values or of malfunctions of corruption, using public office for private gain.

Globally, WikiLeaks to Cobra Post and many other expose reflect positive public interest impact such as cash-for-vote scam or corruption in high places. If one pierces the veil, political undercurrents, power embroils and preferences of such establishments also emerge as relevant factors.

The dubious nature of sting operations has inspired the author to revisit its origins, parallels, comparisons and instances. The phrase 'sting operation' has both positive and negative connotations. The public opinion surveys in India and elsewhere have a mixed perspective. These have never gone totally against sting operations. The dimensions associated with sting operations expose the moral and legal ambiguities and grey areas challenging good journalism.

Basically, a 'sting operation' refers to catching a person while committing a crime by means of deception. The American usage of the term undercover operation is synonymous, 'to set a trap to catch a crook'. One structured approach identifies elements of (a) opportunity or enticement to commit a crime, created or exploited by the police; (b) targeting a likely offender or group for a particular crime type; (c) undercover police officer or surrogate or some climax when it ends well (Williams, 2015).

Sting operation as a tool or technique is not new to journalism to begin with. It is a part of the investigative mechanism, which undercover agents use. It is meant to be used in rare cases by law enforcement agencies to nab a criminal in order to unravel the crime. By practice, prima facie proof of wrongful act and criminal history of the accused are mandatory to validate and propel the operation. Scholars have evaluated 'Operation Greylord', which is hailed as efficient, well-executed in-court sting operation exposing judicial corruption in the United States.

It is difficult to discern how and when exactly it spilled over to journalism. In contrast, journalists are not trained as undercover operators authorised by investigative agencies or lawful authorities. No law recognises them as authorised investigators or as part of an enforcement agency or validates their finding as evidence.

However, many journalists engage in such a risky approach, to serve the public interest, especially when the information is not discernible by searches or requests. Having adopted such a powerful tool without the necessary code of conduct or guideline, journalists often tend to wrongly assume the consequences or abuse it.

Interface with Good Journalism

Good journalism is defined by integrity, objectivity, reliability and authenticity. As said earlier, sting operations pose a situation of tight-rope walking with its thrills and risks. If the performer is neither well-trained nor is cautious in balancing himself/herself to stay focussed, the consequences can be disastrous. Both law and ethics play a complementary role, while adjusting the balance of justice in society as well as in a democracy, in the larger public interest and well-being. They support the goodness aspect of journalism by engaging with the public good through normative framework and value orientation.

Viewed as such, sting operations pose problems, which prevent one from its general approval as well as elimination. The time has come to revisit such a problematic position of sting operations as the grey area fraught with value ambiguities and regulatory gaps, through the criteria of law and ethics by evaluating trends and approaches of the Indian state while converging perspectives from other states and disciplines, wherever relevant.

The Ethico-legal Dimensions

The relevance of sting operations to journalism springs from its power to hold the government responsible. Just as in voting, the public engage in governance by participation in vigilant journalistic avenues of public debates, opinion polls, and so on, where investigative or undercover journalism brings in unreachable exotic delicacies of information.

On the positive side, they check an individual's act against public order and, thereby, check and uncover the working of the government. This makes a government accountable and responsible. They render transparency to governance, which is the cardinal value of good governance. Thus, it serves the public interest, the ultimate goal of good journalism.

On the negative side, sting operations can harm society and individuals. Critics argue that since there is no discernible benefit or impact other than sensationalism and rising TRP rating, profit may have the potential of distorting the truth.

Further, they argue that it is an unholy means to a virtuous end as it violates the privacy and unnecessarily limits the rights of the individual involved. Since there is the use of candid camera or the information is elicited by posing as someone else, they raise the question whether deception is legitimate to draw and tell the truth. Such deployment of false identity, temptation, including the so-called 'honey trap', and the issue getting nuanced with the use of smartphones, pose a difficult ethical and legal paradox to resolve and dilemma to confront.

It involves inducement of 'the stinged' (the author prefers this term to 'bakra' or 'scapegoat') to commit a wrongful act. The essence of such entrapment is the promise of a reward for breaking the law and apprehending when the bait is taken. Such elements blur the line of law and ethics.

Hence, many questions arise. Is this the right method? Is the electorate or populace entitled to such information? Should the forbidden fruit be tasted despite risks? What is the extent of information that the public is entitled to? What are the outer limits of the role, duty, therefore, the freedom of the media? Do the public benefit? Do the media fulfil social responsibility in revealing the one whose rights are violated or invaded or affected? Is this a service to legitimate public interest?

The Indian judiciary has always championed the protection of media freedom. In a slew of cases, it ran as the custodian of the Constitution; recent pronouncements see the swing of the pendulum to the other end. Senior journalists point to the efficacy of sting operations in various cases and lament the caution of the Supreme Court that a journalist indulging in it does it at his/her own risk and may attract prosecution (Chatterji, 2015).

Judiciary in India has often been confronted with these questions (John, 2013) and reflected on these in a variety of cases ranging from the notable *Tehelka* or Operation West End case to the Jindal Group expose. The Delhi judiciary's suo moto action against the media in protecting the innocent victim of 'Live Wire' channel's sting operation in the Uma Khurana case (ALF, 2008; Singh, 2014) and the 19th Law Commission's report on sting operation based on surveys indicate the balancing act of India's regulatory system.

The judiciary is conduit to public interest and sentiments against the current permissive trends. These trends co-exist with proliferating private channels, with their content reflecting a hidden agenda, echoing profit or the ownership's subtle political or business motive, difficulty and disregard of verification indulging in corruption and blackmail, thus totally ignoring self-regulatory norms. The same anguish is reflected by the legal reform deliberations. The storm of grey areas of values and ethics shift the sand of regulatory shores.

The Road Ahead

Truth per se can be a casualty if the media are gagged. This responsible and high-impact profession should not be regulated externally. Rarely, professions are exempted from external regulations. It is based on the assumption of highest responsible behaviour exhibited and required of the particular profession.

The autonomy of such a profession is protected for two reasons: (a) the complexity is so distinct that it requires one with deep knowledge and experience to understand it; and (b) the stakes are quite high to objectively and effectively regulate it (Williams, 2015).

In other words, here also, the public interest predominates. Yet, the profession of journalism engages in the risky approach of sting operation. Can risk be calculated without the fundamental due diligence of law and ethics?

As shown already, sting operation is a risky choice. It should be filtered by the values of good journalism. It should be used judiciously as the last resort to expose the threat to democracy or social evils. As the Law Commission of India has noted, each instance should be decided on a case-by-case basis. By way of caution and protection, permission from the court can be obtained while providing prima facie proof of legitimate public interest involved, while ruling out untoward market appeal or violation of rights.

This cannot be a permissive tool. So much so that it is used even by trained and empowered law enforcement personnel as a 'complicated confidence game planned and executed with great care'.

Journalists should develop such professional expertise with training or collaborate with such expertise which will assume investigative value and legitimacy and take the operation to its logical end of protecting or serving the rule of law. Rather, it will also educate and recast the media's illusion of being one's own judge, jury and juror.

It is the final triumph of law and ethics. As a senior journalist said: 'Sting journalism can never occupy the high moral ground that the rigorous investigation could achieve and deliver for genuine public interest' (Panneerselvan, 2013). It is very difficult to draw a line between expose and falsehood. It is high time the media was reoriented to appreciate and review its own understanding of another elusive abstraction, which runs like an underground spring greening the landscape of truth, namely, public interest.

References

ALF. (2008). Case laws on sting operations in India (Siddarth Narain). Retrieved 26 October 2016 from http://altlawforum.org/?s=sting+operations&x=0&y=0&VGsRKeiwvbXM=.lULAOotW26c&RlgEUujbGJ=Zj9h4Wep%5B%5D&G

AFUsLjBOhSr=Nt1lLwZvI%5BGX&VGsRKeiwvbXM=.lULAOotW26c&RlgE UujbGJ=Zj9h4Wep%5B%5D&GAFUsLjBOhSr=Nt1lLwZvI%5BGX

Chatterji, Shoma A. (2015). Sting operations and the ethics of journalism. Retrieved 21 October 2016 from http://mediamagazine.in/content/sting-operations-and-ethics-journalism

John, Roshan. (2013). Legality of sting operations. *LAW Wire*. Retrieved 21 October 2016 from http://lawinfowire.com/articleinfo/legality-sting-operations

Panneerselvan, A.S. (2013, 16 December). The dilemmas of sting journalism. *The Hindu*. Retrieved 21 October 2016 from http://www.thehindu.com/opinion/Readers-Editor/the-dilemmas-of-sting-journalism/article5463068.ece

Singh, Sandeep. (2014, July–August). An analytical study of move from traditional journalism to investigative journalism. *International Journal of Multidisciplinary Approach and Studies*, 1(4), 353.

Srivastava, Charu. (2016). Role of media in preventing and combating corruption. *Imperial Journal of Interdisciplinary Research*, 2(2), 170.

Williams, A. Rebecca. (2015). An inside job: Using in-court sting operations to uncover corruption in an inadequate self-regulating system. *Georgetown Journal of Legal Ethics*, 28(3), 969.

SECTION IV

Special Areas

14

The Sanctum Sanctorum: Edit Page Specialisation

V. Eshwar Anand

Editors should take a fair, objective and impartial stand on any issue and maintain high professional standards.

The Edit Page occupies a special place in a newspaper. It is called the sanctum sanctorum of a newspaper for the simple reason that it is the most important page in a newspaper and occupies a central position—the 'Holy of Holies'.

To be fair, every page of a newspaper is important and no page can be downgraded as such. However, the Edit Page has its own importance in the overall scheme of things because it is otherwise known as the Editor's Page. It usually contains up to three editorials, but the number may vary from newspaper to newspaper. It also consists of a main article, a second article in the form of a topical piece, interview or middle, and letters to the Editor.

Edit Page: The Opinion Builder

Over the decades, the Edit Page has evolved into a great opinion builder. It not only moulds the public opinion on important issues of contemporary relevance but also influences the decision-making process of the country. Those at the helm of affairs (and not just the common people in the countryside) look to the editorials in newspapers—English or vernacular—on important issues confronting the country. It may be wrong for one to believe that political masters or governments are guided strictly by what editorials say on any particular policy matter or development. However, it would be fair for one to believe that editorials demonstrate the general mood of the country and thus represent the pulse of the people which, in turn, show the line of direction to the political masters on the turn of a particular event.

Arguably, editorials have played a notable role during the freedom struggle in shaping the public opinion. Whenever a government tried to checkmate the media, the Editors cried foul and raised their voice against controversial decisions. The *Tribune*, in particular, was in the forefront of the freedom struggle. Its pithy editorials calling for an end to the British rule shook the high and mighty colonial masters and supplemented the efforts of freedom fighters. Significantly, the *Tribune*, with which this writer was associated for 10 years as the Leader Writer (2001–2011), had brought out an anthology (1881–2006) to record its 125 years of epoch-making contribution to journalism (Nevile, 2008, p.413). This anthology is divided into five sections, each covering editorials and articles during different eventful periods—1881–1905; 1906–1930; 1931–1955; 1956–1980; and 1981–2006. Equally significant, the noted historian V.N. Datta, in another publication, records his impressions of the *Tribune*'s coverage of the nation's long history over a period of 130 years (Datta, 2011, p. 380).

The *Times of India*, too, played a crucial role during the freedom struggle, the political integration of India and attempts to find a 'distinct identity' for India for some of the concerns during that time. Over the decades, through its 'solemn, serious and tongue-in-cheek' editorials, it became an active participant in the transformation of India (*Times of India*, 1989). Other newspapers, too, have done yeoman service to the nation—and the discipline of journalism—by championing the cause of Independence. Many distinguished Editors, through their editorials, have left an indelible impression in the minds of the people. These include, Surendranath Bannerjee, Satchidananda Sinha, Motilal Ghosh, Ambikacharan Bajpai, S. Kasturiranga Iyengar, S.N. Ghosh, Makhanlal Chaturvedi, C.Y. Chintamani and Syed Abdullah Brelvi. In fact, the contribution of English newspapers is as significant as that of language newspapers. Mahatma Gandhi's contributions through his down-to-earth and lucid editorials in *Young India* need no overemphasis. G.S. Bhargava's volume succinctly examines the role of the print media and the Editors during and after the freedom struggle (Bhargava, 2007, p. 217).

The imposition of pre-censorship following the proclamation of Emergency by Prime Minister Indira Gandhi (1975–1977) will always remain a dark chapter in the annals of the world's largest democracy. It is common knowledge how the *Indian Express* and the *Statesman* left their editorials blank in protest against the censorship. As there was no right of appeal during the Emergency, the Editors thought it wise to withdraw the editorials and leave their respective columns blank instead of buckling under pressure from the official censors who were too eager to apply their scissors and keep their political masters and pliant bureaucrats happy. Interestingly, for reasons best known to its management and Editors, the *Times of India* did not play a significant role during the Emergency and the imposition of pre-censorship. No doubt, through its news coverage, cartoons and other features, it sought to reflect the situation during the turbulent times within and outside the country (*Times of India*, 1989).

It goes to the credit of successive Editors of various English and vernacular newspapers that they joined together and spoke in one voice whenever the government of the day—either at the Centre or in the states—attempted to regulate the media and impose censorship of one kind or the other. One remembers the adverse reaction in the media when the then Bihar Chief Minister Jagannath Mishra sought to regulate the press through the Bihar Press Bill (1984). Editorials after editorials strongly condemned the government's conduct and fought tooth and nail until the government was forced to withdraw the controversial legislation.

Prime Minister Rajiv Gandhi's Criminal Imputation and Defamation Bill (1988) was another classic example of how a government enjoying a brute majority in Parliament could run amok and muzzle the media. The editorials in most newspapers against the Bill were so strong and vociferous that the government was forced to retract from its dictatorial path. Had the Bill been passed, it would have abolished presumption of innocence by journalists or others making disclosures construed as defamatory. To check 'irresponsible journalism', it provided for a two-year sentence for first-time offenders and five-year jail for subsequent convictions.

As always, the *Indian Express* (with which this writer was associated during 1987–1996) played the lead role in galvanizing the press throughout the country and raising its voice against the infamous and draconian Bill. The *Indian Express* specifically called for media boycott of Union Ministers supporting the Bill. It asked journalists attending media briefings or other official functions to first ask the Union Ministers whether they supported or opposed the Bill. If the Ministers' response was affirmative, the journalists walked out of the function forthwith. Such was the mounting opposition to this Bill that, to the surprise of top bureaucrats and Union Ministers, Rajiv Gandhi, at short notice, summoned a Cabinet meeting on 22 September 1988 to announce the withdrawal of the Bill (Chawla, 1988).

This Bill generated a heated debate on the Edit Page of various newspapers for quite some time because the Prime Minister was in no mood to retract. He tried every stratagem to pursue the Bill to its logical conclusion so that he could regulate the media and check adverse campaign against his government on Bofors and other issues. He mooted several alternatives such as changes in the Bill as suggested by some media organisations, referring the Bill to a select committee of Parliament, bringing it to the attention of a group of jurists and appointing a joint panel of judges and journalists to examine the Bill. But it did not work and the media were unanimous in their opinion that nothing short of an unconditional withdrawal of the Bill would pacify them.

The Rajiv Gandhi government's another controversial piece of legislation—the Indian Post Office (Amendment) Bill, 1986—also received adverse comments in the editorials. Almost every newspaper and magazine condemned the legislation, maintaining that it was repugnant to the democratic ethos and character of Indian polity. Subsequently, the V.P. Singh government repealed the legislation in 1990. Had Rajiv Gandhi been allowed to have his way, the legislation would have authorised the government to censor personal mail and crush the freedom of speech and expression guaranteed under Article 19 (1) of the Constitution. Interestingly, the then President Giani Zail Singh, too, had serious reservations over the Bill. He was reportedly so unhappy with the draconian legislation that, if reports were to bear scrutiny, he was even contemplating dismissal of the Rajiv Gandhi government, prompting editorials in newspapers such as the *Statesman* and the *Indian Express* to raise the question: Will he, won't he?

Successive governments at the Centre and the states seemed to be no different as far as their attitude towards the media was concerned. And remarkably, they had to beat a hasty retreat and bow before the editorials which condemned measures to tame the media at varying periods of time. How can one forget Rahul Gandhi's close aide and former Congress Lok Sabha Member of Parliament (MP) from Mandsaur, Meenakshi Natarajan's trial balloon during the United Progressive Alliance (UPA) II government in April 2012? Though it was scheduled to be introduced in Parliament on 30 April 2012, surprisingly, she did not turn up at the last minute and the Bill was automatically dropped!

Meenakshi Natarajan's Bill had all the features of a draconian legislation: establishment of a media regulatory authority with powers to ban or suspend coverage of an event that may pose 'a threat to national security from foreign or internal sources'; selection of members of this authority by the Union Information and Broadcasting Ministry and other government nominees; a fine of ₹50 lakh for the offenders; and suspension of a media organisation's operations for a period of 11 months, ultimately leading to the cancellation of its licence. Amazingly, this Bill sought to keep the Right to Information Act, 2005—the UPA government's crowning achievement—out of its ambit (Rahman, 2012).

Delhi Chief Minister and Aam Admi Party chief Arvind Kejriwal, too, cannot be absolved of blame. When he tried to tame the media through a controversial government circular, the Supreme Court stayed it and questioned the propriety of the Chief Minister. The media protested against the circular which sought to prosecute the media and other organisations under criminal defamation charges for defamatory reports against the Delhi government or the Chief Minister (*Indian Express*, 2015).

The Command Structure

Generally, the functions of the Edit Page is entrusted to a Senior Editor. It does not necessarily imply that the Edit Page Editor should always be a senior staffer in the command structure or hierarchy. Promotions come very late in a newspaper and if the Editor is convinced of the capabilities of a particular staffer, even a subeditor can be entrusted with this responsibility. In some newspapers, the person handling the Edit Page is also called the Edit Page Editor.

There is always a core team for writing edits (short form for editorials). In the morning editorial meeting, the Editor-in-Chief allots edit topics on burning issues to individual Editors depending on their areas of specialisation. These could range from national or regional politics, constitutional affairs, legal matters, important court judgements to economy, agriculture, defence, foreign affairs, films and entertainment. The Editor-in-Chief himself chips in whenever he feels strongly about a subject. Sometimes, he also rewrites the entire editorial or edits to the pieces done by his colleagues in order to provide clarity and better perspective. Moreover, when the Editor feels that the edit in question does not represent his views clearly, he either spikes it or tells the writer concerned to rewrite the same.

Editing an edit written by the Editor-in-Chief or by the Edit Page Editor forms a part of the organisation's normal drill and editorial policy. Even the Editor-in-Chief's article, column or editorial will have to pass through the normal editorial scrutiny and no piece is meant for instant publication. If an edit is too harsh on any particular beleaguered Minister, politician or bureaucrat, the Editor-in-Chief chips in and tries to make suitable changes. At the same time, if an edit goes against the editorial policy or is not in conformity with the guidelines issued by the Editor-in-Chief, it is simply not used. There are occasions when the Editor-in-Chief does not assign a subject to the edit writer or leader writer in the morning meeting if he/she has a view contrary to the Chief's views or the overall editorial policy.

In any case, there are always standby edits to fall back on. These come to the rescue of the Editor-in-Chief whenever an edit done in the morning or afternoon falls by evening, when events overtake it. Sometimes, because of late night developments, the chief subeditor or the Night News Editor is appraised of a particular editorial and told to make changes after consulting the editorial writer concerned over phone. To avoid inconvenience, save time and facilitate timely release of the edition, the edit writer also gives the print out of the revised edit to the Night News Editor in the evening itself so that it could be taken in the event of a development.

Some years ago, there were occasions when Senior Editors were summoned to the office late in the night to rewrite the entire edit. Of course, these days, it has become convenient for Senior Editors to email revised or updated edits to the Night News Editor before the edition is put to bed.

No Editor-in-Chief would want to lose control over the Edit Page. At the same time, it is very difficult for him/her to look into the nitty-gritty of this page individually because of too many responsibilities, including day-to-day administrative work. He has to depend upon his senior colleagues to bring out this page without any errors. Consequently, though the Editor is the overall boss, the Edit Page is nobody's monopoly. While one takes care of editing the edits (usually a person who is good at English irrespective of his rank or designation in the office), another takes care of the selection and editing of main articles. Another Senior Editor looks after middles or second articles while the Letters to the Editor section is looked after by yet another Senior Editor.

Selection of Edits

The morning meeting invariably selects the hot topics of the day for the next day's editorial column. At the same time, though the menu for the edits is finalised at 11 AM and the Editors keep themselves busy writing their respective edits, it so happens that no edit selected in the morning goes for print and the edit writers are directed to do fresh edits in the evening or at 9 PM. Sometimes, when Parliament is in session and the government is expected to make an important policy announcement on the floor of the House in the late afternoon or evening, the edit writer concerned is alerted in the morning itself and he/she follows the development closely.

Similarly, if the ruling party of an important state is expected to announce (or elect) its new legislature party leader, a new edit in the evening becomes necessary, especially when the newspaper has the largest circulation among other dailies in the state concerned. Same is the case with an expected judicial verdict either by the Supreme Court, High Court or even trial court at any time of the day. While national newspapers may not be inclined to do an edit on a late evening development promptly for the late city edition, if facts are available, regional newspapers make it a point to carry an edit to be one up in the city or region the next morning.

Sometimes, either the edit writer specialising in judicial matters himself keeps track of the developments and brings it to the attention of the Editor-in-Chief or the latter advices the former to act accordingly. It needs to be emphasised in this context that if the Editor-in-Chief is convinced that a particular judgement is not important enough to merit immediate attention in the editorial column and that some more clarity is required on any legal or constitutional point, the edit writer is advised to wait for a day more instead of rushing in with half-baked ideas.

The order (and the length) of the edits, normally decided by the Editor-in-Chief, depends on the topicality, importance and region. For instance, while the Italian marines case was hardly given any coverage in the editorials by any newspaper (not to speak of its coverage even in the news pages except in a few dailies in the southern states), when the case was investigated in Kerala, it became a hot subject and attained a national character once the Italian government announced that the Italian marines will not return to India after the elections in their country on 22 March 2013. The Supreme Court of India's ruling restraining the departure of Daniele Mancini, Italian Ambassador to India, and the controversy that followed in both India and Italy continued not only to be the lead news on the front page of many newspapers for days but was also covered in the editorials. Newspapers commented on the pros and cons of the Geneva Convention's regulations providing diplomatic immunity and the constitutional legitimacy and rationale behind the Supreme Court's restraining order on the Italian Ambassador.

Honestly speaking, the loss of a human life in any accident is always tragic and no words can compensate the loss. However, such are the ways of newspapers that if the death toll in any accident is in single digit or say, 15, 25 or 35, it may not merit the importance of a lead story on the front page, leave alone an editorial. It is only when the toll crosses 50 or so, the Editor may consider an editorial on the incident, that too, only if the accident has relevance to the readers of the newspaper's circulation area. Obviously, if the accident is proximate to the place of publication, the treatment given to the incident both in the news pages and the editorial column varies substantially.

The *Indian Express* (before its bifurcation) had the provision of using state-specific edits on the Edit Page. While the Edit Page was centralised, controlled by the New Delhi office, Senior Editors or Resident Editors were directed to do edits on subjects highly relevant to their respective states but not at the all-India level. This served three objectives: one, the Editor did not impose unimportant editorials on the readers at the national level; two, it gave due coverage to local or state-specific issues; and three, it published editorials on issues that were more relevant to readers at the national level than ones that were purely of local interest.

In principle, editorials are used on the Edit Page only. However, a few newspapers like the *Indian Express*, the *Hindu* and the *Tribune*, departed from the common practice and use editorials on important subjects on the front page as well. These editorials, called signed editorials, are written by Editors-in-Chief or Editors (the chief functionary of a newspaper) only. There are differing opinions on the front-page editorials. One plausible reason for the latter (only one editorial, either a longish or of normal size of about 350 words on a major development) is that there is no Edit Page on Sunday and the front page is the only important space available to cover opinion on a major development. The other reason is that a development like the demolition of the Babri Masjid was so important that it could not be confined to the Edit Page. Ideally, this writer is of the opinion that editorials should appear in the Edit Page only. This principle is also in consonance with the time-tested policy of making a clear distinction between news and views. While views should appear on opinion pages like the Edit Page and Oped Page (short form for Opposite Edit or Opinion page), opinions in the form of editorials or articles should not encroach upon the news pages, including the front page.

Edit writing is not the only responsibility of Senior Editors. Even though Senior Editors write edits for the next morning's edition, no Senior Editor can claim authorship for the one done by him/her. Edits on the left side of the page do not carry bylines, and for all purposes it is deemed that the Editor (or the Editor-in-Chief) has done them. In other words, Senior Editors do edits on behalf of the Editor. Interestingly, the *Tribune* (Chandigarh), which is not proprietor-controlled and is run by a trust comprising persons of eminence, had at one time followed a system of disclosing the authorship of the edits to the trustees every day. On the left margin of each edit appearing in the first edition of the paper, seals containing the names of the authors of the respective edits were stamped.

Old-timers say, this system was followed for quite some time to keep the trustees informed about the editorial contribution of the respective writers. While releasing the Edit Page after due clearance from the Editor-in-Chief, the Edit Page in-charge would give the list of editorial writers to the production manager who, in turn, would affix the seals of the respective writers next alongside the edits before sending the first edition to the trustees through a special messenger every night. Though this practice was followed scrupulously for decades, H.K. Dua stopped this practice after he took over as Editor-in-Chief in 2002. He emphatically said that the Editor-in-Chief was not bound to disclose the identity of the editorial writers even to the trustees.

Edit Writing Style

There is no stylebook for edit writing. The style may vary from one writer to another and from one newspaper to another. But the general rules of grammar are followed scrupulously. Worthy of mention in this context are the rules of *The Economist's Style Guide* which are followed by most newspapers. For instance, edit writers follow the rules 'Never use a long word where a short word will do' and 'if it is possible to cut out a word, always cut it out' (*The Economist Style Guide*, 1993).

Same is the case with other guidelines such as 'clarity of writing that follows clarity of thought', 'do not be hectoring or arrogant', 'do not be too chatty and too didactic', and 'do not be sloppy in the construction of your sentences and paragraphs' (*The Economist Style Guide*,

1993). Suffice it to mention, these rules are applicable in every piece of writing—be it the main article, middle, letter to the Editor or even in general day-to-day correspondence.

Today, the writing style should be as simple as possible. The days of Victorian English are over. Ornamentation and flowery language are no longer appreciated or encouraged. As the newspapers have a large presence in the rural areas, the writer should write in simple English so that he/she does not force the reader to reach out to a dictionary. What is the use of a bombastic word if the readers do not understand its meaning? At the same time, Editors, while writing their own pieces or editing content, take due care of felicity of expression and stylistic presentation of views.

Essentially, the opinion should be direct, crisp and down to earth. Even if the writer wants to criticise a public figure, it must be done politely and decently without causing hurt to the person. Arguably, Editors have their own likes and dislikes, and it is in the public interest that they take a fair, objective and impartial stand on any issue in tune with the highest professional standards of journalism.

In an edit, there is no scope for giving too many facts or statistics. Otherwise, analysis will suffer. An edit is a comment and not a news report. If the writer indulges in statistics, where is the space for comment or analysis? In that sense, it can be said that statistics is like the swim suit of a blonde: What it reveals is suggestive, but what it conceals is vital. At the same time, it may sometimes be necessary for the edit writer to quote official figures (if available) to buttress an argument, but this will have to be precise, logical and powerful. An argument not backed by facts looks weak with feet of clay and will not impress the readers.

Edit writers should always stick to the word limit. Otherwise, it becomes a challenge for the Edit Page Editor to accommodate all the edits in the allotted space. When the edit content far exceeds the space, the normal practice in newspapers is to kern the content or reduce the point size of the letters and carry the whole content somehow. The readers may not know this trick of the editorial department, but this is bad production technique.

Moreover, small print is a strain on the eye and since readers read the editorials first, it is better to use a bigger point size and stick to it. Ideally, the Edit Page Editor, without resorting to mechanical subbing, should try to edit the content on the screen judiciously so that the meaning of a point is not lost or left incomplete while editing the content.

The use of visuals has become a modern-day practice in most newspapers. These are carried to break the monotony and provide relief to the eye. While advance planning is necessary for articles, visuals for edits will have to be arranged the same day. Once the Editor-in-Chief clears the schedule of the articles for a week or fortnight, the Edit Page Editor gets in touch with the design department to get visuals and illustrations ready.

Edits: Two Case Studies

Indisputably, edit writing is a specialised skill and one masters the art of doing edits only over a period of time. As this is a thoroughly professional job, one would do well to examine the manner in which edit topics are handled by Senior Editors. As discussed earlier, edits always reflect the Editor-in-Chief's views in particular and the editorial policy of the newspaper in general. In view of the immense interest they have generated in the country in recent times, it would be worthwhile to examine two recent case studies—Nitish Kumar's exit from Bihar's Mahagathbandhan (Grand Alliance) and re-entry into the National Democratic Alliance camp; and Ram Nath Kovind's election as the 14th President of India. If anything, they exemplify differing styles and treatment of the topics by various newspapers without disturbing the focus or the dominant theme of the edits. This writer does not want to reproduce the edits, but analyse them, with his own comments in the beginning.

Case Study I: Bihar and National Politics

A thrill-a-minute developments in Bihar on 26 July 2017 evening starting from Nitish Kumar's resignation from the post of Chief Minister to his swearing in as the new Chief Minister the next morning under a new coalition with the Bharatiya Janata Party (BJP)-led National Democratic Alliance were not entirely surprising. Apparently, for quite some time during the 20-month regime, Nitish Kumar was feeling uncomfortable in the company of Lalu Prasad and his family. He himself confessed before the media after submitting his resignation to the Governor that day in and day out, he was subjected to various kinds of pressure and interference from Lalu Prasad and his family and, consequently, it was becoming impossible for him to continue in office. With too many cases of corruption filed against Lalu Prasad and his company, the shrewd political instinct in the Chief Minister convinced him that his association with the former will become a liability for him both in terms of electoral politics and governance. The filing of FIR against his erstwhile Deputy Chief Minister and Lalu Prasad's son, Tejashwi Yadav, in the land-for-hotels case was the last straw in the camel's back. Ever since the FIR was filed, Nitish tried many times to impress upon Lalu and his son to come clean on the matter, but to no avail. As Lalu's Rashtriya Janata Dal was the largest coalition partner in the government, Nitish had his own limitations in peremptorily sacking Tejashwi because of his corruption taint. He thought the course he took on 26 July 2017 was the only alternative before him to wriggle himself out of the crisis and chart out a new course of action in the interest of Bihar and his own political future. His cosying up with Prime Minister Narendra Modi and others in the ruling dispensation made things easier for a quick and smooth transition.

Undoubtedly, the new political realignment in Bihar is bound to have its echo in national politics. As the Mahagathbandhan in Bihar lies shattered, the possibility of a formidable opposition to the Narendra Modi-led NDA government in the 2019 Lok Sabha elections seems remote. The Grand Alliance in Bihar in 2015 had amply demonstrated that if the Opposition parties joined hands under one banner and made their caste calculations perfect and foolproof, no Modi government could pose a challenge to them. This is not going to happen anymore. The worst victim of the July tremors is the fate of the Congress which will now find it very tough to improve its image. Indeed, it has never shown any inclination or interest to salvage its reputation ever since its drubbing in the 2014 Lok Sabha elections. Devoid of a strong leader at the helm who can take on the mighty Modi government's bull by its horn, it has been losing state after state, reducing itself to the status of a rump across the political spectrum. It would be wrong for one to blame the BJP and the Prime Minister or even the BJP President Amit Shah for the Opposition's troubles. If the ruling dispensation at the Centre has been planning to strengthen the BJP's units in all states in the run-up to the 2019 elections, how can one grudge about it?

The writer selected six national newspapers for the analysis of the Bihar developments. These are, the *Telegraph,* the *Times of India, Hindustan Times*, the *Indian Express*, the *Hindu* and the *Tribune*. In the editorial, 'Private math', the *Telegraph* comments on Nitish Kumar's selective choice of 'inner conscience' (*Telegraph*, 2017). He was aware of the Rashtriya Janata Dal leaders' dubious background and criminal antecedents when he successfully fought with them in 2015 Assembly elections and cohabited with them in the government for 20 months. What happened to his 'inner conscience' then? The BJP is back in the game in Bihar today only because of Nitish Kumar's 'selective righteousness'. While the latest developments in Bihar are bound to be interpreted as a shot in the arm for the Prime Minister, these may curtail Nitish Kumar's prime ministerial ambition.

The *Times of India* focussed its edit entitled, 'Break point', on the implications of Nitish Kumar's U-turn on national politics (*Times of India*, 2017). Commending his exit from the Mahagathbandhan, it hailed his decision as a 'bold move against corruption'. While internal contradictions marred the 20-month regime, Nitish Kumar's move is a great moral booster for the BJP which will reap good harvest in the 2019 Lok Sabha elections. As the Mahagathbandhan experiment, supposed to be a 'template' for Opposition unity, has failed, the Opposition will have to recalibrate their strategies and come out with a fresh approach to tackle the Modi challenge.

Hindustan Times editorial fixed accountability on the Congress for the changeover in Bihar (*Hindustan Times*, 2017). Arguing that the Congress had never tried to recover from the drubbing in elections to three states—Rajasthan, Madhya Pradesh and Chhattisgarh—the edit maintains that it hardly posed a challenge to the BJP in the 2014 Lok Sabha elections. When 'powerful poachers are on the prowl', the 'sin of silence' is inexcusable, it says, maintaining that the Congress should only blame itself for its refusal to learn lessons from successive defeats.

The *Indian Express* maintains that the developments in Bihar are against the mandate in 2015 Assembly elections (*Indian Express*, 2017). People voted for the Mahagathbandhan then and the best course for Nitish Kumar was to seek a fresh mandate. Why did his 'inner conscience' not tell him so, it asks, pointing out that 'opportunistic politics' was the reason behind his decision to cling on to power even at the cost of probity in public life. Close on the heels of the BJP's success in cobbling together majority support in Goa and Manipur, notwithstanding its failure to win the Assembly elections in the two states, the edit commends the 'tactical acumen' of the BJP managers in capturing yet another state.

The *Hindu*, in its editorial, declares the BJP as the winner in the latest round. It is unconvinced about Nitish Kumar's stand on probity in public life (*Hindu*, 2017). Since corruption charges against Lalu Prasad Yadav and his family members was not the primary reason behind Nitish's move, it doubts his new experiment. How long will it last, asks the editorial, maintaining that it is a serious setback to Opposition unity. Since 2005, Nitish Kumar may have taken steps to build support for himself among marginalised sections such as women, more backward among the Other Backward Classes, Dalits (the Mahadalits) and Muslims (Pasmanda Muslims). However, it would be premature to comment how they would vote for him in the next elections.

The *Tribune*, in its editorial, bemoans the fact that the alternative narrative that the Mahagathbandhan had sought to present lies shattered with the collapse of the government (*Tribune*, 2017). It squarely blames the 'familiar indecisiveness' of both Sonia Gandhi and Rahul Gandhi to resolve the differences between the Lalu and Nitish camps. Nitish Kumar understood his limitations, curtailed his prime ministerial ambition and settled for the post of Chief Minister. Having maintained that the Central Bureau of Investigation (CBI) raids on Lalu Prasad's family properties had helped the Modi government, it criticises the use of the CBI as the 'new instrument of political management'.

Case Study II: The New President of India

The election of Ram Nath Kovind as the 14th President of India has generated considerable interest in the country. Though his victory does not come as a surprise because of the numbers of the ruling coalition in the electoral college that elects the President, his election once again brings to the fore his role and powers under the Constitution. Undoubtedly, the President occupies a place of pride and honour in the country. He is considered a symbol of stability and continuity of the world's largest democracy. He may be a ceremonial head under the Constitution. However, he has his own importance inasmuch as the nation is governed in his name. He enjoys untrammelled powers when the Lok Sabha elections throw up a hung house or when the government of the day loses the majority support in the Lok Sabha. Even otherwise, as the head of the Constitution, he exercises immense moral authority during crisis situations and can guide the government on the course of action to be taken. Increasing misuse of Article 356 dealing with promulgation of President's rule in states is one issue the new President will have to deal with tact and due diligence. His predecessor, Pranab Mukherjee, may have strictly followed the rule book, once again like all others in the past, in signing the proclamation for President's Rule in Arunachal Pradesh and Uttarakhand in 2016 'on the aid and advice' of the Union Cabinet, following receipt of reports from respective Governors. Though some Governors are on the mat these days for their blatantly partisan role in crisis situations, the President's explicit role is willy-nilly scrutinised whenever the higher judiciary declares the proclamation as *null* and *void* and ultra vires of the Constitution. Such is the extent of scrutiny that the role of an upright President A.P.J. Abdul Kalam in signing the Union Cabinet's order from Moscow, when he was away on an official visit, to dissolve the Bihar state Assembly on 22 May 2005, following Governor Buta Singh's infamous recommendation, which drew severe strictures from the Supreme Court, continues to dominate the political discourse even today.

Though the presidential election passed off peacefully and both Kovind and his opponent, Meira Kumar, conducted themselves in a highly dignified manner during their respective campaigns, it did leave a tinge of bitterness as both the major political formations—the NDA and the UPA—sought to project it as a Dalit versus Dalit contest. Both formations may have demonstrated their Dalit credentials and their priority to social inclusivity. However, the fact remains that it is ultimately for the electoral college to pick up the right candidate in an election where there is no party whip and the voters—comprising MPs of both Houses of Parliament and Members of Legislative Assembly (MLAs)—have the right to vote according to their conscience. The new President was a senior lawyer, twice MP (Rajya Sabha) and former Governor of Bihar. Thus, he is expected to bring to the Rashtrapati Bhavan his rich experience in jurisprudence, parliamentary system and constitutional norms. For Kovind, it is a challenge to believe and an opportunity to prove. While his experience will, certainly, keep him in good stead in the exercise of his powers, the media, political scientists and constitutional experts will evaluate his performance as the President based on his track record in the next five years.

For examining the Presidential election, the writer has selected six national newspapers for analyses. These are, the *Times of India*, *Hindustan Times*, the *Indian Express*, the *Hindu*, the *Economic Times* and the *Statesman*.

The *Times of India*, in its editorial, argues that Ram Nath Kovind's Dalit and political considerations are well known—he is a Dalit himself and was once the BJP spokesman and an RSS activist (*Times of India*, 2017). Now that he has entered the Rashtrapati Bhavan, he has got an opportunity to rise above all considerations and prove worthy of people's expectations in the exercise of his functions and powers. Indisputably, by making Kovind the President, Prime Minister Narendra Modi is eyeing the consolidation of the Dalit vote in favour of the BJP in the 2019 Lok Sabha elections. Presenting the mantle of Uttar Pradesh leadership to Yogi Adityanath was the first step in Modi's plan for achieving this. Mr Kovind's election is the second.

The *Hindu*, in its editorial, stressed the need for the new President to rise above partisan politics and exercise his moral authority in influencing the government on important issues confronting the country (*Hindu*, 2017). Though the BJP, having selected him for the highest post, signalled its socially inclusive agenda, Kovind is expected to 'distinguish between settled conventions and questionable precedents' while taking decisions as the head of the state. The office of the President is not strictly a ceremonial post. He has the primary duty of acting in a fair and objective manner whenever he is called upon to exercise his discretionary powers during a constitutional crisis.

The *Economic Times*, in its editorial, describes Kovind as a political novice compared with his predecessor, Pranab Mukherjee, and even his opponent in the Presidential election, Meira Kumar, who was the Lok Sabha Speaker (*Economic Times*, 2017). Even though his CV is 'pretty thin' and he is an 'unknown quantity to most people', his election gives him an opportunity to rise in stature through impeccable and nonpartisan conduct. He should particularly be careful regarding the 'presidential integrity' while signing the order of proclamation of President's Rule on the advice of the Union Council of Ministers for the simple reason that the Supreme Court not only took serious exception to the manner in which Article 356 was misused in Arunachal Pradesh and Uttarakhand but also restored both the dismissed governments.

Hindustan Times, in its editorial, maintains that the President should rise above petty considerations and perform in accordance with the provisions of the Constitution (*Hindustan Times*, 2017). Kovind's election may be interpreted as a sign of Dalit empowerment, but Dalits need more than such tokenism. What they need are education, health care and employment. Dalits are tortured in some places and the government should address the issue of their social ostracisation and casteist conflicts in some states. As the President is also the Supreme Commander of Defence forces, he should refrain from being a 'divisive figure' to set the 'right benchmark for the future'.

The *Indian Express*, in its editorial, comments that for the first time in the annals of Indian history, the President, the Vice-president and the Prime Minister have the Sangh Parivar background (*Indian Express*, 2017). Consequently, it enjoins a greater responsibility on the part of the President to act as a great moral force and a unifying factor to preserve and protect the Constitution and safeguard the institutions. No doubt, the judiciary has been stepping in during crisis situations. However, in view of recurring incidents of mob violence and lynching in the name of cow in some states, notwithstanding the Modi government's commitment and determination to tackle them firmly, the President's role and intervention, his constitutional limitations notwithstanding, become all the more challenging.

The *Statesman*, in its editorial 'Pathetic whining', took exception to the manner in which Congress MPs Ghulam Nabi Azad and Anand Sharma criticised Kovind for his failure to include Jawaharlal Nehru's name in his address after being sworn in as the President in Parliament (*Statesman*, 2017). Defending Kovind, the editorial maintains that the President has the liberty of extolling the virtues of any national leader, including Pandit Deendayal Upadhyaya, and no one can dictate terms to him only because references to Nehru would satisfy their political masters. Criticism of the President would be justified if he erred in taking wrong decisions such as the misuse of Article 356 and not if he does not laud Nehru's services.

Main Articles

It is said that a newspaper's reputation depends largely on the quality of the editorials and articles on its Edit Page. How does an Editor get good articles? It is not just by contributions alone. Indeed, no Editor can maintain the standards of this page by waiting for contributions. A good Editor, of course with the help of his/her equally resourceful colleagues, constantly tries to commission articles on current topics from experts. Moreover, an article penned by an expert has greater credibility than a person who does not have sound knowledge on the subject he is handling.

The Edit Page represents the personality of the Editor-in-Chief of a newspaper. Its image mostly depends upon his stature and contacts. In the 1980s, the *Statesman* (Calcutta and New Delhi) was one of the popular newspapers in the country mainly for the kind of editorials and articles it published on its Edit Page. It had a wide ranging list of contributors for this page—academics, research scholars, jurists, administrators, bureaucrats, ambassadors, industrialists, scientists and top politicians. Moreover, the panel it used to carry for the main article (a dotted single-column box in the middle of the article providing a gist of the piece together with an introduction) was popular among the readers. This panel was helpful in many ways. Office-goers and students, who were in a hurry to reach their destinations in the morning, used to get the essence of the article by having a glance at the panel.

On the face of it, selection of main articles for the Edit Page may appear to be too easy for the Edit Page Editor. But it is a difficult assignment. As most articles are well written, it is a challenge for him to select the best. Of course, the Editor-in-Chief will have the final say on whether or not a particular article should find a place on the Edit Page or pushed to Oped Page or returned to the contributor with regrets.

In the 1980s, the *Statesman* had a unique system of informing the contributors by post whether or not their articles have been accepted for publication. Invariably, the contributors (including this writer) used to receive this communication within 10 days of receipt. If the article is accepted, he/she received an envelope. With the newspaper's insignia, it had a white card with this communication in italics: 'The Editor presents his compliments and thanks for offering ... (the title of the article) ... which he will publish when space permits.' However, if the article is rejected, it had this communication in italics: 'The Editor presents his compliments and regrets his inability to use the enclosed article for the offer of which he expresses thanks.'

Articles used in the Edit Page are known for their value, quality and merit. Undoubtedly, the writer or contributor will have to be a person of standing. Just as newspapers sometimes carry front-page editorials, articles also appear on front page for their worth and significant contribution to knowledge. For instance, if there is an important Supreme Court judgement, the Editor or the Editor-in-Chief would love to use an article by legal luminaries like Fali S. Nariman and Soli J. Sorabjee on the front page—as a flier or as an anchor—than confine it to the Edit Page. Special treatment to such articles has its own advantage. In addition to the front page lead and another spot story on the same subject, the opinion piece by a constitutional expert in the front page will add to the quality of debate and discussion.

Newspapers such as the *Statesman, Hindustan Times,* the *Hindu,* the *Tribune,* the *Times of India* and the *Indian Express* invariably rope in academics (university professors or even research scholars) to deliver Edit Page articles. For Editors feel that if a subject is handled by an academic, he or she will do justice to the article, examine the issue from various angles free of bias. At least this was the impression obtained in the 1980s as far as the editorial policy of a few newspapers such as the *Statesman* and *Hindustan Times* was concerned.

Word count has always been a challenge for Edit Page writers. It's not a new phenomenon. It has been there for quite some time. When this writer joined the print media as a freelancer for the *Statesman* and *Hindustan Times* in the 1980s, the Editors had advised him to keep the length of the Edit Page Main Articles to 1700 words, which was considered an honour. If a piece deserved more space, it was split into a two-part article. This writer had also done full page and half-page articles for the Oped Page. Nowadays, readers seem to have no patience to read longish pieces. Consequently, the length of Edit Page Main Articles has come down to 500 words in a few papers like the *Times of India.* Sadly, the latter has downgraded the Edit Page status to Page number 18 instead of the usual Page 8 or 10. Significantly, though Edit Page is reserved for experts and specialists these days, there is ample scope for doing longish pieces for Oped Pages in some newspapers.

Over the years, though the policy of commissioning experts to write articles by and large continued, the proliferation of writers in various fields has become a challenge for Editors. It was felt that while not all writers can be accommodated on the Edit Page, a way out should be found to give them an opportunity to express their views. This led to the emergence of the Oped Page. The Oped Page came in handy for Editors to cover a representative of views from this section of society–good writers with a specialist touch, but not so eminent as to be given prominence on the Edit Page. The introduction of Perspective Page and Oped Page on Sunday in some newspapers such as the *Tribune* also came to the rescue of the Editor-in-Chief to make the best use of a good number of articles on these pages.

While the introduction of Oped Page has helped Editors cover diversified views on various subjects, this has also led to some resentment among regular in-house editorial writers whose first preference is always the Edit Page. Experience has shown that Senior Editors do not always come forward to do an Oped Page article, but agree to do an Edit Pager whenever advised by the Editor-in-Chief.

In recent times, newspapers such as the *Tribune* have expanded the scope of both the writers and the opinion pages. In the past seven years, the *Tribune* has made the Oped Page a specialised page. The Edit Page layout of this newspaper has more or less remained intact. During Raj Chengappa's editorship, the Oped Page was confined to one particular theme (on week days) such as governance, defence, foreign policy, agriculture, economy and society. Significantly, in-house editorial writers were encouraged to plan and write for these pages. Of late, the *Hindu* has also expanded its space for contributors. While its Edit Page continues to be restricted for experts, contributions are encouraged on the Oped Page and the features page. In the Sunday edition of the *Hindu*, many articles are published.

Remarkably, the *Indian Express* and the *New Indian Express* are doing well. Sometimes, the Oped Page of the *Indian Express* seems to have greater readability in terms of its articles and columns than the Edit Page. The articles are exhaustive and are invariably penned by experts from Harvard University, London School of Economics and Political Science and the John F. Kennedy School of Government.

Unfortunately, while some newspapers have downgraded the Edit Page, some have scrapped it altogether. The *Times of India*'s Edit Page is one of the best in the country, but as mentioned earlier, it appears on page 18 in a 24-page edition. Ironically, though it was one of the first newspapers to introduce the Oped Page with brilliant articles and features, it scrapped it years back for reasons best known to it. Even its Sunday Magazine, which was one of the best in the country a few decades ago, does not carry articles on burning issues anymore. *Times*

Life, the new avatar of Times of India's Sunday Magazine focusses on films, fashion, society and entertainment. Newspapers such as *Daily News and Alliance* (DNA) and *Sakal Times* have no Edit or Oped Pages. Moreover, not all newspapers carry three editorials. The *Times of India* uses only two edits (the second one is too short), the *Telegraph* has one or two edits and *Deccan Chronicle* has one. While the *Hindu's* two editorials are exhaustive and take up the entire column, the *Indian Express* (north) carries three edits on weekdays. The *Tribune* has now reverted to two edits on weekdays.

The Oped Page in some newspapers gives a comprehensive view of a particular theme from various angles, including facts on file in the form of timelines, boxes, illustrations, graphics, charts, visuals, cartoons and special features. Nowadays, the focus is more on how to package the articles with good visuals and graphics rather than following the same old mould of a fixed format and layout. During Raj Chengappa's editorship of the *Tribune*, the layout of the Oped Page changed every day—it was indeed a tribute to the talents of the designers.

This is true in the case of news pages as well. Today, almost all newspapers face this challenge—how best to package the news with a good design element. There is no problem with content at all. The reporters burn the midnight oil to do special stories. And news agencies are everready with their reports. But the challenge is the design element and layout. Not surprisingly, it is not the desk but the graphic artists who do the pages. One does understand the limitations of graphic artists. And it is for this reason that they are adequately briefed by the News Editor, the chief subeditor (or Senior Editors as the case may be) while pages are made. In some newspapers, Senior Editors sit with the designers or artists when pages are being made to ensure that the content is free from errors.

Letters to the Editor

This is another important column on the Edit Page. A lot of attention is given to it because it is said to provide the feedback to the Editor-in-Chief on the quality of news reports, editorials and articles covered by the newspaper. As it represents the pulse of the readers, the Editor-in-Chief vets the letters that get published.

Another reason for the importance attached to this column is the fact that letter writers voice their concerns over a number of issues ranging from social, economic and political to education, science and technology, defence, agriculture and women's empowerment. These writers are also knowledgeable and give official figures to buttress their arguments on topics such as economic growth and planning, corruption, bureaucratic control and foreign policy. Consequently, this column is not only seen as an 'important source of information' but also a 'compelling force of intervention' (*Times of India*, 1988).[1]

It goes to the credit of the *Times of India* that many eminent personalities used to contribute letters to its Editor on various issues to this newspaper. They include Mahatma Gandhi, Bal Gangadhar Tilak, Gopal Krishna Gokhale, Jawaharlal Nehru, Mohammad Ali Jinnah, Acharya J.B. Kripalini, Jayaprakash Narayan, Indira Gandhi, J.R.D. Tata, Nani Palkhivala, Minoo Masani and Sir Ratan Tata. This shows the attention they used to give to this column. While writing letters on topics of current interest, these writers were not guided by any personal or populist considerations. The letters were written with a view to improving the state of the nation and in the public interest. Clearly, this continues to be the sole intention of most letter writers.

On an average, a newspaper receives about 100 letters every day. It is not possible for an Editor to use all of them for reasons of space. On any given day, one can hardly accommodate four or five letters. Thus, it is a bit of a challenge for the Letters Editor to select a few letters for the day's page. Keeping in view the increasing number of letters that he/she receives every day, the Letters Editor cannot afford to be complacent and is expected to weed out the unnecessary ones on a daily basis. Otherwise, their number would multiply the next day, thus increasing his workload considerably.

To hit the bull's eye, the letters will have to be brief and to the point. There is no problem with style or grammar. The Letters Editor will take care of it. But the letters cannot be long. Sometimes, when the Letters Editor comes across good but longish letters, he/she just paraphrases it. Care is taken to ensure the original flavour of the letter.

In principle, a letter is normally considered for publication only if it has a view different than that of an editorial, article or news report and is critical of a policy decision of the government. Laudatory letters are not encouraged. Even when many readers write on a particular theme, only a few are published, that too, carrying different viewpoints on the same theme.

---

[1] It has brought out an excellent volume on Letters to the Editor. It contains letters written by such eminent personalities as Mahatma Gandhi and Jawaharlal Nehru.

The Letters Editor will have to tread with caution while selecting letters. He cannot select a letter that seeks to inflame communal passions or advocates treason. One has to respect the opinion of a citizen or reader, but it cannot go to the extent of preaching or giving a call for sedition. Similarly, one has to be careful for any comment that may be defamatory. The Editor and the publisher would attract penal action in accordance with law if a letter is found to be defamatory. There are clear-cut guidelines from the Press Council of India and the Editors' Guild of India and the Editors would do well to conform to these guidelines.

When readers complain against any authority or official for any arbitrary action or decision, it is better to drop the name of the official concerned in the letter. Otherwise, the official's personal reputation may be harmed if the complaint is found to be untrue, and he/she may file a defamation suit against the Editor. In any case, it is better if the Letters Editor rewrites complaints of this kind for brevity and clarity. Owing to increasing pressure on the news pages, sometimes clarifications on news reports, factual inaccuracy in reports or articles, inadvertent omission of bylines, and so on, are also included in the letters column.

In recent times, the pressure on the Letters to the Editor column has increased so much that the Editors have found different ways to provide space for readers' views—by opening up news pages and organising debates with logos such as Forum, Debate, Discussion; by withdrawing the second article on the Edit Page; or by devoting a full Oped Page. For a while, the *Tribune* used the Oped Page to accommodate Letters to the Editor. However, this column was back on the Edit Page as the Editor felt that the Edit Page was indeed the right place for letters.

While letters need to be given their rightful place on the Edit Page, the Editors cannot afford to carry anonymous letters anymore. True, decades ago, newspapers published letters signed 'Pro Bono Public', 'Repose', 'Young Lady', 'Reform', 'Trident', 'Sufferer', 'False Economy', 'Vox Populi', or abbreviations such as ABC, XYZ or AKT. However, the thumb rule today is that if a reader does not have the courage to stand up for his comment and disclose his identity and address to the Editor-in-Chief, his/her letter should not be used. Not surprisingly, newspapers and magazines these days insist that every letter should carry the full name of the writer, postal address, contact number and e-mail address. Encouragingly, the Editors of some newspapers play a proactive role in making this column more interesting, lively and intellectually stimulating. Contact numbers and e-mail ids of readers not only help as effective bridges of interaction with the Editors from time to time but also make readers consider themselves as important stakeholders in the management of news and opinions in the media.

References

Bhargava, G.S. (2007). *The press in India: An overview*. New Delhi: National Book Trust.

Chawla, Prabhu. (1988, 15 October). Conceding defeat. *India Today*, New Delhi.

Datta, V.N. (2011). *The Tribune 130 years: A witness to history*. New Delhi: The Tribune and Hay House.

Hindustan Times. (2017b, 21 July). The office of the president. *Hindustan Times*.

———. (2017a, 28 July). Fall in Bihar. *Hindustan Times*.

Nevile, Pran. (2008). *The Tribune 125 years: An anthology 1881–2006*. New Delhi: Hay House.

Rahman, Shafi. (2012, 4 May). Rahul Gandhi's aide Meenakshi Natrajan's proposed bill seeks to gag the media. *India Today*.

The Economic Times. (2017, 21 July). Ram Nath Kovind. *The Economic Times*.

The Economist Style Guide. (1993). Style guide. *The Economist*, London, p. 5.

The Hindu. (2017a, 21 July). The new President. *The Hindu*.

———. (2017b, 28 July). The shift in Bihar. *The Hindu*.

The Indian Express. (2015b, May). SC stays Delhi Government's anti-media order. *The Indian Express*.

———. (2017a, 21 July). President Kovind. *The Indian Express*.

———. (2017b, 28 July). Opportunities. *The Indian Express*.

The Statesman. (2017, 28 July). Pathetic whining. *The Statesman*.

The Telegraph. (2017, 28 July). Private math. *The Telegraph*.

The Times of India. (1988). Feedback: Letters to the Editor of the Times of India. *The Times of India Sesquicentennial*, Bombay.

———. (1989). Forefront. *The Times of India Sesquicentennial*, Bombay.

———. (2017a, 21 July). President Kovind. *The Times of India*.

———. (2017b, 28 July). Break point. *The Times of India*.

The Tribune. (2017, 28 July). The drama in Bihar. *The Tribune*.

15

Keeping Confidences: Political Reporting

Neerja Chowdhury

> Building relationships of trust and respecting people's confidences are the sine qua non for good political reporting for a print journalist.

If I were to distil what has stood me in good stead as a political reporter over the past 30 years, it is credibility, contacts and legwork.

It goes without saying that an interest in the country's politics is a natural prerequisite for any political journalist. Many have asked me whether I find reporting on the country's politicians a depressing affair because they are a discredited lot today. I have, in many ways, found reporting on Indian politics to be educative and entertaining. No day is a dull one; nor is one day like another.

Indian politics, which mirrors the plurality and vibrancy of the nation, is like many *nautankis* (folk theatre) rolled into one. Covering elections, which every political reporter does during the course of his/her career, teaches you so much about India which no degree or doctorate can.

Credibility is the prized possession of any journalist, more so of a political reporter. This simply means that whatever you write, for whichever medium, is taken seriously because over the years a journalist acquires a reputation for accuracy and objectivity. That is why today readers not only want to know 'what' has appeared in a newspaper but 'who' has written the report. The answer to 'who' is crucial in helping them make up their minds on how much credence they should give the report.

There was a time when people tended to believe the information appearing in newspapers as gospel truth. 'But this has appeared in the newspaper,' the readers would insist. Today that faith in newspapers and broadcasters has been eroded. People have come to realise that agendas or personal considerations decide what news gets published or broadcast. Or that the publication of a report may be the result of 'paid news', where politicians and parties or corporate companies pay money to get items published, with media houses even offering packages they can opt for. So much so that one newspaper had on its front page two news items placed alongside, each predicting the victory of two contending candidates.

There are many elements that determine 'credibility'. Accuracy is one of them. Opinions can vary. So can emphasis in a story. One reporter may start her report with one piece of information, yet another may give something else primacy. That is understandable, for there will be a certain element of subjectivity. But facts are sacrosanct.

Often the placement of a story can either enhance the value of a news item or virtually 'kill' it. The reporter, in most cases, has little say on the placement of the story, and this is usually the prerogative of the Editor or the editorial team which decides what goes where. A newspaper can put an item it wants to play up on Page 1 and bury an equally important one in the inside pages if it wants to detract from its value.

We all have our opinions, our ideological inclinations and electoral preferences. But a political reporter has to be scrupulously fair to all, more so when the report involves someone whose views you disagree with. It is this that contributes to the credibility of the reporter.

It is easier today to ensure accuracy of information than was the case in the past. In this day and age of Google, Facebook, Twitter and other technological breakthroughs, it takes only seconds to check the spelling of a name, the designation of a person, or get the complete profile of a person or the history of an event.

When I started my career in political reporting in 1987, newspaper libraries were not so well equipped. We would often spend hours checking simple facts. I remember once it took me two hours to merely check how Dr Subramanian Swamy spelt his name. For, if you got one small thing wrong in the story, every other piece of information would become open to question.

I remember one scoop that I had chanced upon, on the yet-to-be published Kuldip Singh Commission report which had indicted Ramakrishna Hegde for irregularities in the allotment of land when he was Chief Minister of Karnataka in the mid-1980s. I listed it for use, insisting that it could not wait even for a day because somebody else might get hold of it. Even before I finished writing my piece, the Editor came into the office carrying Hegde's resignation as Deputy Chairman of the Planning Commission, a position he occupied in 1990. Somehow, Hegde had got wind of the fact that the *Indian Express* had got hold of the report and wanted to mitigate the damage. Both the stories, of Hegde's indictment and his resignation, were carried side by side in the next morning's paper.

But, knowing how critical accuracy is for a report, I could barely sleep that night when the story went to press. Knowing the implication the story would have, I began to question if I had heard my 'source' right? So I telephoned him at 11.30 PM to double-check. Again, at 1.30 AM, more doubts assailed me. So I called the gentleman again to make doubly sure about some other piece of information I had used.

Today, social media has enabled responses of politicians to a development known instantly and the media picks them up. In fact, politicians have put whole teams in place that react to events with speed. One of Prime Minister Narendra Modi's successes is attributed to his effective use of social media to reach out to the younger generation. So was the case with the Anna Hazare–Arvind Kejriwal movement against corruption, which created the ground for the 2014 change of government. Congress politicians later lamented that they had not been as quick to discern the use of social media, but they are fast changing.

However, there is a flip side to this story. This trend of dependence on social media to know the responses of politicians to situations is increasingly giving a go-by to the old system of interviews, where you can counter question a politician. With instant blogs and tweets this is no longer possible; it is now a one-way conversation with them.

Credibility also ensures balanced reporting. Almost always there are two sides to any story. I have learnt over the years that no matter how reliable your sources, almost all of them give information selectively. That is why corroboration becomes essential. It is equally important to record the other side of the story, even if the person may be telling untruths. That is for the reader—or the viewer—to judge. It is the skill and hard work of a reporter that can help separate the wheat from the chaff.

What helps a political reporter strike a balance is when he/she covers not just one political party but can write about parties across the spectrum. If you cover one party for a length of time, you may start to see events through one lens—and it is very easy to do this—and this is something to guard against. It also helps to talk not just to the people at the top in government or in a party but also with functionaries and grass-roots workers who can provide a very different perspective.

Network of Contacts

If a political journalist has found a job in a reputed media house, it must be because of the vast network of contacts he/she has managed to create. Contacts do not happen overnight, but are critical to political reporting, particularly when it comes to reporting for the print media. Undoubtedly, a TV journalist often stands for hours sometimes—and you see hordes of them hanging around, say outside Parliament, in the hope of catching politicians coming out of the building to get a sound byte from them.

In some way a print journo's job begins where the TV journalist's job ends. The print journalist has to go beyond the news, for the reader would want to know more about the story that broke on her TV screen the previous night. The newspaper story has to answer more than 'what', 'where' and 'when' and try and answer questions of 'how' and 'why'. Of course, with 24×7 news channels and evening panel discussions much of this gets discussed, making the task of the print journalist even more difficult. That is why TV is often referred to as an on-the-record medium and print is increasingly seen as an off-the-record medium.

Political journalism thrives on 'contacts' and it involves years of building relationships of trust when those in positions of authority feel comfortable talking to a journalist in confidence. Just as a political reporter is called to read many newspapers carefully every day so as to be on top of the latest political situation, it is part of his/her job to meet as many people as possible during the course of his/her work.

This is now being done increasingly on the telephone, but really it is not a substitute for a one-to-one conversation where views, body language, and not just what is said but also what is unspoken can become a story, and what is more, the relationship is less transactional. The more the people a reporter meets and is in touch with, the more she will be able to create a network of 'sources' who will ensure a flow of information, and may give 'tip offs', which can lead to scoops or breakthroughs or 'breaking news' before others get it. This is greatly prized in a profession which is highly competitive.

Developing a network of contacts can take years before people start to trust a journalist and talk freely. Respecting people's confidences is the sine qua non for good reportage. If something has been conveyed in confidence, it must be respected. If the 'source' has said that the information given can be used in an article but without attributing it to the person that too must be respected. Sometimes it can be tempting to use a piece of given information and it may even make a sensational story. This will not only be a betrayal of trust, but the reporter may end up killing the goose that lays the golden eggs.

While it is important to keep information truly off the record, it is also necessary that it is not bandied about at parties or in groups. For by boasting at a party that an 'X' politician had given you a 'Y' piece of information, the journalist may be able to show off his/her high-level contacts, but it can make the going tough for the 'source'. For that piece of information may work against him, if it gets back to his party leaders and they take a dim view of his 'indiscretions'.

Sometimes, if a story creates embarrassment for the government or for an individual politician, leading to action against him or her, the reporter may come under pressure to reveal his/her source. Though the law in India does not give journalists a legally backed right not to reveal the identity of their sources, it is the reporter's professional right, I believe, not to do so.

If the paper faces litigation on account of his/her story, the reporter can tell the Editor about the identity of his/her source, but doing everything possible to protect the person who has trusted him/her with information.

This is not always easy. One day, as I was walking into the office of the *Indian Express* in New Delhi, also known as New Delhi's Fleet Street, the receptionist accosted me by saying that the Prime Minister wanted to speak to me. I thought it must be a call from the Prime Minister's Office. I picked up the receiver and heard the words, 'Maain Atal Bihari Vajpayee bol raha hoon' (I am Atal Bihari Vajpayee, speaking). I was taken aback, and it took me a few seconds to recover. The Prime Minister referred to a story I had written on the front page that morning. He asked me who had given me the information. It had created enormous problems for him. For his parliamentary managers had persuaded an irate Opposition to return to the House after disrupting it for several days but my story had put the fat in the fire again. I assured him that I had spoken to more than one person. Taking a couple of names, he asked me if they were the ones who had given me information. I said, 'Please excuse me, but I cannot reveal the identity of my source.' This was difficult to say, and I felt very bad and embarrassed. At the other end of the line was after all the Prime Minister of India.

It is a fact that 'leaks' of information often take place when 'thieves' fall out. People who give you information may well have motives for releasing it, to fix an opponent or embarrass someone they had fallen out with.

For the reporter, it is the accuracy of the information made available that is important, not the motive for leaking it.

Legwork

Any political journalist will tell you that there is simply no substitute for legwork. That is why it is important to be interested in politics and current affairs, and as a colleague put it, to have an 'insatiable curiosity' about it to be able to work hard and enjoy it. It can mean long hours. It can mean being called at any time if something major breaks out.

During the 1980s and 1990s when the era of coalition politics had set in and governments were being made and unmade with a rapidity— these years saw the decline of Rajiv Gandhi, the rise of V.P. Singh, the enthronement of Chandra Shekhar for four months and then the return of a minority government of the Congress led by P.V. Narasimha Rao, and the 'government of chief ministers', led by H.D. Deve Gowda and then I.K. Gujral—those of us who were covering politics rarely went home before midnight.

Political reporting entails a relationship between the politician and the political journalist. Since the reporter meets and talks to politicians frequently, over the years they may become friends. Politicians need journalists to get across their views to the voters and journalists need political information to keep their readers and viewers informed, public opinion being so critical for a democracy. But there has to be dignity and mutual respect because both have a role to play in a democratic polity.

16

Monetised Media: Media Ethics

Kamlendra Kanwar

The business–government nexus has resulted in a decline in hard-core reporting and an increase in soft features, many of which are sponsored news.

There is much that has changed in journalism in India over the years like in any other profession. Some changes have been for the better and some for the worse. There is far more variety in newspapers and television channels today than there was a couple of decades ago. In print journalism, production techniques and processes have improved so much that newspapers and magazines look slicker than ever before.

The real watershed has been the advent of private television channels, which has deeply affected the way news is purveyed even in the print medium. Added to that is the digital revolution with many niche and general websites making space for themselves. It is difficult to surmise whether it is now a crowded news market or a no-holds-barred jungle of news sources with little sense of direction.

While there have been a few positives, one aspect of the profession that has witnessed a perceptible deterioration is journalistic ethics. Unfortunately the tribe of 'black sheep' in the profession is increasing and there is no check on this negative trend.

Money Is King

Professionalism has suffered as money has become king. It is sad that commercial considerations override editorial freedom and commitment to public good today. Increasingly, newspapers are doctoring news to suit big advertisers, suppressing negative news about them while playing up positive news about them beyond proportion.

In pre-Independence days and the early decades after Independence, journalism was a mission. Youngsters who joined the profession were usually idealists who looked upon the job as a means to serve society and the nation. Salaries in the profession were abysmally low then, and so those who took up journalism did so for the love of it.

The good news for youngsters aspiring to a career in journalism is that journalists are not paid a pittance as they were a couple of decades ago. Today salaries by and large are a lot better and growth opportunities have opened up, especially in big cities.

There has been a proliferation of newspapers and electronic channels with the result that aspirants can look forward to a wide array of jobs. Gone are the days when journalists stuck to the same job for decades. There is much greater mobility now with increased opportunities and many more new avenues.

Journalism courses, too, have improved. There is a wide choice of institutions offering courses relating to various aspects of journalism. While most of them are run-of-the-mill, there are some that conform to international standards and are churning out well-rounded journalists with their skills duly honed. While the English media has stuck roots, there is a mushrooming of vernacular media. But the downside is that satisfaction levels have suffered and the journalist stands devalued in the eyes of the avaricious owners in relation to the bigwigs of the revenue-earning departments. The days of the supremacy of the Editor are virtually over.

Back in the 1950s, Prime Minister Jawaharlal Nehru had warned journalists that the freedom of the press did not mean freedom from government control alone. It meant freedom also from the control of business, both overt and covert. Today, while business exercises its own influence over the media, governments too wield considerable influence through their massive advertising budgets. It is not unusual for governments in states to deny advertisements to media outfits that are critical of them. Indeed, government advertisements are an effective means to twist the arms of newspaper owners who in turn twist the arms of Editors to extract submission. The days of the powerful Editor, who defied unethical instructions, and in many cases, staked his job to uphold principles, are now over.

There used to be a big hue and cry in the media over the whims of proprietors, especially where shown the door for their uprightness. Today's Editors are forced to cave in to pressure: there is no organised support from the rest of the media and from people at large.

With all these influences, what we are seeing in the media today is a decrease in hard-core reporting as a proportion of the whole and an increase in soft, entertainment features, many of which are sponsored news. Hard-core reporting is usually with an axe to grind. Clearly, corporates are wary of supporting the media that regularly criticise their products or discuss corporate wrongdoing. They would rather support the media that put readers and audiences in a passive, non-critical state of mind, making it easier to sell things to.

D.R. Mankekar, a much-respected Editor of the *Times of India* in the 1950s and 1960s, who in his autobiographical work, *No, my son never*, recounted his travails as an Editor in a fictional manner to his son who wanted to become a journalist. He asks his son, who expresses his intent to become a journalist, whether he wishes to follow in his footsteps after seeing what he had gone through. But to his utter surprise, the son reaffirms that he will choose no other career because of the eventful and exciting incidents and encounters that his father had experienced.

In fact, journalists who leave the profession for better salaries and working conditions invariably return to journalism despite its pitfalls because the grass looks greener on the other side but is not as green as it seems. Today's breed of journalists by and large lack the idealism that characterised those of the past decades. That is because while monetary compensations are much greater now, the average journalist is not prepared to stick his/her neck out to fight for the truth.

A guilty conscience about unethical conduct and an inability to conform to the path of right conduct disturb many mediapersons even as they wilt under the pressure of a system in which values have been subverted.

'Editorial Products'

The growing synergy between media marketing, on the one hand, and advertising and public relations (PR), on the other, has created an array of 'editorial products'—different forms of paid content, advertorials that look like editorials, sponsors creeping into the editorial content of sponsored programmes, 'PR-friendly' events and awards, and new mechanisms for generating 'internal PR' within media organisations.

It is not unusual to find reviews of films, eating places and even doctors' skills written in a calculated design to act as 'plugs' for those who pay for favourable reviews. The consumer gets cheated in the process but newspapers, magazines and TV news channels do not seem to bother about their credibility.

In most newspaper outfits, the Editor has to act according to the preferences of the advertising manager. All sorts of innovative advertisements are designed where the advertiser encroaches on what was earlier considered inviolable editorial space. Advertisement jackets where editorial space begins from what is effectively Page 3 are now commonplace.

Almost every major film production now has media partners who ensure good reviews for the film and promote it through other means that violate the sanctity of impartiality. When people watch a film because it has got a high rating in a particular newspaper or TV programme and then find the movie disastrous, they lose faith in the medium itself.

In 2005, the Press Council of India, which functions as a watchdog body, was mandated to draw up 'norms of journalistic conduct'. Although it has only recommendatory authority and has no powers to pull up those who violate the norms, it is nevertheless a guide for those who want to play by the rules.

In his Preface to the 2005 edition of 'Norms of Journalistic Conduct' issued by the Press Council of India, Press Council Chairman Justice K. Jayachandra Reddy said:

> There was a time when journalism was a mission. Soon it became a profession and is now run as a full-fledged business activity like any other enterprise. Journalism has expanded its role and activities and has also grown in power. Codification of its work ethics is, therefore, an imperative need.

Many of the guidelines that the Press Council laid down are violated routinely. Since there is no mandated body to punish the wrongdoers and, mercifully, in the absence of any governmental control or regulation, it devolves on journalists to exercise self-restraint.

Accuracy and Fairness

The Press Council lays emphasis on accuracy and fairness. The norms enunciated by it state clearly that 'The Press shall eschew publication of inaccurate, baseless, graceless, misleading or distorted material. All sides of the core issue or subject should be reported. Unjustified rumours and surmises should not be set forth as facts.' All these are sanctimonious statements but they sound hollow when seen against the fact that they are violated routinely.

The Press Council of India's guidelines for Norms of Journalistic Conduct on pre-publication verification say:

> On receipt of a report or article of public interest and benefit containing imputations or comments against a citizen, the Editor should check with due care and attention its factual accuracy apart from other authentic sources—with the person or the organisation concerned to elicit his/her or its version, comments or reaction and publish the same alongside with due correction in the report where necessary. In the event of lack or absence of response, a footnote to that effect may be appended to the report.

If reporters, subeditors and Editors of newspapers and magazines were to adhere to these basic guidelines, both fairness and accuracy can be achieved. But there is a long way to go to make this an acceptable principle in this age of sensationalism.

With regard to coverage of communal incidents, the Press Council has given useful guidelines. It says:

> News, views or comments relating to communal or religious disputes/clashes shall be published after proper verification of facts and presented with due caution and restraint in a manner which is conducive to the creation of an atmosphere congenial to communal harmony, amity and peace.

> Sensational, provocative and alarming headlines are to be avoided. Acts of communal violence or vandalism shall be reported in a manner as may not undermine the people's confidence in the law and order machinery of the State. Giving community-wise figures of the victims of communal riot, or writing about the incident in a style which is likely to inflame passions, aggravate the tension, or accentuate the strained relations between the communities/religious groups concerned, or which has a potential to exacerbate the trouble, shall be avoided.

While these norms are followed by and large, it cannot be denied that some publications transgress the limits. It would be in the fitness of things to have an effective deterrent against violations because in the absence of a deterrent, the tribe of violators is bound to increase. It is, therefore, imperative that the Press Council is empowered to punish the recalcitrant newspapers and journalists. Or, a separate self-regulatory body consisting of right-thinking individuals from the media should be constituted.

The electronic media, too, has some soul-searching to do. Managed by relatively younger people, TV news channels display a rare sense of enterprise. Investigative journalism has been given a perceptible boost by some of them though there is weight in the argument of some critics that they have heightened the tendency for 'trial by the media'.

Also, there is too much negativity in the 24×7 news channels. Rarely do the channels come up with inspiring, positive stories. The result is that there is a mood of despondency that has gripped the nation. Scams must be unravelled as is being done but there is a need for profiles in courage, stories of enterprise and achievement.

All said and done, there is still a lot in the journalistic profession that a journalist can be happy and proud of. The reporter must continue to look under the carpet but he or she must be responsible and rooted in the soil. He or she must cross-check facts and give a fair hearing to a person/persons who is/are likely to be aggrieved by the report. Journalists must have a nose for news and a 'feel' for society. The reporter must stay clear of inducements and must establish a reputation for incorruptibility and objectivity. He/she must research well his/her breaking stories.

Good subeditors are rare to find. They are an extremely valuable part of any newspaper. They must not only have a broad vision and a deep understanding of issues—local, regional, national and international—but also have a good command over the language. It is not the business of subeditors to inject their own views into the reporter's copy. They must stay steadfastly loyal to the spirit of the copy but must not fight shy of looking at copy with a critical eye to detect and correct factual errors.

Losing Track of Objectivity

It is the responsibility of Leader Writers to represent the policies of the newspaper or journal without losing track of objectivity and integrity. Indian editorials are still seen as sober and balanced expressions of opinions. By and large, there is a sense of propriety in judging contentious issues although this cannot be said of all major newspapers.

The language Press keeps its finger on the pulse of the region and the nation, reflecting the reality. Generalisations are odious but reporters in vernacular newspapers tend to sensationalise their news stories.

However, they have their ears to the ground, which is not always the case with the English-language media.

With the mushroom growth of media, malpractices are bound to take root. There is a general lack of commitment to old style ethical standards. There is an increasing trend towards making a quick buck.

All said and done, it is still a wonderful profession but a lot depends on what path a particular journalist takes—the path of ethical conduct which gives a great deal of job satisfaction or the path of wheeling and dealing and deception which may bring monetary returns but trouble the conscience.

In the rat race that now characterises the media, especially the electronic media, sensationalism has virtually taken over from credible, well-researched news. Distortion of news permeates the election scene, too. During the 2014 general election, there was a plethora of complaints that candidates, especially those belonging to bigger parties, were planting stories favouring them in an effort to influence the result.

Pre-poll surveys and 'opinion polls' are fast losing their credibility as political parties increasingly use poll survey agencies to project things in a way that benefits them. While there are still some credible and well-collated surveys, in the public mind they are tarred with the same brush.

Likewise, business interests are furthered through newspaper campaigns and many companies sponsor campaigns for a price. There is a trend of sponsored features in news channels where specific agendas are catered to. To what extent are such features allowed to steer away from the avowed policy of the channel is a moot point.

In 2014, the concept of paid news in reporting came to the fore. This amounted to a serious erosion in the time-honoured principle not to camouflage advertisement content or business promotion as hard news. While there was a big outcry in media circles against this pernicious trend, the result was that while it was taken away from public focus it re-surfaced in an insidious form.

It is not as though these practices have not crept into the media in the United States, Britain and Europe. While they are being tolerated, there is a credibility-conscious section that is frowning upon such practices which are diluting the very essence of journalism. The American media are indeed the fountainhead of sensationalism just as they showed the way for the use of new technology.

An animated debate is on throughout the free world against the growing challenge to ethical standards. Yet, it must be admitted that people at large are becoming increasingly insensitive to negative media trends.

Nevertheless, it would be prudent for journalists to recognise the need to do a course correction to ensure that the profession retains a measure of sobriety and a sense of responsibility. Credibility needs to be propped up more than ever before.

The laws against defamation need to be re-defined and new standards set within the profession. While any form of regulation imposed by governments are anathema, we need to accept higher standards of self-regulation.

There is indeed a case for giving more teeth to the Press Council of India so that the recalcitrant newspapers, magazines and digital media are brought under a stricter code of conduct and held accountable.

If malpractices are not checked, we will be setting dangerous standards for future generations. We need to do some soul-searching to recognise the ills that have crept into the profession.

Let us face it—for every system to succeed, there must be some checks and balances. There is a crisis of accountability in our democracy today.

We must accept more rigorous self-regulation or else we may fall victim to governmental regulation, which will be calamitous.

Even as there is no outright censorship or governmental interference with press freedom, self-censorship imposes a legitimate threat to plurality of views in national discourse. Laws should exist not only to protect the space for the media to act independently but also to guard against the co-option of the media by the executive.

The rapid growth in media organisations along with increasing commercial pressures has meant that objectivity in reporting has suffered significantly. The lack of punitive powers with the Press Council of India means that it 'cannot levy fines or order the withdrawal of advertisements by government agencies, leave alone place errant journalists behind bars.' Hence it is rendered ineffective in placing any cost on those violating journalistic ethics.

In the case of television news, the News Broadcasting Standards Authority (NBSA) looks into violation of code of ethics laid down by the News Broadcasters Association (NBA). However, the problem with this self-regulatory body is that its membership is voluntary and 'out of 135 news channels in the country, only 28 news broadcasters owning 57 news channels are members of the NBA.' A large number of television news channels continue to be beyond the ambit of any regulation by virtue of not being part of the NBA.

In such a situation, the two self-regulating media bodies are at best, toothless tigers.

The privilege of protection of identity of sources used by journalists is an important element in how they unearth the truth. However, in

India, there are no statutory rights accorded to journalists to protect their sources. In fact, in a court of law, a journalist may be held in contempt of court for not disclosing his/her sources. This makes uncovering the truth tenuous. The law makes speaking the truth a risky choice between future harassment by those being exposed and putting up with injustice and wrongdoing in society.

17

Blurring the Lines: Visual Journalism

Gagan Prakash and Manju Singh

New ethical standards are needed for photojournalism as digital manipulation of news photographs is becoming the norm.

Visual journalism can have an immediate impact on national and international opinion and decision-making. Whereas printed news stories reach their targeted readers several hours after an event has occurred, high-speed digital applications deliver the information instantly to readers' mobile phones. Not only printed news, even news photographs have a tough time catching up with the moving images on television news channels (Patterson & Wilkins, 2010).

Visual journalists often face a dilemma whether to show an image or not. Their decisions define the line between what information is right for public consumption and what is harmful. These decisions are often tied to the ethical decision-making process, which may include ethical education, formally laid codes of ethics, personal experiences and values. This chapter examines the decisions needed to draw a line between the ethical and unethical approach in covering news, the contemporary trends in visual journalism and the challenges faced by photo journalists and video journalists.

New Media Tools

The convergence of a mixed media of traditional newspapers and broadcast stations with digital and Web-based media has resulted in the rapid growth of journalism. Convergence of various media formats is an old discussion. The relevant question in the digital era would be: How new media tools and online news platforms affect the traditional media and the public? The section below describes the proliferation of news media over the years and the various trends in journalism drawn from history.

Like any other form of communication, journalism has also changed with developments in information technology. From newspapers to television, from television to Web broadcasts, technology has not only provided new tools but also upgraded old ones. Newspapers have gone online and formatted for mobile devices.

The abundance of news sources could result in a possible fragmentation of the news audience. Audiences cannot be expected to sit down and watch television news programmes as they get news updates on a variety of media platforms and communication devices.

The convergence of media has given rise to competition. If a journalist does not have the ability to report for print, broadcast and the Internet synchronously, he will be left behind in the race to break news or post a video or picture. The recent trends in journalism such as the convergence of media tools, the race to deliver news first and the treatment of the public as one of the information source creators rather than as receivers have given rise to ethical risks.

Mass Media as the Fourth Estate

The concept of mass media in India has always been correlated with the concept of authority in many ways. The first use of the term 'fourth estate', according to scholars, is attributed to Alexis de Tocqueville, who, while determining a new classification of authorities, deemed the written press to be the Fourth Estate (De Tocqueville, 1835). The older literature that focussed on studying the Fourth Estate (Faucher, 1957; Paillet, 1974; Ulmann, 1935) addressed in general the written press as a domain, which affects the political, cultural and social life. Such periods witnessed no audio and visual mass media, compared to the situation at the beginning of the second half of the twentieth century.

According to Hidri (2012), many researchers in the field of sociology and communication literature believe that controlling society, upbringing and transferring heritage, achieving social solidarity, enhancing social criteria and mobilisation are among the most prominent functions of the mass media. Such functions are seemingly independent, but they are closely interrelated and sometimes concurrent. For example, social solidarity can be achieved by enhancing and promoting the social criteria. Mobilisation can never be achieved except by controlling society. Hence, this package of functions form a closely connected system that reveals the nature and levels of media action.

Ethical Dilemma

The technological developments since the 1990s have reduced the time gap between the happening of a news event and the distribution of information relating to that event. Photographs or videos of an event are uploaded almost as the event is taking place. The live transmission of information raises a few questions relating to media operations: Should a visual journalist shoot or not shoot? Is it relevant for the public? Do people need a particular piece of information or not? (Patterson & Wilkins, 2010).

The process of transmission and involvement of consumers in the creation and distribution of news could throw up unwanted errors, an unorganised information matrix and breaches. With changing media platforms, it is also important to recognise the gaps in existing media laws and ethics. In the digital age, video journalists find themselves caught between delivering to open information platforms, where news and audience are treated as targets, and playing the role of a salesperson trying to meet the target of achieving maximum news and maximum audience in minimum time.

With changes in the form of media, the ethics governing them have also undergone some changes. However, ethics drawn from sociocultural constructs remain unchanged. The International Federation of Journalists (IFJ) has codified ethical practices in journalism and some of them are relevant to visual journalism as well.

The first duty of a visual journalist is to respect the truth and the public's right to the truth. Only fair methods should be used to obtain news information, photographs and visual content (Press Council of India, 2010). A journalist should avoid facilitating discrimination based on race, sex, sexual orientation, language, religion, political or other opinions and national or social origins in news stories, photographs and video productions (White, 2008).

Plagiarism, malicious misrepresentation, libel, slander, unfounded accusations and accepting bribes in any form are serious professional offences. It is a challenge to uphold some of the ethics relevant to visual journalism in this age and time (Altun, 2011).

Balancing the Right to Privacy with Newsworthiness

John Berger, in his book *Seeing is believing*, says that a picture is an interpretation of reality, not reality itself. According to him, if a dozen photographers are asked to photograph a scene, most of them will produce different interpretations of reality.

For instance, when Tyler Hicks, winner of the Pulitzer Prize for Breaking News photography, covered the Westgate Mall massacre in Nairobi, Kenya, there were other photographers as well at the spot. But his interpretation of reality was different from that of the others. Berger says: 'Not only does the camera differ from the eye in its ability to manipulate angle, light and focus, but cameras also capture an isolated reality by presenting us with a slice of life, free from context.'

Media consumers generally believe that the photographs they see are true because their eyes cannot deceive them. From this assumption, a possibility of manipulation is not suspected (Shutter Release, April 2010).

No story is complete without a visual. The visual is so crucial to a story that this creates pressure on photojournalists. In their rush to shoot a strong image to accompany a story, photojournalists have to take some tough decisions. The most basic but important decision is whether to shoot or not to shoot. Many a time, the subject is not in any position to deny access to the photographer and many a time the subject is wounded or in grief. These situations call for some tough decisions on the part of the photographer (Pulitzer Prize, 2013).

Two territories are problematic to visual journalists: the right to personal space and the right to preserve the subject's information, such as joy or grief, from the public gaze (Goffman, 1959).

The irony is that somebody's misfortune is good fortune for visual journalists. In fact, visual journalists happen to get many assignments that involve encroaching into a subject's privacy.

Case I: What Comes First? Journalism or Humanity?

In 1994, the South African photojournalist Kevin Carter won the Pulitzer Prize for his disturbing photograph of a malnourished Sudanese child being stalked by a vulture. That same year, Kevin Carter committed suicide.

Without knowing the facts surrounding Carter's death, his suicide may seem shocking. It is believed that Carter received piles of criticism for his photograph. The picture was taken at Avod in Sudan where Carter found a toddler struggling to reach a food station. When she stopped to take some rest, a vulture came into the scene with its eyes focussed on the girl. Carter took over 18 minutes to take a satisfactory photograph. He waited for the right timing and right angle before chasing the bird away. The photograph was published in the New York Times in March 1993. Within a few days, it sparked a wide reaction and people wanted to know about the girl and whether Carter had assisted her. The New York Times, however, issued a statement giving information that the girl made it to the food station, but the statement lacked details (Wakeland, 2013).

For months, Carter was bombarded with questions about why he did not help the girl and was criticised for using her as an object of his photograph. The St. Petersburg Times (Florida) commented on Carter thus: 'The man adjusting his lens to take just the right frame of her suffering, might just as well be a predator, another vulture on the scene.'

However, it is not only photographers who are always at the edge and succumb to pressure. Editors are equally responsible for the choice of images that disturb society. Editors generally argue that it is not necessary that every decision has to be made on the field. They also believe that not every photograph of grief needs to be ruled out just because a few subjects are vulnerable. Where to draw the line should be made known to people who often cross it. Moreover, it is the photographer's job to cover the event as it is. So the people who often cross the line should be the ones who draw it.

A photographer covering victims of tragedy faces the dilemma of treating every subject as an end and not merely as a means to an end. We may agree that powerful pictures of accidents might compel a driver to drive with caution, but if that photograph comes at the expense of a victim's privacy, is it necessary to use that image? Bovee in the essay titled 'The ends can justify the means—but rarely' puts forward some questions to help the photographer find an answer to questions relating to ethics. He asks whether the means that a photographer uses are truly and morally evil or merely distasteful. Is the end a real good or something that merely appears to be good? Is it possible to have the same good using other means and whether these means withstand the test of publicity?

Case II

The Wall Street Journal's crime reporter Daniel Pearl was abducted in Pakistan on 23 January 2002, and a month later, FBI officials received a video entitled 'The slaughter of the Spy Journalist, the Jew Daniel Pearl.' This video made it clear that Daniel Pearl was murdered by those who had kidnapped him. It had Daniel Pearl giving a message on his Jewish roots and reading a statement condemning the United States' foreign policy, which clearly was a message from the extremists who killed him. The video then showed a man decapitating Daniel Pearl and holding his head aloft. The whole video was available to the US news media. An edited version of the video, depicting propaganda by Pakistani terrorists, was broadcast on CBS evening news. But it opened the doors for others to show the more graphic parts of the tape. The fears of Daniel Pearl's family came true on 31 May when *Boston Phoenix* published a link to the video. In no time this video got 40,000 hits (Photo 17.1).

The controversy over the contents of the video snowballed when *Phoenix* published photographs of Daniel Pearl talking into the camera before he was killed and his decapitated head. When criticised by the government, the editorial team compared the footage of Daniel Pearl's murder with widely used images of the Challenger space shuttle explosion and the 9/11 World Trade Center footage (Patterson & Wilkins, 2010). These instances raised many concerns about the policies and ethics of visual journalism.

In 1990, the freelance photographer Gregory Marinovich took photographs of a mob of African National Congress supporters killing a man believed to be a Zulu spy. Marinovich and Associated Press reporter Tom Chen followed the incident in which the man was stoned, stabbed,

Photo 17.1
Phoenix fix

Courtesy: i-kinja.

doused with gasoline and set on fire. The series of photographs stirred an intense debate among Editors and critics. Some Editors questioned the photographer on his role and some did not show any interest in the photographer. The photo series had many gory photographs. One of them, used widely in the print medium, showed the man being set on fire.

Los Angeles Times and *Dallas Morning News* carried the photograph in colour on their front page. Some newspapers carried photographs of the man being stabbed. One photograph showed a knife being stuck into his head. The *St. Paul Pioneer Press* ran this photograph in colour on its front page. After looking at the image, The News Editor Joe Sevick said: 'I look at the moment that the photo freezes on film, rarely do you see a photo where a knife is about to go into somebody.' Most of the controversial photographs were given the go-ahead by the management and were only finalised at the desk. Some newspapers play it safe. They do not carry gory pictures of victims of their areas in their local editions but allow them to appear in other editions. Around 41 newspapers carried at least one of the Marinovich pictures and very few Editors protested against their visual content.

Staging Video and News Photography

Every photographer aims 'to capture that perfect moment'. The perfect moment can be filled with numerous possibilities. For instance, if a photograph covering a birthday party excludes an annoying child from the frame, it will be the first stage of manipulation in capturing a scene.

What to include and what not to include in a frame is a question that a photojournalist always asks himself. Tampering with the subject is rearranging reality. This ethical issue of staging or rearranging the frame is not new; this problem has remained unresolved for more than a century.

The issues of faking and manipulation are more closely related to news photography than any other visual communication tool. There are two possibilities: the mirror photograph and the window photograph. The mirror photograph is subjective recreation of reality. The window photograph is as objective as it can be, untouched by the bias of the lens or any other tool.

Case III: Staging—The Major Ethical Turn

In 2010, Haiti was rocked by a massive earthquake that claimed over 300,000 lives. A week after the earthquake, a 15-year-old girl, Fabienne

Cherisma, died in a police firing. The police had claimed that she was running away with some expensive paintings, and would not stop even after warnings, forcing them to take the hard decision.

This case sparked debates about media ethics when photographs of the victim appeared in various media platforms as there were many photographers covering the aftermath of the quake. However, the major ethical question arose when photographers changed the position of the body to capture a perfect image. Note the paintings' placement in Photos 17.2 and 17.3. The painting on the extreme right is differently placed in the second photograph. This is a clear example of tampering with the subject.

If you look closely at the photograph taken by Nathan Weber (Photo 17.3), it is very similar to what the *St. Petersburg Times* said about Kevin Carter's baby girl and vulture photograph. Photographers aiming their cameras towards the dead girl are no better than vultures waiting for the right moment to pluck their prey. Is composition more important than reality, and is it important to make things look organised and beautiful?

The photograph taken by James Oatway is an example of the window photograph where he captures the moment with no alterations (Kim, 2011).

Photo 17.2
Tampering with the subject

Fabienne Cherisma, a 15-year-old girl, was shot dead by the police for stealing paintings in Haiti, 2010.
Courtesy: James Oatway.

Photo 17.3
Composition more important than reality?

Photographers surround Fabienne Cherisma's body after she was killed by the police.
Courtesy: Nathan Weber.

Electronic Manipulation and Editing

The history of image editing or photo manipulation is long. Manipulation began with art tools such as cropping and pasting. In recent times, it has moved on to darkroom manipulation such as burning and dodging and airbrush in recent times. Digital photography and digital imaging go a step further and allow sophisticated changes to be made in an image after it is captured. Computer editing has become so easy to do that anyone who knows Adobe Indesign, Adobe Photoshop and similar software can easily manipulate images. In fact, digital imaging has changed the meaning of photography from 'drawing with light' to image management.

Editors must look into the ethical ramifications of the use of manipulated images. A strong editing tool used by both Television and News Photography Editors these days is morphing. By using this tool they can cut image information from one image and paste it on another (Patterson & Wilkins, 2010).

Case IV

Editing and manipulation of news photographs is a more serious offence than manipulating feature photographs. Thewire.in examined the unethical practices in photojournalism by publishing two photographs: one by the famous photographer Mary Ellen Mark (Photo 17.4a) and the other by the award-winning Kolkata photojournalist Souvid Datta (Photo 17.4b). While Mary Ellen Mark's photo dealt with transgender people in Bombay in 1978, Souvid Datta's photograph captured the violence in Kolkata's sex industry in 2014.

Souvid Datta, who until 2014 was an inspiration to upcoming photographers in the field of documentary photography, was caught in a major controversy. His work on violence in the city's sex industry won him some prestigious awards like Magnum Photos award before experts in the industry came across Mary Ellen Mark's photograph.

In his photograph, the image on the right was taken by him in 2014, whereas the image on the left was taken in 1978 by Mary Ellen Mark. This image became an example of unethical practices in photojournalism (Basu, 2017).

During an interview to *Time* magazine, he admitted that he had digitally manipulated the photograph by copying a part of the image taken by Mary Ellen Mark and pasting it on his photograph.

Visura, an agency which had funded his projects, launched an investigation into his practices.

To conclude, it is important to understand that ethical practices in visual journalism are changing and that new ethical standards are needed. Experts in the field have laid down a code of ethics and drawn a line between ethical and unethical behaviour and actions of visual journalists.

However, the line between ethical and unethical is getting blurred with the advent of new technology. Photo manipulation often goes unnoticed as modifying scenes and taking photographs with a better composition are accepted in news photography. If digital manipulation of photographs become the norm, it would be difficult to spot reality in news photography.

References

Altun, Fahrettin. (2011). Media ethics and discourse of impartiality. *Turkish Journal of Business Ethics*, 4(8), 18–24. Retrieved from http://web.a.ebscohost. com/ehost/pdfviewer/pdfviewer?sid=630eef54-08b5-4a79-b0ac-5d4f55868c 04%40sessionmgr4004&vid=2&hid=4112

Basu, Shome. (2017). Souvid Datta's plagiarised photos point to an industry that needs higher standards. Retrieved 21 November 2017, from https://thewire. in/132854/souvid-datta-photography-plagiarism/

Photo 17.4

Digital manipulation in visual journalism: (a) Transvestites getting dressed in a courtyard, Falkland Road, Bombay (1978); (b) Sex industry in Kolkata (2014)

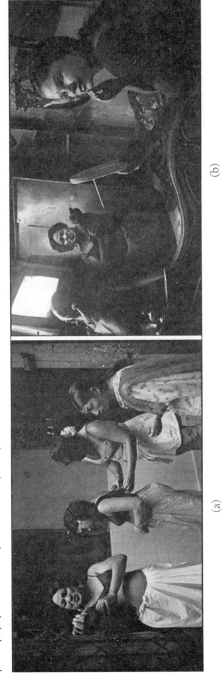

(a)

Courtesy: Mary Ellen Mark.

(b)

Courtesy: Souvid Datta.

De Tocqueville, Alexis. (1835). *De la démocratie en Amérique [Democracy in America: Historical critical edition*; vol 1]. Paris: Michel Lévy Frères.

Eric, Kim. (2011). Is this photo ethical? Retrieved 21 November 2017, from http://erickimphotography.com/blog/2011/04/07/is-this-photo-ethical/

Faucher, Jean-Andre. (1957). *Le quatrieme Pouvoir: La Presse de 1830 a 1930 [The fourth power: Press from 1830 to 1930]*. Universite de Michigan: L'Echo de la presse et de la publicite.

Goffman, Erving. (1959). *The presentation of self in everyday life*. Garden City, NY: Doubleday Anchor Books.

Hidri, Abdallah. (2012). The Fifth estate: Media and ethics. *UAE Journal of Arab & Muslim Media Research, 5*(1). Retrieved 21 November 2017, from https://web.a.ebscohost.com/ehost/pdfviewer/pdfviewer?sid=73dce5f1-1c6f-472a-ba6b-20fd59691b70%40sessionmgr4005&vid=4&hid=4112

Paillet Marc. (1974). *Le journalisme: Fonctions et langages du Quatrieme Pouvoir [Journalism: Functions and language of the fourth power]*. Paris: Denoel.

Press Council of India. (2010). Norms of journalistic conduct. Retrieved 21 November 2017, from http://presscouncil.nic.in/OldWebsite/NORMS-2010.pdf

Shutter Release. (2010, April). Ethical issues in photography. Retrieved 21 November 2017, from http://www.iconicphoto.com/pdf/ethical_issues_in_photography_0305.pdf

Smith, Kevin Z. (2012). Misrepresentation: An ethics tragedy. *Quill, 100*(3), 44. Retrieved from https://web.a.ebscohost.com/ehost/pdfviewer/pdfviewer?sid=c5e80182-3f85-4884-b6b8-b17e1b267da4%40sessionmgr4004&vid=7&hid=4112

Topping, Seymour. (2013). History of the prizes. The Pulitzer Prizes. Retrieved 21 November 2017, from http://www.pulitzer.org/historyofprizes

Ulmann, André. (1935). *Le quatrième pouvoir: Police [The fourth power, the police]*. Paris: F. Aubier.

Wakeland, Kelly A. (2013). Pulitzer Prize winning photographs and the rhetoric of 'Poignant Presence': What brings the war home? San Luis Obispo: California Polytechnic State University. Retrieved 21 November 2017, from http://digitalcommons.calpoly.edu/cgi/viewcontent.cgi?article=1147&context=comssp

White, Aidan. (2008). *To tell you the truth*. Belgium: International Federation of Journalists. Retrieved 21 November 2017, from http://ethicaljournalisminitiative.org/pdfs/EJI_book_en.pdf

18

The Probing Mind: Research in Journalism

Ruchi Jaggi

> Cultivating a research aptitude from the very beginning is imperative to sound journalistic expression.

Introduction

Research is inherent to the practice of journalism. It helps understand, explore, uncover, improve, influence and contextualise issues and perspectives. Research provides journalists with sources of data, knowledge and explanations that can make their reporting more authoritative and useful to readers, listeners, and viewers (Colvin, 2008).

Journalism education has evolved both in terms of the number and range of courses. It has, in fact, come a long way from the generic and vocational newsgathering and reporting courses and now includes an array of sophisticated and specialised streams. Journalism education has indeed inspired young students to enter the news world with more knowledge and confidence to explore new ideas and challenging issues, and to ask tough questions. By honing the students' writing skills and storytelling techniques, this training has become further value-laden. However, such training is also delimited by its very nature as it may not be enough in the age of new media, where a new story develops every minute and a new perspective emerges with every click.

Today's journalists not only have to be well-informed but should also have the prudence and skills to package the information in diverse ways for diverse reader/user engagement. It is also extremely important to distinguish between the terms education and training. Nuanced understanding based in theoretical rigour is extremely significant when we look at journalism studies as an educational pursuit. Knowledge of language, political science, sociology, even psychology and marketing, engagement with subjects such as gender, class and caste, and the ability to observe, reflect and argue are the core of this field (Jaggi, 2017).

It is in this revolutionary era of information overload that journalists may just not feel adequate with traditional training and conventional ideas of journalistic practice. As John Wihbey (Managing Editor of the Shorenstein Center research portal—Journalist's Resource) puts it:

> But in a wired age, where knowledge on all topics is accumulating and proliferating, a new kind of fear should be persistent for journalists: Not knowing what you are talking about. Or put more practically, not doing your research. There is little excuse these days for being uninformed and caught unaware. Expectations are being raised all around us. (Wihbey, 2012)

It is precisely in this context that a research aptitude becomes indispensable to survive and thrive in contemporary journalism. Instilling this aptitude in journalism students from the very beginning orients them towards a substantial, intelligent and successful professional pursuit forever.

Lamble (2004), in his research paper, 'Documenting the Methodology of Journalism', curates from a multitude of scholars to reflect upon the extensive and multidimensional character of a discipline like journalism. A critical review of the following text (which is a selected amalgamation from Lamble's piece) attempts to situate the field of journalism as intense, complex, and drawing from and contributing to a host of other disciplines and subjects.

Yin is one of many academics who have recognised that there is a close relationship between journalism and history (Yin, 1989). Philip Meyer was another. He said 'it used to be' that journalism was referred to as 'history in a hurry' (Meyer, 1979, p. 14). Back in 1949, Wilkerson observed: '... the journalist is himself [sic] the historian of the present, and the record which he puts together will, when used with critical discretion, furnish valuable source material for the scholar of the future who delves into the history of our times' (Wilkerson, in Nafziger & Wilkerson, 1968, p. 11).

And, in order to portray his subject against the panorama of the times, the writer must have a good background in many fields but particularly in history, economics, sociology and political science (Wilkerson, in Nafziger & Wilkerson, 1968, p. 15).

Brucker adopted a similar theme 30 years ago when he suggested that: 'Whatever the age, whatever the accompanying paraphernalia of civilisation, it is always the journalism of the day that tells us most of what we know about it' (Brucker, 1973, p. 14).

In fact, obvious connections between the discipline of law and studies of communications inspired one of the earliest attempts at identifying a methodology of journalism. Writing in 1949, United States journalist, academic and media studies theorist Frederick Siebert said that research in the field of law and communications fell within the ambit of the 'immediately related fields' of journalism, law and political science (Siebert, 1949, in Nafziger & Wilkerson, 1968, p. 34). In more contemporary times, Ericson (1996) implied there were very close epistemological and methodological links between law and journalism, or 'law and news' as he put it. He said the two disciplines have common purposes.

Lamble's scholarly disposition emphatically articulates the position of journalism as not just an effective social commentary but a critical juncture where social sciences, humanities as well natural sciences (sometimes) converge. Hence, this specialised character of the field makes thorough research and reflection a prerequisite for intelligent, responsible and meaningful practice of journalism.

The Research Aptitude

With the proliferation and omnipresence of news media, the reader/listener or, to put it more comprehensively, the audience is no longer primarily seeking information. It is the structuring of information in apt contexts with interesting perspectives that gives an edge to a news item. This perspective is based on knowledge and experience, which emanate from extensive reading, writing and forming of opinion. In a nutshell, an interesting story that holds the attention is the result of long durations of hard work put in by the journalist in researching, reviewing and reflecting. Hence, developing a right research aptitude from the very beginning becomes imperative to sound journalistic expression.

The columns or television presence of some journalists are noteworthy in this context. The opinions of columnists are respected and sought after. The screen presence of TV anchors, their personal charisma, command over the language, and control of thought flow may be some of the reasons that make these journalists impressive. However, what makes them actually stand out is their knowledge base and years of research and reflection upon the multiple facets of different subjects. This expertise does not come from random research. Only an impeccably well-structured research procedure cultivated as second nature or, in other words, the cultivation of the right research aptitude, can produce a good columnist or television anchor.

Background Research

The cornerstone of strong journalistic practice is researching and referencing. However, there is no one model that encapsulates the various stages of research for journalism either sequentially or comprehensively. At the very outset, I would like to argue that there cannot be a single model. What emerges in this section is, in fact, a discussion on different approaches that have been envisaged and refined over time by practitioners and academics.

The different subdomains of journalism have varying approaches to conducting research. However, as clichéd as it may sound, the cardinal research principle for any story begins at the stage of 5Ws (what, when, where, who, why) and 1H (how). A truism was immortalised by one of the world's great early journalists, Rudyard Kipling, when he wrote:

> I keep six honest serving-men,
> (They taught me all I knew);
> Their names are What and Why and When
> And How and Where and Who.
> I send them over land and sea,
> I send them east and west.... (Kipling, 1986, p. 291)

Who did what, when and where they did it, how and why it happened … these are, in fact, the very essence of the most courageous acts of journalism throughout history. They require a journalist's knowledge and a journalistic understanding of the matter at hand (Lamble, 2004).

Researching for an article begins with gathering information by various means so that the writer has a strong foundation of knowledge. A journalist should have a thorough understanding of why a story should belong to a certain timeline. An in-depth research into the sequence of events that took place before a particular story broke out is necessary to contextualise the news item in the appropriate temporal framework.

It is imperative that the journalist begins with a central question. This will help align the story around a focal point and structure the research required to do it. Thorough and structured research of this nature will provide not only vital information to the audiences but also sound evidence and hard-hitting facts that give an edge to the story.

As simple as it may sound, even the basic journalistic practice cannot be executed without in-depth research. Journalists use interviews as a popular method to collect information. Choosing the right interviewees—experts, officials, witnesses, social scientists, physical scientists or whoever is required for the story—requires smart research and homework. Similarly, if the journalist is able to observe the subtle nuances and subtexts in any event, even something as plain as a press conference or seminar can provide the scoop. However, this is possible only when a journalist is well prepared with information and knowledge before he/she attends the event. Here again, background research becomes an indispensable tool.

In the contemporary era, when in-depth and specialised journalism has become the unwritten rule, journalists should understand social science research methods to develop their interpretation and analysis. Informing their audiences about research findings, polls, surveys, political campaign statistics, development figures, scientific research reports and similar data of a specialised and sophisticated nature in a form that is understandable and useful requires knowledge and understanding of the social research techniques on the part of journalists.

Research in the Digital Age

The current catch phrase in journalism is 'the defining moment'. Simply put, the phrase means how has a story or an event defined a specific medium or brand name (Harper, 2003). Online journalism has dramatically altered the traditional role of a journalist. Harper argues that online journalism places far more power in the hands of the user, allowing the reader to challenge the traditional role of the publication as the gatekeeper of news and information. The user can depend on the gatekeeper to select and filter the news in the traditional manner or drill down to the basic documents of a story. In short, the user can look over the shoulder of the reporter by researching the original documents and easily comparing the stories of various publications as well as searching the archives for previous stories on the topic. This articulation situates the critical role of intensive research in journalism even further.

Besides being a platform to practise journalism, which is redefining its practice, the Web has emerged as the largest research platform as well. Journalists make use of search engines—general and academic, web pages, web articles, web encyclopedias, e-books, blogs, discussion threads, web archives, and now social media—to research all possible dimensions in a subject.

However, the Web poses a significant challenge in terms of credibility and accountability. It is very important that a journalist evaluates the authority of the information retrieved from the Internet. Reliability and affiliation of the web page from where information is retrieved, timeliness of content, status of hyperlinks on the page (whether they are still active), author of the page, author's affiliation, whether the content is written as part of advertising or promotional initiatives are some of the points that a journalist should check when using the Internet for research. The need for such a check could, for instance, arise when a journalist uses the popular online encyclopedia, Wikipedia. If Wikipedia provides any figures or information that does not have further reference to a primary source, it should not be used. A professional journalist will always check the facts before making them public.

Using Research Papers and Reports

Using research papers and reports can add a lot of substance when a journalist is doing a specialised story or handling a sensitive subject. Using the statistics or arguments from such documents can enhance the standard of the story and bring out fresh perspectives. However, more often than not, research reports either get lost in translation or are so laden with jargon that audiences lose interest in them.

A journalist should answer one basic question before incorporating or reproducing research data—how is a certain research meaningful to the issue in question or even to an ordinary member of the audience? The answer to this question can be the decisive factor for including or excluding the research report.

The use of a research study can lend meaningful insights to any story, be it crime, business, sports or even entertainment! For instance, successful sports columnists always quote from record statistics to add weight to their opinions. A usual feature on films released in the festive season can become insightful and analytical if trade reports of the films released during the same season in the past five years are retrieved and researched. Interesting patterns on box-office success, star power, mainstream vs parallel cinema debate, marketing gimmicks, among other themes, can emerge. This can take the otherwise linear entertainment story to another level altogether.

However, it is important for journalists to attribute these reports or statistics to their rightful sources. Journalists should be patient enough to allow themselves to get interested in a topic and develop relevant expertise before moving on to the stage of using scholarly or applied research references.

Summing Up

John Wihbey says that 'in an overcrowded marketplace, it is ultimately about turning out the highest-value work on a given news topic'. This statement articulates a coherent needs analysis in the current journalistic practice. That it is an era of specialisation and only in-depth and different ideas will attract audiences is a reality.

Hence, the challenge to train students in this competitive environment is far greater than it was before.

'Looming in the background is this issue of rising knowledge, even as schools struggle to figure out how to embed deeper research content into their classrooms,' says Wihbey, in the context of journalism training.

Innovation, both in terms of technology and research capabilities, can give the students an edge. Wihbey articulates it succinctly: 'The intellectual component—though complex at one level, involving fluency with numbers and with some academic concepts (think correlation)—can be broken down into a single mantra: make a "research review" a core habit for students.' He argues that the same analytical skills embedded in the research review habit will make for better questions, more rigorous scrutiny of assumptions, and higher-level journalism [sic].

There is no doubt that systematic and in-depth research is the backbone of competent and professional journalism.

References

Brucker, H. (1973). *Communication is power: Unchanging values in a changing journalism.* New York: Oxford University Press.

Colvin, R.L. (2008). The Hechinger Institute guide to education research for journalists. Retrieved 15 November 2012, from http://hechinger.tc.columbia.edu/primers/Guide%20to%20Education%20Research%207-2008.pdf

Harper, C. (2003). *Journalism in a digital age.* Retrieved 21 November 2012, from http://web.mit.edu/m-i-t/articles/harper.html

Jaggi, R. (2017). Taking the plunge. Retrieved 5 August 2017, from http://indiatoday.intoday.in/story/engineering-fashion-law-mass-communication-management/1/992903.html

Kipling, R. (1986). The elephant's child. *Just so stories.* New York: Exeter Books.

Lamble, S. (2004). Documenting the methodology of journalism. *Australian Journalism Review, 26*(I), 85–106.

Meyer, P. (1979). *Precision journalism: A reporter's introduction to social science methods* (2nd ed.). Bloomington and London: Indiana University Press.

Nafziger, R., & Wilkerson, M. (Eds). (1968). *An introduction to journalistic research*. New York: Greenwood Press. Originally published in 1949.

Wihbey, J. (2012). *Sure journalists need to know digital tools, but they really need to know how to do digital research*. Retrieved 22 November 2012, from http://www.niemanlab.org/2012/09/sure-journalists-need-to-know-digital-tools-but-they-really-need-to-know-how-to-do-digital-research/

Yin, R.K. (1989). *Case study research design and methods*. Newbury Park, CA: SAGE Publications.

19

The Big Story:
Investigative Journalism

Abhay Vaidya

Journalists work in the public interest and it is not just our business but duty to the nation to bring things to light.

Newspapering deals with small daily bites from a fruit of indeterminate size. It may take dozens of bites before you are sure it's an apple. Dozens and dozens more bites before you have any real idea how big the apple might be. It was that way with Watergate.

—Ben Bradlee, Executive Editor of the *Washington Post* who supervised the Watergate investigations

If one were to consider the importance of a story by its impact, then investigative journalism would clearly emerge as the highest form of journalism. I consider it as such because no other form of journalism requires the kind of courage, effort and persistence that investigative journalism does.

A classic example is the Watergate scam of the 1970s. Brought to light by journalists Bob Woodward and Carl Bernstein of the *Washington Post*, this story of political espionage at the Democratic Party headquarters at the Watergate complex by members of the Republican Party was not broken in a day. Starting with the follow-up of what appeared to be a simple burglary, it was painstakingly uncovered story by story, over nine months 'before other engines kicked in' such as the Senate Watergate Committee hearings and follow-ups by other newspapers.

The Watergate scam is hailed as an iconic piece of investigative journalism because it was unprecedented in its impact: It forced the resignation of President Richard Nixon under the threat of impeachment, and the tremors were felt all over the world.

India's '2G spectrum scam' unearthed by J. Gopikrishnan of the *Pioneer*, was in many ways a solitary effort, similar to the Watergate story. Once the story exploded after going to the Delhi High Court as a result of a public interest petition, all news organisations, big and small, had no option but to do regular follow-ups. In 2011, *Time* magazine ranked the 2G expose as the second biggest story of 'Abuse of Power' just under the Watergate scam. It is now a different story that the Central Bureau of Investigations (CBI) failed to prove its own charges and all the 18 accused were acquitted in the case in December 2017.

Originally pegged as a scam estimated at a staggering ₹1.76 lakh crore, within a year, the 2G scam was overtaken by what came to be known as 'Coalgate' involving the questionable allocation of coal blocks in India. The Comptroller and Auditor General (CAG) of India, in a draft report that found its way in a report in the *Times of India* in early 2012, estimated the loss to the tune of ₹10 lakh crore. The Supreme Court of India declared the allocation of coal blocks right from 1993 as illegal and arbitrary.

It is one thing for a journalist to get hold of a file of confidential documents and break a big story and quite another to smell a story with a sharp nose for news, gather evidence to validate the story and write it skilfully after checking and cross-checking the facts. The heart and soul of investigative journalism lies in the latter.

The Bofors scam is another big story in the history of investigative journalism in India which was first exposed by Swedish Radio in April 1987. The radio station filed a report stating that the Swedish firm Bofors AB paid kickbacks of ₹64 crore to top Indian politicians and defence officials for getting a ₹1,500 crore contract for supply of 410 155-mm Howitzer guns. The story was aggressively followed up and investigated further by Chitra Subramaniam of the *Hindu* who later took the story to the *Indian Express*. This expose led to the defeat of Prime Minister Rajiv Gandhi in the 1989 elections.

When a Story Goes Wrong

The flip side of investigative journalism can be devastating. If a story in this genre goes wrong and is challenged for accuracy, it can backfire heavily on the journalist concerned. It can lead to a defamation suit, demands for heavy compensation, a public apology, resignation of the journalist(s) concerned and the accompanying loss of credibility.

One prominent example would suffice as an illustration: The well-known Editor Vinod Mehta had this to write in his memoirs, *Lucknow Boy*, about a bitter experience when he was Editor of the now defunct the *Independent* published by the Times of India Group:

> On October 19, 1989, I put out a front-page story headlined, 'Y.B. *Chavan, Not Morarji, Spied for the US*'. The Prime Minister's Office and the Ministry of Home Affairs promptly issued a press release calling our report 'false, baseless and mischievous'. I had no leg to stand on. On October 24, 1989, *The Independent* printed a front-page 'apology' signed by me withdrawing the story and the allegations made in it. I didn't try to defend some part of the story since the core claim had proven to be false. It was a straightforward, blunt expression of regret. A day after the apology appeared, I resigned.

Significance of Investigative Journalism

The powers that be always want status quo. In India, a strong 'corruption nexus' exists between politicians, bureaucrats (including police officers) and businessmen. The dramatis personae in most scams hail from these three streams, a perfect example being the 'Railgate scam' allegedly involving Pawan Kumar Bansal, Railway Minister in the United Progressive Alliance (UPA) government. Given a choice, this nexus would like to keep its corrupt deals, frauds and land grabs under wraps. If someone tries to expose a fraud, he/she receives various forms of threats, including threats of physical violence.

As journalists we work in the public interest and it is not just our business but duty to the nation to bring things to light. One of the first lessons that we learn in journalism is that our loyalty is to the reader/viewer of our newspaper/television channel and not to the Editor/publisher or channel owner. An analogy would be, although the CAG of India or the Chief Election Commissioner and other bureaucrats are appointed by the government, their loyalty is to the Constitution of India (and by implication the people of India) and not to the government which appointed them or pays their salary.

The *Washington Post* in its charter on Standards & Ethics says clearly: 'The newspaper's duty is to its readers and to the public at large, and not to the private interests of the owner.'

Amidst all its flaws and deficiencies, Indian journalism has had its great moments from time to time. At the same time, it disappoints us with a strong trend of 'Page-3 journalism', which began in the late 1990s, and the unethical practice of 'paid news', which became rampant in the first decade of the new century.

Investigative journalism is critically important for a democracy if it is to be vibrant, robust and healthy. It can be pursued only in the environment of a free press. This was recognised more than two centuries ago by Thomas Jefferson, one of the founding fathers of the United States. He observed most eloquently that if he were forced to choose between 'a government without newspapers' and 'newspapers without a government', he would have no hesitation in choosing the latter.

Eminent jurists and commentators from India and across the world have underscored the significance of press freedom, and by implication, investigative journalism, in various landmark cases. In *Grosjean vs American Press Co* (1935), it was observed that 'the newspapers, magazines and other journals of the country ... have shed and continued to shed more light on the public and business affairs of the nation *than any other instrument of publicity....*' The judge observed that 'a free press stands as one of the great interpreters between the government and the people. *To allow it to be fettered is to fetter ourselves*' (emphasis mine).

What Is Right, What Is Wrong?

It is important to remember that an investigative story should be done in the public interest. Thus, the illicit affair of a lawyer–politician filmed in flagrante delicto by his driver on his mobile-phone camera cannot be used as source material for an 'investigative' story. The video clip did find its way into the Internet and news organisations would have liked to run it but for a restraining order brought by the lawyer–politician.

Journalists following high ethical standards cannot pay bribes, cannot offer favours or arrange for sexual favours as was done by *Tehelka* in 2001 while exposing a defence equipment purchase scam. Army officials involved in the scam demanded prostitutes from journalists posing as businessmen and *Tehelka* not only did the needful but also filmed the act using spy cameras. Although *Tehelka*'s senior journalists Aniruddha Bahal and its then Editor-in-Chief Tarun Tejpal defended their actions by describing them as 'minor transgressions', such practice would be unacceptable to the best news organisations around the world.

In exceptionally rare cases, journalists pursuing investigative stories are allowed to mask their identity. The use of spy cameras has become acceptable in sting operations by TV or print journalists.

However, there cannot be ethical transgressions. The world's biggest media baron, Rupert Murdoch, had to shut down his 168-year-old newspaper, *News of the World*, after a public outcry in the United Kingdom over journalists and private detectives hacking telephone voice mails of the royal family and other celebrities and bribing the police for information.

Communicate Clearly

A thumb rule in investigative journalism is that one has to communicate clearly and precisely. An example of what happens when you don't follow this rule is the controversy over the *Indian Express* story of 10 June 2012: The January night Raisina Hill was spooked: Two key Army units moved towards Delhi without notifying government. This story, filed by Shekhar Gupta, the newspaper's then Editor-in-Chief, and two others, was about the panic in the government over what seemed like a coup attempt. Although the story did not use the c-word, it left the reader confused whether a coup had been attempted. The story came in for much criticism from other Editors and senior journalists for being sensationalist and irresponsible.

Scope for Investigative Journalism

It is important to note that investigative journalism is a broad term and not all stories under this genre will lead to the fall of a government. If the stories are of a political nature and have a high impact then there is a consequence to the government. Take the case of the resignations of Maharashtra Chief Minister Ashok Chavan (in November 2010) in the wake of the Adarsh Housing Society case, and Union Minister A. Raja and Dravida Munnetra Kazhagam (DMK) Member of Parliament (MP) Kanimozhi following their arrest by the CBI in the 2G scam, and the suspension of Suresh Kalmadi, a Congress MP, following corruption cases relating to the 2010 Commonwealth Games in Delhi. Most corruption stories are partially political in nature because politicians help in the manipulation of the system; they bend the rules to favour their relatives, businessmen and others who pay bribes and kickbacks.

However, investigative journalism is a skill set and can be applied to any stream of journalism—be it political reporting or beats such as health, crime and court, education, defence, rural affairs, banking, sports, entertainment and real estate or even general reporting. The Uttar Pradesh National Rural Health Mission (NRHM) scam, which falls in the health beat, is estimated at ₹10,000 crore and has led to at least five murders in cover-up operations.

What Makes a Fine Investigative Journalist?

It is a desire to unravel the truth, and bring it before the public, that drives an investigative journalist. He/she cannot do it without qualities such as passion, curiosity, initiative, courage, determination and patience. Pursuing a story, gathering evidence, piecing them together and writing the story take time. Often there is pressure from seniors and influential people within and outside the news organisation. It is only with passion, courage, determination and patience that a journalist can pursue such stories. Curiosity is important because you then ask questions about what is happening around you:

- Why are there only two bidders for this tender? Who are these bidders? What are their connections? Readers' convenience was given top priority.
- This toilet block in the Planning Commission premises looks like it is out of a 7-star hotel. How much did it cost?
- Who are the allottees in the Adarsh Housing Society?
- Who is behind this education trust that has got a prime piece of land at a throwaway price?

There are other qualities that an investigative journalist needs such as flexibility to drop and pursue fresh leads; ability to work with others who have subject expertise; good reporting and research skills and a sense of fairness and ethics.

Pioneer journalist J. Gopikrishnan, who exposed the 2G scam, has said in an interview that he was offered 'mind-boggling' bribes and that 'corporate lobbyists and A. Raja's people even asked me to stop informing the Editor and end the series abruptly'. At the same time, 'there were several politicians who enlightened and encouraged me. Some bureaucrats and police officials also guided our investigations.'

In 2012, the investigative reporter Sara Ganim, at 24, became one of the youngest American journalists to win a Pulitzer. She has been described as a tenacious reporter with grit and gumption and with countless hours of 'thankless shoe-leather reporting', all pointing to qualities of passion, determination, persistence and patience.

Dealing with Difficulties

Not all news organisations, publishers and Editors welcome investigative stories. It would, therefore, be good to check with the chief reporter or the Editor whether or not to pursue a story. This is the first hurdle that needs to be crossed.

Convinced that you have a strong story idea, a good Editor would take you off routine work and give you the time and support that you need to pursue your story. Stories need to be checked, cross-checked and verified, almost always with a field visit. Pictures need to be taken wherever possible. If the story involves investments by companies, politicians, their relatives or others, getting details is not easy. Often 'sources' help us with these documents and critical information as has happened in most scams.

If you approach the company directly, the company officials are likely to get in touch with the marketing department of your news organisation which, in turn, will ask you to drop the story. This is what happens in many organisations. Often investigative reporters have got critical documents from searches at the Company Law Board office, by using the Right to Information Act, 2005, or by taking the help of trusted activists and sources in the bureaucracy.

Here is an illustration: The controversy around the Lavasa lake city project in Maharashtra involving Sharad Pawar, who was Union Agriculture Minister in the UPA government, is now well known. However, it was in 2006 that this journalist brought the Lavasa project before the public through a series of investigative reports in the *Times of India*.

The starting point for the story was a piece of gossip from a Pune architect who said, 'Go and see what is happening in Mulshi. Mountains are being excavated, forests are being cut....' A field visit to the construction site was undertaken with the help of a rural reporter and some villagers from Dasve. Pictures were taken secretly, evading the attention of private security at the construction site. Internet trawling revealed that the Lavasa project had been nominated for top US awards for New Urbanism—something that was not known in India. The clinching details about investments from the Pawar family in the project, now publicly accepted, the background of the project and the numerous permits granted to the project by the Maharashtra government were obtained through certified documents filed with the Union Ministry of Corporate Affairs.

Thus, what began as a conversation about 'something happening in Mulshi' turned out to be a big story involving a top politician, a controversial township project in the backwaters of a dam and the Maharashtra government. It was only a few years later that the project came under intense scrutiny after cases were filed in the Bombay High Court by the Union Ministry for Environment and Forests and some public-spirited activists.

Some Case Studies

This writer would like to present two case studies of investigative stories that were supervised by him as Resident Editor, *Daily News and Analysis* (DNA Pune), during 2008–2012.

Pune 'Water Affidavits' Scam

In mid-2009, DNA, Pune, carried a series of investigative stories by freelance commissioned journalist Ritu Goyal Harish on the 'Water Affidavits' scam of Pune. The stories established how people residing in housing societies in the fringe areas of Pune had been cheated of civic water supply by the Pune Municipal Corporation (PMC) and were forced to depend on tanker water. The stories revealed that the PMC had secured 'water affidavits' from builders stating that the builders would bear the responsibility for water supply. These 'water affidavits' were never disclosed to buyers at the time of purchasing the flats. The series of stories relating to the scam required numerous field visits, multiple interviews, discussions with experts and access to critical documents such as the water affidavits themselves. This story was worthy of consideration for the Ramnath Goenka Award for Journalism in the Civic Reporting category.

Environmental Degradation in Mahabaleshwar

In 2009, DNA, Pune, published a series of stories on the environmental degradation in the Mahabaleshwar hill station. The stories were done by

Rahul Chandawarkar, then a freelance journalist, who was commissioned by DNA. Chandawarkar undertook a number of field visits, conducted multiple interviews and took telling photographs to substantiate his stories. There was strong background research and interviews with experts and officials. The stories were carried prominently by DNA to maximize impact. Not surprisingly, the series was selected for the 2009–2010 Ramnath Goenka Excellence in Journalism Award in the Environmental Reporting category.

The Press is regarded as the fourth pillar of democracy because it acts as a watchdog. It can function effectively if journalists are trained better and encouraged to undertake investigative work.

20

Areas of Neglect: Media and Development[1]

H.K. Dua

The media, guided by a profit motive, have failed to focus on issues that concern the masses.

The Indian press, despite enormous difficulties, played a major role in the freedom struggle and in the awakening of the nation. As education took root and spread, although slowly, the press and the area of freedom began to grow.

Leaders such as Bal Gangadhar Tilak and Mahatma Gandhi launched their own publications such as *Kesri*, *Young India* and *Harijan* to carry the message of freedom to their followers and the people.

Less important leaders in many parts of the country started their own newspapers, magazines and occasional publications. Freedom fighters in district towns, too, came out with publications aimed at opposing the British Raj and mobilising the people to fight for the liberation of the land.

As education was limited to a small section of people, the circulation of these publications was small. Yet, the press spread the message

[1] This article, published in the Souvenir of the Press Council of India on National Press Day on 16 November 2007, is reprinted with permission from the author and the Press Council of India.

to different parts of the country and created a body of opinion makers, many of whom joined the freedom movement. Like the movement for freedom, newspapers, small and big, too grew in number and influence.

The British did not like the growth of the Indian press, particularly those sections that supported the freedom movement. The more intense the freedom movement turned, the harsher became the British rules in suppressing it.

The attitude of the British towards the press was similar to its policy towards the freedom movement: tolerate it when it became weak; crack down when it gained momentum. Those sections of the press that praised the British were feted; the papers that chose to voice the people's aspirations were suppressed. Publishers and Editors who fought for freedom were sent to jail. Their printing presses, often housed in cottages and small buildings, were seized and locked.

Yet, the brave men and women carried on. More and more publications began to come up under different titles. A kind of guerrilla journalism grew and it often rattled the British authorities, who, in turn, adopted greater repressive measures. Hide-and-seek journalism came to rule the hearts and minds of the readers who would wait for their favourite newspapers.

The fight for the liberation of the country and all that went into it was the predominant theme of the newspapers and periodicals of the pre-Independence era. Yet, the leaders of the period and the press, by and large, came to the conclusion that India would not be able to come into its own until and unless it also thought about the content of 'freedom' and what it should mean for its people, most of whom were poor, weak and for long suppressed under foreign rule and, in Mahatma Gandhi's words, 'the loneliest and the lost'.

Like many political leaders, several small and not-so-small publications felt that simply throwing out the British would not bring real freedom to India and that a struggle had to be mounted to fight poverty, ignorance, caste, superstition, and all that kept India divided, weak and subjugated.

Many enlightened people looked ahead. They felt that the people, while fighting the British, should also aim at rooting out whatever made India miss the economic progress of the kind the West had made since the Industrial Revolution. Why could India not raise the standard of living of its people? If the West could do it, why not India? Many such questions ran through their minds.

The British believed the press was often subversive. The idea of building a modern, united and strong India thus became the subtext of the idea of freedom. The people, too, came to believe that the political aims could not be achieved without fighting societal ills. Hence, some newspapers began attacking the caste system that has held India in its grip for hundreds of years, superstition, ignorance, the lack of education, health care and housing, unemployment and all the ills that bred despair among the people.

In essence, the aims of the freedom struggle—building a new nation, modern and free from social and economic ills—consciously and otherwise, began to converge. These were reflected in the debates in the Constituent Assembly and, after Independence, in the Constitution adopted in 1950. The Constitution—a noble document—gave the people Fundamental Rights, provided institutions such as Parliament and an independent judiciary and guaranteed the freedom of the press. At the same time, the Directive Principles of State Policy enshrined in the Constitution gave it social and economic aims.

Come Independence and the press began breathing fresh air, growing fast. Over the years, the press has indeed expanded. Newspapers have become larger in size and expanded their reach. The quality of production has improved tremendously. TV news channels are competing with one another and the print media for attention. But the sense of mission that pervaded the growth of the press before Independence is no longer the guiding spirit for the majority of the media organisations. Newspapers and TV news channels are definitely bright and slick, but the soul is missing in them.

Campaign Against Caste

It is a pity the press in India is no longer attacking caste, which has kept the country far behind the rest of the world. Practically, no part of the country is free from its cancerous influence. No section of society, irrespective of religious affiliation, has been able to get rid of this all-pervasive phenomenon where the accident of birth decides the future of a child or a family.

Before Independence, there were attempts at fighting casteism and untouchability. But after Independence, these issues, which should have been taken up by the enlightened sections of society, particularly the press, have remained neglected. Conscious of its duty, the press occasionally wakes up to the dangers casteism poses to the growth of modern India, but there is no sustained campaign to erase the institution of caste from the Indian psyche.

Despite the fact that education and economic activity have grown, the Indian mind has somehow remained stuck on caste, and this manifests itself in the daily lives of the people. The press merely analyses how politicians use caste to win elections, form and undo governments or control their decision-making.

While most people in the print and broadcast media are aware of the havoc caste has played in the growth of the nation as a more equitable and just society, the media has not taken it up as a major campaign issue. It has merely accepted the status quo, hoping that the spread of education and economic growth will, over a period of time, lead to the eradication of caste. Experience of the past decades shows it is a misplaced belief.

The press has, during the past few years, taken up corruption as an issue but only when a big scandal has broken out. Its impact on the daily life of a citizen—seeking a job or in getting a ration card or water and electricity connection—is seldom highlighted. The impact of corruption is felt more by the poor and illiterate people than on the educated and moneyed. In several states, even the job of primary school teacher cannot be found without greasing the palms of officials or elected representatives.

Lately, criminalisation of politics in India is focus of media attention, but the presence of mafia dons in many state legislatures is increasingly accepted as an unavoidable phenomenon and not as something that needs to be abhorred and stopped. Some sections of the press paint the criminals indulging in decision-making in a better light, which they hardly deserve. The seriousness of the dangers these elements pose to the political system is not fully comprehended by the media.

It is a pity that the press is unable to focus its attention on areas of vital concern to the people not because of constraints but because of its insensitivity to the human condition.

In several states, there are schools, but no teachers. If there are teachers, there are no blackboards. The dropout rate in schools is very high in many states. In some states, the teachers do not even go to the school; instead, they farm out their work for a consideration.

Health care in rural areas, if at all available, is elementary. Often primary health centres have no doctor or nurse on duty and face a short supply of medicines and equipment.

In most parts of India, in villages particularly, clean drinking water is not available. There are no toilet facilities for the majority of the population. But these grass-roots problems are not reported by the media for they do not make a catchy story.

The media have got accustomed to giving more space and time to the activities of politicians of varying degrees of integrity and competence. Pages in newspapers are filled with their inane speeches. TV news channels also give more time to ordinary politicians and unwittingly project them as leaders of some consequence. Their fleeting successes are magnified as major achievements. Larger-than-life images are painted. The lives of these men and women, who may not even find a place in the footnotes of history, seem to matter more than issues that affect the voiceless people.

Essentially, the problem is that political parties and politicians are hogging the headlines, not the people. A limited India is being reported, not Bharat. The advent of Page-3 journalism, focussing on the party life of a handful of people in big cities and celebrities adept in catching the media's attention has pushed the common folks and their problems out of the media's concern and attention. The media are busy reporting the Shining India, expressing an occasional and condescending concern for the welfare of the people.

The media's fascination for the Shining India and the celebrities that make up Page-3 is not necessarily to brighten up newspapers and TV screens; rather it is advertisement revenue that this India fetches, far different from the mundane world of citizens of Bharat who lead simple lifestyles and cannot afford trendy kitchen gadgets or fashion wear that only the upwardly mobile-middle class can afford. Profit has thus become a vital, if not the sole, motive of most media organisations.

In essence, the commercial interests of the expanding industry of newspapers and TV channels, which is served by an urban India, keep the media's attention away from the villages. With India making economic progress, although at a slow rate, the divide between rural and urban areas is getting blurred. However, in the media, the dividing line continues to remain sharp. With urban India remaining the focus of its attention, the media fails to study the other India existing in its villages.

Like urban India, which is changing at a faster rate, rural areas are also changing, although slowly. With pressures on land increasing, more people are joining the ranks of the youth who are in search of jobs. The despair of the jobless is leading to alienation, discontent and anger, which the media are unable to understand. In several states, naxalite violence has become a major problem, but the media fail to make an effort to understand what impels a young man to become a naxalite.

The youth who are not attracted to the romantic appeal of a violent revolution are joining hands with the local mafia, caste *senas* and other such groups seen wielding lathis and guns in the countryside of Bihar. The media are not trying to understand or report these inconvenient facts. This is mainly because they do not make a glamorous story that brighten up the pages or the TV screens. Also, it requires that extra effort, which the media are not inclined to make because of their skewed concerns and priorities.

No one can deny newspapers and TV channels the right to earn profits for their survival and growth. But the view that a daily newspaper is just a commodity to be sold with the sole aim of earning profits is increasingly overtaking the basic functions of the press, which are to serve society by informing it, analyse public affairs and enable the readers to make their own judgement on matters that affect them.

The press, guided solely by profit motive, is forgetting its essential concerns. The neglect of the interests of the people might lead to its losing public support, which is essential in a vibrant democracy. The leaders of the media—Editors, publishers and proprietors—need to examine whether they are on the right track.

21

Partner in Development: Development Journalism

V. Eshwar Anand

The media cannot indulge in partisan politics if they are to fulfil their role as an agent of social change and development.

Though development journalism as a concept and discipline is not new, it has acquired a new dimension under Prime Minister Narendra Modi. The National Democratic Alliance government, which he has been heading since May 2014, has been virtually rewriting every aspect of development planning, administration and governance. This, in turn, has multiplied the responsibilities of journalists and made their job all the more challenging.

A significant change in New Delhi's Yojana Bhavan is the scrapping of the 65-year-old Planning Commission. With the constitution of National Institution for Transforming India (NITI) Aayog on 1 January 2015, the planning set-up at the top has undergone a drastic overhaul. While the Prime Minister heads this body, all Chief Ministers and Lt. Governors of Union Territories are on its Governing Council to evolve national development priorities with the involvement of the states. Dr Rajiv Kumar, noted economist, has replaced Dr Arvind Panagariya, eminent economist and Professor of Columbia University, as its Vice Chairman. The full-time members of the NITI Aayog are V.K. Saraswat, former Secretary, Defence Research and Development Organisation (DRDO), and Bibek Debroy, reputed economist. Its ex-officio members are Finance Minister Arun Jaitley, Home Minister Rajnath Singh, Railway Minister Suresh Prabhu and Agriculture Minister Radha Mohan Singh. The Special Invitees to the panel are Union Ministers Nitin Gadkari, Smriti Irani and Thawar Singh Gehlot.

The NITI Aayog has been set up with a view to fostering a spirit of 'cooperative federalism'. The Prime Minister sums up its mission thus: 'Through Niti Aayog, we will bid farewell to a "one-size-fits-all" approach towards development. The body celebrates India's diversity and plurality.' The NITI Aayog has a Regional Council to tackle issues relating to more than one state/region. The panel serves as a government think tank on key policy issues. It has a resource centre on good governance and best practices.

The scrapping of the Planning Commission on 13 August 2014 and the creation of the NITI Aayog did not come as a surprise. In his Independence Day address to the nation, the Prime Minister announced that the Planning Commission would be abolished. On 9 December 2014, he interacted with the state Chief Ministers and Lt. Governors on the contours of the new panel. Earlier, the Planning Secretary Sindhushree Khullar, who later took over as the first Chief Executive Officer of the NITI Aayog, in a Cabinet Note suggested five changes that outlined its identity, structure and function. While the name envisages the spirit of development and knowledge-based work of the body, there is a cut down on the routine staff, replaced by a handful of specialists with domain competence and expertise, according to the Cabinet Note. Currently, Amitabh Kant is its CEO.

The NITI Aayog works on the model concession agreement of public–private partnership (PPP) projects across sectors as the Union Government is keen on roping in private players for infrastructural development. It seeks to limit its functions to key areas such as infrastructure, mining and targeted implementation of the government's flagship programmes. The experts in the new institution, primarily from the social sector, deliberate on the key changes in over a dozen flagship schemes and introduce these changes over a period of time to ensure that the targeted outcomes are achieved (Sharma, 2014). Earlier, the Centre had received many suggestions on the name and role of the new body. In addition to the NITI Aayog, names such as Sustainable Development Commission, National Development Agency, Social Economic Development Commission and

Bharat Pragati Lakshya were suggested. The NITI Aayog is also deemed as the secretariat for the Inter-state Council which was under the Union Ministry of Home Affairs and met rarely during the United Progressive Alliance (UPA) I and II governments.

To be fair, the Planning Commission, set up by a Cabinet Resolution in 1950, played an important role in the programmes of national reconstruction with no less than the Prime Minister as its Chairman. The Deputy Chairman, often a political stalwart or eminent economist, held the rank of a Cabinet Minister. Its most important functions were fixing targets for sectoral growth and allocating resources. In a scholarly article, Mihir Shah, a former member, Planning Commission, makes a strong case for continuing the Planning Commission's role in 'mediating' Centre–state relations and striving for a more devolved economy and polity in the country. He succinctly describes seven key roles of the Planning Commission which need to continue under the NITI Aayog, especially because of their 'extremely positive role'. These are

> Pioneering an inclusive planning process; facilitating and mainstreaming reform; pushing decentralised planning forward by emphasising the principle of subsidiarity in recognition of the deep diversity of India; rationalising the centrally sponsored schemes and introducing greater flexibility within them; being the spokesperson of the States at the Centre; coordinating across, if not breaking down departmental silos within the Government of India as also arbitrating disputes by taking a more long-term and holistic view of issues; and providing an independent evaluation and critique of government programmes and policies. (Shah, 2014)

Encouragingly, during successive NITI Aayog meetings, the Prime Minister availed himself of the opportunity to interact with the Chief Ministers on the planning and economic problems confronting their respective states. The first conference convened by him on 9 December 2014 discussed the contours and modalities of the NITI Aayog. It was not only an attempt by the Centre to keep all the state governments in the loop but also seek their help and guidance in streamlining and strengthening the planning process. While Chief Ministers representing NDA-ruled states endorsed the Centre's proposal on the expected lines, those from the UPA-ruled states have opposed it. The best defence of the new panel, perhaps, came from Odisha Chief Minister Naveen Patnaik who backed it to the hilt and pledged support to pursue the idea to its logical conclusion.

Patnaik maintained at the Chief Ministers' Conference that the planning process and distribution of resources during the past six decades had not entirely been guided by merit and necessity which has resulted in a serious imbalance in development across states and unsatisfactory performance in human development indicators. Proliferation of centrally sponsored schemes had gradually eroded the flexibility of the states in designing development programmes suited to the specific needs of the states concerned, he maintained. Giving examples of how Odisha was deprived of its legitimate share in the past, Patnaik said that though his state had contributed over ₹14,000 crore annually or about one-tenth of the total revenue of the Indian Railways, the Railways had not ploughed back even 20 per cent of the collected revenues into the state. Consequently, the railway density in Odisha at 15 kilometres per thousand square kilometres remained significantly lower than the national average of 20 kilometres, he said (*Pragativadi*, 2014). The national highways constitute only 2 per cent of the total road network and handle about 40 per cent of the traffic on road.

Similarly, three-fourths of total gram panchayats in Odisha do not have a brick and mortar bank branch. Financial inclusion will remain a dream if three-fourths of the state does not have a proper banking system. No other state or region in the country faces natural disasters with such frequency and magnitude as Odisha faces almost every alternate year. The same is the case with Andhra Pradesh and even Jammu and Kashmir. One should view seriously the horrific impact of the natural disasters in these states that cause colossal loss of infrastructure, lives and livelihood of people requiring huge time, effort and resources to rebuild people's lives and the states' economy. Patnaik focussed on how cyclonic storms such as the Super Cyclone (1999), the Phailin (2013) and the Hudhud (2014) wreaked havoc on the planning process and resources of the state. There is no second opinion that the resource allocation planning needs to take note of these factors. Indeed, Odisha's demand for the status of a special category state together with adequate flow of central resources to address increasing inter-state disparities should be seen in the context of how repeated natural disasters have perpetuated poverty and underdevelopment in that state.

The NITI Aayog Governing Council met for the first time on 8 February 2015. All Chief Ministers with Legislative Assemblies and Lt. Governors of Union Territories are members of this council. The Prime Minister said that the priorities before the NITI Aayog are 'growth, investment, jobs, poverty alleviation, decentralisation, efficiency and no delay in execution of projects'. Identifying poverty elimination as the biggest challenge, he said it will forge a model of 'cooperative and competitive federalism' (ndtv.com, 2015). The meeting set up three important sub-groups of Chief Ministers: one to look into the rationalisation of 66 centrally sponsored schemes and recommend which ones 'to continue, which to transfer to states, and which to cut down'; another for skill development and creation of jobs within states; and another to create an institutional framework to make Swachh Bharat a 'continuous initiative'. There is no doubt that NITI Aayog merits a fair trial.

Significantly, under Dr Arvind Panagariya's leadership, the NITI Aayog has released the Ease of Doing Business Enterprise Survey Report, 2017, which has made a slew of recommendations on labour reforms. The Report's finding that regulatory reforms did not help cut red tape in India's businesses should serve as a warning signal to the powers that be at various levels and introduce necessary course corrections (Mishra & Prasad, 2017). Moreover, a developing economy like India cannot afford to view its emphasis on regulatory changes lightly for the simple reason that these hold the key to 'faster urbanisation' which, in turn, will not only help absorb surplus agricultural labour but also give a boost to the economy (*Times of India*, 2017).

Dr Panagariya's main focus during his stint at the NITI Aayog was job creation with reasonably better wages. His key concern was employment, employability and the entire concept of skill development. He opines that this issue can be effectively pursued to its logical conclusion if each ministry does its job properly and efficiently (Bhan, 2017). The NITI Aayog has also recommended a National Level Overseas Employment Promotion Agency and overhauling of the University Grants Commission Act. More to the point, in a letter to the Department of Economic Affairs and the Human Resource Development Ministry on 7 August 2017, Amitabh Kant recommended amendments to rules that 'restrict' private investment in higher education (Chopra, 2017).

In a major move, the Centre scrapped the Five-Year Plans, paving the way for a 15-vision document, to be drafted by the NITI Aayog. Speculation was rife for quite some time that the Twelfth Five-Year Plan (2012–2017) was on its way out (*Economic Times*, 2015). The midterm appraisal of the Twelfth Plan was not done though it was due after the completion of two-and-a-half years. The NITI Aayog is primarily engaged in outcome-based monitoring of all government programmes and ministries on a yearly basis. The first 15-year vision document started in 2017–2018. In addition, there will be a seven-year National Development Agenda, which will lay down the schemes and goals to achieve the long-term vision.

The Five-Year Plans have had a chequered history. Owing to the failure of the Third Five-Year Plan (1961–1966), the government declared a plan holiday in 1966–1967, 1967–1968 and 1968–1969 and brought out three annual plans during this period. In 1978, the Janata Party government led by Morarji Desai rejected the Fifth Five-Year Plan

(1974–1979) for political reasons. No Five-Year Plan was implemented from 1989 to 1992 owing to political instability.

One cannot altogether dismiss the rationale behind the Centre's professed intentions of streamlining the development process and give the states their legitimate place in the overall scheme of development. Undoubtedly, the planning and development machinery has been top-heavy with excessive concentration of power and authority in the Centre, giving very little independence to the states. Centralisation of power had been accentuated for reasons such as the adoption of planning as a strategy of national development in which investment decisions determined by the Union Government set the priorities for state budgets.

Although India is a federal state, the Centre continues to call the shots at every stage of planning and development. Clearly, the dice is heavily loaded against the states in this game of federal supremacy and one-upmanship. Indeed, a close look at the Indian Constitution would suggest that there is no mention of the word 'federal'. Dr B.R. Ambedkar's logic for the use of the word 'Union' was simplistic. Having picked it up from the British North-American Act of 1867, he and a few other members of the Constituent Assembly were in favour of the word 'Union' on the grounds that the basic law would provide for a Union in which the states would have no right to secede (Anand, 1985a, 1985b). Equally interesting is the fact that the Indian Constitution does not use the word 'Centre' anywhere. The Justice M.M. Poonchi Commission, which succeeded the Sarkaria Commission of the 1980s, was called the Commission on Centre-State Relations (2010) (Government of India, 2010).

Over the years, in the name of cohesion and integration, the decision-making process has been over-centralised and the states had very little freedom in selecting their own priorities. First, the overall national plan has itself been converted into a multipurpose plan with several types of objectives being given equal priority. As a result, purely social objectives are forced to compete with other objectives—cultural, educational, political and economic. Secondly, the allocation of outlays in different sectors tends to converge on averages worked out by the Centre for the entire country. In successive Five-Year Plans, difficulties of this approach have been shown in no uncertain terms. As a portion of the total outlay must be earmarked for certain types of programmes in every sector, others which need higher priority in the regional or local context and background tend to get neglected. Thirdly, even after 12 Five-Year Plans, no satisfactory arrangements have been evolved to apportion the total investment in the different regions of the country according to their needs of growth, stability and social justice. The thin spread of limited resources over a large variety of items has not only reduced the overall rate of economic growth but also created bottlenecks for which quick solutions are difficult to find (Anand, 1985a, 1985b). Fourthly, the states are so dependent upon the Centre that they will have to look at it for everything under the sun: be it for seeking the Centre's permission for borrowing from the market (though the states are permitted to do this under Article 293 of the Constitution, it is circumscribed under Article 293(3)); obtaining discretionary transfers through central sector and centrally sponsored schemes; or pleading for rectifying the imbalance between the tax and expenditure responsibilities assigned to the Centre and the states (Debroy, 2012).[1] The Centre's new strategy merits a fair trial. It remains to be seen whether it will promote 'cooperative federalism' in letter and spirit and strengthen Centre–state relations.

Too Many Gaps

Over the decades, the process of consultation between the Centre and the states has been sketchy and perfunctory. For one thing, the Centre seems to have failed to address the issue of decentralisation comprehensively. The Constitution (73rd and 74th Amendment) Acts notwithstanding, there are too many gaps in the decentralised governance ambit—political, administrative, fiscal and economic. For another, the issue of decentralisation and devolution within the State and realistic empowerment of the third tier of governance has not been examined properly.

It is nobody's case that the Centre has done little to empower the states in planning and development. But the bane of development has been the Centre's step-motherly attitude towards the states, especially those ruled by non-Congress parties. There is no denying that no nation can progress without empowering women. And gender will have to be made an integral part of the planning process. The Modi government would do well to respect inclusive growth in the new planning process which, indeed, is an important mandate of the Indian Constitution, implying that the social sectors and initiatives for empowerment of tribals and other vulnerable sections should not be adversely affected by

---

[1] A state may not without the consent of the Government of India raise any loan if there is still outstanding any part of a loan which has been made to the state by the Government of India or by its predecessor government, or in respect of which a guarantee has been given by the Government of India or by its predecessor government.

any resource constraint. As most problems encountered by the states are unique and state-specific, efforts need to be stepped up to tailor developmental plan programmes to meet their local needs.

If Prime Minister Narendra Modi is deeply distressed over the manner in which the planning machinery had been run all along, the reasons are not far to seek. In many cases, before introducing a piece of legislation in Parliament, the Centre has not consulted the states even when the subjects directly form a part of the Concurrent List in the Seventh Schedule of the Constitution. Again, surprisingly, there is no time limit prescribed for processing a Bill passed by a state legislature. The latter sends the Bill to the Governor who, in turn, forwards it to the President. The system is so open-ended that the state legislature is completely kept in the dark and it does not get to know the follow-up action either from the President or the Governor.

It is a travesty of six decades of planned development that the Centre has always been treating the states as vassals and not as equal partners of development. While the Inter-State Council Secretariat in the Union Ministry of Home Affairs has been ineffective, states have no formal representation in the National Development Council, the National Integration Council, the Planning Commission and the Finance Commission. All these bodies have been politicised to the core with members nominated by the Centre.

The existence of a constitutionally demarcated jurisdiction for the states is the test of a federal system. In a federal Constitution, State autonomy has, apart from the political, three other important dimensions. One, autonomy is a condition for self-expression, expression of a sense of identity which is strengthened by regional history, local tradition, language and culture. Two, autonomy is a condition for the effective use of resources. This presupposes that all state governments—irrespective of party affiliations—must have the freedom to determine their own priorities in planning. And three, autonomy is a condition for operational efficiency. The states provide an important level for the implementation of developmental plan programmes to tackle the gigantic problems of poverty, unemployment, agriculture, education and culture.

Moreover, in the context of a federal polity, state autonomy has a narrow connotation inasmuch as it does not connote 'polyphonic federalism' but 'cooperative federalism'. Thus, the Centre and the states must be seen as two levels from which the tasks of economic development can be carried out simultaneously.

Empowering States

The Centre's acceptance of the Fourteenth Finance Commission's recommendation to transfer a higher share of central taxes to states was aimed at empowering them by improving their financial position. This will also help achieve the goal of cooperative federalism in letter and spirit. At a time when it is being increasingly felt that the states should be viewed as equal partners in the national project of development, the Centre's decision can be regarded as an important step towards this end. It is also a 'paradigm shift' in Centre–state relations and will usher in a new phase of 'fiscal federalism' by enhancing the states' financial autonomy and independence. Fourteenth Finance Commission Chairman Y.V. Reddy has privileged tax devolution as the channel for transfers and scrapped the arbitrary distinctions between 'Plan' and 'Non-Plan' spending. Successive governments at the Centre were using conditional 'Plan'-related transfers as an instrument to sanction funds to states subscribing to the political philosophy of the Centre and exercise control over foes and allies (*Indian Express*, 2015). In a letter to the Chief Ministers, the Prime Minister said how the country was moving away from the peculiar philosophy of rigid centralised planning, forcing a 'one-size-fits-all' approach on states (*Economic Times*, 2015).

In the Union Budget 2015–2016, Finance Minister Arun Jaitley referred to this decision and said that the big jump in the proportion of the money that will devolve to the states is first of its kind as their share of taxes will rise from 32 per cent of the divisible part of the Centre's tax collections to 42 per cent. The total devolution to the states in 2015–2016 was ₹5.25 lakh crore as against ₹3.48 lakh crore in 2014–2015, representing an increase of ₹1.78 lakh crore (*Economic Times*, 2015).

Arvind Subramanian, Chief Economic Adviser to the Government of India, has termed the Finance Commission recommendations as a 'watershed in Centre–state relations' as these will help strengthen states. The greater devolution to states will make them more accountable while giving the common man a greater say in government schemes. Subramanian said, the common man will be benefitted because this will give more power to states to decide on what to spend. 'Now how to spend money will not be taken by New Delhi but by each State,' he said (*Indian Express*, 2015).

Jaitley's Assertion

Arun Jaitley has said that Centre's discretions in devolution have come to an end following its decision to redefine the entire architecture of

Centre–state relationship (*Business Standard*, 2015). In his Budget speech, he asserted that notwithstanding the reduced 'fiscal space' for the Centre, the government has decided to continue supporting important national priorities such as agriculture, education, health, Mahatma Gandhi National Rural Employment Guarantee Act (MGNREGA) and rural infrastructure. There will be no change in the government's decision to continue all programmes targeted for the poor and the under-privileged. 'In keeping with the true spirit of cooperative federalism, we have devolved a 42 per cent share of the divisible pool of taxes to States,' Jaitley said. Giving statistics on the extent of devolution, he said the states' share has increased to ₹5.24 lakh crore in the financial year 2015–2016 as against the 2014–2015 revised estimates of ₹3.38 lakh crore. The Centre will transfer another ₹3.04 lakh crore by way of grants and Plan transfers. Further, the total central assistance (Plan and non-Plan) for states and Union Territories stands at ₹2.10 lakh crore for 2015–2016, down from ₹2.83 lakh crore from the revised estimates of 2014–2015. The assistance under the Plan expenditure stands at ₹2.04 lakh crore as against the revised estimates of ₹2.78 lakh crore. And the non-Plan share has been increased to ₹5,611 crore as against the revised estimates of ₹5,224.24. Meanwhile, the number of Centrally Sponsored Schemes has been reduced to 61 from 66 in 2014–2015 (*Business Standard*, 2015).

Chidambaram's Viewpoint

Interestingly, former Union Finance Minister P. Chidambaram, while appreciating the Finance Commission's recommendations and the Centre's acceptance, has maintained that he has always been stressing the need to significantly increase the states' share of taxes and duties collected by the Centre and that the central schemes must be 'very few' as also 'fully funded' by the Centre (Chidambaram, 2015). He said there would have been no problem had the states done their work properly with regard to their share of taxes and duties transferred to them and their own resource mobilisation. Giving his perspective on the subject during his stint in New Delhi's North Block, Chidambaram said that though the Centre made it clear to the states that they will have to implement their respective Plans, draw up their own State Plans (including non-Plan schemes for which they wanted money from the Centre), there was friction between the Centre and the states. The latter drew strength from Article 275 of the Constitution that deals with grants from the Centre to the states. The Planning Commission did act as the 'arbiter' but was not of much help because of the states' insistence on higher share of central funds.

One of the terms of reference of the Fourth Finance Commission was to recommend 'the principles which should govern the grants-in-aid of the revenues of the States.' Consequently, in the Union Budget 2014–2015 presented to Parliament on 17 February 2014, Chidambaram announced restructuring the Centrally Sponsored Schemes into 66 programmes and the release of funds for these schemes as 'Central assistance to State Plans'. This, he claims, has resulted in a dramatic raise in the central assistance to State Plans from ₹136,254 crore in 2013–2014 to ₹338,562 crore in 2014–2015—a fact duly acknowledged by Chidambaram's successor, Arun Jaitley, when he presented his regular Budget in July 2014 (Chidambaram, 2015).

Subsequently, the Fourteenth Finance Commission raised the states' share of taxes and duties from 32 per cent to 42 per cent (which the Modi government has now accepted); recommended grants for revenue deficit, disaster relief and local bodies; and suggested a separate institutional arrangement for grants to sectors such as health, education, drinking water and sanitation. Chidambaram says this has not only resulted in 'more untied funds' to the states but also imposed greater financial responsibility on them.

Equally important is Chidambaram's reference to the Finance Commission Member Abhijit Sen's note of dissent: he has been against a drastic shift from the past practice. As Sen feared that any disruption of the existing plan transfers will have 'very serious effects' in the first year of the award period, he called for an abeyance of greater devolution to the states in the first year of the award, and maintaining the level of the states' share at 38 per cent until a separate institutional arrangement is put in place. According to Chidambaram, while the Commission Chairman and other members left it to the wisdom of the government to take a final call on 'the transition path', the Modi government has 'played safe'. He says that though the government has accepted the recommendation for raising the states' share to 42 per cent, in respect of grants-in-aid of revenue and Revenue Deficit grant, it has accepted it only 'in principle' (Chidambaram, 2015).

States' Concern

Some states are not happy with the Finance Commission recommendations. Andhra Pradesh Chief Minister N. Chandrababu Naidu, for instance, is peeved at the fact that the commission is silent on the concerns of the state, which was divided in June 2014 to grant state-hood to the Telangana region. He said 'the Finance Commission has not taken care of development needs of Andhra Pradesh and treated it on a par with other states. It did not help Andhra Pradesh get a level-playing field.' A statement released by his government on the Facebook page of the Andhra Pradesh government said that the central government is required to address the development needs of the state following the creation of Telangana as India's 29th state. The state government said that the Finance Commission had addressed only the revenue expenditure needs (administration and maintenance costs of governance) rather than 'the massive development requirements of the new state without a capital city, without the ecosystem for development and without major growth engines' (Varma & Mishra, 2015).

Bihar Chief Minister Nitish Kumar, too, was unhappy with the recommendations (i.e., before he patched up with the Bharatiya Janata Party (BJP) on 26 July 2017 and started his new innings as the Chief Minister with the BJP's help). He had even hinted at approaching the Supreme Court for 'justice'. Now that he is friends with the Prime Minister and the BJP, it remains to be seen how he would deal with the issue. Initial estimates showed that Bihar would face about 1.3 per cent point loss in share in overall amount due to the Fourteenth Finance Commission recommendations as compared to the Thirteenth Finance Commission report. Under the latter report, Bihar's share in the overall amount was 10.9 per cent which will go down to 9.6 per cent as per the former report. This implies a reduction of 1.3 per cent for Bihar, according to Kumar (Zee News, 2015).

He said that the Prime Minister's letter indicated that all additional benefits Bihar was getting by way of plan money as per the Gadgil–Mukherjee formula, the Backward Region Grant Fund (BRGF) following the bifurcation of the state to form Jharkhand from it and the Union Government share in central schemes were being subsumed in the 10 per cent hike recommended in the central taxes share. 'This means a loss to Bihar,' he said. Bihar would go to the Supreme Court if Bihar was not compensated for the loss, among others, by ending fund under BRGF which was devised by a law made by Parliament under which the state was getting additional fund since the Tenth Plan period (Zee News, 2015).

Similarly, the Naveen Patnaik-led Biju Janata Dal government in Odisha is sore with the Finance Commission report. It asked why the commission is silent on the funds sanctioned to the state for the development of the Koraput–Bolangir–Kalahandi (KBK) region (*Headlines Today*, 2015). Stating that Odisha's share in tax devolution would come down from 4.78 per cent to 4.60 per cent, the Chief Minister said this would involve a loss of about ₹4,600 crore over a period of five years because of the inclusion of new criteria such as demographic changes, that is, population as per 2011 census and deletion of the criteria of fiscal discipline (*Outlook*, 2015). 'We are being penalised because of our good performance in fiscal discipline and population stabilisation initiatives,' Patnaik lamented. The net positive impact to Odisha would be minimal after the increase from 32 per cent to 42 per cent in case of central taxes, he said, adding there has been a substantial decrease in overall plan outlay of the state and also at the overall national level (*Outlook*, 2015).

According to a study, nine of the 29 states will be at a disadvantage following the Finance Commission's recommendations. These are Assam, Bihar, Himachal Pradesh, Odisha, Rajasthan, Telangana, Tamil Nadu, Uttar Pradesh and Uttarakhand. The Commission has assigned 7.5 per cent weightage to forest cover for inter se determination of the shares of taxes to the states. The weightage for population carries 17.5 per cent, demographic change 10 per cent, income distance 10 per cent and area 15 per cent. Uttar Pradesh has complained that the new criteria will hit the state hard (Shekhar, 2015). In all, 19 states stand to gain from the recommendations. These include Arunachal Pradesh, Chhattisgarh, Maharashtra, Madhya Pradesh, Karnataka, Jharkhand and Jammu and Kashmir. Nonetheless, if nine states complain that they are in a position of disadvantage and that the Finance Commission has not done justice to them in its recommendations, it would only be fair if the Prime Minister, as the Chairman of NITI Aayog, addresses the problem with the attention it deserves. It is the Centre's duty to assuage the feelings of the states and convince them of the Union Government's efforts to establish a level-playing field for all states without any discrimination.

The Finance Commission has a five-year term. The Fourteenth Finance Commission's recommendations are valid from 2015 to 2020 (Mishra, 2017). While the Modi government has kick-started the process of constituting the Fifteenth Finance Commission, its recommendations will be implemented for the period starting 1 April 2020 to 31 March 2025. According to well-established practice, a Finance Commission is set up two years before the end of the period for which it sets rules for devolution of taxes. Given the flexible attitude of the Union Government to hear the grievances of the states with an open mind in tune with its philosophy of cooperative federalism, it should not be a problem for the Centre to formulate fiscal policies in the larger interest of all the states irrespective of the party in power.

Media's Responsibility

As the Modi government is desirous of ushering in significant changes in the national economy, planning, development and governance, journalists have a responsible role to play in development journalism. The Centre's decision on demonetisation and its aftermath have multiplied the responsibilities of journalists. To write with authority and credibility, they need to have a grasp of the development process and mechanism at the Centre, state and district level. It is not enough if journalists merely collect data for a story or feature on, say, demonetisation or the Land Acquisition Act. They need to have adequate background information on such issues. If stories are not backed by authentic facts and figures, they will not be credible enough to convince the reader. The government, too, will not take the reports seriously if they are not well researched.

The big-ticket programmes, launched by the UPA government (2009–2014), did not give it votes and help it return to power for a third term. If the Congress and its allies have been decimated in the Lok Sabha elections, it is because of rampant corruption, policy paralysis and inefficiency at various levels and not due to any conceptual or structural flaws of these schemes.

The duty of a development journalist is to inform and educate the reader. At the same time, he/she should write in a manner that would attract the attention of the government and the powers that be. Otherwise, it will be a futile exercise. While the journalist handles a story, he/she needs to examine the issue from various angles and perspectives without any bias. In principle, journalistic writing should be free of bias of any kind.

Depending upon its topicality and relevance, any scheme or programme can become a subject for a front-page lead, flier, anchor, feature, editorial or article. Essentially, journalists should keep their eyes and ears open and act accordingly. Though a journalist is expected to question the political masters or officials on a particular scheme, he/she need not be arrogant and play an adversarial role. Even if a development journalist is required to make a critical appreciation of a particular scheme or piece of legislation, it can still be handled or examined from a positive frame of mind. However, if a journalist has negative thoughts, the report or feature in question will not help society and serve the intended purpose.

The GST Act

As the Prime Minister Narendra Modi emphasised in his address to the nation on 15 August 2017, on the occasion of Independence Day, the

Goods and Services Tax (GST) Act is the biggest reform of his government. The nature, scope and magnitude of this legislation are such that it is bound to play an important role in development journalism. If implemented effectively, it is bound to fulfil the objectives and goals of fiscal cooperative federalism and thus usher in new vistas of cooperation between the Centre and the states.

West Bengal's U-turn on GST following the Centre's decision on demonetisation did raise doubts about the roll out of the new architecture. However, at the Hindustan Leadership Summit in New Delhi on 2 December 2016, Arun Jaitley made it clear that the Centre and the states were constitutionally bound to put in place the new GST architecture within one year of the legislative enactment by Parliament, that is, on 16 September 2017. Otherwise, there will be no taxation and there will be a constitutional vacuum. He repeated his caution on 17 December 2016, when he said that states that delay GST would lose the right to collect tax.

It augurs well that the Centre successfully rolled out the final GST Act on 1 July 2017, that too, at a special midnight session of Parliament notwithstanding opposition by a few states such as West Bengal and Kerala who have been up in arms with the Centre over its decision on demonetisation. Calling it a 'double whammy', they wanted the GST exercise to be differed as it would 'harm' their respective states' finances. There were also other problems such as who will have the exclusive control over all traders—the Centre or the states? West Bengal, Kerala and Tamil Nadu wanted control over all traders with an annual revenue threshold of less than ₹1.5 crore. The Centre, however, did not yield as it felt that it would be left with a very small pool of traders. On the contrary, it was in favour of dividing traders in a fixed proportion between the Centre and the states irrespective of the threshold. It was also in favour of dividing only those traders who were to be audited in the new GST regime.

Encouragingly, at its meeting on 23 December 2016, both sides—the Centre and the states—agreed to a compensation formula with the Centre committing itself to absorb any revenue losses incurred by the states on account of transition to a new indirect tax regime. The GST Compensation Bill, passed on 23 December 2016, will provide legal backing to the Centre's proposal to compensate states if their revenue growth rate were to fall below 14 per cent in the GST's first five years. The base year for calculating the revenue is 2015–2016.

Subsequent meetings of the GST Council, especially on the issue of dual control or cross empowerment and reduction of tax rates, were equally crucial. The one on 11 June 2017 was significant inasmuch as the GST Council cut tax rates for as many as 66 items. Of the 133 representations received seeking reconsideration, the Council revised downwards the rates on 66 items—from cashew nuts, packaged foods such as sauces and pickles, agarbatti, insulin, school bags, children's colouring books, cutlery to a few tractor components. Despite some differences, it was not a problem for both sides to agree on two less contentious issues—the Central GST Bill and the Integrated GST Bill. According to the schedule, Parliament will have to pass all the Bills after which the states, too, must individually pass their respective state-level GST Bills.

Despite the Trinamool Congress leaders' dissenting voices on the GST and, more important, their efforts to rope in other Opposition leaders to stall the move, there were no hurdles before the Modi government. It brought the new architecture as a money bill, much to the chagrin of the Rajya Sabha where it is in a minority, and thwarted any opposition to it in Parliament. There is no denying that the coming months are an acid test for the Modi government to concretise the GST in letter and spirit.

The GST is considered a 'destination-based tax'. It will subsume various indirect taxes at the Centre and in the states such as excise duty, service tax, value-added tax, entertainment tax and luxury tax. In essence, it will ensure an integrated tax regime and thus promote efficiency, check tax evasion and broaden the tax base. According to Shaktikanta Das, former Secretary, Economic Affairs, Government of India, if the GST Act is implemented properly and efficiently, it will add 2 per cent to India's gross domestic product (GDP). For 2016–2017, the Central Statistical Organisation has put the figure of GDP growth rate at 7.1 per cent. For the current year, 2017–2018, the Government of India expects the figure to touch 7.5 per cent. Das says, it will touch 8 per cent and will thus give a boost to the economy (ndtv.com, 2017).

As the GST is said to be a progressive tax reform, there is so much at stake and development journalists will get ample opportunities to do as many stories. Significantly, Symbiosis Institute of Media and Communication's (SIMC) journalism students have been writing on various aspects of GST Act in the in-house publication, Ink. This writer believes that every aspect of the new reform will unleash new forces and provide further leads for research, study and investigation. For instance, the establishment of a legal framework and preparations of information technological infrastructure is as challenging as the change management covering the training of officials and staff and outreach and consultation with trade and industry.

The GST Act envisages a three-tier structure: the Central GST, the state GST (in all states), and the Integrated GST. While the first two tiers are self-explanatory as to their jurisdictional limits, the third is unique and special as it is based on the concept of 'one tax, one nation'. It shall be levied as 'Dual GST' separately but concurrently by the Union (CGST) and the states (SGST). Of course, Parliament will have the exclusive power to levy IGST on inter-state trade or commerce (including imports) in goods or services.

According to a presentation by the Revenue Secretary to the Government of India, Hasmukh Adhia, the recommendation of model GST laws by the GST Council, Cabinet approval of the CGST and IGST laws by the Centre and SGST laws in all states, passage of these laws by Parliament and notification of GST rules are all steps in line. The wash-out of Parliament's winter session in 2016 because of obstruction by the Opposition on the issue of demonetisation delayed the GST rollout by a few months. Registration for existing and new dealers is equally an important process. While no fresh registration was required for existing dealers (the existing indirect taxes such as value-added tax, service tax, entertainment tax will be integrated with the GST system), new dealers ought to register online for which PAN numbers are required for both the Centre and the states. Each dealer gets a unique GSTIN and registration is done in just three working days. The registration process itself will be made easier and without hassles in due course of time, according to Adhia. On the one hand, most average taxpayers use only four forms for filing their returns for supplies, return for purchases, monthly and annual returns. On the other, small taxpayers do so on a quarterly basis (Ministry of Finance, 2016). See Table 21.1 for the GST challenges.

The Congress' opposition to the Centre's decision to bring forward the model GST legislation as a Money Bill in Parliament and thus prevent a thorough discussion in the Rajya Sabha (where the BJP is in a

Table 21.1
The GST challenges

1. Calculation of revenue base of the Centre and the states
2. Compensation requirements of the Centre
3. GST rates structure
4. List of exemptions
5. Consensus building on a model GST Bill
6. Threshold and compounding limits
7. Empowerment to mitigate effects of dual control

Source: Presentation of Revenue Secretary to Government of India, 2016.

minority) seemed misplaced and unwarranted. Under Article 109 of the Constitution, there is a special procedure in respect of Money Bills. No Money Bill can be tabled in the Rajya Sabha. After the Lok Sabha passes a Money Bill, it is transmitted to the Rajya Sabha for its recommendations. However, the Rajya Sabha will have to return it to the Lok Sabha within 14 days, failing which the Bill will be deemed to have been passed by the Rajya Sabha. Its recommendations are also not binding on the Lok Sabha. The Congress would do well to understand that the procedure that the Modi government was following with regard to the GST legislation did not give it any scope for one-upmanship and trampling upon the powers of Parliament. Union Finance Minister Arun Jaitley, in his reply to the debate on the GST Bill in the Rajya Sabha, coined a new term, 'veto over veto' with regard to the powers being enjoyed by the states in the GST regime. Having underlined the importance of cooperative federalism and the effective cooperation between the Centre and the states, he said even if the Centre tried to veto a particular provision and asserts its supremacy in lawmaking, the states could 'veto over the veto' by virtue of their strength and overall majority in the GST architecture. Technically, the Centre has only one-third of rights vis-à-vis two-thirds of the states in the GST regime. Of course, it requires all the leadership skills, political sagacity, persuasive skills and administrative acumen of the Centre to convince the states and build up consensus on important issues such as uniform tax rates and compensation to manufacturing states likely to be affected by the legislation.

The GST architecture is beautifully designed and it would take a few months for it to stabilise. As it is a comprehensive reform, there are bound to be teething troubles which are in no way a reflection on the conceptualisation of the legislation itself. The argument that people are not aware of the GST system does not cut ice. According to Prakash Kumar, CEO of GST Network (GSTN), people will gradually understand the system just as they are able to file income-tax reforms online without any glitches. He said whenever there was a glitch, people unnecessarily became apprehensive. The 'fear of the unknown' prevented them from going ahead with the reform and joining the mainstream, he said (Kumar, 2017).

As on 1 August 2017, three lakh people filed their GST returns. Complaints with respect to digital signature certificates are being attended to on a war footing by the GSTN. More important, Prakash Kumar says that not everyone needs to use digital signature certificates. Others can do it through the one-time password (OTP) method. Even otherwise, while the OTP method usually takes time to deliver, GST OTP is delivered within 15 seconds. He says that while the Centre has been closely monitoring cyber traffic security, there has been constant upgradation of the system in terms of security equipment, firewall and intelligence. Intelligence alerts are being issued from time to time to monitor security. There is no denying that compliance of the GST Act will help make the system sustain itself (Kumar, 2017).

Meanwhile, the GST Council at its meeting in Hyderabad on 9 September 2017 has set up a minister-level committee to oversee the GSTN's technical and operational issues, including the traders' concerns. Calling them 'transient challenges', Arun Jaitley has said that the panel comprising finance ministers of a few states will interact with GSTN for a 'smooth transition' (Seth, 2017).

Land Acquisition Act

The Right to Fair Compensation, Resettlement, Rehabilitation and Transparency in Land Acquisition Act, 2013, also called, the Land Acquisition Act, 2013, was the UPA-II government's answer to forced acquisitions, the previous legislation's silence on rehabilitation and resettlement of displaced families, low rates of solatium and the urgency clause—which allowed complete dispossession without prior notice to the project-affected families—under the colonial and anachronistic 1894 land acquisition law. It is the brainchild of the UPA chairperson Sonia Gandhi and Congress vice-president Rahul Gandhi. Jairam Ramesh, who was Rural Development Minister in the UPA government, is also one of the architects of the Act (Ramesh and Khan, 2014).

After the Modi government assumed office in May 2014 following its thumping victory in the Lok Sabha elections, it decided to rectify some anomalies in the legislation. It proposed some amendments in the Act through an Ordinance, or executive order, on 29 December 2014. The Centre took the Ordinance route as it was deeply concerned over the adverse fallout of the land acquisition procedures in the earlier legislation on defence, infrastructure and rural power projects. The amendments to the Act through the Ordinance sought to strike a balance between farmers' welfare and the strategic and developmental needs of the country. They were also meant to mitigate 'procedural difficulties' brought about by the original law in 2013. Another aim of the amendments was to speed up developmental and security-related projects without compromising on the benefits/compensation to be given to farmers.

The Modi government had been maintaining that the land law required amendments to help farmers and give a boost to industrialisation. Notwithstanding stiff opposition to the Ordinance and a new amended law by parties led by the Congress in the 2015 Budget session of Parliament, the Prime Minister stood his ground, implying that the Union Government was in no mood to retract from its stated position. Modi said the land Bill would benefit the farmers, and the amendments brought in by his government were based on suggestions from Congress Chief Ministers (*Mail Today*, 2015). Subsequently, Arun Jaitley, while replying to the debate on Motion of Thanks to the President's Address, emphatically declared in the Rajya Sabha that the government was committed to go ahead with the amended legislation (*Indian Express*, 2015).

Of all the political parties opposed to an amended land law, the objections of the Aam Admi Party, which returned to power in the February 2015 Delhi Assembly elections after decimating both the Congress (which did not win a single seat) and the BJP (which had to contend with just three seats) in the 70-member House, need to be mentioned. The following data (five points) are based on the Background Note prepared by the Aam Admi Party.

1. **No emergency:** The Ordinance violates the basic spirit of why it is needed. There was no emergency in the case of the land legislation. The Centre should have waited till the commencement of the Budget session of Parliament from the last week of February 2015.

2. **Back to 1894 Act:** The amendments proposed by the Union Government will nullify the gains of movements against forced land acquisition and displacement. The nation will return to the days of the 'draconian' 1894 Act.

3. **Annulment of the Act itself:** The proposal to exempt five categories of acquisition from the procedural requirements of the 2013 Act will give a free hand to politicians, bureaucrats and builders to manipulate the situation and mint money. This will virtually lead to the annulment of the Act itself.

4. **Speaker's endorsement:** The BJP, too, supported the passage of the 2013 Act in Parliament. The present Lok Sabha Speaker, Ms Sumitra Mahajan, headed a parliamentary committee that cleared the Land Acquisition Bill in 2013. Why this sudden U-turn by the new government?

5. **No fair chance:** The 2013 Act has not been given a fair chance so far. Most states have not framed rules necessary for its implementation. How did the Modi government come to the conclusion that it is impractical without even a trial?

It would be noteworthy to mention seven points dealing with the reservations expressed by Yogendra Yadav, noted political scientist, Swaraj Abhiyan leader and former Aam Admi Party leader:

1. **Against farmers:** The new Bill will not safeguard the interests of the farmers.
2. **Statute misuse:** In the name of infrastructure, the government can acquire land for private educational institutions and private hospitals as well, which were specifically excluded by the original Act (Amendment to Section 1 b(i)).
3. **Exemption of defence:** 'Defence' has now been defined to include any project vital to 'national security' and 'defence production'. This definition can include all kinds of infrastructural projects and privately owned projects (insertion of new Section 10A).
4. **Limits the benefit:** The original Act gave relief to farmers whose lands were acquired a few years ago, but where the process was not completed, farmers were to be given the benefit of compensation under the new Act. Now the amendment limits this benefit to only those few cases where the delay was not due to any judicial order or pending case (Amendment to Section 24(2)).
5. **Immunity to officials:** Earlier, the Head of the Department was held responsible if the violation of the Act took place with their knowledge and connivance. The Amendment removes this provision and provides immunity to government officials under Section 197 of the Criminal Procedure Code. According to Amendment to Section 87, there won't be any action against a government official for violating this Act without sanction from the government.
6. **Retention without utilisation:** The original provision of returning the land to the original owner, if not utilised within five years, has been removed. Now the government can retain the land for longer without utilising it, if the 'period specified for the project' is longer (Amendment to Section 101).
7. **Removal of difficulty:** The government has given itself the power of 'removal of difficulty' for five years instead of the original two years (Amendment to Section 113). The Modi government has annulled every 'positive feature' of the 2013 Act, which was passed with the BJP's support.

Surprisingly, the Congress, during the debate in Parliament against the Land Acquisition Ordinance, did not come forward with any comprehensive note on why it was opposed to the proposed amend-ments to the 2013 Act. Former Union Commerce Minister and Congress leader Anand Sharma had been in the forefront of the Opposition attack in Parliament on the Modi government's policies. Not surprisingly, he had called for status quo and maintained that nothing short of with-drawal of amendments to the land law, originally passed by Parliament during the UPA dispensation, will satisfy the Opposition.

Interestingly, Arun Jaitley exposed Sharma's double standards on the issue in the Rajya Sabha on 26 February 2015. Referring to some former UPA minister's (including Sharma's) view that the provisions of the land acquisition law would affect infrastructure projects, he read out a letter written by Sharma to then Prime Minister Dr Manmohan Singh in this regard. In the letter dated 25 May 2012, Sharma, in his capacity as the Union Commerce Minister, had argued that the law (which was passed by Parliament in 2013) would 'not only make the cost of land exorbi-tantly high but also make acquisition proceedings well-nigh impossible' (*Indian Express*, 2015). Going a step further, Sharma had said 'the insis-tence on consent of 80 per cent of the project-affected families would seriously delay acquisition and in many cases halt essential infrastructure projects' (*Indian Express*, 2015).

Sharma's response to Jaitley's revelation in the Rajya Sabha debate was weak, unconvincing and did not hold water. He said while he stood by what he had written in the letter, his objection to the proposed amendments was that it asked the government to acquire land for private parties in certain cases. Amusingly, after the debate, he told journalists outside Parliament that Jaitley should not have revealed in Parliament a Union Minister's 'privileged communication' to the Prime Minister (*Headlines Today*, 2015).

Such are the ways of politicians! When they are in the government, they speak in one voice. When they are in the Opposition, they speak in a different voice. Opposition for opposition sake has become the biggest hurdle in development.

The Ordinance on land acquisition, a temporary order, needed the approval of both houses of Parliament to come into force as a constitu-tional amendment to the Land Acquisition Act. There was no problem for the BJP and its allies who command a comfortable majority in the present Lok Sabha—first time in 30 years. However, they did not have the required numbers in the Rajya Sabha. A constitutional amendment can be passed only if an amended Bill has the support of at least two-thirds of members present and voting in Parliament. Even after the pas-sage, half of the states will have to ratify the Bill before it is sent to the President for his assent.

The government tried for an all-party consensus on the amendments to the land acquisition legislation, but without success. An eight-member committee appointed by BJP President Amit Shah held consultations with various farmers' groups and associations to allay their apprehensions and the imperative need to go ahead with the amendments. The National Democratic Alliance, too, tried to pacify parties such as the Shiv Sena, an ally of the ruling coalition, opposing the move. As voices against it grew louder, the Shiv Sena's boycott of an all-party meeting and its overall attitude towards the legislation were indicative of the fault lines within the alliance over the issue. In the light of the civic elections in Maharashtra, the Shiv Sena tried to outsmart the BJP and regain its lost ground in the Lok Sabha election.

The BJP had been maintaining that it would have to amend the legislation for speedy infrastructural development without compromising the interests of the farmers. After the BJP won the Lok Sabha election, the issue triggered a confrontation between the government, non-governmental organisations (NGOs) and industry. As the Opposition did not allow the government to go ahead with the proposed amendments in the winter session of Parliament in 2014, it was forced to promulgate an Ordinance. Indeed, this had been the stand of the government. One should see the manner in which the Centre was consulting various stakeholders on the issue.

More important, even before the proposed amendments came to the fore and the Ordinance was promulgated, Union Rural Development Minister Nitin Gadkari had convened a conference of Revenue Ministers of all states in New Delhi on 27 June 2014. At this conference, many recommendations were made. Some of these, in a nutshell, were as follows (Tewari, 2014; counterview.org, 2014):

1. **Consent clause:** The Consent Clause [Section 2(2)] should be re-examined, as ownership of land vests with the government in PPP projects. The consent clause should be removed from PPP projects. Alternatively, consent requirement may be brought down to 50 per cent.

2. **Elaborate definition:** Definition of 'affected family' [Section 3(c)] needs to be re-examined as it is very elaborate and includes 'livelihood losers' working in the affected area for three years prior to acquisition of land and whose primary source of livelihood is affected. The Act provides for rehabilitation and resettlement (R&R) benefits to the affected families. Hence, the provision is likely to be misused in the absence of clear criteria for determination of affected families.

3. **Delegate to UTs:** Posers of 'Appropriate Government' [Section 3(e)] which are with the central government should be delegated to the Union Territories.

4. **Scrap SIA:** Mandatory social impact assessment (SIA) study (Sections 4 to 9) should be done away with; and SIA should be confined to large projects/PPP projects as it may delay the acquisition process.

5. **Food security:** The provision to safeguard food security (Section 10) by development of 'culturable wastelands' in lieu of acquisition of 'multi-cropped irrigated land' needs to be amended as states such as Delhi, Goa, Himachal Pradesh and Uttarakhand do not have any wasteland for the purpose.

6. **A heavy burden:** The Retrospective clause (Section 24) which stipulates that land acquisition proceedings would lapse in case compensation is not paid or physical possession is not taken should be modified. Payment of compensation as per new Act to the persons specified in Section 4 notification under old Act leads to increased burden on the state exchequer. The provisions of Section 24 need to be amended as it is leading to litigations.

7. **Time limits:** The litigation period or period of stay/injunction should be excluded while calculating the prescribed time limits for completing various proceedings under the Act, for instance Section 24(2), Section 25.

8. **Market price:** Section 26 should be re-examined as determination of market price of land based on 'agreements to sell' will lead to speculation in land prices. As such, at present the compensation paid is higher than market value in Himachal Pradesh, Lakshadweep and Kerala.

9. **Preliminary notification:** In Section 30(3), the date from which an amount of 12 per cent of market value is to be given, should be calculated from date of preliminary notification under Section 11 and not from Section 4 notification which deals with SIA study as stipulated in the Act presently.

10. **Value calculation:** It also contravenes Section 69(2) of the new Act which deals with determination of award by authority and stipulates calculation of 12 per cent of market value from the date of preliminary notification under Section 11.

11. **Urgency clause:** Under the Urgency Clause (Section 40), the powers to determine 'any other emergency' should also be exercised by the state government concerned. At present, the urgency clause is restricted to 'the defence of India or national security or for any other emergency arising out of natural calamity or any other emergency with the approval of Parliament'.

12. **Private purchase:** Section 46 stipulating R&R obligation in case of private purchase beyond limits specified by the state government should be deleted. The jurisdiction of authority (Section 51) should be restricted to dispute resolution only and not be on determination of award.

13. **Stringent punishment:** Penalty Provisions (Sections 84–90), including imprisonment of six months extendable to three years or with fine or with both for the government servants are too stringent and may lead to harassment of civil servants.

14. **Unutilised land:** Section 101 dealing with return of unutilised land to the original land owners or heirs should be deleted.

15. **Enhanced cost:** The clause specifying sharing of 40 per cent enhanced cost with original land owners (Section 102) when the land is transferred on higher consideration should be deleted as it leads to disputes.

16. **Lease amount:** Under Section 104 of the Act, a formula for calculating 'lease amount' may be given, as a formula has been prescribed for calculating compensation value.

17. **Relief and rehabilitation:** There should be threshold for relief and rehabilitation entitlements in the Second Schedule and infrastructural amenities in the Third Schedule.

18. **Land for land:** Under the Second Schedule, the provision of 'land for land' should be re-examined.

19. **Fourth Schedule:** State-specific Acts dealing with land acquisition should be included in the Fourth Schedule exempting the enlisted Acts from provisions of the new Act.

Indeed, the Modi government's intention to amend the Act was never in doubt. The Mid-Year Economic Analysis 2014–2015 had called for 'better drafting of the Act to avoid confusion and litigation through rules and notifications, urgent (and politically non-controversial) measures needing legislation and other measures'. It says, reforms that can be undertaken without central legislation include issuing notification exempting the special Act; modifying the SIA rules to focus more on the poor land owners; prescribing a high limit for private purchases of land; and allowing states to modify some provisions of the Right to Fair Compensation and Transparency in Land Acquisition, Resettlement and Rehabilitation Act, 2013 (*Indian Express*, 2014).

Arun Jaitley gave ample indication of the government's thinking on the Land Acquisition Act when he said that some changes to the Act might be necessary. Addressing the India Global Forum in New Delhi on 22 November 2014, he said that the government will first try to reach a consensus with political parties and if it was not possible, it would go ahead and take a decision (Roche, 2014). Significantly, while delivering the keynote address at the 2014 edition of Economic Times Awards for Corporate Excellence in Mumbai on 29 November 2014, Jaitley was more vociferous on his criticism of the Act when he said that it was full of 'flaws and absurdities' and hence needed to be revamped. He said the land law needed a fresh look. The myriad restrictions on land acquisition were applicable not only to the private sector but even to defence and national security. Consequently, even for acquiring land for a cantonment or a seaport, land acquisition, under the present law, is very difficult. 'Should we or should we not look at this very important law?' Jaitley asked the captains of industry (*Times of India*, 2014).

To buttress his argument against the present amended land law, Jaitley narrated an interesting discussion he had with Andhra Pradesh Chief Minister Chandrababu Naidu when he met him regarding the new capital city for his state. Chandrababu Naidu told him that the Centre would help him build a beautiful capital city for Andhra Pradesh, but no private school, private hotel or club could be in Andhra Pradesh because all these would come under the land acquisition law.

It would be worth recollecting Professor Amartya Sen's observations during the Nandigram and Singur episodes in 2007 when he said that there should be no restriction on the acquisition of agricultural land for purposes of industrialisation. Interestingly, Professor Sen said that global cities such as Manchester, London, Munich, Paris, Pittsburgh, Shanghai and Lancashire came up on fertile agricultural land (Kumar, 2014).

Be that as it may, there were reasonable concerns over the 'consent clause' in the Land Acquisition Act as some state governments have complained to the Centre that acquiring land from farmers for industrialisation was becoming extremely difficult for them. Some NGOs and farmers' associations have also voiced fears on the plight of farmers.

The Modi government's decision to allow the Second Ordinance on the Land Acquisition Act to lapse on 31 August 2015, notwithstanding its commitment to amend it during the 2014 Lok Sabha election, needs to be viewed in the light of the Prime Minister's line of thinking that there was no point in pursuing a piece of legislation amid the Opposition's hue and cry over the issue. Apparently, the decision was based on the NITI Aayog's recommendation that the matter of enacting a law on land acquisition should be left to the discretion of the state governments since the subject is in the Concurrent List.

Even though the Modi government was interested to go ahead with its amendments, it would not have succeeded because of lack of numbers in the Rajya Sabha. It also felt it was politically prudent to allow the Ordinance to lapse and restore the status quo in the context of the Bihar Assembly elections. (It is a different story that the BJP lost the elections in Bihar.) For one thing, the Modi government felt that its first mission was to assuage the feelings of farmers in all states and win their hearts amid the hostile campaign by the Opposition led by the Congress. For another, it did not want to give a hand to the Congress to intensify its agitation however unreasonable it may be, against the amendments. The Prime Minister wanted to convince the farmers that he and the government had an 'open mind' on the issue and that it would never hurt the sentiments and interests of the farmers. Subsequently, the government pledged to implement the rules to benefit the farmers for 13 types of land transaction that were exempt under the original 2013 law. These include acquiring land for national highways, metro rails, atomic energy plants, mines, petroleum and mineral pipelines.

Rajasthan Legislation

A discussion on the Land Acquisition Act will remain incomplete without reference to the Rajasthan Land Acquisition Act passed by the state Assembly in September 2014. Development journalists should understand that since the Rajasthan government is a BJP government headed by Vasundhara Raje Scindia, the policymakers involved in the exercise of drafting the amendments to the Central Act took cognisance of the Rajasthan legislation.

The Rajasthan Act is said to be 'business-friendly' and ushers in major reforms in labour laws. With a view to putting investments in the state on the fast track, it overrides the provisions of the central law. The consent clause is one of the two elements the law picks up from the 2013 central legislation, which requires the consent of 80 per cent of the project-affected families for private projects and the consent of 60 per cent for PPP projects (Sethi & Makkar, 2014).

However, where the Rajasthan Act has differed with the Central Act is that it makes exception for all projects that can be called or interpreted as infrastructural projects. In all, the state law defines 25 types of projects as infrastructural projects covering sectors such as roads, power lines, highways, water supply and telecommunication lines.

Interestingly, the state law also includes schools, colleges, hospitals, housing projects, sports, tourism, industrial parks and special economic zones. Indeed, the 25th category in the Rajasthan legislation has been left 'open-ended' so that the state government could classify any other project as an infrastructural project at a later stage at its discretion without inviting trouble under the consent clause.

Equally interesting, the state legislation does away with the need for a SIA and other processes. If reports were to bear scrutiny, the state government will save 18 months on an average in acquiring land as compared to the central law. It has also diluted the compensation and rehabilitation and resettlement package.

The Rajasthan law is also said to be 'draconian' than the 2013 central law. Having derived powers under the Criminal Procedure Code, anyone obstructing a public servant from carrying out his duties of acquiring land will receive a punishment of six-month imprisonment or a fine of up to ₹3 lakh as against the punishment of a month's imprisonment and a fine of ₹500 under the central legislation.

Clearly, the issue of land acquisition is important for development journalists. For instance, a development journalist can take a stand for or against the consent clause that requires 80 per cent consent of the affected families (for private projects) and 70 per cent consent (for PPP projects) before the land is acquired from them. However, the ends of justice will be met only if the development journalist concerned covers the views of all stakeholders—the farmers, the villagers, the officials, the experts and the government. More important, he should also give his own views and suggestions.

Doubtless, legislations such as this are a bonanza for development journalists. The kind of resistance the proposed amendments were facing from the Opposition, the slew of recommendations made by the Revenue Ministers, Jaitley's reference to Chandrababu Naidu's apprehensions and the Rajasthan legislation—each one of them can be an important subject for examination and research by development journalists. Each one of them can be a potential subject for a front-page story, feature, editorial or article.

Farmers' Agitation

The agricultural sector and farmers' issues, particularly after the firing in which six farmers were killed in Mandsaur in Madhya Pradesh on 5 June 2017, are going to be a major challenge for the Modi government in the coming months. To mollify farmers in his state, Madhya Pradesh Chief Minister Shivraj Singh Chouhan announced an unprecedented ₹1 crore relief to the kin of each farmer, allegedly killed in police firing. Farmers in almost every state are demanding loan waiver, though it is bad economics and has a short-term benefit. It is common knowledge Tamil Nadu farmers staged a 40-day protest at New Delhi's Jantar Mantar demanding a better deal for them. It all started with Uttar Pradesh Chief Minister Yogi Adityanath's announcement of loan waiver to farmers in his state. Soon farmers in other states followed suit and demanded similar relief. Maharashtra Chief Minister Devendra Phadnavis announced similar relief though his government is yet to come out with the modalities of relief.

The Government of India needs to make its stand clearer on the issue of loan waiver without yielding to the orchestrated and unreasonable demand by the Opposition. Similarly, a decision on minimum support price (MSP) for farmers, another issue of serious concern, brooks no delay. Interestingly, the BJP had included MSP in its 2014 Lok Sabha election manifesto. Indeed, the M.S. Swaminathan Committee Report, as far back as 2006, had recommended that MSP for crops should be at least 50 per cent more than their cost of production (PRS Legislative Research, 2017). However, in an interview, BJP President Amit Shah said on the eve of the Modi government's three years of completion in office that 'no government can meet the Swaminathan formula for calculating the cost of production' (Munshi, 2017). Several farmers' unions intensified their protests against the Mandsaur incident and demanded loan waiver as well as MSP. The government needs to decide on the two ticklish issues keeping the larger interest of farmers in mind. It cannot afford to dilly dally on the issue anymore as it is bound to have an impact on the Assembly elections in the near future. The Centre should also bestow attention on the various recommendations of the Swaminthan Committee and implement them with a sense of urgency. There is no need to appoint another committee to look into these recommendations.

As agriculture is a critical sector having a bearing on the economy, development journalists have an important role to play in highlighting farmers' distress. Unfortunately, television channels cover this crucial sector only when there is a firing. As far as possible, development journalists should factor in experts' views on such matters in order to infuse a specialist touch to the story or article in question. Reports and articles that include experts' views on the subject will have greater readability and credibility than those that are sketchy. Moreover, the government will attach greater value to experts' opinions and comments published in newspapers and periodicals.

The Pradhan Mantri Jan Dhan Yojana

The Pradhan Mantri Jan Dhan Yojana (PMJDY) continues to hog the limelight. Following the Centre's decision on demonetisation, huge deposits to the tune of crores of rupees in zero-balance accounts have been reported from some parts of the country. This is cause for concern (*Times of India*, 2016). Apparently, some holders of these accounts are being encouraged to receive 'unaccounted money' by some unscrupulous people who, in turn, are trying to convince them to make best use of these deposits in clearing loans and repaying them after six months or so with or without commission (Dev & Dubey, 2016).

The same report, quoting Pankaj Saxena, a bank manager, says that 40 per cent of commercial banks in Agra District of Uttar Pradesh consist of three banks—the State Bank of India, Canara Bank and Gramin Bank. In all, 75 per cent of Jan Dhan accounts in general and 1.7 lakh Jan Dhan accounts in particular in these banks have seen 'abnormal transactions' since 9 November 2016 (Dev & Dubey, 2016).

Some unscrupulous people and middlemen are particularly targeting farmers who are holders of Kisan Credit Cards and had borrowed loans from banks. They are being offered the invalid currency to pay their crop loans. The Government of India stepped in and acted in time. It has introduced three measures to prevent its misuse. These are, namely, a withdrawal limit of ₹10,000 per month after duly ascertaining the genuineness of such withdrawal, a deposit limit of ₹50,000 and making these accounts Aadhar-linked. Moreover, taking the Reserve Bank of India's observations seriously, the Centre has ordered a probe on the 'sudden influx' in Jan Dhan accounts. In view of attempts by some people to give respectability to demonetised notes and sabotage the scheme to check black money, the media have the responsibility to do special stories to ferret out the truth. As the general public has evinced interest in the scheme following demonetisation, the PMJDY deserves adequate coverage. If implemented properly and effectively, this 'blockbuster' social uplift scheme is expected to ameliorate the condition of poor people by bringing them into the financial mainstream and freeing them from the clutches of rapacious moneylenders.

The PMJDY is aimed at checking corruption. The programme will 'break the vicious cycle of poverty and debt and boost the economy', the Prime Minister has said (*Economic Times*, 2014). Encouraged by the success on Day 1, he had shortened the time for achieving the 7.5 crore new accounts to five months from six. His direction to the Finance Ministry to complete the task by 26 January 2015 worked wonders. By opening 11.5 crore new accounts in a very short span, the scheme has achieved a coverage of 99.74 per cent of all households in the country (*Times of India*, 2015). According to the Union Finance Ministry, in September 2014 itself, 40 million or 4 crore bank accounts have been opened under this scheme (pmjandhanyojana.co.in, 2016).

It is a unique scheme because the Centre has topped up each account with a life insurance cover of ₹30,000 adding to the ₹1 lakh accidental insurance benefit already available under the account that will come bundled with a Ru-Pay-enabled debit card. While all banks have completed the work by 26 January 2015, they have also assured that the account holder, after six months of satisfactory operations, would be eligible for ₹5,000 overdraft facility. Subsequently, these account holders also became eligible for sanction of micro pensions (*Economic Times*, 2014).

Significantly, Arun Jaitley said in his Budget speech that the government would move from Jan Dhan (financial inclusion) to Jan Suraksha (social security). He announced half a dozen social security schemes that would lead to a universal social security scheme. These schemes such as the Pradhan Mantri Suraksha Bima Yojana, the Atal Pension Yojana, the Pradhan Mantri Jeevan Jyoti Bima Yojana were also rolled out on the platform of the Jan Dhan Yojana under which 12.5 crore bank accounts have been opened up. Jaitley said the government will utilise the vast postal network with 154,000 points of presence spread across the villages to help the beneficiaries (Sharma, 2015).

While lauding the Jan Dhan scheme for the new government's initiative, the media should not overlook the fears expressed in some quarters. And it is here that development journalists should step in and do careful study of how the scheme is being implemented on the ground and do appropriate follow-ups. Former Reserve Bank of India Governor Raghuram Rajan said: 'We need to make sure that the scheme does not go off track. The target is universality, not just speed or numbers. We need everybody in the system' (Ghunawat, 2014). He said the system would go waste if we generated a system of 'duplicate accounts' like the same people already having accounts opening new accounts. The scheme would not serve the intended purpose if some others, instead of the genuine 75 million households, got accounts, he warned (Ghunawat, 2014).

Interestingly, the media, too, raised similar fears after the scheme was launched on 28 August 2014. Ray, for instance, feared that some beneficiaries who enrolled under the PMJDY 'may have accounts elsewhere and could have been persuaded to open new ones because of the attached insurance cover' (Ray, 2014). This makes it imperative for the officials of the respective banks to do comprehensive screening of the account holders so that only the right ones get the benefit. If there is no proper screening, the whole purpose of helping the poorest of the poor will be defeated.

Meanwhile, in its eagerness to push through its financial inclusion plan, the Modi government has finalised the life insurance cover to be provided to the beneficiaries under this scheme. Significantly, contrary to expectations, the insurance cover has several riders, implying that not all those who have opened an account under the scheme would be eligible for life insurance (Surabhi, 2014).

According to the guidelines, for starters, the ₹30,000-life insurance cover would be limited to just one account holder per family. The person should normally be the head of the family or an earning member of the family and should be in the age group of 18–59. While the beneficiary will have to exit the life insurance scheme at the age of 60 years, the cover is available at present only for a period of five years till 2019–2020 after which the government will review.

The guidelines also mention that the life insurance would be available only to those people opening a bank account for the first time between 15 August 2014 and 26 January 2015. To ensure that the scheme helps the deserving lot, the Centre has excluded various categories of people from the scheme. These include central and state government employees, people whose income is taxable under the Income-Tax Act 1961 or TDS is being deducted from the income and their families. These guidelines need to be given adequate publicity in the media in public interest. However, more than the guidelines, what is important for development journalists would be to investigate how this scheme is working on the ground and whether it would really make any practical difference to their quality of life.

Interestingly, in response to a Right to Information (RTI) query on the status of the scheme, the data provided by the Department of Financial Services, Government of India, to the effect that 75 per cent accounts opened under the PMJDY have 'zero balance' have created a flutter in November 2014 (Pandathil, 2014). Moreover, according to the data available on the PMJDY website, as on 13 November 2014, banks have opened 7.25 crore accounts with a balance of ₹5,611.2 crore. Of these, about 5.48 crore accounts or 75 per cent have zero balance.

The media cannot afford to miss such reports in the interest of fair and responsible journalism. If most accounts have a zero balance, how will the scheme help the needy and deserving? How many of them will get the promised insurance cover and overdraft facility? Questions are bound to be raised on the efficacy and utility of the scheme if most account holders have a zero balance. See Table 21.2 for the status of the scheme as on 30 November 2016. Table 21.3 is equally significant. It gives the latest information on the total number of beneficiaries in various categories of banks and, more important, the balance in beneficiary

Table 21.2

Progress report of accounts opened under the *Pradhan Mantri Jan Dhan Yojana* as on 30 November 2016 (all figures in crores)

Bank Categories	Rural	Urban	Total	No. of Rupay Cards	Aadhar Seeded	Balance in Accounts	% of Zero-Balance Accounts
Public sector banks	11.44	9.07	20.51	15.60	11.51	57,939.75	22.93
Regional rural banks	3.79	0.62	4.41	2.95	2.07	13,682.12	20.10
Private banks	0.52	0.34	0.86	0.81	0.37	2,699.69	34.92
Total	15.75	10.03	25.78	19.36	13.95	74,321.55	22.85

Source: www.pmjdy.gov.in/account

accounts. The information in Tables 21.2 and 21.3, according to the Government of India, is based upon the data as submitted by different banks.

The Sansad Adarsh Gram Yojana

The Sansad Adarsh Gram Yojana (SAGY) was launched by Prime Minister Modi on 11 October 2014. Under this scheme, every Member of Parliament (MP) would adopt a gram panchayat and develop it as a model for other villages. While Lok Sabha MPs can adopt a panchayat within their constituencies, Rajya Sabha can adopt any panchayat in the state they represent. According to the guidelines, for inclusion under the scheme, a village must have a population of between 3,000 and 5,000 in the plains and between 1,000 and 3,000 in hilly areas.

It is a boon for development journalists because it covers a myriad of areas—agriculture, health, education, sanitation, environment and livelihood. More to the point, the panchayats selected under this scheme will get priority for developing infrastructure under existing schemes such as the National Rural Health Mission, the Sarva Shiksha Abhiyan, the MGNREGA and the Integrated Child Development Programme.

The plan envisages a model village with schools that have toilets, computers, libraries and laboratories; basic health facilities for complete immunisation, gym and yoga centres; household toilets for all; and facilities for solid and liquid waste management. Health volunteers would visit every house to promote personal hygiene. The panchayats will hold meetings on issues related to development, women and children. They can also organise functions to felicitate achievers and village elders. The Prime Minister sought to expand the scope of the scheme to the states by saying that the state governments could emulate the programme by asking each Member of Legislative Assembly (MLA) to adopt a panchayat.

Experts have stressed the need for effective coordination between multiple agencies for the success of this scheme. Undoubtedly, if there is no proper coordination, especially between the Centre and the state, a scheme of this nature and scope, far from serving the intended purpose, will not succeed. Significantly, the Prime Minister has said that SAGY would aim at a 'bottom-to-top approach', adding that the scheme would be 'demand-driven, not supply-driven'. As he has focussed on location-specific development under this scheme, development journalists get an opportunity to closely monitor the implementation of the scheme at various stages of execution and to what extent it has helped in the socio-economic transformation of the villagers concerned.

Table 21.3

Progress report of accounts opened under the Pradhan Mantri Jan Dhan Yojana as on 7 June 2017 (all figures in crores)

Bank Categories	Total Beneficiaries	Beneficiaries at Rural/Semi-urban Centre Bank Branches	Beneficiaries at Urban/Metro Centre Bank Branches	No. of Rupay Cards	Balance in Beneficiary Accounts
Public sector banks	23.19	12.67	10.52	17.9	50,777.34
Regional rural banks	4.70	3.99	0.70	3.54	11,679.33
Private banks	0.92	0.56	0.37	0.85	2,092.49
Total	28.81	17.22	11.59	22.29	64,549.16

Source: www.pmjdy.gov.in/account

The Prime Minister has said that every MP should adopt one village each by 2016 and another two by 2019. They should focus on providing modern and better services and infrastructure. 'We are nearly 800 MPs. If before 2019 we develop three villages each, we reach nearly 2,500 villages. If in the light of this scheme, the states also introduce a similar scheme for MLAs, then 6,000–7,000 more villages can be added,' Modi said (ndtv.com, 2014a; also see ndtv.com, 2014b, 2015).

The Prime Minister has adopted Jayapur village in the Rohania Assembly segment of his Varanasi Lok Sabha constituency. In 2002, the Rashtriya Swayamsevak Sangh adopted this village under the Ideal Village Scheme, and focussed on tree plantation and animal husbandry promotion. Modi intends to develop this village further under SAGY.

Arun Jaitley has adopted Karnali Gram Panchayat villages comprising Karnali, Pipaliya, Vadiya and Baglipura. Karnali, known for the ancient Kuber Bhandari temple, has the potential to become a major tourist spot (IBNlive.com, 2014). Congress President Sonia Gandhi has selected Udwa village from Jagatpur block in her Rae Bareli Lok Sabha constituency and Rahul Gandhi has chosen Deeh village in Jagdishpur block in Amethi constituency (*Times of India*, 2014).

Union Minister of State for Commerce Nirmala Sitharaman has chosen two villages in East Godavari district of Andhra Pradesh. Similarly, actress-politician and Lok Sabha MP (Mathura) Hema Malini has adopted Raval village in Uttar Pradesh. Interestingly, she said though people of this village, only 9 km away from Mathura, had been chanting *Radhe Radhe* for decades, they were completely neglected. She said she would develop this village in a manner that it would symbolise women's empowerment. Development work started in this village on 17 November 2014 (Phukan, 2014).

Cricket icon and Rajya Sabha MP (Nominated) Sachin Tendulkar, after a discussion with the Prime Minister, has adopted Puttamraju Kandriga village in Potti Sriramulu of Nellore district in Andhra Pradesh. This village was one of those that were ravaged by the Hudhud cyclone. Sachin Tendulkar has pledged to redevelop the entire village.

Interestingly, five BJP MPs from Maharashtra have adopted 'developed' villages such as Thane, Palghar, Raigad and Konkan under the SAGY, inviting criticism from the Congress. However, these villages are classified as 'urban' and thus disqualified for adoption under the scheme. Subsequently, the Union Ministry of Rural Development advised them to select nearby areas for 'redevelopment'. For instance, when Rahul Shewale, MP (Mumbai South Central), wanted to adopt an area in Pune district under the SAGY on the grounds that it was his native place, the

Ministry politely told him that it did not qualify for development and that he should instead select a village either from Dahanu or Thane in Maharashtra. He has now selected the Gungwada Gram Panchayat in Dahanu village of Thane district. He has approached researchers and scientists from the Bhabha Atomic Research Centre to help him with technical solutions to address the issues in this village (Phadke, 2014). Similarly, Gopal Shetty, MP (Mumbai North), wanted to develop two villages in Vasai. However, the District Collector has requested him to take up Gorhe village for development and he has since accepted the suggestion.

Unfortunately, despite SAGY's positive features, reports suggest that its performance has been unsatisfactory. In a letter to the Prime Minister, Union Rural Development Minister Birender Singh has said that several MPs have complained that they were unable to implement SAGY successfully in the absence of dedicated funding for the scheme. The MPs say, SAGY, at present, 'depends entirely on the convergence of various existing schemes' (Nair, 2016). The Agriculture Minister himself has endorsed the view of these MPs, maintaining that SAGY needs to have separate funding. Though increasing the MP Local Area Development fund could be solution, it was beyond his powers, he said. As an alternative, he has suggested a ministry funding of ₹50 lakh per every Adarsh Gram towards the estimated cost of ₹2 crore to ₹12 crore required for the development of each village under SAGY (Nair, 2016).

Though SAGY has given an opportunity to the MPs to evince interest in the villages and strive for their integrated development, reports are not encouraging. According to the Rural Development Ministry sources, during Phase II of SAGY, only 60 out of 795 MPs have chosen a model village for development. Considering the fact that about 2,200 villages need to be adopted in SAGY's first three phases by 2019, the Prime Minister needs to intervene to rejuvenate the scheme and make it more acceptable for MPs. The deadline for every MP to nominate a village for Phase II has lapsed on 31 January 2016. However, very few Lok Sabha and Rajya Sabha MPs have come forward to adopt villages (Kumar, 2016).

In view of various doubts raised over the success of SAGY as well as the MPs' Local Area Development Scheme (MPLADS), development journalists need to study the implementation of the scheme carefully without being carried away by the official handouts, press releases or statements by ministers. On the whole, issues of poverty, sanitation, disease, illiteracy and social inequality are prevalent in the villages and towns and the media would do well to cover them to improve the quality of life in the countryside.

Beti Bachao, Beti Padhao

The launch of two progressive schemes—Beti Bachao, Beti Padhao and the Sukanya Samridhi Account—by the Prime Minister on 22 January 2015 at Haryana's Panipat is another example of the Centre's concern for the girl child and the decline in child sex ratio (Dhawan, 2015). While the first is aimed at encouraging birth and education of girls and tackling the low child sex ratio of 918 girls for 1,000 boys, the second scheme envisages providing bank accounts to girl children below 10 years with more interest and income tax benefits (Ghosh & Sandhu, 2015).

The Beti Bachao, Beti Padhao scheme is timely because a girl child is still regarded by many families in the countryside as a burden and as a liability. The country may have made rapid advancement in science and technology as also produced brilliant women administrators, politicians, scientists, academics and scholars. Yet, there has been no change in the mindset of some families towards the girl child (Joshi, 2015). This largely explains the skewed sex ratio and disturbing practice like female foeticide. The worst sex ratio in the country is in Haryana's Mahendragarh district where there are only 775 girls per 1,000 boys, according to 2011 Census figures. In all, 12 of its 21 districts are gender-critical. Dozens of villages across Haryana have a child sex ratio of under 600.

True, Haryana's child sex ratio (girls per 1,000 boys in the age group 0–6), though far below the national average of 918 girls per 1,000 boys, has been improving over the last five calendar years. Consider these figures of sex ratio in Haryana during the years mentioned within brackets: 837 (September 2010), 828 (2011), 847 (2012), 864 (2013) and 872 (2014) (Government of Haryana, 2015).

However, according to official figures compiled by the Haryana government in collaboration with the Registrar General and Census Commissioner to the Government of India, Ambala district's progress has taken a sudden downturn.

Until the beginning of 2014, it was improving its sex ratio before it started to plunge. Consider these figures of sex ratio in Ambala district during the period mentioned within brackets: 860 (March 2013), 889 (May 2013), 876 (July 2013), 890 (September 2013), 909 (November 2013), 1,012 (January 2014), 959 (March 2014), 913 (May 2014), 899 (July 2014) and 888 (September 2014).

Not surprisingly, the Prime Minister, while launching the scheme, not only deprecated this but also stressed the need to end this pernicious practice. Maintaining that he had come to Panipat 'like a beggar' and was 'begging for the lives of daughters', he said that a state like Haryana which produced a woman astronaut like Kalpana Chawla, the first woman to have travelled to space, 'other Kalpana Chawlas are killed in the wombs of their mothers' (Ghosh & Sandhu, 2015). According to the action plan of the Beti Bachao, Beti Padhao scheme, it seeks to promote early registration of pregnancy and institutional delivery; ensure panchayats display gudda–guddi board with number of newborn boys and girls every month; hold panchayats responsible for child marriage; and create parliamentary forum of MPs representing 100 districts.

Experts say, strict enforcement of the Pre-Conception and Pre-Natal Diagnostic Techniques (PC-PNDT) Act and surveillance of pregnant women and dodgy doctors may improve the child sex ratio to some extent. However, for a long-term solution, root causes of the menace such as dowry, female foeticide and crimes against women will have to be eliminated with a sense of urgency.

It augurs well for Haryana that the latest figures show a negation of the skewed sex ratio in the state—a fact which has been duly acknowledged by the Centre. For the first time in 10 years, the girls' number in the state has crossed the 900-mark. How did Haryana's sex ratio improve after a decade? Several factors are responsible for the upward trend. These include, among others, affirmative action and mid-term correction; strict enforcement of regulatory measures; and increasing cases against illegal sale of medical termination of pregnancy kits (Dayal, 2016).

In Maharashtra, District Collectors have been given strict guidelines to improve the sex ratio at birth (SRB) in 10 gender-critical districts in the state at least by 10 points every year. The 10 districts are: Beed, Jalna, Jalgaon, Ahmednagar, Aurangabad, Buldhana, Washim, Osmanabad, Kolhapur and Sangli. Beed in Marathwada region is notorious for female foeticide. The child sex ratio in Beed district has plummeted alarmingly to 807 girls per 1,000 boys. After the district administration strictly enforced the PC-PNDT Act, the figures gradually climbed to 858 girls per 1,000 boys. The guidelines to improve the gender gap include improving nutrition for the girl child and reducing the number of underweight and anaemic girls below five years of age (Mascarenhas, 2015).

Under the Sukanya Samridhi Account, launched by the Prime Minister, an account is opened in girl child's name any time before she attains the age of 10. While minimum deposit required is ₹1,000, any amount in multiple of ₹100s can be deposited subsequently up to a maximum of ₹1.5 lakh in a year. The Centre will provide a monthly rate of interest of 9.1 per cent for the savings account. Interestingly, no income tax will be charged. While 50 per cent money can be withdrawn by the girl child after 18 years, the account will remain operative till the girl attains the age of 21 years. This campaign is being initially implemented in 100 districts, including 12 in Haryana, of the country where the sex ratio is very poor.

Smart Cities

The Centre's Smart City Mission to develop facilities in 100 select cities has been hogging the limelight for quite some time. It has announced 90 cities to be developed as smart cities. On 28 January 2016, it announced the inclusion of the first 20 cities in Phase I of the mission. These are, Bhubaneswar, Pune, Jaipur, Surat, Kochi, Ahmedabad, Jabalpur, Visakhapatnam, Solapur, Davangere, Indore, the New Delhi area, Coimbatore, Kakinada, Belgaum, Udaipur, Guwahati, Chennai, Ludhiana and Bhopal. These cities were selected from a list of 97 city plans submitted by states during a competition held in December 2015.

On 25 May 2016, the Centre added 13 more cities in Phase I of the mission. These are, Warangal (Telangana), Dharmashala (Himachal Pradesh), Chandigarh, Raipur, New Town Kolkata, Bhagalpur (Bihar), Panaji, Port Blair, Imphal, Ranchi, Agartala and Faridabad (Haryana).

On 20 September 2016, the Centre added 27 cities to the Smart City Mission. These are Agra, Ajmer, Amritsar, Aurangabad, Gwalior, Hubli-Dharwad, Jalandhar, Kalyan-Dombivili, Kanpur, Kohima, Kota, Madurai, Mangaluru, Nagpur, Namchi, Nashik, Rourkela, Salem, Shivamogga, Thane, Thanjavur, Tirupati, Tumakuru, Ujjain, Vadodara, Varanasi and Vellore. While the first 20 cities had proposed a total investment of ₹50,802 crore, the 13 cities in the second lot have proposed ₹30,229 crore. The third set of cities proposed projects worth ₹66,883 crore under the Smart City Mission.

On 23 June 2017, the Centre announced another set of 30 new cities taking the total number of smart cities announced so far to 90. It has sanctioned ₹57,393 crore for the 30 new cities. Of this, ₹46,879 will be for developing core infrastructure and ₹10,514 crore for technology-based solutions for better governance, smooth service delivery and optimal utilisation of infrastructure. While the Centre is in the process of selecting 10 more new cities under the Smart City Mission, the total budget of the smart city project has risen to ₹2 lakh crore for 90 cities.

These cities were selected on the basis of a set of criteria. These include, among others, implementation of e-governance and an online grievance redressal mechanism; putting all government expenditure online for public; track record of paying timely salary to employees; and track record of urban reforms and citizen participation. Figure 21.1 is a graphic representation of all the essential features of a typical smart city.

According to the United Nations, India will add 404 million people to its cities—which is the equivalent of one Sao Paolo or two Singapores a year for the next 36 years (Menon, 2015). How would India meet the requirements of the increasing population and manage so many cities if it does not provide urban services like education, health care, security and government services without being smart with limited resources?

According to the Draft Concept Note for 'Smart Cities Scheme', the Union Urban Development Ministry dwells on the pillars of institutional infrastructure including governance, physical, social and economic amenities, and how the centre of attention for each of them should be the citizen (*Times of India*, 2015). The Note observes that the first pillar of institutional infrastructure including governance itself has been neglected by successive governments. As the structure in its present form does not focus on citizen participation, the Smart Cities Scheme seeks to rectify the anomaly in a manner that people would get the feel of the ownership of the town or city they live in. Procedures are cumbersome and there is a need to have a second look at them so that citizens are not only involved in the decision-making process but also ensure that they

Figure 21.1
Smart city: Blazing a new trail

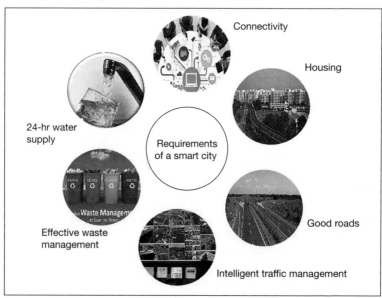

Source: Prepared by author with permitted images from google images.

do not find it difficult to secure the public services they seek. For example, the Ministry notes that when it comes to handling the basic traffic and transportation system, issues of parking arrangements, traffic lights, street lights, and fleet of buses are handled by various departments. It makes the situation more complex for the citizens.

Among the benchmarks for smart cities, besides efficient public transport, water supply, electricity and Wi-Fi connectivity, there is also a need for civic bodies to formulate building and parking standards. Clearly, each benchmark set under the Smart Cities Scheme can be a subject matter for study, scrutiny and analysis by development journalists. Essentially, there are five important benchmarks under the scheme. These are transportation, water supply, solid waste management, sewerage and sanitation and health care facilities. The special components for each one of these benchmarks are as follows:

1. **Transportation:** maximum travel time of 30 minutes in small and medium-size cities and 45 minutes in metropolitan areas; continuous unobstructed footpath of 2-m width; dedicated and physically segregated bicycle tracks; high quality and high frequency.
2. **Water supply:** 24×7 supply of water; 100 per cent household with direct water supply connections; 100 per cent metering of water connections; and 100 per cent efficiency in collection of water tariff.
3. **Solid waste management:** 100 per cent households covered by daily door-step collection system; 100 per cent collection of municipal solid waste; 100 per cent segregation of waste at source; and 100 per cent recycling of solid waste.
4. **Sewerage and sanitation:** 100 per cent households should have access to toilets and be connected to the waste water network.
5. **Health care facilities:** Availability of telemedicine facilities to 100 per cent residents; 30 minutes emergency response time; one dispensary for every 15,000 residents.

Prime Minister Narendra Modi has laid down norms for his ambitious project, some of which were discussed at a national conference of State Urban Development Secretaries in January 2015. Mr Modi wants the designated bodies to take up 'doable items' and inculcate 'smart solutions' rather than take up a 'mega wish list' as envisaged in the Draft Concept Note (*Times of India*, 2015). Some state governments have earlier pointed out to the Union Government that urban local bodies (ULBs) should not be made to understand and implement all tasks such as Information Technology-based solutions, 24×7 power and water supply, total sanitation, quality public transport and effective waste management at one go since they lack the capacity to implement (Dash, 2015). The Prime Minister is believed to have advised the officials concerned that 'doable initiatives will build confidence of municipal bodies and will encourage and enable them to take up more such initiatives' (*Times of India*, 2015).

The issue in question is to what extent the mission would succeed. The idea of covering at least one city from each state under the mission is good. A special purpose vehicle (SPV) is envisaged for each city to implement the plan. Though the ULB, the state government and the Centre will sign the SPV, it is not yet clear to what extent the Centre will assist the project. This is particularly true in the case of ULBs which do not generate enough resources on their own for various reasons. These are some of the issues which development journalists need to examine. They should do proper research and get to the roots of the problem. This is the way by which the media can bring the issue to the attention of the government and the people who matter for timely course corrections.

In an accompanying article, Dr Yogesh Patil and his team of researchers comprising Sneha Kumari and Gahana Gopal examine the question of environment and sustainability with special reference to the Smart City Mission and the expectations from the media in this context.

Debate over the futility over this ambitious project in the name of overall development of cities and towns is out of sync with the present times. If the media is satisfied that the government—whether at the Centre or in the states—has initiated a worthwhile programme, one which is aimed at improving the quality of life and keeping pace with the changing times, the media should do fair, objective and dispassionate reporting without taking an adversarial role. Suffice it to say that the media cannot indulge in partisan politics if they are to fulfil their role as an agent of social change and development.

Smart Villages

Interestingly, Andhra Pradesh Chief Minister Chandrababu Naidu has come forward with his own scheme to foster villages in the state under a new banner—Smart Villages. While putting in place a plan for developing smart cities in consonance with the central scheme, the SAGY, Mr Naidu wants to develop villages in his own way, which, according to him, have been reduced to the status of 'old age homes'.

More important, there is a conceptual difference between the Prime Minister's model of developing small villages under the SAGY and

Mr Chandrababu Naidu's programme. Adoption of villages by the MPs is the main component of the SAGY. However, in Andhra Pradesh, the government will rope in corporate houses and philanthropists to make the villages 'smart'. The Andhra Pradesh programme is aimed at stopping migration of workers to far off places for livelihood, checking suicides and improving livelihood options in the villages (*Times of India*, 2014).

The Smart Village Scheme will focus on, among other things, construction of latrines, strengthening the rural health system, reducing the dropout rate in schools to zero, reducing infant mortality rate, providing safe drinking water, providing employment by imparting suitable skill development to harness the local resources, improving road connectivity, extending special help for rural artisans, encouraging folk arts, and eradication of child labour and child marriages.

The first phase of the programme began on 1 January 2015. In all, 309 villages with a population of above 10,000 have been included in the programme. There are 16,883 villages spread across the 670 Mandals in Andhra Pradesh. The Chief Minister held a meeting with senior officials to discuss the contours of the new scheme. The officials and the staff will be trained in a series of workshops to get familiar with the Smart Village concept. The programme would have two strands—one continuous and the other seasonal which would be confined to activities such as rainwater harvesting and addressing the school dropout issue and other farm-related works.

Swachh Bharat Abhiyan

The Prime Minister's Swachh Bharat Abhiyan (SBA), launched on 2 October 2014, received adequate coverage in the media—print and electronic. The Clean India campaign is bound to be in the limelight for quite some time, particularly because of the kind of people it is attracting. However, to be fair, this scheme should look beyond photo opportunities. The real challenge before the government is to sustain it. The government's pledge to remain committed towards cleanliness and devote time for this will have to be honoured by one and all on a daily basis.

There is no doubt that the media has got an opportunity to spread awareness among people on cleanliness. To begin with, newspapers would do well to cover different areas in a town or city and report, with an illustration or two, on how the civic/municipal authorities are keeping the roads and streets neat and clean.

Garbage disposal in big cities and towns has become a big menace and overflowing garbage bins are a poor reflection on the lack of civic awareness on the part of the citizens.

The media may have been justified in covering the controversy surrounding Congress MP Shashi Tharoor following his acceptance of the Prime Minister's invitation and pledge to commit himself to Clean India. However, while doing so, it would do well to focus on the scheme rather than deflecting public attention from it. It is not important what programmes did successive governments launch earlier. What is of utmost importance for the media is to examine how the government is implementing it on the ground.

The government announced in October 2014 that it would spend ₹2 lakh crore on building more than 111 million toilets. It had invited contributions to a new Swachh Bharat Kosh (Clean India Fund). Giving an account of its progress, while presenting the Union Budget in Parliament on 28 February 2015, Arun Jaitley said that the government is committed to build six crore toilets in the country. Expressing satisfaction over the record of progress, he said that 50 lakh toilets have already been constructed during 2014–2015. However, Swachh Bharat is not only a programme of hygiene and cleanliness but, at a deeper level, a programme for preventive health care, and building awareness, he said, calling it a 'game changer' which has been transformed into a 'movement' (*Economic Times*, 2015).

Jaitley has also introduced Swachh Bharat Cess at a rate of 2 per cent or less on all or certain services. Donations made to the Swachh Bharat Mission and Clean Ganga Fund are eligible for deduction under the Income Tax Act. However, the contribution to Swachh Bharat Kosh as part of the corporate social responsibility activities by companies is not entitled to tax exemptions.

The media would do well to focus on this and other areas such as garbage disposal, sewage clearance and solid waste management so that it will truly help develop the neglected villages. In view of its importance, the media would do well to keep politics off this scheme.

Development journalists should specifically monitor how the municipal authorities are measuring up to the task. Monitoring is virtually non-existent. Unfortunately, no civic authority monitors the system of daily garbage clearance. The result: overflowing garbage bins in cities and towns and throwing of garbage and kitchen waste on the roads as a daily habit. This is in sharp contrast to the system that obtains in foreign countries. Let us not speak of the systems in vogue in developed countries such as the USA or the UK. They are far more advanced than those in countries such as China and South Africa.

This writer was amazed to see the regular and methodical manner in which garbage was lifted by the municipal staff in Cape Town (South Africa), Chengdu (China) and Bandung (Indonesia). Inquiries revealed that it is the responsibility of the respective apartment welfare associations (in residential areas) and heads of departments (government/ private office buildings) to ensure that the garbage, neatly packed, is kept at the designated places before 8 AM every day, well before the arrival of the corporation vehicles. Why cannot India emulate these best practices? No excuses, please. If the Chief Secretary (in the case of the Secretariat building) or the Police Commissioner (in the case of the Police Commissionerate) is made accountable for lapses on the part of his staff for daily garbage clearance, it will work wonders. Here is a rider. The municipal authorities cannot abdicate responsibility even if the work of garbage clearance is handed over to private contractors or agencies.

Though it is considered rude to spit in public in many countries, India seems to be an exception. Even state guest houses are not free of this malaise. This writer was surprised to see how *paan*-chewers have stained the staircases of Uttar Pradesh government's State Guest House in Lucknow despite warning boards here and there.

The state of other government buildings is far worse. Walk into any government building like the Road Transport Office in Pune, Pimpri-Chinchwad, or a District Hospital at Rayagada or Berhampur in Odisha. Shockingly, shabby walls, broken furniture in staircase corners and corridors, and old files and records will greet the visitors to most government offices. The situation may have improved in Delhi after the SBA was launched by the Prime Minister and the proactive role played by Union Ministers and Secretaries to the Government of India. But why confine media coverage to offices in Lutyen's Delhi and other metros alone? To begin with, let newspapers (and television channels) start a campaign on the poor maintenance of government buildings in all sub-divisions, collectorates and hospitals. The situation will, certainly, change for the better.

Water ATMs

Development journalism covers a vast area. For a comprehensive coverage, the media must not confine themselves to major subjects dealing with Five-Year Plans, plan allocation, Centre–state relations and constitutional imperatives. Any subject that affects the community or the common man can be picked up for scrutiny, analysis and coverage. The media should give some positive strokes, too. For instance, there was an interesting piece of news in August: villagers in a water-starved Rajasthan hamlet rejoiced when they got 20 litres of potable water for ₹5 through water ATMs (India Abroad News Service, 2014). Under Cairn India's Jeevan Amrit Project, kiosks with reverse osmosis (RO) plants have been installed to provide safe drinking water in Bhakarpur, Kawas, Guda, Jogasar, Aakdada and Baytu to help as many as 22,000 people. Admittedly, it is a good PPP model in which Cairn India has joined the Rajasthan government's Public Health Engineering Department, Tata Projects and village panchayats of the respective beneficiary villages to supply drinking water to people.

Rajasthan is known for erratic rainfall and large variation in its distribution pattern. The average annual rainfall ranges between 100 mm in Jaisalmer and 800 mm in Jhalawar. Not surprisingly, the water ATMs have come as a boon to the villagers. Reports suggest that they are becoming popular day by day and more and more people are purchasing the smart cards to avail themselves of the benefit. A significant development in this context is the report that the number of water-borne diseases such as diarrhoea in children and cases of joint pain caused by high fluoride content in drinking water have come down (India Abroad News Service, 2014).

SIMC Study

Encouragingly, SIMC, Lavale, Pune, has taken the initiative to train budding journalists on development journalism through rural survey projects and RTI. This programme was spearheaded by the late Dr Dileep Padgaonkar, former Editor of the *Times of India*, and R.K. Laxman Chair Professor in the Faculty of Media, Communication and Design, Symbiosis International University. A first of its kind in the country, this project is unique and significant for the simple reason that media houses seem reluctant to spend money to cover the developments in the countryside.

Dr Padgaonkar was of the opinion that the media was yet to grasp the fact that the Big India Story was being scripted in the countryside. The rural areas attract attention only during elections or when natural or man-made calamities overwhelm the population. As attempts to understand and appreciate the trends and processes shaping rural India are few and far between, SIMC has taken up the task of developing skills journalists need to track the changes occurring in villages. These skills involve an intimate knowledge of local economic and social structures, local cultures and religious beliefs, local needs and aspirations.

Students of SIMC's Journalism Department visit villages in Maharashtra from time to time and file reports on the socio-economic changes affecting the population. They meet the villagers, politicians, teachers and officials and gain hands-on experience on the state of affairs in the villages and the status of various developmental schemes meant for the villages. The reports, brought out in in-house periodical, *Ink*, and a special volume, cover a wide range of issues such as the plight of sugarcane cutters, the lack of facilities in schools, the link between the midday meal scheme and declining dropout rate in schools, the condition of farmers, the living conditions of workers and health care. The essence of these reports is not only to pinpoint functional drawbacks or inadequacies in the system but to help rectify them so that the villagers would be able to lead a hassle-free life. Remarkably, the reports, written without prejudices or ideological biases, present a picture that is refreshingly different from the sort of news reports that feature in the columns of newspapers, periodicals and on television channels (Anand, 2014).

Right to Information

Significantly, students of SIMC make best use of the RTI for seeking information from the government. SIMC and other constituent schools—Symbiosis Law School and Symbiosis School of Economics—file RTI petitions in the Pune Municipal Corporation and offices of the Maharashtra government to know about the execution of various developmental programmes in cities, towns and villages.

They are trained by eminent social activists such as Aruna Roy, Nikhil Dey and Vinita Deshmukh and former Central Information Commissioners Wajahat Habibullah and Deepak Kapoor on how to file RTI petitions and elicit response from the government. As part of the R.K. Laxman Chair Initiatives, a seminar on RTI is organised every year at Symbiosis International University. This seminar is used to inculcate the RTI spirit in the students. Having been aware that the RTI has sometimes been misused to settle business, political or other scores, SIMC students participate in thorough discussion on such misuse. Sadly, the RTI has seldom been used for good purposes.

Thanks to RTI activists, dozens of instances of lack of probity in public servants have been brought to the notice of the public at large. The courts have taken swift cognisance of such instances. Charges have been filed, trial conducted and judgements passed with commendable speed. Such activism has not been without its dangers. RTI activists have been subjected to intense pressure and on occasion even killed. This testifies the huge potential of RTI to reform the system of governance to make it transparent, accountable and efficient. SIMC focusses on the RTI to better understand the legal and procedural issues involved in procuring information from officialdom in order to highlight issues that affect the community and society.

SIMC students do not wish to spread themselves too thin. Attention is riveted on how journalists can use RTI to improve civic amenities. This includes infrastructure as well as services: condition of civic infrastructure, services such as power supply and health care and the conditions of public buildings.

Writing Skills

Writing development stories calls for specialised skills. In development journalism, one cannot afford to do uneven reports. A development journalist ought to be free and frank in his opinion. He/she should write with utmost sense of responsibility.

Such reports should also be refined to the core. As officials always toe the government line, journalists should ask questions very carefully and be extremely sceptical of what they hear from them. Moreover, questioning alone won't do. The journalist should always do proper research to get to the root of the problem without resorting to shortcuts.

The beauty of a development story lies in its specificity. If a journalist is specific and focussed throughout, the story will grip the attention of readers from the beginning to the end. Plain editorialising won't do. A development story must be dramatic enough to pinpoint things.

Sometimes, journalists collect more data than required for a particular story. In that case, they need to make the best use of the available data for doing more stories replete with major and minor problems and grievances. True, these stories will be appreciated for their comprehensive coverage and worth. But then, reports of this nature will have to be structured more professionally.

Data collection is only one part of the duty of a development journalist. A lot of attention needs to be given to writing the story effectively by collating the data in an organised manner.

Development journalists could choose some villages around their area, subdivision or district and follow developments there over a period, jot down various developments in governance, economy and reforms through field visits, analyse and report them from time to time for whichever slot the Editor of a publication may deem fit.

Development journalism is people-centric and hence an important tool in the hands of journalists for ushering in socio-economic change.

While journalists are welcome to do critical appreciation of any story in the countryside, town or city, the media, as a whole, should not play an adversarial role. It ought to play a friendly and cooperative role in tasks of nation building even while criticising the government for failures or lapses, if any. Otherwise, it will miss the wood for the trees. While the government of the day at the Centre and in the states, which enjoy the trust and confidence of the people for a five-year term, needs to be given an opportunity to function in accordance with the provisions of the Constitution, the media should not lag behind in their mandated task of pinpointing the lapses of the government and stemming the rot in the public interest.

References

Anand, V. Eshwar. (1985a, 15 May). States of the Union: Building cooperative federalism. *The Statesman*, Calcutta.

Anand, V. Eshwar. (1985b, 19 December). Poverty and development: Alternatives to centralisation. *The Statesman*.

Anand, V. Eshwar. (2014). *Development journalism: A catalyst for positive change.* Revised paper presented at IRC-2013: International Relations Conference on India and Development Partnerships in Asia and Africa: Towards a New Paradigm, Symbiosis International University, Pune, India, in collaboration with the Policy Planning Division, Ministry of External Affairs, Government of India, (14–15 December 2013); *Procedia—Social and Behavioral Sciences*, 157(24 November), 210–225.

Bhan, Shereen. (2017, 29 August). Creation of jobs which pay good wages is priority No. 1: Panagariya. *Mint*.

Business Standard. (2015, 1 March). Arun Jaitley's interview with Lok Sabha television on the Union budget. *Business Standard*.

Business Standard. (2015, 1 March). States empowered with additional funds. *Business Standard*.

Chidambaram, P. (2015, 1 March). Fourteenth Finance Commission: Generous to a fault—across the aisle. *The Sunday Express*, Pune.

Chopra, Ritika. (2017, 2 September). Change laws that curb foreign investment in education: NITI Aayog. *The Indian Express*.

counterview.org. (2014, 2 August). Gujarat civil society protests move to drop provisions related with consent and social impact assessment while acquiring land. Retrieved 1 October 2014, from http://counterview.org/2014/08/02/gujarat-civil-society-protests-move-to-drop-provisions-related-with-consent-and-social-impact-assessment-while-acquiring-land

Dash, Dipak. (2015, 26 January). PM wants 'smart cities' to take up doable items. *The Times of India*.

Dayal, Sakshi. (2016, 2 November). Haryana gets PM pat for negating skewed sex ratio. *The Times of India*, p. 6.

Debroy, Bibek. (2012). *Gujarat: Governance for growth and development*. New Delhi: Academic Foundation, p. 33.

Dev, Aditya, & Dubey, Yogesh (2016, 13 November). 'Dead' Jan Dhan accounts get richer by ₹170 cr. *The Times of India*.

Dhawan, Himanshi. (2015, 23 January). 2 schemes launched to give girls fair deal. *The Times of India*.

Ghosh, Abantika, & Sandhu, Khushboo. (2015, 23 January). We are worse than 18th century: PM on foeticide. *The Indian Express*.

Ghunawat, Virendrasingh. (2014, 15 September). What Raghuram Rajan fears is the duplication of accounts and their usage. *India Today*, Mumbai.

Government of Haryana. (2015). *Child sex ratio figures*. Chandigarh: Government of Haryana.

Government of India. (2010). Report of the commission on Centre–State relations. Retrieved 1 September 2016, from http://interstatecouncil.nic.in/volume1.pdf

Headlines Today. (2015, 26 February). *Headlines Today*.

IBNlive.com. (2014). Jaitley to visit Karnali village in Gujarat. Retrieved 15 January 2018 from http://www.business-standard.com/article/pti-stories/arun-jaitley-to-visit-karnali-village-in-gujarat-115010801159_1.html

India Abroad News Service. (2014, 31 August). *Water ATMs: Villagers rejoice as they get 20 litres of potable water for ₹5*. Noida: IANS.

Joshi, Vishal. (2015, 23 January). Modi calls for putting end to female foeticide. *Hindustan Times*.

Kumar, G. Pramod. (2014, July 15). How Modi's version of Land Acquisition Act will be industry friendly. Retrieved 12 January 2018 from http://www.first-post.com/india/how-modis-version-of-land-acquisition-act-will-be-industry-friendly-1619729.html

Kumar, Prakash. (2017, 6 August). NewsX.

Kumar, Vikram. (2016, 8 February). SAGY loses steam in second phase. *Mail Today*, New Delhi.

Mail Today. (2015, 24 February). Land bill: BJP forms 8-member panel to talk to farmers. Retrieved from https://www.indiatoday.in

Mascarenhas, Anuradha. (2015, 24 January). Collectors in districts with low count of girls told to push them 10 rungs up. *The Indian Express*.

Menon, Anil. (2015, 26 January). Smart Cities are the way ahead for us. *The Times of India*, p.12.

Ministry of Finance. (2016). Presentation of Revenue Secretary to Government of India. Retrieved 11 October 2016, from finmin.nic.in/press/2016 _next step_04082016

Mishra, Asit Ranjan. (2017, 8 February). Modi Govt. begins process to constitute 15th Finance Commission. *Mint*.

Mishra, Asit Ranjan, & Prasad, Gireesh Candra. (2017, 29 August). Regulatory reform fails to cut red tape for businesses in India, says NITI Aayog. *Hindustan Times*.

Munshi, Suhas. (2017, 7 June). The past, present and future of farmers' protest in MP. CNN-News18.

Nair, Shalini. (2016, 9 May). SAGY: Minister seeks PM's intervention to salvage scheme. *The Indian Express*, New Delhi.

ndtv.com. (2014a, 16 October). Sachin Tendulkar adopts village, PM Narendra Modi delighted. Retrieved 4 February 2018 from https://www.ndtv.com/india-news/sachin-tendulkar-adopts-village-pm-narendra-modi-delighted-680200

ndtv.com. (2014b, 10 November).

ndtv.com. (2015, 8 February).

ndtv.com. (2017, 4 May). Economic affairs secretary on GST, digital economy on demonetisation (Interview by Vishnu Som). Retrieved 16 June 2017, from http://www.ndtv.com/video/news/the-buck-stops-here/economic-affairs-secretary-on-gst-digital-economy-and-demonetisation-456303

Outlook. (2015, 28 February). *Outlook.*

Pandathil, Rajesh. (2014, 13 November). 75% of Jan Dhan accounts empty. Retrieved 22 November 2017, from http://www.firstpost.com/business/economy/75-of-jan-dhan-accounts-empty-modis-pet-scheme-may-be-missing-its-objective-1996183.html.

Phadke, Manasi. (2014, 8 December). Confused no more, MPs pick villages to adopt. *The Indian Express*, Pune.

Phukan, Rumani Saikia. (2014, 15 November). Model villages adopted under Modi's SAGY. Retrieved 22 November 2017, from https://www.mapsofindia.com/my-india/society/model-villages-adopted-under-modis-saansad-adarsh-gram-yojana.

Pragativadi. (2014, 8 December). *Pragativadi*, Bhubaneswar (in Odiya).

PRS Legislative Research. (2017). Swaminathan report: National Commission on farmers (2006). Retrieved 17 June 2017, from http://www.prsindia.org/parliamenttrack/report-summaries/swaminathan-report-national-commission-on-farmers-662/

Ramesh, Jairam, & Khan, Muhammed. (2014, 1 August). Give 2013 law a fair chance. *The Indian Express*.

Ray, Atmadip. (2014, 1 September). PM's Jan Dhan Yojana: Fake accounts may cloud the plan. *India Today*.

Roche, Elizabeth. (2014, 10 November). Will take action on reforms with or without political consensus. *Mint.*

Seth, Dilasha. (2017, 9 September). Ministers' panel to resolve GSTN issues: Arun Jaitley. *Business Standard*, Mumbai.

Sethi, Nitin, & Makkar, Sahil. (2014, 15 September). Rajasthan Assembly to push land bill. *Business Standard*, New Delhi.

Shah, Mihir. (2014, 30 August). The 'New' Planning Commission. *Economic and Political Weekly*, 49(35).

Sharma, Yogima Seth. (2014, 28 August). Cabinet Note proposes new identity, role for Planning Commission. *The Economic Times*.

Sharma, Yogima Seth. (2015, 1 March). Jaitley proposes Universal Social Security Scheme, Pension Schemes. *The Economic Times*.

Shekhar, Kumar Shakti. (2015, 27 February). ibnlive.com.

Surabhi. (2014, 14 December). Life insurance cover under Jan Dhan comes with riders. *The Indian Express*, Pune.

Tewari, Ruhi. (2014b, 15 July). Government seeks to make it easier to acquire land. *The Indian Express*, New Delhi.

The Economic Times. (2014, 29 August). PM 'Jan Dhan' Yojana launched; 1.5 crore bank accounts opened in a day. *The Economic Times*.

———. (2015a, 15 January). *The Economic Times*.

———. (2015b, 25 February). States to get higher share of Central taxes. *The Economic Times*.

———. (2015c, 1 March). Six crore toilets and Swachh Bharat Cess. *The Economic Times*.

The Indian Express. (2014, 20 December). Land Acquisition Act needs clarity. *The Indian Express*.

———. (2015a, 26 February). United States of India: Finance Commission award gives meaning to cooperative federalism. *The Indian Express*, editorial.

———. (2015b, 26 February). Finance Commission proposals to empower Centre–State relations. *The Indian Express*.

———. (2015c, 26 February). *The Indian Express*.

The Sunday Times. (2014, 30 November). Land takeover laws flawed, to be revamped: FM. *The Times of India*, p. 12.

The Times of India. (2014a, 14 November). Sonia, Rahul adopt villages under Modi's Model Village Scheme. *The Times of India*.

———. (2014b, 9 December). Plan to change. *The Times of India*, editorial.

———. (2014c, 27 December). Next up: Smart Villages. *The Times of India*, Hyderabad.

———. (2015a, 5 January). Smart Cities Draft Note highlights parking needs. *The Times of India*, Pune.

———. (2015b, 25 January). Next phase of Jan Dhan to offer credit, insurance. *The Times of India*. Also see pmjandhanyojana.co.in.

———. (2016, 13 November). Centre to probe sudden influx in Jan Dhan accounts. *The Times of India*.

———. (2017, 28 August). Let our cities rise: NITI Aayog provides a useful roadmap for reforms and faster urbanisation. *The Times of India*.

Varma, Gyan, & Ranjan, Mishra Asit. (2015, 26 February). Concerns of Andhra Pradesh ignored: TDP. *Mint*.

Zee News. (2015, 27 February). Fourteenth Finance Commission Recommendations a "Loss" for Bihar: Nitish to PM Modi. Retrieved 4 February 2018 from http://zeenews.india.com/news/india/finance-commission-recommendations-loss-for-bihar-nitish-to-pm-modi_1553649.html

22

On the Ecological Footprint: Media and Environment

K. Jayanthi

Issues concerning the environment and ecology will continue to dominate the discourse in the media in the years to come.

The scope of environmental writing in India has widened today to include a multitude of human activities that are harmful to the ecology. People's struggles of the 1970s and 1980s to save forests and natural resources, and campaigns in the subsequent decades against soil and water contamination and air pollution opened new vistas for news writing and offered new perspectives for long-form writing on environmental issues. What journalists lacked by way of insight into a subject that had moved from nature watching to depletion of natural resources to industrial pollution to the thinning of the ozone layer was compensated for by inputs from and, sometimes writings of, conservationists, environmental activists and scientists. This helped put the issues in perspective. Of course, there was always the danger of blurring the lines between journalism and activism while reporting on arguments against consuming nature for man's selfish ends or achieving economic growth without employing sustainable measures to protect the biological diversity of forests and wetlands and the rights of communities that depend on forests for subsistence.

The urban landscape, with issues such as pressures on groundwater use and land for housing, provided a different set of challenges for the metanarrative of development discord. This was evident when torrential rains pounded Mumbai in 2005 and Chennai in 2015: Both the metropolitan cities were victims of years of bad development and encroachments along waterbodies and waterways. In the case of Chennai, the aftermath of the floods of 2015 threw up another important issue—the need for water conservation and management—as the city missed its tryst with the monsoons in 2016. At the global level, Cape Town, South Africa, is already facing a severe water crisis.

Writing on Nature

The 1970s and 1980s were the periods of the dam versus development debate, which was the bedrock of environmental journalism in India. As opposed to this, in the previous decades, writing on nature consisted of articles based on keen observation of the megafauna, birds and other wildlife, written by naturalists and conservationists, such as M. Krishnan for the *Statesman* and Zafar Futehally for the *Times of India* and *Deccan Herald*. Such stories were often relegated to the magazine or feature sections of newspapers. But the readership they generated and the awareness they spread about wildlife and conservation were significant.

An article written in 1930 (reprinted in 2008), by the ornithologist Salim Ali, describing the breeding season of insectivorous birds in the monsoon season and 'the caterpillars which also appear at this time in devastating hordes', underlines the built-in checks and balances present in nature:

> Thus, it is that Providence had devised the most efficient automatic control agencies. Were it not for the check exercised by man's feathered friends at this crucial period, a time would soon come when not only crops but all vegetation would cease to be. Such is the astounding rate at which insects multiply that no power of man's invention alone would ever be capable of stemming the overwhelming tide of their numbers. (Ali, 2008)

Man's use of synthetic chemicals to wage a war against worms and insects was eloquently questioned by the American biologist Rachel Carson in *Silent spring* (1962). The work inspired the environmental movement through the concerns it raised about the huge human and environmental costs of the indiscriminate use of pesticides, particularly

DDT. She won her fight against DDT. The pesticide, which was used extensively to control malarial mosquitoes, was banned in the United States. But researchers began to formulate a less toxic but equally effective pesticide for farmers. The American multinational Union Carbide came up with sevin, whose main component was methyl isocyanate, or MIC (Mukherjee, 2002, p. 10).

This deadly liquid added new dimensions to environmental writing in India. In the early hours of 3 December 1984, water leaking into one of the tanks holding liquid MIC in Union Carbide India Limited's pesticide plant near the Bhopal railway station caused pressure and heat to build up. The runaway reaction ejected a safety valve and toxic gas escaped and enveloped vast areas of the city. For thousands of people that night death was immediate. The impact of the gas on the health of the survivors was immense. The closed pesticide plant continues to pose a health risk as remediation efforts have been slow. The last word has still not been written on what is considered the world's worst disaster.

A slew of regulations came into place after the Bhopal gas tragedy: The Environment (Protection) Act, 1986, in accordance with the decisions taken at the 1972 Stockholm Conference of the United Nations to protect and improve the human environment and prevent environment pollution; the Manufacture Storage and Import of Hazardous Chemical Rules, 1989; the Public Liability Insurance Act, 1991; The National Environment Tribunal, 1995; and the Chemical Accidents (Emergency Planning, Preparedness, and Response) Rules, 1996.

The Endosulfan Story

The severe health hazards posed by another insecticide, endosulfan, became visible only over a period of time. For close to 20 years, from the 1980s, the Plantation Corporation of Kerala (PCK) had resorted to indiscriminate aerial spraying of endosulfan over 2,000 hectares of cashew crops under its cultivation in the upper reaches of the hills in Kasaragod district to win its war against the tea mosquito, a pest affecting the yield. The first alarm was raised by a medical doctor practising in the area who noticed 'unusual maladies' in his patients. He shared his suspicion of a connection between repeated exposure to endosulfan and illnesses with the local people (Joshi, 2001). The media and civil society woke up to the health crisis when it became clear that the instances of birth defects, diminished intelligence among children and cerebral palsy were not isolated.

The Supreme Court ordered a ban on aerial spraying of endosulfan in the PCK area in 2001. On 10 January 2017, the court asked the Kerala government to provide compensation to all the victims. Clearly in line with the polluter pays principle, the court asked the state government to 'initiate legal proceedings to recover the compensation money from pesticide companies responsible for the production and sale of the highly controversial but cheap agrochemical' (Rajagopal, 2017).

Giving a slightly different perspective to the issue in *Frontline*, its science correspondent R. Ramachandran posited:

> A plausible explanation for the range of observed health effects in Kasaragod is the indiscriminate aerial spraying of endosulfan. Though risk evaluation of endosulfan is still evolving with better understanding of host interactions, the diverse effects reported in Kasaragod are a great deal beyond the documented effects of acute toxicity.... At present this association is, as the Kerala government report says, at best more by way of elimination of other possible causes. This assumed causal link with endosulfan needs to be established by a properly designed epidemiological study. This, unfortunately, has not happened till date despite media reports that began to surface about a decade ago. (Ramachandran, 2011)

The risk in reporting environmental issues is that there is a tendency to press the panic button. A lack of knowledge of science among most reporters who handle the environment beat and an inability to analyse scientific data are major handicaps to producing informed reports. While on the subject, it would be pertinent to note how a reporter jumped the gun when he stated that 'many parts of the world have fallen prey to this pesticide [endosulfan] that has affected a lot of humans, animals and the environment' (*Hindu*, 2015).

A broad-brush picture of environmental issues will miss the intricacies of the forces at play. An understanding of the policies and regulations concerning the environment is essential for writing a nuanced report. The basic tenet of journalism is to inform, but there is a growing tendency to rush to inform.

Environmentalism

Environmental communication, or environmentalism, plays a significant role in mobilising awareness among those affected by development and industrial activities: forest dwellers to fight for their rights; the dam displaced to fight for resettlement and compensation; villagers to fight against overexploitation of water aquifers by Coca-Cola at its plant in Plachimada, Kerala; townspeople of Tamil Nadu to protest against contamination of groundwater by untreated effluence from tanneries. These public awareness campaigns needed media coverage to get the attention of policymakers.

Environmental activists get media space, which they use effectively for agenda building. The Save Silent Valley campaign was able to spread awareness about the need to conserve the unique biodiversity of Silent Valley, the evergreen forests in Palakkad district of Kerala and a part of the Nilgiri biosphere, and more importantly, its famous inhabitant, the lion-tailed macaque. The Kerala Sashtra Sahitya Parishad helped raise awareness about the impact of deforestation and pollution through folk songs and plays (Gadgil & Guha, 1995).

The Narmada Bachao Andolan, a movement started in 1985 to protest against the construction of dams across the west-flowing Narmada river, organised rallies, marches and 'jal satyagrahas', which involved dam-affected villagers and supporters of the campaign staying immersed in the river water for periods of time.

In the middle of January 2017, Chennai, Tamil Nadu, witnessed a massive mobilisation of people under the 'We do jallikattu' banner through the social media platforms. Although it was not strictly an environmental agitation, it sought to highlight important environmental issues affecting the state—drought, farmer suicides, the Cauvery dispute and sand mining. Beach and river sand mining, granite quarrying from farmland and hillocks and bauxite mining have been rampant in pockets of Tamil Nadu and have wreaked havoc on the ecology (Rajasekharan, 2015).

Urban Environment

Nowhere is the pressure on the environment more evident than in our cities and metropolises, which continue to witness development in the form of road widening and construction of flyovers, metro rails and other structures that showcase a developed urban landscape. The urban biodiversity is under threat with steady contamination of its soil with urban waste and dumping of solid and liquid waste in lakes and swamps (as witnessed in Chennai, for instance) or release of raw sewage into lakes (as in the Bellandur lake in Bengaluru), which has resulted in heavy frothing, dispersal of toxic froth onto roads and residences nearby and occasional fires (Johnson, 2018). Urban waste disposal, water supply, depletion and groundwater and unsuitability of groundwater for human consumption are issues that need the media's attention.

Following the Tamil Nadu government's decision to allow the Kamarajar Port Limited 'to divert 1,000 acres of the hydrologically sensitive Ennore wetlands for industrial installations', the environmental activist Nityanand Jayaraman came up with a unique campaign to inform the public about the role of the wasteland, referred to as poramboke in local parlance, in maintaining Chennai's groundwater aquifers and preserving its topography. A video showing the creek in all its glory and featuring the Magsaysay Award winner and Carnatic musician T.M. Krishna singing the 'Chennai Poramboke Paadal', was released on YouTube. Jayaraman and Krishna followed this up with an article in the *Hindu* asserting the ecological importance of the creek for the city:

> Much of the creek looks dry year-round, when visible waterspread is only 1,000 acres. But when cyclonic weather pushes the sea surging landwards, or when rainwaters from the two rivers come rushing to meet the sea, the waterspread in the creek swells to its majestic fullness. Come rain or storm surge, the availability of room for the rain or sea water to stay is what keeps the city from going under. The creek offers another protection too. It buffers the rich aquifers of the Araniyar-Kosasthalaiyar Basin from the sea, and keeps salt water from invading groundwater resources that supply several hundred million litres daily to Chennai even during the worst droughts. (Jayaraman & Krishna, 2017)

When Arundhati Roy, and later Aamir Khan, joined the anti-Narmada dam agitation, they lent a similar celebrity voice to people's campaign. 'I grew interested in what was happening in the Narmada Valley because almost everyone I spoke to had a passionate opinion based on what seemed to me to be very little information. That interested me too, so much passion in the absence of information,' Arundhati Roy wrote in *Frontline*, using 'the craft and rigour of writing fiction' to narrate the human, social and 'environmental costs' of the dam.

Journalists of a previous generation were constrained by an inability to gather scientific data. Added to this was the scientific community's unwillingness to speak to the media. Today, there is no dearth of information; young scientists are more than willing to share information. Serious environmental writing has become the passion of young journalists. It has also become a fad.

Going Green

One noticeable trend in environmental communication is the green culture that has taken hold of it. The go-green attitude has given rise to a new line of writing, shorn of the language of advocacy of the previous decades. There are as many eco-fashion writers today as there are dedicated environmental journalists. Writings showcasing green styles and trends with a liberal dose of 'eco-friendly' words thrown in get ample column space in feature supplements. 'Organic' is the other pet word of these green writers. This is the age of eco-consciousness. And feature pages reflect this in their own style. Here is a sample of stories with some interesting headlines that appeared in the *Hindu Metro Plus* between 3 and 9 August 2017: 'Herbs in your bed', a story that talks about bed linen made with organic cotton and natural dyes consisting of 'medicinal herbs' (Rao, 2017); another, 'Dude, where's the soil?', was about a couple cultivating exotic vegetables through hydroponic farming with the aim of making 'nutritious food', free of chemicals and pesticides, available to everyone', with the writer chipping in with 'their loyal clientele vouch for it being free of pesticides and harmful chemicals' (Borah, 2017); and there was 'Vegan vanity fair' on vegan fashion (Shah, 2017); and 'Hit the reset button' on how mainstream fashion is adopting eco-friendly and ethical ways (Adlakha, 2017).

These trends may pass, but issues concerning the environment and ecology will continue to dominate the discourse in the media in the years to come.

References

Adlakha, Nidhi. (2017, 12 August). Hit the reset button. Waterproof corsets and deconstructed shirts from recycled cotton will be part of restart fashion at Lakme's Fashion Week's Sustainable Day. *The Hindu Metroplus Weekend*, p. 10.

Ali, Salim. (2008). Stopping by the woods on a Sunday morning. In Abdul Jamil Urfi (Ed.), *Birds of India: A literary anthology* (pp. 246–247). USA: Oxford University Press.

Borah, Prabalika M. (2017, 17 August). Dude, where's the soil? Using hydroponics, a farm is growing improved varieties of salad leaves, veggies, berries and flowers. *The Hindu Metroplus*, p. 4.

Gadgil, Madhav, & Guha, Ramachandra. (1995). Ideologies of environmentalism. In *Ecology and equity: The use and abuse of nature in contemporary India* (p. 100). London: Routledge.

Jayaraman, Nityanandan, & Krishna, T.M. (2017, 27 July). Time to change course: Chennai city will have no future if plans to fill the Ennore creek go ahead. *The Hindu*, p. 10.

Johnson, T.A. (2018, 23 January). Growth gone rogue: Why Bengaluru's Bellandur lake keeps catching fire, *The Indian Express*. http://indianexpress.com/article/explained/bellandur-lake-pollution-growth-gone-rogue-why-bengaluru-lake-keeps-catching-fire-5035220/

Joshi, Sopan. (2001, 28 February). Children of endosulfan. Several unusual diseases afflict Kerala village. Residents blame aerial spraying of the pesticide endosulfan by the Plantation Corporation of Kerala. *Down to Earth*, online edition.

Mukherjee, Suroopa. (2002). *Bhopal gas tragedy: The worst industrial disaster in human history—A book for young people*. Chennai: Tulika Books.

Rajagopal, Krishnadas. (2017, 11 January). Effects of endosulfan devastating: SC. *The Hindu*, Chennai, p. 8.

Rajasekharan, Ilangovan. (2015, 24 July). Mother of all loot. *Frontline*.

Ramachandran, R. (2011, 3 June). Lethal mix. *Frontline*, p. 16.

Rao, Subha J. (2017, 19 August). Herbs in your bed. Introducing the country's go-to brands for non-toxic bed linen infused with essential oils and flowers. *The Hindu Metroplus Weekend*, p. 7.

Roy, Arundhati. (2000, 8 February). Cost of living. *Frontline*, pp. 65–66.

Shah, Gayathri Rangachari. (2017, 19 August). Vegan vanity fair. Take your luxury accessories with you on the road to eco-consciousness. *The Hindu Metroplus Weekend*, p. 5.

The Hindu. (2015, 20 February). Endosulfan—the spray of death. *The Hindu*, online edition.

23

Smart Initiatives: Smart Cities

Yogesh Patil, Sneha Kumari and Gahana Gopal

On critical issues pertaining to the urban environment with special emphasis on smart cities.

In the past several decades, issues such as global warming, climate change, melting of polar icecaps, aridity, greenhouse effect, acid rain, extinction of plant and animal species, and developments such as damage and destruction caused by floods, hurricanes, tornadoes and tsunamis have constituted recurrent themes in environmental writing.

Media have a crucial role to play in making people aware of the environmental problems and the impact they have on every aspect of life. The main role of the media is to disseminate the right information to the masses. However, it has been documented that awareness creation on key environmental issues is not comprehensively recognised by all media institutions. Thus, the increasing trend of combating environmental deterioration is not properly supported by adequate information dissemination. There is a need to assess the role of the media to bring about a positive change in the attitude of the public and problems encountered in relation to coverage and accessibility to communities.

This chapter examines critical issues of urban environment, with special focus on smart cities vis-à-vis municipal solid waste (MSW) in the light of the Narendra Modi government's commendable initiative to develop smart cities in the country. As this issue will become increasingly important in the coming months, the chapter is expected to sensitise and enlighten the media so that they can improve their coverage on issues concerning the urban environment and contribute to spreading awareness among the people and policymakers in order to make planet earth a better place to live in.

Conceptualisation of Smart Cities

Smart cities are about providing high quality of life for the inhabitants along with various user innovations for experimenting as well as validating future services. Sustainable and efficient cities also demand smart energy management, smart environment and climate, smart waste management and water management practices, which are the pressing issues of the current times. Development in these areas will not only help improve the overall economy but also ensure sustainable environment which will, in turn, promote the quality of life.

The concept of smart city was evolved in the early 1990s to signify the role of the Internet, technology and innovation, and media and communication towards reducing greenhouse gas emissions and improving the energy efficiency of urban areas, optimisation of water usage, and infrastructure for education, innovation and quality of services (Schaffers et al., 2011).

In the twentieth century, it was observed that degradation of the environment was strongly associated with urbanisation and industrial development. The heart of the problem lies in an unbalanced growth in urban settings, industries and energy use, which have given rise to increase in MSW generation (Grodzinska-Jurczak, Tarabuła & Read, 2003).

Over a period of time, in most cities in India, inefficient management of MSW has had a deleterious effect on human health, and the ecology and environment. Therefore, addressing the issue of MSW management holds the key to development of smart cities. In general, the vision of smart city is confined to 'technical excellence', which will ultimately lead to digital economy.

Smart Cities and Waste Management

Lack of clarity in concept misleads any process. In the case of smart cities, the cities will be smart only when smart energy management, waste management, and protection/conservation of natural resources and their utilisation in the urban environment are done properly and efficiently. Though due consideration has been given to this aspect in the smart city project, it does not seem to be effective.

Ecological and green city mechanisms should be provided alongside technologies. Multiple utilisation of plastics, which inversely attack the environment, should be prohibited. People's participation will play a crucial role in this. The authorities should help people understand the main concept of smart city and involve them in the process of achieving sustainable urban environment (Grodzińska-Jurczak et al., 2003).

A city with high technological efficiency and improper waste management and energy utilisation will never lead to a smart recognition. Mandatory acts need to be enforced properly to involve all housing societies, industries and institutes in waste management. Industries should focus on treating the waste and should be prevented from dumping effluents and waste on open dumping sites outside their premises.

Local government bodies have limitations in providing waste management facilities in societies in view of problems caused by the techniques and attitudes of the people. This situation can be changed through the involvement and cooperation of both the parties. New innovative spaces should be provided in the cities for encouraging young talents for developing new techniques and processes/systems to make our cities more safe and environment friendly. Closer interactions with citizens can provide mutually acceptable solutions for the projects. Participation of people in interactions and meetings will help them put forward their own ideas which will, in turn, help decision-makers.

Smart city is basically the taxonomy of several domains such as natural resources, energy, transport, living government, economy, technology and the Internet. Its main aim is to improve economic, social and environmental sustainability.

Information and Communication Technology (ICT) has helped use a mixture of right data of right policies to make morning traffic run smoothly. Researchers have identified six smart city domains: transportation and mobility, natural resource and energy, government, buildings, way of living and economy, and people. According to researches, transportation and mobility, and natural resources and energy are the two top priorities for development of a smart city. Inherently, the energy component includes the waste management aspect as well.

It can be seen from Figure 23.1 that a smart city is composed of three important dimensions—technology, institution and people—which are surrounded by waste management at every step (Nam & Pardo, 2011). As a result of rapid industrialisation, population growth and urbanisation, the management of MSW in India has slackened off. As the volume

Figure 23.1
Dimensions of a smart city

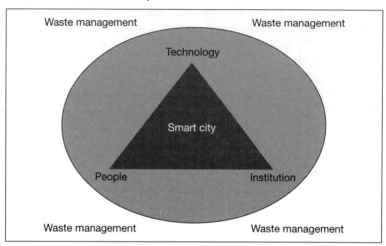

Source: Author.

of MSW generation in India has reached its peak, its management has become a major social problem for living in a smart city. With rapid change in the living standard of humans, waste accumulation and management has become unmanageable, leading to transmission of diseases.

Indisputably, solid waste management has become an issue of major concern for developing a smart city. It is known to be an important contributor to many environmental problems such as climate change (i.e., from emissions of greenhouse gases from landfills) to stratospheric ozone depletion (from emissions of halocarbons in discarded cooling systems or in-use foams), human health damages (from exposure to chemicals and particles during waste collection and treatment), ecosystem damages (from emissions of heavy metals to air, soil and surface water) and resource depletion (due to currently inexistent or inefficient recycling systems for certain key minerals or metals). The management of these wastes is essential for making a smart city (Gasc, 2016). Let us understand, in a nutshell, the various dimensions of smart cities.

Technology

Technology is getting invented and innovated at every step. It includes smart technology, mobile technology, virtual technology and digital network, which has made the life of common man much easier. Technology fulfils some of our basic needs for day-to-day life, and so sustaining life without technology is becoming more and more difficult (Yigitcanlar, 2009).

Institutional

Today, institutions have an important role to play in the development of smart cities. The government has designed several policies, rules and regulations to ensure clean surroundings. This will perhaps help reduce diseases and illnesses, by providing clean and fresh air. Prime Minister Modi has launched the Swachh Bharat Abhiyan to make India a better place to live in. In this context, the municipal corporations and urban local bodies (government bodies) are making every effort to address the issue of cleanliness across the country. The Swachh Bharat Abhiyan has guided them to look into the number of households in a city, the number of slum areas, the number of toilet constructions, the number of chronic spots for waste disposal, user fees for waste pickers and also the management of wastes in a particular sector.

Human

The smart city project is incomplete without people's participation as in the case of Environmental Impact Assessment (EIA) of infrastructure projects. Human and social capital are key aspects to be taken into account for building a smart city (Webler et al., 1995).

Cities

Cities are engines of economic growth, education, employment and innovation. Thus, they attract people from rural areas who migrate to seek better opportunities. In the next two to three decades, nearly 80 per cent of the rural people are expected to migrate to cities. This will lead to an imbalance in the socio-economic conditions and sustainability. Problems faced by cities include pollution, traffic, unhygienic conditions and an unequal standard of living. This led to the starting of a new project called the Smart City Mission to provide future viability, prosperity and socio-economic growth (Batty et al., 2012).

The conceptualisation of a smart city varies from city to city, state to state and country to country. The development of smart cities matching European standards is a difficult task. But we can, certainly, raise the bar of a smart city through a concerted approach and societal cooperation. Smart city is not confined to providing Wi-Fi and other technological facilities. People of developing India would like to enjoy all facilities such as a well-defined infrastructure, Wi-Fi network, transportation, and safety and security to all citizens. But many people would also like to have a sustainable environment with proper sanitation, waste management, controlled pollution and, consequently, a healthy and educated society.

The Smart City Mission is bound to face environmental and socio-economic challenges. 'Smart' in the nomenclature of the Smart City Mission does not mean smart technological steps, but smart routes for development as well as smart steps for maintaining sustainability. Each movement will include environment friendly aspects as its backbone. Environmental aspect simplistically implies that the waste generated from one output should be utilised as an input for another generation of the product. Researches have pointed out that environment sustainability is at the heart of the development of a smart city.

Role of Symbiosis International University

As economies develop and grow, so does consumerism. The major fallout of consumerism can be the inefficient ways of managing waste generated before, during and after consumption. Emerging markets like India can learn from the mistakes of other nations that have already reached critical limits of environmental degradation and check them at the right time.

Significantly, Symbiosis International University (SIU), Pune, has established the Symbiosis Centre for Waste Management and Sustainability (SCWMS) in Pune. The new centre aims to be a pioneer in building knowledge, disseminating awareness and improving practices in sustainable waste management.

The objectives of the SCWMS are (a) to develop cutting-edge, need-based strategies and technologies in waste management for societal benefit; (b) to recover economically (valuable) important resources (like energy) from waste for the benefit of society; (c) to undertake quality academic and market need-based research in waste management areas; (d) to impart education and training for practitioners in waste management and environmental protection industries; (e) to provide need-based consultancy services to government, non-government and industry/corporate sector; and (f) to facilitate cooperation between members and professional bodies, industry, regulators and the environmental research community.

The SCWMS has started operating and maintaining the existing biogas plants and sewage treatment plants across various SIU campuses. The efficiency of these plants has improved considerably by resolving several technical problems. In addition, the SCWMS is creating awareness on waste management among students, faculty and staff of SIU.

Further, the SCWMS has joined hands with the Pune Municipal Corporation in its Smart City Mission with a special focus on the management of MSW in Pune city. In this regard, the SCWMS undertook the following projects: environmental impact analysis of the Pune Municipal Corporation's biogas plants; awareness and training of solid waste management among the MSW personnel; and high-end validation survey of 76 *prabhags* (areas) of Pune city with respect to sanitation and waste management. For this project, apart from the SCWMS, two other institutions are involved: the Gokhale Institute of Politics and Economics (GIPE) and the Centre for Environmental Education (CEE), both situated in Pune.

The Symbiosis Institute of Operations Management (SIOM), Nashik, on behalf of the SCWMS, has prepared the development plan report for the mobile biodigester toilet projects for the Kumbh Mela. This project was funded by the Defence R&D Establishment, Government of India, Gwalior. Another project, called 'Project Shuddi', in human biowaste management was carried out under a collaborative network involving three organisations: Reckitt Benckiser Indian Pvt. Ltd, New Delhi; Charities Aids Foundation, New Delhi; and Indian Infoline, Thane.

Towards a Sustainable Smart City

Communication through media is a successful intermediate between a source and receiver. Along with development and modernisation, people's priorities have changed. Innovative works carried out by different segments of society should be disseminated through the media so that people will be familiar with the functions.

The Ganga Action Plan (GAP) project in Varanasi, a commendable initiative, had a flying start only because of media support. The role of mass communication in creating awareness and spreading information on sustainability initiatives in cities can seldom be over-emphasised. Indeed, it will help others to follow and promote similar techniques.

In India, millions of tonnes of MSW are generated every day. Approximately 1 tonne of MSW emanates annually from each household with five members. In a developing country like India, MSW contains

40–60 per cent of organic fraction, which is relatively rich in plastic. This has led to efficient management of municipal waste.

Recently, the media played a crucial role in highlighting the health hazards from the dumping of wastes in New Delhi. The media have helped people realise the threat posed by waste to smart cities. This has led to offices and households segregating wastes into dry and wet wastes. Dry wastes are sent for recycling or reuse, whereas wet wastes comprising kitchen wastes are used for making fertilizer, compost and biogas. Through the media, people have responded to the problems of MSW management for developing a smart city. The media have created a better understanding of the need for an efficient waste management system for the smart city project. All media channels should telecast smart city programmes on a daily or weekly basis, and there should be an exclusive section for telecasting smart city projects.

The media can access news and information relating to smart energy, smart technology and smart city easily and can connect several construction companies to develop a Make in India concept.

Newspapers and magazines do cover issues concerning adequate water supply, assured electric supply, public transport, housing, sustainable environment, safety, sanitation, health, education, IT connectivity, governance and solid waste management, which are the key parameters for the development of a smart city. Advertisers are encouraged to promote the Smart City Mission at exhibitions. Indeed, these advertisements have been useful in popularising the concept. Radio, television and social media sites have also helped promote the mission.

There is a project called Broadcast Asia whose main focus is to provide solutions to problems relating to survival in a smart city. Several regional, national and international conferences are also being organised to promote the smart city concept. These conferences have bridged the gap between conceptualisation and people's perception about the smart city.

Social media sites go a step further. They have the capacity to capture the mood of the audience and take powerful actions to develop a smart city. This, in turn, will help engage new concepts such as collaboration, communication and innovation.

Millions of people are connected through Facebook, LinkedIn and Twitter, which has made social media analytics easy. People get to know about developments on smart city through a chain of networks.

Interestingly, the nineteenth century is regarded as the century of empire, the twentieth century as the century of nation-states and the twenty-first century as the century of cities. A smart city is the self-computing of technology in an efficient manner for tackling problems such as scarcity of resources, inadequate infrastructure, energy shortage, price instability, droughts, floods, forest fires, health care, education, transportation and waste management.

Figure 23.2, a blueprint of a smart city, clearly depicts a smart city as a sustainable place. A smart city is not only composed of technology such as Wi-Fi and radio-frequency identification (RFID) but also public safety, education, transportation, fire house, media and communication, and waste management (Washburn et al., 2009). The concept of biogas is an efficient measure to reduce waste and utilise vegetable and agricultural wastes as a source of biogas. The pipe of this biogas plant has been connected to houses and commercial estates and is used for the purpose of cooking as well as for electricity (Abushammala et al., 2016). This whole concept can be called smart thinking. A city is not fit for living if its wastes are not managed properly. This concept of smart city can only reach builders and common people through media and communication. Therefore, the media have a very important role in building a smart city. Social media, as one of the fastest growing marketing platforms, has spread the concept of a clean and smart city (Alcatel-Lucent Market and Consumer Insight Team, 2013).

The authors firmly believe that the issue of waste management is getting neglected in the overall smart city concept. No city can become smart, clean, green or sustainable unless its waste management aspects are handled meticulously.

In Indian cities, currently, there are numerous issues relating to waste management which include segregation of wet and dry wastes, improper

Figure 23.2
Blueprint of a smart city

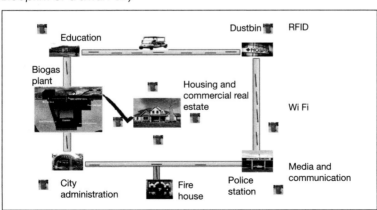

Source: Author.

disposal of waste on the road side, overflow of dustbins, capacity of collection vehicles, transfer and transport of garbage, treatment, nuisance in terms of smell/odour, disease and leaching, and lack of awareness among masses.

Role of the Media

Clearly, there are several issues of solid waste management in the urban settings in India which need to be addressed on a priority basis. The role of the media in this regard has become all the more important. Unfortunately, the media in India are not mature enough to assess issues on environment properly and scientifically. They seem to have a superficial knowledge on environmental issues. Media professionals, unless having a science and research background, do not seem to be aware of the legislative, economic and scientific aspects of the environment, because of which they are unable to create a positive impact among the masses to bring about necessary corrective actions. There is hardly any newspaper or television channel that covers environment regularly.

The media cover development issues only when there is a major ecological or environmental disaster or when there is an important judgement by the Supreme Court or High Courts against violation of environment or pollution laws.

The authors firmly believe that the Government of India will have to intervene to sensitise the media on issues of urban environment. This is an onerous task which cannot be left to non-governmental or similar organisations. The Government of India should organise orientation programmes for media professionals in universities and research institutions from time to time to educate them on diverse and critical issues of the environment. The University Grants Commission (UGC), the All India Council for Technical Education (AICTE) and the Council of Scientific and Industrial Research (CSIR) should grant fellowships for journalists interested in specialising in environment. Those selected for the fellowship could be attached to universities such as SIU so that they could do some realistic and meaningful research on the environment.

Not long ago, there was an impression that the establishment of a smart city would lead to the destruction of thousands of trees, contributing to climate change. These arguments are no longer valid. On the contrary, a smart city can be a boon for the world with the involvement of the environment and the media (Caragliu, Del Bo & Nijkamp, 2011).

The authors have designed the blueprint of a smart city, which must include all the best possible facilities and, more important, be able to manage wastes. If the government resorts to felling of trees to develop a smart city, it should undertake massive afforestation to compensate for the loss of forest cover and promote environmental sustainability. The true concept of a smart city can be evolved if society is well aware of its purpose and goals. This would be possible if the media get involved in the gigantic exercise.

References

Abushammala, M.F., Qazi, W.A., Azam, M.H., Mehmood, U.A., Al-Mufragi, G.A., & Alrawahi, N.A. (2016, March). *Generation of electricity from biogas in Oman.* Paper presented at the 3rd MEC International Conference on Big Data and Smart City (ICBDSC), 1–3.

Alcatel-Lucent Market and Consumer Insight team. (2013). Getting smart about smart cities understanding the market opportunity in the cities of tomorrow. Retrieved from http://www.tmcnet.com/tmc/whitepapers/documents/whitepapers/2013/6764-getting-smart-smart-cities-marketanalysis.pdf

Batty, M., Axhausen, K.W., Giannotti, F., Pozdnoukhov, A., Bazzani, A., Wachowicz, M., & Portugali, Y. (2012). Smart cities of the future. *The European Physical Journal Special Topics, 214*(1), 481–518.

Caragliu, A., Del Bo, C., & Nijkamp, P. (2011). Smart cities in Europe. *Journal of Urban Technology, 18*(2), 65–82.

Gasc, M. (2016, January). *What makes a city smart? Lessons from Barcelona.* Paper presented at the 49th Hawaii International Conference on System Sciences (HICSS), 2983–2989.

Grodzinska-Jurczak, M., Tarabuła, M., & Read, A.D. (2003). Increasing participation in rational municipal waste management—a case study analysis in Jaslo City (Poland). *Resources, Conservation and Recycling, 38*(1), 67–88.

Nam, T., & Pardo, T. A. (2011, June). Conceptualizing smart city with dimensions of technology, people, and institutions. In *Proceedings of the 12th Annual International Digital Government Research Conference: Digital Government Innovation in Challenging Times* (pp. 282–291). New York: ACM.

Schaffers, H., Komninos, N., Pallot, M., Trousse, B., Nilsson, M., & Oliveira, A. (2011, May). Smart cities and the future internet: Towards cooperation frameworks for open innovation. In J. Domingue et al. (Eds.), *The future Internet assembly* (pp. 431–446). Heidelberg: Springer Berlin.

Washburn, D., Sindhu, U., Balaouras, S., Dines, R.A., Hayes, N., & Nelson, L.E. (2009). Helping CIOs understand 'smart city' initiatives. *Growth, 17*(2).

Webler, T., Kastenholz, H., & Renn, O. (1995). Public participation in impact assessment: A social learning perspective. *Environmental Impact Assessment Review, 15*(5), 443–463.

Yigitcanlar, T. (2009). Planning for smart urban ecosystems: Information technology applications for capacity building in environmental decision making. *Theoretical and Empirical Researches in Urban Management, 4*(3), 5–21.

SECTION V

Reporting and Editing

24

Keeping It Simple: Techniques of Editing

Vinaya Hegde

Copy Editors come across a minefield of mistakes when subbing copy, but turning a badly written copy into a cogent report can be satisfying.

Provided you do not mind the relative anonymity of it—given that the Copy Editor does not get credit in print alongside the reporter's byline—copy-editing can be a very satisfying job. Very few things can beat the high of turning a jumbled morass of information into a cogent report that is readable and actually conveys some meaning.

The most satisfying copy—in terms of allowing you to show your competence—is what is called 'mofussil' copy (or copy which comes from district/rural correspondents). You are forced to literally sculpt a story out of a mass of information thrown in higgledy-piggledy.

Crime Reports

The most challenging copy, however, generally comes from those on the crime beat or police beat. Copy Editors will agree that crime copy is often a minefield, and you will need total concentration when you tackle it. The following examples will bear me out.

Bodies of unidentified persons being found in groves or deserted areas are not uncommon occurrences, and the desk routinely gets at least one such report every day. However, while stating that the person's identity and other details are not known, the report will declare his or her age with absolute authority. So, the report will say, for example, 'The body of a 25-year-old man was found …' as if the reporter is privy to the dead man's date of birth! The accurate way of putting it would be to say: 'The body of a man aged about 25….'

Those on the crime beat usually have a partiality for what they like to call 'police station limits'. In most reports, the emphasis in the opening sentence is more often than not on the police station limits in which the crime took place, rather than on the crime itself. Gently relegate the police station limits to a more innocuous position. Remember, the reader is more interested in knowing what happened, and in which area, first, rather than in which particular police station limits.

Shoot-outs are pretty frequent affairs. Criminals fire at a police party. And the police 'return the fire'. Almost as if they are conscientiously returning a library book that was long overdue. Remember, they 'return fire'.

Drunken driving being common, frequently pedestrians die when they 'come under the wheels' of a car or bus or lorry. This is translation, verbatim, from Hindi or one of the other Indian languages. The phrase 'knocked down' or 'run over' (by a car or lorry) should be preferred.

Names, especially longish ones, seem to feature in most crime reports only to test the alertness of the desk. Assume the protagonist of the story is called 'John Jani Janardhan'. The opening para will introduce him as Janardhan, and as the story meanders, he will be referred to variously as John or John Jani or John Jani Janardhan or Jani Janardhan or John Janardhan or J.J. Janardhan or John J.J.—as many permutations and combinations as are humanly possible. If he has an alias, it gets merrier. The alias or pet name also pops up once in a while, perhaps for variety. The caption (in case a photo goes with the story), has an entirely different variation, referring to him may be as Johnn Jaanni Janaardhan or even Johannan Janardhanann. If there is more than one person involved, and the dramatis personae share the same surname, God help you!

Even simple names like 'Rajiv' metamorphose to 'Rajeev' or 'Rajiva' in subsequent paras and then miraculously regain their original spelling by the time you reach the last para.

Always stick to *one* spelling. Make sure that names are spelt the same way *everywhere*: in the brief on Page 1, in the main story in an inside page, in the box within the main story and in the caption which goes with a related picture. And make sure that the same spelling is used when there is a follow-up story the next day. Remember, this rule is not only for crime reports. Consistency is important everywhere.

Punctuation

Punctuation matters. A lot. A report in the *Times of India* (2012a) on a burglar raping a Spanish woman has this sentence: 'The thief shinned up a drain pipe and entered the third floor flat where she has been residing for four months through an open window.' If it weren't so tragic, you'd laugh. For, the sentence implies that 'she has been residing for four months through an open window'. A comma after 'months' would have conveyed the intended meaning—that the 'thief entered ... through an open window'.

The hyphen is one of the most taken-for-granted punctuation marks, used and dropped at random. Reports speak of 'pro and anti-FDI lobbies'. The correct usage is 'pro- and anti-FDI lobbies' (with a space immediately after the hyphen which follows 'pro'). Similarly, a diet rich in fruits and vegetables is a 'fruit- and vegetable-rich diet' (with a space after the hyphen which follows 'fruit').

Style Sheet

Spare some time to study the style sheet of the publication you work for. Is it 'Mr KS Anand' or 'Mr K S Anand' or 'Mr.K.S. Anand' or 'Mr. K. S. Anand' (with spaces in between)? Is it 'geo-political' or 'geopolitical'? 'Cooperation' or 'co-operation'? Is it 'State' or just 'state' (as in 'the S/state of Maharashtra')? Is it ₹1,005 or ₹ 1,005, or $1,005 or $ 1,005, (with a space between $ and the number) or $1,005 m or $ 1,005 m? Familiarise yourself with the style sheet and stick to it. At the risk of sounding like a parrot, I repeat, consistency matters.

Captions

Giving captions is an art. Coaxing information out of photographers is an art. Make it a point to properly identify the person in the photo, even if he or she is a universally recognised face like, say, Barack Obama. If you get a picture of a top cop handing over charge to his successor, do *not* assume that the reader will figure out who is who, and give a casual caption saying, 'DIG Xxx handing over charge to his successor Yyy.' Identify the two properly—whether Xxx is the person on the left or if Yyy is the person on the right. Second, if there are only two persons in a caption, and you have identified one of them as, perhaps, 'Mr X (left)', then do not emphasise that Mr Y is on the right. When there are just two of them in the frame and if you have said that X is on the left, logic says that Y must be on the right. If there is a line-up of people in a photo, it suffices to say 'from left' or 'from right' while identifying them. 'From left to right' (or vice versa) is redundant.

It is not difficult to spot captions given carelessly, in any edition of most newspapers. Look at this example from the City Express supplement of the *New Indian Express* (2012). The caption under an ink sketch by a schoolboy in this Children's Day special reads: 'Studying in 9th standard, HAL Public School, Aditya Varma started sketching when he was in the third standard. Here is an ink sketch of little Krishna stealing butter.'

Let us see what is wrong with it: (a) There is no consistency: it is '9th standard' but 'third standard'; (b) There is no mention that it is Aditya who has drawn the sketch. 'Here is an ink sketch of little Krishna stealing butter' does not necessarily mean that Aditya drew it. (c) There is no period at the end of the sentence. All this screams *carelessness* in capital letters. A crisp, simple way of putting it would have been: 'Aditya Varma, a Class 9 student of HAL Public School, started sketching when he was in Class 3. Here is his ink sketch of little Krishna stealing butter.'

Editing Features

While 'subbing' features, ensure that the voice of the writer/author is not drowned out. Of course, some stories will need to be rewritten drastically, but try as far as possible to retain the voice of the author.

Let the voice of the character speak, especially if he/she is being quoted, or if the story is written in first person. If it is a lay person or a child who is speaking and the quote has been translated from the local language, use appropriate words. Consider this story from the City Express supplement of the *New Indian Express* (2012), a first-person account (as told to the reporter) of a young girl, a Class VII student, who lives in a slum. Sample the language of the report:

> I *realise that I am extremely lucky to be able to go to school.…* I want to live in a 'proper house' and not the tin shed I *today call home, which is only an extenuative for a slum.…* Surrounded by dirt, filth and sewage water, I can't wait to grow up and get out.… My father, X Lewis is the president of Dr. B.R. Ambedkar Youth Social Welfare Association, who has been fighting for the rights of the *EWS quarters' residents for more than a decade* (emphasis mine).

This certainly is *not* the voice of the young girl. It is the patronising voice of the reporter that you hear. Some small changes would make a world of difference and allow the girl's voice to come through:

> I know I am very lucky that I am able to go to school.... I want to live in a proper house and not in the tin shed where we live now. I want to live in a clean area, not in a slum.... Our slum is surrounded by garbage and sewage water. I want to grow up fast and get out of here.... My father, X Lewis is the president of the Dr B.R. Ambedkar Youth Social Welfare Association. He has been fighting to improve our area.

A report in the *Times of India* (2012b) on the plight of garment workers in Bangalore, featured a semi-literate worker who spoke of how she had to rush to work early every morning after sending her children to school and finishing all her household chores, as being late even by a few minutes meant a pay cut. 'The first casualty is breakfast,' she was quoted as saying. Semi-literate workers do not speak like that in real life. 'On most days I don't have time to eat anything before I go to work,' is more like the way she would have said it in the vernacular.

Even if the reporter gives a 'smart' quote like the first one, feel free to alter it suitably to suit the tone and feel of the story—without, of course, changing the meaning.

Always use a simple word if one is available, and more importantly, one that the reader will understand. One of the first feature stories I edited, as a raw apprentice subeditor, was about a fruit vendor from a village in Tamil Nadu. Eager to show off my knowledge, I changed the name of the fruit he sold, to 'mud apple' wherever it appeared. (We edited laboriously on paper printouts those days. Which meant we learnt the hard way—for the News Editor could fling badly edited copy back at you with unerring aim!) The NE circled all the mud apples in the copy. 'What are these?' he asked. 'That is the English word for chikkoos, Sir,' I answered proudly. 'I know that. But do all your readers know that?' he demanded. Sadly, but wisely, I laboriously changed all the mud apples back to chikkoos and retained the rural flavour of the story which my mud apples had killed.

Headline Licence

The much-touted 'headline licence' does allow you to take liberties with headlines, but punctuation matters, even in headlines.

A story in the *Times of India* (2012c) on Indian Institute of Technology (IIT)-Madras graduates rejecting cushy job offers was headlined: '82 L/year job? Sorry not interested'

There is a vital comma missing. It is like saying: '82 L/year job? Anita not interested'. It should have been: '82 L/year job? Sorry, not interested'. The comma after 'sorry' is crucial if the correct meaning is to be conveyed.

Another example of how a comma can make that vital difference in meaning: 'Moms-to-be cut out fat' would mean pregnant women are consuming less fat. On the other hand, 'Moms-to-be, cut out fat' is advice to pregnant women to consume less fat.

Common Errors

There are some standard phrases which figure with unfailing regularity in raw copy. When an official refuses to give his reaction on a certain matter, the reporter will declare that the official 'could not be reached for comments'. When you pass comments, you make remarks, perhaps unflattering ones. The way idle boys sitting on a compound wall do. But the Foreign Secretary, or Defence Secretary, for that matter, don't pass 'comments'. At least, we hope they do not! They may perhaps refuse to comment, that is, refuse to give their reaction to the issue at hand.

'Rs 35–37 crore' is erroneously used to convey the meaning 'between ₹35 crore and ₹37 crore'. It actually means any sum between 35 rupees and 37 crore rupees. '₹35 crore to ₹37 crore' or '₹35 cr–₹37 cr' is more accurate.

The sequence of words in a sentence can change the meaning dramatically. Most newspaper reports dealing with any issue needing resolution, refer to 'concerned officials'—and not to 'officials concerned' as they should. While 'concerned officials' means officials who are worried or concerned (about the people or the issue at hand), 'officials concerned' means the officials who are in charge of, or perhaps relevant to, the department/issue at hand. For example, if there is an outbreak of gastroenteritis in an area, officials of the health department would be the 'officials concerned'—regardless of whether they really are concerned or not. However, if a pregnant woman standing in a queue to vote collapses, and the officials manning the polling booth rush her to a hospital, they would be 'concerned officials'.

Similarly, if a couple of cops have been accused of inappropriate behaviour, say, extortion, and the police chief promises action against them, you do not say that he assured 'action against the responsible policemen'. This would imply that he is going to punish dutiful cops! It should be 'policemen responsible' (for the inappropriate behaviour).

What to Do

Be fastidious and meticulous. Count, check and double-check. An eye for detail is invaluable. Pick up any edition of any newspaper any day, and more often than not, you will see a sum of ₹16 lakh or perhaps ₹16 crore in the headline becoming simply ₹16 in the second or third para or in the detailed report in an inside page. Such gaffes are easily avoided. Always do a quick count when a figure is mentioned and a break-up given.

A spellcheck helps, though a blind spellcheck certainly will not. For example, the rogue word in the following sentence can easily slip through the most stringent spellcheck: 'The official assured that action would be taken, and asked the people to bare with him.' Remember, the eye has the propensity to take certain things for granted, in the process making you see things the way you think they are, unless you are paying very careful attention. (The late Ramakrishna Hegde, one of the most popular Chief Ministers of Karnataka, would testify: his surname would appear as 'Hedge' pretty often, in almost every English newspaper in the state!).

While editing hard news reports, ensure that the language is crisp and businesslike.

Colloquialisms and words used in informal conversation are taboo. If a gang of pickpockets has been active in crowded buses and the police promise action, do not say: 'Police assured that the guys would be caught soon.' Prefer 'men' or 'culprits'. Avoid long-winding sentences, especially in the intro, like this one:

> Sacked CWG Organising Committee chief Suresh Kalmadi will face trial for allegedly abusing his office and causing loss of over Rs 90 crore to exchequer in a Games-related graft case before a Delhi court which ordered on Friday framing of cheating and conspiracy charges against him. (*Times of India*, 2012d)

Forty-six words which make the reader want to desperately come up for air. (And 46 only because the vital 'the' before 'exchequer' is missing— else, it would have been 47!) Remember, the narrow width of a newspaper column makes the sentence seem much, much longer than it actually is.

Editing is subjective to a large extent. No two Copy Editors would edit a report the same way. However, all good Editors do follow the same basic guidelines.

Make reports coherent; ensure there is no superfluous word or sentence. Pull in all the slack.

The KISS principle works well for the Desk. Keep It Simple, Silly! Use simple words. Remember, you edit not to show your erudition, but to communicate news clearly and concisely to the reader. No one wants to reach out for the dictionary while reading the newspaper.

Stick to the story, make sure you do not cut out vital info. And if vital info is missing, make it a point to badger the reporter for it. A good Editor asks questions. Ask plenty of questions. The reporting team will respect you for it, because eventually, they are the ones who will get the credit for a good story well written.

And finally, remember, news reports or stories are 'copy', not 'copies'. Copies are replicas.

References

The New Indian Express. (2012, 14 November). Their lives, their wishes, their dreams. City Express supplement of The New Indian Express, Bangalore edition, p. 1.

The Times of India. (2012a, 6 November). Guard ignored Mumbai victim's cries. The Times of India, Bangalore edition, p. 8.

———. (2012b, 3 December). Why Gauri's kid can't get a pink frock. The Times of India, Bangalore edition, p. 1.

———. (2012c, 4 December). ₹82 L/year job? Sorry not interested. The Times of India, Bangalore edition, p. 7.

———. (2012d, 22 December). Kalmadi to face CWG graft trial from Jan 10. The Times of India, Bangalore edition, p. 1.

25

Word Artist at Work: Subeditor's Role

Amar Chandel

> The art of making copy come to life is still the sole responsibility of the subeditor.

Even in the good old days, when most of the tasks in the publishing industry were done without the help of computers, the job of editing was considered a thankless one. It was jocularly said that the subeditors' job was similar to that of a janitor. What they cleaned up would be hardly noticed; what escaped their hawk eyes would be frowned upon.

Subeditors spent their lives confined to grubby newsrooms, poring over reams of copy to correct grammar, syntax and spelling errors, polish up the language, and give brilliant and imaginative headlines, which mostly their peers noticed. On the other hand, those in the reporting stream were the glamour boys. They were the ones who got to visit exotic places (well, horrible ones, too), got to meet interesting people and, above all, had the smug satisfaction of seeing their names in print.

Role of Subeditors

Although unsung and unseen, the role played by subeditors in the production of a newspaper/magazine is unmistakable. Subeditors bring order to the chaotic writing done under the tremendous pressure of daily deadlines. In fact, it is amazing how a mistake escapes the notice of a reporter but gets detected by the sub; how a shoddily written copy gets refined in the hands of a subeditor and becomes more readable. It is the sub's job to check and double-check the content to avoid factual errors and language mistakes, and make the copy accurate.

The general belief is that the role of the subeditor has somewhat diminished with the use of computers for writing, editing and typesetting. Nothing could be farther from the truth. Actually, the desk has a much more central role today in the production of a newspaper or magazine, considering that in most publications the proofreading section has been scrapped. Subeditors are the last line of defence. They provide the vital link between what is written and what is printed.

Editing copy online has its benefits and dangers. While the computer can highlight even minor errors in punctuation and spelling, it can also introduce the most horrendous ones if the subeditor is not alert while running the spellcheck or the search-and-replace option. It is a wild animal whose efficacy is determined by how dexterously its handler can manoeuvre it.

In other words, while the mechanical burden of checking spelling and grammar has been admirably borne by the computer, the art of making copy come to life is still the responsibility of the subeditor.

Structure of the News Desk

Before we go into the layered nuances of this art, we need to focus on the structure of the news desks or the editorial department. The top rung in most publications is held by the Editor-in-Chief, Executive Editor or just Editor. The next in the hierarchy could be a Managing Editor or Acquisition Editor responsible for commissioning stories. These roles may overlap in small publications but could be elaborate in large ones.

The next in line are mid-level Editors who may head various sections such as sports, commerce and technology. The person in charge of the news section is typically a News Editor. He/she is assisted by chief subeditors, senior subeditors and subeditors, working as a team in the laborious process of copy tasting, editing, revising, page-making and checking the typeset pages before they are printed.

Most of the stories, generally called copy, come either to the News Editor's or chief sub's desk. The chief subs work in rotation in three or two shifts of six to seven hours. It is under the command of the chief sub on night duty that the edition is put to bed.

The News Editor/chief sub takes a quick look at the copy, given the phenomenal flow of copy from various sources, to decide whether they are worth publishing.

Copy tasting is a skill that is developed and honed over a long period of time, keeping in mind factors such as the news story's relevance to the place of publication and the nature of the publication and its topicality. As one example, an accident occurring in Guwahati may be an important news for newspapers published from Assam but may appear only in brief in a newspaper in Gujarat, if at all.

The chief sub will pass on the selected copy to the senior subeditor or subeditors, who are also called Copy Editors in some publications. Traditionally, senior persons on duty handle important stories themselves and pass on the relatively less significant ones to junior subs.

One of the most important tasks of the desk is giving headlines to draw the reader's attention to the story. Long, clichéd or straight headlines can put off readers. Subs who are capable of giving catchy, clever and smart headlines are a valued lot. To recall, a headline given by a colleague for a story about the hardships faced by owners of apple orchards in a state simply stated:

Apple growers in a jam

Giving the essence *of the story in a few words* is an art, and it is an essential skill that a subeditor acquires over time.

Space is at a premium in almost all publications. Some portions of a story may have to be lopped off while fitting it in a page. So, the subeditor has to ensure that the copy conforms to the time-tested 'inverted pyramid' structure, which simply means that the most important facts appear in the first few paragraphs while the least important details go to the very bottom so that even if they are removed, for want of space, the story is not incomplete.

At the same time, it is necessary to ensure that there are no unanswered questions and the story is fair, balanced and objective.

The printed word has a lot of sanctity. Most of the readers take published material as gospel truth. So it has to be not only factually correct but also provable. The subeditor must avoid libel. It is always better to err on the side of caution. Missing a story is bad; printing a wild allegation is far worse.

Keeping control over all these parameters is like learning to ride a bicycle. In the initial days, when you concentrate on the handle, you are unable to focus on the pedals, and when you learn to manipulate both, you forget to apply the brakes. But by and by, all actions get synchronised, making the art of bicycle riding a joy.

Autocorrected Howlers

As mentioned earlier, proofing tools such as Spellcheck, Spelling and Grammar, and Look Up available in computing have made the work of subeditors easy. But these options are like a double-edged sword. The programme can not only detect mistakes, it can also introduce language errors. The computer gives the subs a false sense of security that it can do the job for them. The synonyms it offers for a word you may wish to replace may not always be relevant to the context. The computer will clear a word if it is grammatically right, even if it is not the appropriate usage in a particular sentence.

Equally dicey is the autocorrect option. Clicking this option will result in automatic corrections of say an Indian word to a similar-sounding English word. You may type Rama and the autocorrect will convert the word to ram in a blink. Such auto-corrected howlers have appeared in various newspapers because the subs concerned were not alert enough.

The subeditor's responsibility has increased because with the advent of computers, proofreaders are on the way out. Previously, the edited story was sent to pre-press for composing. As the compositors were prone to introduce mistakes in the copy while typing, the copy was proofread word by word and letter by letter. Now, the edited copy goes to press without any human intervention. So, it is the responsibility of the sub to ensure that the copy/pages are in perfect order.

The subs have the additional responsibility of making the pages—a task earlier handled by paste-up men and before them, imposers. So, knowledge of layout and design is an essential prerequisite for an Editor at every level. In many organisations, the printer has been re-designated as Production Editor and the layout artist as Design Editor.

Pictures and graphics have become an integral component of publications. While big organisations appoint Photo Editors and layout artists/designers to take care of the visual element, subs are generally expected to choose pictures, write photo captions and also come up with ideas for graphics.

In short, a subeditor should be a well-read person whose worldview is formed on the basis of knowledge, experience and wisdom.

A subeditor should have a passing knowledge of almost every subject under the sun and a thorough grasp of at least one subject, be it films, music, sport, environment or literature so that whenever a story on his/her area of interest comes up for editing, it is he/she who gets to make the copy more readable and free of factual errors.

26

Newsmakers at the *Statesman*: Desk's Duties

Uttam Sen

Editing a newspaper and keeping the production cycle going smoothly
hinge on a news desk's capabilities.

Editing a newspaper can be as thankless as it can be entertaining and
rewarding. Beginning with the junior-most slot on the desk[1] where
a subeditor[2] had to manually convert Fahrenheit to Celsius in the day's
weather report from the Meteorological Department to making sense of
reports sent by stringers from small towns and press handouts, there was
both pain and pleasure.

A newsroom[3] could be a hothouse of high drama and spontaneous
comedy when the stakes were high in a leading national edition (particularly before the onset of television). Consider for instance, the exasper-
ated Editor's caveat that 'Babu English' had to be rectified at all times.
The casualty in a real-life cops-and-robbers story had not 'received a
hail of bullets', vide the police press release, as if they were a 'bouquet of
roses', but had been simply 'shot'.

---

[1] Desk is the department of a newspaper that writes, edits or releases news.

[2] A subeditor is a person who checks and edits copy.

[3] Newsroom is the room in a newspaper office where stories are written and
edited.

The heat of the moment could lead to uproarious verbal transpositions. An Editor who shared his surname with a celebrity was, in effect, intimated of his own unexpected demise by an inadvertent interchange of first names by a hassled chief sub[4] calling from the desk. The Editor, an unflappable person with a quiet sense of humour, came down to share the joke with his interlocutor (and possibly inspect the latter's condition).

Journalism of the Elite

This is the unexceptional side of nostalgia stretching back more than three decades to the news desk of a foundational English language publication in the country. The origins of print journalism of the 'elite' English language variety can be traced to the endeavours of Robert Knight, a Unitarian Englishman who arrived in Bombay (now Mumbai) as a small-time merchant in 1847 and channelled a genuine concern and curiosity about the country into 'creating' the *Times of India* in Bombay and founding the *Statesman* in Calcutta (Hirschmann, 2008). Both the newspapers led the field in India (and arguably figured among the best in the world) for more than a century. The former still tops global circulation charts. One among several noteworthy facets of Knight's persona was his English middle class education and upbringing, in which the liberal ethic advocated universal humanism.

The quality of life in his childhood London neighbourhood of Lambeth had improved as a result of the new thinking of the nineteenth century. Lambeth rode the crest of reform from enfranchisement in 1832 to the lifting of mercantilist restrictions and protective tariffs. Knight himself went beyond King and country to identify so deeply with the Indian condition (for which he thought self-governance was the remedy) that he incurred the wrath of the colonial establishment. But his word was taken seriously even in Whitehall.

Enlightening the benighted became his, and his publication's, theme, though more in the image of the people themselves than as European reform. For example, he was not an advocate of Western education at the expense of the vernacular. He did not want people to lose their integrity of thought or character. Arguably, the alchemy through which the common man's travails and the objective reality of the ruler, sometimes local elite, figured in parallel set the tone for a tradition of substance.

---

[4] The chief subeditor is in charge of bringing out the edition.

It is for us to pick up the threads. Even today, journalism without a larger motif can be a non-starter. For historical reasons, newspapers, journals and so on had become the vehicles of political and social awareness in the Western idiom and Indian nationalism in the late nineteenth and early twentieth centuries (McQuail, 2000, p. 22).[5]

Wholeness of Print

Political leaders were more often than not practising journalists. Pune provides glowing illustrations. Without a substantive raison d'être, print journalism is tottering in the West, whereas it is booming in India.[6] The inescapable feature, particularly in the newly emergent middle and mercantile classes rooting for the newspaper despite the electronic media's larger-than-life presence, is the ineffable human quest for the wholeness that print provides and a priceless property that the pioneers had discerned.

---

[5] According to McQuail,

> The late 19th century bourgeois newspaper was a high point in press history and contributed much to the modern understanding of what a newspaper is or should be. The 'high-bourgeois' phase of press history, from about 1850 to the turn of the century, was the product of several events and circumstances. These included: the triumph of liberalism and the absence or ending of direct censorship or fiscal constraint; the forging of a business-professional establishment; plus many social and technological changes favouring the rise of a national or regional press of high information quality.

The *Statesman* and the *Times of India* uncannily fit the bill because of the Knight connection and the influences he embodied.

[6] The dispersal of erstwhile monopolies in which major productions alone had access to government advertisement, influence and news. Power and politics have grown more diffuse, and news caters to a relatively wider base, though still liable to the charge of elitism. The resilience of the new off-set printing presses makes the setting up of plant and machinery at diverse locations relatively easy. Countless new publications have sprouted, particularly in the vernacular. Somewhat contradictorily, giant rotary machines with more than a million copies on each run have overtaken the older apparatuses and are thriving on the support of a growing market and advertisements where economies of scale are required. Publications such as the *Times of India*, the *Hindu* and *Hindustan Times* are proving that traditional lineages are not necessarily impediments.

The news vendor's varied lot, striving for mastery of the text under any circumstance, was a fundamental regimen. The English novelist Graham Greene's recipe for successful writing was 10 years at the desk, apparently the voice of experience judging by his own stint in the *London Times* (except that it appears to have lasted half the recommended time; Green, 1999).[7]

The basics were to first get a sense of the copy, preferably jot down a headline alongside, capitalise the name of the place on the top left of the copy and insert the date before launching on the text (latter-day datelines have dispensed with the date!). The news had to be sourced to a news agency or the newspaper's own correspondent, according to house style. This could be in the form of a line below the heading for a staffer, and the name of the agency woven into the text at the end of the first paragraph.

The Workflow

The chief sub has a computer terminal today to which copies are electronically transferred from the subeditor's terminal. The latter vets the copy for language, facts and so on, with half a mind on the positioning of the story on the page, that is, its alignment with other items of the same nature, display according to its importance, the font size of the heading and so on. The word processor is a dream come true for the desk, with electronic facilities to correct, transpose sentences and even split the screen to check facts from a relevant source. The versatility of newspaper editing software available today is in theory augmenting the news desk's capabilities.

However, its full-blown adaptation in addition to the catalogue of existing duties makes the resultant agenda a big task. In the old days, these functions were executed by hand and took more time. Staffers on the local beat, including those belonging to the political bureau, could be consulted for clarifications. Political correspondents and news reporters in the national capital or the states were also sounded out. Technically, the chief sub conferred with the Editor for about 10 minutes on the final plan. But the going was smoothest when the Editor had the confidence to leave the Night Editor (as the chief sub is sometimes called) with the last word.

In-house legend had it that Oxbridge scholars began their careers as 'galley boys' and made their way to the top with a thorough understanding

---

[7] *A sort of life* is Greene's autobiographical volume.

of the newspaper's production cycle.[8] The process continues today, but with nomenclature taking a bit of a back seat. The Editor, Resident Editor or Associate Editor could be interchangeably executing the functions of the chief sub of old.

If the big picture was the chief sub's responsibility, now it is not a case where the mill cannot grind with water that is past. On a visit to the *Times of India*'s office in Mumbai a few years ago (it was selection to the *Times of India*'s trainee journalist scheme that brought me to journalism), I found its Resident Editor slotting the night's stories on the dummy.[9] The gentleman had no qualms about telling his juniors that he had cut his teeth at Statesman House. 'Some things don't change,' he had told me. Conscientious Night Editors go through all competing editions through the day, follow telecasts and develop the night's stories in their mind's eye.

The newspaper is a continuous process, and succeeding shifts of subs create files on developing stories through the day in tandem with news agencies that keep updating their inputs. Senior subs, usually the night chief's deputy and the next in line, integrate these stories for the lead and second lead, the anchor and other important stories, sequencing scattered events, sometimes rewriting bits and pieces, and consulting reporters and political correspondents;[10] they could even have to recast a running story altogether when events take an unexpected turn.

Some leading newspapers have adopted the practice of employing sleek columnists and word spinners to touch up the final Page 1, with the right turn of phrase and language to make the finished product a virtual fashion statement, often quite magnificently, demonstrating the wonders that literary skill and technology can perform together.

The night chief usually turns up about an hour before the rest, goes through the copy that are ready and fits the stories on his dummy. The much-preferred functional, modular design had stories as well as photographs etched in rectangles and squares. Unlike in a magazine, there would be a standard template with some tinkering when the need arose.

A document itemising the pertinent information about something can serve as a gauge for accurate production. The newspaper, as it was,

---

[8] The reference was probably to young men in the hot metal era who carried the molten lead in trays to the flat-topped stand on which the pages were laid out prior to printing.

[9] The dummy is a set of pages with the position of text and artwork indicated for the printer.

[10] The story between the lead stories that held the page together both in make-up and content.

provides the basic pattern and, more often than not, is still shaping the existing product. But it is also a flesh-and-blood creation that could fade away without the adrenalin of the human element and the wider perspective.

References

Green, Graham. (1999). *A sort of life*. London: Vintage.

Hirschmann, Edwin. (2008). *Robert Knight: Reforming Editor in Victorian India*. New Delhi: Oxford University Press.

McQuail, Denis. (2000). *Mass communication theory*. London: SAGE Publications.

27

Chasing the Story: Reporter's Responsibilities

Uttam Sengupta

> There is no substitute for cultivating new contacts, which alone can ensure
> a steady stream of fresh stories.

'How do you recruit reporters', asked Gour Kishore Ghosh. The well-known journalist and writer from Kolkata had arrived in the middle of the interviews we were conducting at the Patna office of the *Times of India*. His seemingly innocuous question caught me off guard.

'Why, Gour *da*', I explained innocently, 'we shortlist candidates on the basis of their academic record, then call them for a written test and hold a group discussion, followed by an interview'.

The Magsaysay award winner shook his head and asked: 'What do you achieve by holding group discussions?' I said: 'We try to form an opinion about their communication and persuasive skills; their ability to ask questions and hold the attention of others in a discussion'.

Group discussions also exposed their clarity of thought and the depth of their understanding and demonstrated how curious or nervous they were by nature. But I had no time to add the details because Gour *da* was clearly sceptical.

'What you need to do', he said, 'is to just send them out to the streets. Ask them to go wherever they want, visit whichever place they want to visit'. Let them return after four or five hours and then ask them to report

on what they have observed. You would immediately be able to make
out who had the makings of a reporter, he said with his eyes twinkling.

The News Sense

A curious mind, a questioning nature and a lively interest in everything
around him are what distinguish a good reporter from an average one.
Gour *da* had made his point.

Allow me to recall the story of a fabulous reporter and a close friend,
who unfortunately died young. Had Niraj Roy still been alive, he would
have been a star. He was then a struggling, junior reporter with *National
Herald*, a newspaper which barely existed in New Delhi. Its printing
quality was poor. The staff were ill paid and the management had lost
interest in the newspaper. In short, it was a recipe for disaster.

I was then a young professional in a small town and had come to the
national capital to attend a seminar. The organisers had put me up at the
Young Men's Christian Association (YMCA) on Jai Singh Road. I called
Niraj and invited him over for breakfast the next day. He lived alone and
so happily agreed to my suggestion. But the next day, he failed to turn
up. There were no mobile phones those days. After waiting for an hour
or so, I gave up, had my breakfast and went to the seminar.

Niraj turned up after 9 PM that evening instead of 8 AM as agreed. He
said he had boarded a bus at 7 AM, but when the bus was moving past
the All India Institute of Medical Sciences (AIIMS), he was struck by the
sight of hundreds of people cooking and eating outside the hospital.
Impulsively, he got down from the bus and began talking to the people.

They were all attendants of patients, and they had no place to stay. They
had come from faraway villages and could not afford to stay in hotels. So,
they would cook a modest meal on the pavement and sleep there at night.
Niraj was moved enough by their plight to spend several hours recording
their stories. He spoke to the doctors, met the patients and then called up
his office and persuaded his boss to send a photographer. He took down
copious notes and went back to the office to file his report.

When he told me the whole story, both of us were excited enough
to miss sleep and chat through the night. And at 5 AM we rushed to the
nearest newspaper vendor to see how the report had appeared in the
newspaper. I was a little disappointed to find that his story had spilled
over beyond a page and a half. No attempt had been made to display
it properly. A few photographs had been carelessly thrown in. The

reproduction was poor and it was clear that the report would possibly be read by only the two of us. But what a moving story it was. Niraj was also the first reporter in our generation to befriend the prostitutes on GB Road and write on their lives.

'Can you believe it', I remember him telling me, 'these girls, after a long night of servicing God knows how many clients, would actually go out to take a dip in the Yamuna, return to have a cleansing bath, worship and pray before eating and getting to sleep'.

A reporter needs to have a similar sense of wonder—I refuse to call it news sense, which is too prosaic—to succeed in the business of reporting.

Authentic Information

'Reporting' is the business of acquiring, assimilating and communicating authentic and credible information and knowledge. Efforts are required to acquire information. Information is to be collected or gathered and sifted for accuracy and relevance. They must be authentic and attributable to a source or sources. Such information or knowledge needs to be put in the right perspective. Backgrounds are necessary to understand the context, and the significance of the information needs to be explained.

Even before a reporter sets out to collect information, he needs a certain degree of clarity on why he is embarking on the task. Why is the information he seeks so important and for whom. Above all, what is it that is new and has not been said before. Clearly, it is important for the reporter to know what has been published or produced on the subject, especially in recent times, and the contemporary debate or discourse on the subject so that he does not unwittingly report what is already known and available in the public domain. Call it the 'homework' that a reporter needs to do even before he sets out to collect information, attend a press conference or report a seminar, political rally or cultural event.

This has become easier with Internet accessibility. A quick search on the subject and the people involved is helpful to prepare for the exercise. To buttress the point on why such homework is important, an example may suffice. In daily newspapers, the newsroom is generally flooded with reports on visits by Ministers or the Chief Minister to various districts or by Union Ministers to the states. Very often, the Ministers repeat what they had said earlier in the State or at the national capital or at other events in other places. It is not unusual for reporters to have missed the earlier reports. Very often, therefore, they report statements and facts that their newspapers or channels had reported earlier. Many such reports get spiked, while some go through the desk because the subeditors might have missed reading the reports or were too lazy to check.

Doing the Homework

The homework also equips the reporters with the ability to zero in on new aspects of an old story. I have always told reporters that just as poets have been writing poetry on a limited range of subjects (nature, life and death, love and suffering, and war and peace) for hundreds of years in various languages, mass media also are essentially concerned with governance and the people. Law and order, health and education, schemes and employment, crime and punishment, and expenditure and development are some of the broad areas of concern that reporters are expected to cover.

But very few reporters make an effort to do their homework. Even those who have beats to follow are no exception. And that is where the malaise lies. For example, I once quizzed a reporter who covered the municipality. She was a gutsy reporter who had specialised in reporting on financial irregularities. This essentially meant listening to the disgruntled, collecting documents and writing half-truths. But the reporter had no idea of the basics. It was fine to report on who was being favoured, but it was far more important to learn why supervision was lax, whether there were structural or human weaknesses and how they could be plugged. The reporter could not remember the annual budget for the municipality, the number of people it employed, the number of sections it had or even the number of projects it had completed. Without an understanding of such basic information, one cannot rate and assess the municipality or grasp what is right or wrong with it.

I see reporters flaunt 'documents' to prove their point on television. But documents do not impress me because they almost always tell only part of the story, not the whole. Moreover, documents can easily be forged and one must make sure he/she is not taken for a ride.

I remember a report carried by all the newspapers barring the *Times of India*, Patna, which I was editing at the time. On the face of it, it was a straightforward report. A local court had ordered the police to inquire into the complaint that a schoolteacher's wife had been raped by an official of the examination board. Newspapers had been provided with copies of the court order, a copy of the complaint petition and the medical report of a lady doctor.

I asked the report to be held back because my suspicion had been aroused by the large number of spelling mistakes in the medical report. I wonder how could a doctor make so many mistakes while spelling medical terms. There was no mobile connectivity in those days and it was already late in the evening. The doctor was not at home and most of the reporters had already left the office. We resisted the temptation of running the story without checking with the doctor first. When we contacted her the next day, the doctor was shocked and denied having examined the victim or written the medical report. She said the letter-head was not hers though it carried both her name and address.

Fewer Contacts, Fewer Stories

I often quote a former Director General of Police to highlight one of the key distortions that has crept into reporting. The police officer recalled that in pre-Independence India, officers in charge of a police station were required to maintain a diary and record all the information they gathered on the beat in their area. They would ride a bicycle and often stop by to chat with people, have tea or meals with them and exchange gossip. This way they would come back to the police station with information about disputes and discontent and brawls and scandals brewing in the area, and about petty crimes and criminals. 'But now officers move in vans and jeeps from one point to another and drive back to the police station. They have less contact with people and hence are ignorant of what is happening on the ground', he explained.

Something similar has happened with reporting. It is comfortable to rely on mobile phones and emails. The number of reporters who rely on Google for information has grown. Also, reporters now move in their own cars and this has reduced their interaction with people a great deal. They meet fewer strangers and, as a consequence, hear fewer new stories. Most of them tend to move in herds, attend the same press conferences, meet the same officials and party spokesmen, access the same documents, and share the same stories. They often travel together and cover the same election rallies at the same places. Therefore, while the number of reporters has gone up dramatically, new grounds, let alone stories, are rarely broken. There is no substitute for cultivating new contacts, which alone can ensure a steady stream of fresh stories.

Acquiring New Skills

The new reporters not only require old skills like asking the right questions to the right people at the right time, but they need to acquire new skills like making use of the Right to Information (RTI) Act to access information, using research techniques and making sense of the obscure. However, the ability to mingle with people is a quality that a reporter must never lose.

'People do not exist to give you news or information', I was told by the late Chanchal Sarkar, the then Director of the Press Institute of India. Reporters, he had painstakingly explained, needed to understand and respect people and the work they do. 'It is only when they sense that you are making an effort to understand their work, their work-related problems and their frustrations that they will develop respect for your work and needs', he had said.

Until then, we had been trained to respect nobody. There should be no holy cows; journalism should not be a respecter of anyone, we had been taught. Sarkar had clearly meant people and not people in power. One need not respect the trappings of power, but unless one understands the work and responsibilities of people in power, reporting is bound to remain superficial.

One reason why there is such an enormous gulf, not just between reporters and the general public but also between reporters and the people in power, is often the reporter's inability to honour confidentiality and remain discreet. The temptation to boast or blabber is hard to resist, but the reputation of such people precedes their physical movement, shutting doors and windows of information. In short, reporters must learn to talk less and listen and observe more.

28

The Adventure of Reporting: Reporting and Writing

Ramesh Menon

Reporters should be adept at collecting information and aim at being master storytellers without losing sight of news values.

Try searching for a reporter who is bitter about his or her job and you should not be surprised if you don't find one. Reporting is one of the most exciting careers today. Every day holds a promise as one never knows which story will emerge from the shadows. There is excitement in the air all the time for a diligent reporter who can find a story anywhere and everywhere.

Each day provides a new learning experience. No other profession can offer such a rich platter in terms of learning. On Monday, you could be covering the prevalent political culture; on Tuesday, the popularity of traditional medicine; on Wednesday, it could be about growing teenage crime; on Thursday, the growing alienation among India's neighbours; on Friday, it could be about the need for economic reforms; on Saturday, it could be about the new gadgets that are capturing the imagination of the young. At the end of the week, the reporter has a bagful of new experiences and insights.

No wonder, reporters find their lives happening all the time. The glamorous part is that they get to meet exciting people, travel widely and be present at all the hot spots in the course of newsgathering. The tough part is that they work 24×7; there are no designated working hours for a reporter, and no off day. Forty years of reporting has been a roller-coaster adventure for this writer. It was not only educative but enjoyable as well. One saw action almost every day. There was not a single boring day.

Competition for Content

Across print, television and the new media, reporting today has become one of the most challenging jobs in journalism. There is a lot of competition to provide good content. A reporter has to constantly get content that is different and exclusive, and, more than anything, present it well. Good reporting is crucial, but it is effective writing that enhances the worth of a report. Good writing can come only out of good reporting. Writing is mostly a craft, and any craft, you will agree, can be learnt.

Even veteran reporters are continually driven crazy trying to figure out how a story will affect their readers. They wonder how to focus the stor. What to add and what to leave out. What words to use to set the right tone. But at the end of the day, it is the organisation of information that will matter for the story to make an impact.

The press baron William Randolph Hearst famously observed: 'News is something somebody wants suppressed. All the rest is advertising.'

In the course of newsgathering, you will realise that people are telling you only what they want published about themselves or an issue in which they have a vested interest.

To get the real story, a reporter would have to sniff around, dig deeper and remain constantly alert. Keen observation and good listening skills are two attributes that are useful in newsgathering. It is also important for a reporter to be an extrovert. Being filled with curiosity about anything and everything helps a reporter dig out information more easily. All these call for excellent communication skills.

The Importance of Sources

No reporter can survive without sources or contacts. It is sources that help reporters get stories, build angles to them, write exclusives and investigate difficult stories. Sources are a reporter's lifeline. Information does not come looking for reporters; reporters have to go looking for it. News stories and feature ideas often emanate from sources. A reporter gains from developing and maintaining good sources. You cannot write great stories unless you have great contacts or sources. When a reporter cultivates a source, a professional relationship based on trust develops and they keep in constant touch, and in some cases even become good friends. Sources provide tips on what is happening, and the reporter follows them up.

However, all information has to be checked and counter-checked. Be always alert as you could become a victim of planted stories that vested interests float to manipulate events or further their own interests.

To understand how to write news stories effectively, let us quickly look at some news values that make a piece of information newsworthy. If you analyse various news stories in a newspaper or magazine, you will realise that almost all of them have a certain style of storytelling. You will notice that the news points come right at the beginning and the writer tells the story bit by bit, weaving all the facts together.

Conflicts Make News

Conflict punctuates all our lives. All around us, there are different types of conflict. Countries, governments, workers, communities, families and individuals are often caught in conflict. As conflict governs our lives, it makes news. It is something we want to read about. It is something we want to identify. Any conflict makes news. So, when writing the story, you must learn to weave in elements of conflict into the story. It is this tension and drama that grabs the attention of the reader.

Human interest stories have always captivated us and will continue to do so. They are in many ways the story of our lives, our society and our world. Anything that touches our heart is a great news story. Human interest stories must be written with great care and sensitivity. The writers must empathise with the characters and bring out heart-tugging emotions. Human interest writers have to have good writing skills as they cover wide-ranging issues that affect ordinary people.

For a story to be newsworthy, it needs to be timely. The bigger the scale, the bigger the story. Timeliness also provides you a news peg to hang your story on.

Whether we like it or not, celebrities drive the news agenda. The Page 3 section of most newspapers and tabloids are filled with stories of ordinary and mundane things that concern celebrities.

It is a fact of life that negative news will get more attention. Open any newspaper or magazine and you will see that bad news makes more interesting stories than good news. This is true because bad news fits most of the criteria that governs news values.

Once a story has been covered, it is likely that it will be covered again and again on the same day on television as it develops and impacts society. For example, the report on corruption in the Commonwealth Games held in India got tremendous coverage as the story began to develop and more scandals started surfacing. Then, other corruption scandals surfaced, and they too got coverage and got linked to each other as they all dealt with corruption. Reporters covering the scandal had to keep tabs on the developments, investigate independently and keep the interest in the story alive for months.

Exclusives

Newspapers and magazines give prominence to exclusives. Reporters must look out for quirky or funny stories. It could be about pigeons bred by a school that are abnormally fat as they are being fed fast food left over by the students. It could be about a leopard that has strayed into the city. Obviously, such stories have to be written well.

A good reporter keeps the news values in mind when writing a story. The greatest challenge today is to attract the readers' attention and keep them engaged. We are passing through times when the attention span of readers is decreasing. The only way to keep their attention is with good content and good writing. The content should be structured and presented in a logical way. It has to be precise and clear, and written in a simple style.

Keep your audience in mind when you write. They have to understand what you are trying to say. Use full forms and not abbreviations. Do not use jargons. Keep your sentences short.

While writing a news feature, make an impact in the very first paragraph with a keen statement. For example: 'Every two minutes, one person dies of tuberculosis in India.'

The reporter must try to explore the concept 'News you can use fully'. The news report or news feature must have tips the reader can use. For example, if you are writing on the harmful effects of pesticides, you can tell the reader that washing vegetables can be effective in removing a large amount of pesticide residue as most of it is water soluble.

Marshalling Facts

There is a general feeling among students that the main job of a reporter is to collect facts and not dwell so much on the writing of the story as it is the job of the desk to beat it into shape. That might have been the case many years ago. It is not so now. Reporters are expected to write well. They have to be good storytellers by not only marshalling facts but by putting them together in a logical fashion using effective language and writing tools.

How can a reporter do this? Once all the facts are gathered, it might be a good idea to roughly write down the points. Then, on another piece of paper, these points can be written down in a logical order. The quotes can be fitted in at the right places. A good description of the incident or the place is essential so that the readers can visualise the narrative. It is important to 'show' and not 'tell'. Let the sounds and smells come alive in your writing as they provide a sensory experience to the reader.

People are always interesting. Get them to talk in your stories. It adds credibility to the story. Sometimes, getting a character to narrate his or her story can have a magical effect on the story. Eyewitness accounts are arresting. It is critical to identify the people who are in your story. Readers want to know who they are so that they can evaluate what they are saying or doing.

Your writing gains credibility when you attribute the facts to your sources—be they authorities, experts, eyewitnesses, victims or even ordinary people. It is their views, expressions, joy or anguish that lifts your story from the ordinary to the exceptional.

Quotes help the reader understand and identify with the story. Readers feel that they are being spoken to by characters in action. Quotes reveal the emotion of the people involved and help the reporter 'show' rather than 'tell' what is going on. Quotes help to construct the personalities of the characters in the stories. The audience gets a feel of the people they are reading about. A good reporter works hard to get quotes as they are crucial to storytelling.

Gather as many quotes as you can, and then pick out the most effective ones that can carry the story forward. It is absolutely unethical to change a quote to suit the focus or the strain of your story. Do not manufacture quotes as it is unethical to do so.

Quotes go a long way in supporting your storyline. Take care to get the names and other details right. Many of us can be quite careless with spellings of names, places and things. Often we take them for granted. People can get offended if their names are spelt wrong.

Compelling Narratives

Traditional reporting is changing as modern newspapers and magazines rely heavily on feature style/writing. Narrative journalism is increasingly making an impact. A good narrative is remembered as it describes in such graphic detail and answers questions that get raised in the minds of the readers. Powerful news stories rely on compelling narratives.

Always explain the dimensions of the story by writing it in the simplest way possible so that people understand it in the right perspective. Journalists often ignore the basics. As they understand it perfectly, they assume that everyone does. That is why mainstream business stories are difficult to fathom. As journalists, we do not write for ourselves. We are paid to make difficult concepts simple for readers.

Sculpting Your Lead

While writing a news or feature story, one of the most important things to work and rework is your lead or the opening paragraph. Your first sentence has to be a clincher. Do not take it lightly, as it is the first impression you are making. More importantly, it is going to decide if your story is going to be read or not. It is worth spending time sculpting your lead. There are numerous ways of writing a lead:

- It can be a combination lead where two types are mixed together like a summary and a question.
- It can be a question you are asking.
- It can be a quotation that is striking.
- It can be a description of a place or event.
- It can be a gripping narration.
- It can be a teaser designed to deliberately confuse the reader before you unravel the story.
- It can be a bullet lead which is just one sharp sentence.
- It can be an anecdote that is remarkable.

Writing leads is an art. You can perfect it with practice. After a point in time, the lead will jump out of your mind almost immediately when you start writing. It might help to consider these points.

It is worth spending time sculpting your lead. There are numerous ways of writing a lead:

- Carefully organise and choose the right words that will make the right impact.
- Keep your lead short.

- Let nouns and verbs do the work of providing the impact. Nouns and verbs show something while adjectives and adverbs tell.
- Never go beyond the facts to grab your reader's attention. Instead, make the words serve the facts.
- Never try to exaggerate.
- Read your lead loudly.
- If it does not sound right, write it again.
- Never settle for the first lead you write.
- The more you rewrite your lead, the sharper it gets.

Writing is a process that begins with thinking and ends with tinkering. Doing it well requires dedication, hard work and a willingness to rewrite it many times.

Whether you are writing for print, broadcast or the Web, the second paragraph of your story should expand on what your lead contains. In fact, work the transitions along as you write from paragraph to paragraph as it should flow smoothly. Your story must have a beginning, which is the lead; a middle, which is the main part of the story; and a conclusion, which smoothly rounds off the story.

Art of Interviewing

Interviewing is the heart of information collection. Good news writing largely depends on the kind of interviews you have. If you have people talking about controversial issues making relevant points, you will see the story spring to life. That is why it is important you meet the right people and ask the right questions. You can easily do this if you do some background research before the interview. Prepare a set of questions. But instead of just asking questions, turn it into a conversation so that the interviewee feels comfortable and opens up. Listen carefully. Most reporters get so carried away by their personalities that they talk all the time.

If you want to interview someone on India's space programme, for example, you must know everything about the space programme. When did it start? Who were the brains behind it? What has it achieved? Where has it failed? What foreign collaborations are being worked out? What is the future of the Indian programme?

It is answers to these questions that give you material to write.

Good reporters love conducting interviews as they learn so much from it. It is one of the biggest rewards of being a reporter.

The media is changing rapidly and so are the challenges for reporters. But a good reporter will take these challenges in his stride as they only demand more passion and dedication.

Bibliography

Agarwal, U.C. (2010). *Governance and administration: An insider's view*. New Delhi: Indian Institute of Public Administration/Kanishka.

Ahuja, B.N. (2009). *Theory and practice of journalism*. New Delhi: Surjeet Publications.

Baru, Sanjaya. (2014). *The accidental Prime Minister*. New Delhi: Penguin/Viking.

Bhargava, G.S. (2005). *The Press in India: An overview*. New Delhi: National Book Trust.

Bhatt, S.C. (1993). *Broadcast journalism: Basic principles*. New Delhi: Har Anand.

Chopra, Shaili. (2014). *The big connect: Politics in the age of social media*. New Delhi: Random House India.

Christians, Clifford G, Rotzoll, Kim B, Fackler, Mark, McKee, Kathy Brittain, & Woods, Robert H. (2006). *Media ethics: Cases and moral reasoning*. Boston: Pearson.

Dale Jacquette. (2010). *Journalistic ethics: Moral responsibility in the media*. Upper Saddle River, NJ: Pearson.

Divan, Madhavi Goradia. (2013). *Facets of media law*. New Delhi: Eastern Book Company.

George, T.J.S. (1990). *Editing: A handbook for journalists*. New Delhi: Indian Institute of Mass Communication.

Gupta, Shekhar. (Ed.). (2006). *India empowered*. New Delhi: Penguin.

Hakemulder, Jan R., de Jonge, Fay A. C., & Singh, P.P. (2005). *Broadcast journalism*. New Delhi: Anmol.

Hargreaves, Ian. (2005). *Journalism: A short introduction*. United Kingdom: Oxford University Press.

Hicks, Wynford, & Holmes, Tim. (2002). *Subediting for journalists*. London: Routledge.

Jaisingh, Hari. (2005). *No, my Lord! A window on India's realpolitik*. New Delhi: Siddharth Publications.

Jeffrey, Robin. (2010). *Media and modernity*. New Delhi: Permanent Black.

Joshi, Uma. (2005). *Textbook of mass communication and media*. New Delhi: Anmol.

Kamath, M.V. (2008). *Professional journalism*. New Delhi: Vikas.

———. (2009). *The journalist's handbook*. New Delhi: Vikas.

Karlekar, Hiranmay. (1992). *In the mirror of Mandal: Social justice, caste, class and the individual*. New Delhi: Ajanta Publications.

Kohli-Khandekar, Vanita. (2013). *The Indian media business*. New Delhi: SAGE Publications.

Lewis, Jon E. (Ed.). (2003). *The mammoth book of journalism*. New York, NY: Carroll and Graf.

Loo, Eric. (Ed.). (2009). *Best practices of journalism in Asia*. Singapore: Konrad Adenauer Stiftung.

Lorenz, Alfred Lawrence, & Vivian, John. (1996). *News reporting and writing*. New Delhi: Pearson.

McKane, Anna. (2006). *Newswriting*. New Delhi: SAGE Publications.

McKenzie, Robert. (2007). *Comparing media: From around the world*. New York: Pearson.

Menon, Ramesh. (2014). *Modi demystified*. Noida: HarperCollins.

Neelamalar, M. (2010). *Media laws and ethics*. New Delhi: PHI Learning.

Padgaonkar, Latika, & Singh, Shubha. (Eds.). (2012). *Making news, breaking news, her own way*. New Delhi: Tranquebar.

Pandey, Rajesh. (2009). *Citizen journalism*. New Delhi: Adhyayan.

Parthasarathy, Rangaswamy. (2009). *Journalism in India*. New Delhi: Sterling.

———. (2010). *Basic journalism*. New Delhi: MacMillan.

Quraishi, S.Y. (2014). *An undocumented wonder: The making of the great Indian election*. New Delhi: Rainlight/Rupa.

Raman, Usha. (2010). *Writing for the media*. New Delhi: Oxford University Press.

Rai, Vinod. (2014). *Not just an accountant: The diary of the nation's conscience keeper*. New Delhi: Rupa.

Ravindranath, P.K. (2010). *Indian regional journalism*. New Delhi: Authors Press.

Roy, Prannoy. (2016). *More news is good news*. Noida: HarperCollins.

Sardesai, Rajdeep. (2014). *The election that changed India*. New Delhi: Penguin.

Saxena, Sunil. (2006). *Headline writing*. New Delhi: SAGE Publications.

Sorabjee, Soli J. (1976). *The law of press censorship in India*. Mumbai: N.M. Tripathy (Pvt.) Ltd.

———. (1977). *The emergency, censorship and the press in India, 1975–77*. London: Writers & Scholars Educational Trust.

Thakurtha, Paranjoy Guha. (2012). *Media ethics: Truth, fairness and objectivity*. New Delhi: Oxford University Press.

Vaidya, Abhay. (2017). *Who killed Osho?* Noida: Om Books International.

Varghese, B.G. (2010). *First draft: Witness to the making of modern India*. New Delhi: Tranquebar.

Vilanilam, J.V. (2003). *Growth and development of mass communication in India*. New Delhi: National Book Trust.

good number of PhD research scholars registered with SIU. He was also Member, Board of Examinations, SIU.

He had contributed articles for national and international publications, presented papers, moderated discussions and presided over national and international conferences. He was nominated to the Advisory Council, World Education Congress, 2017.

He was Member, International Organising Committee and the Board of Editors of the International Conference on Nation-Building 2017: Innovative Solutions for Sustainable Social, Economic and Political Development held in Bangkok, Thailand (28–30 May 2017). He also organised the First International Conference on Media and Communication at SIMC (6–8 October 2016).

Dr Anand was a recipient of the National Education Award (India's Best Professor Teaching Journalism and Mass Communication) for 2015 and 2016, and the Best Paper Award (Reforms and Best Practices) Honorable Mention at the Tenth International Conference on Public Administration held at the School of Political Science and Public Administration, University of Electronic Science and Technology of China, Chengdu, in October 2014. He also received New Delhi's India International Centre Award, the Olive I. Reddick (Senior) Prize and the Karpoor Chandra Kulish Award for Excellence in Print Journalism.

Jayanthi Krishnamachary, co-editor of this volume, is a senior Editor in print journalism with over three decades of experience.

An alumnus of Madras Christian College, she has an MA in English and holds a postgraduate diploma in journalism.

She started her career in journalism with a brief stint in the *Mail* in Chennai. She moved to Bengaluru in 1981 to join the *Indian Express* where she left an indelible impression as desk chief, at the mofussil desk and news desk.

She moved to the *Indian Express*, Chennai, in 1990, where she rose to the position of Deputy News Editor. In addition to her various responsibilities on news desk, she edited *Expressweek*, a weekly supplement, and the cinema and culture pages. Jayanthi joined *Frontline* in 1998, where she is presently a Senior Deputy Editor. She has attended the Neiman Foundation's Conference on narrative journalism.

She is currently pursuing her doctoral degree in English.

Contributors

Ranjona Banerji has been in the media for over 30 years. After a short stint in advertising, she moved to journalism and worked with a variety

About the Editors and Contributors

Editors

V. Eshwar Anand was a senior Editor with an academic bent of mind. He did his BA (honours with distinction) from Rayagada Autonomous College, Odisha, and MA, MPhil and PhD in political science from Berhampur University with a fellowship from the American Studies Research Centre, Hyderabad.

He held senior editorial positions in the *Indian Express*, *Deccan Herald* (both Bengaluru) and the *Tribune* (Chandigarh). Before joining the *Indian Express* in 1987 and as a research scholar, Dr Anand contributed Edit Page articles in the *Statesman* and *Hindustan Times*.

He was a specialist in public administration and constitutional law with primary focus on legislature, executive and judiciary. He also wrote on media laws, ethics and communication, integrity institutions, public policy and governance, electoral reforms and development administration. He was associated with programmes organised by top institutions such as the Supreme Court of India, the Election Commission of India, the Central Information Commission, the Second Administrative Reforms Commission and prominent NGOs such as the Association for Democratic Reforms and the National Election Watch.

He was Professor of Journalism and Media Studies at Symbiosis Institute of Media and Communication (SIMC), Symbiosis International University (SIU), Pune, where he taught editing and reporting, media laws and ethics, development journalism, democracy and political parties, integrity institutions, constitutional law and elections.

As Member, Academic Council, and Board of Studies, Faculty of Media, Communication and Design, SIU, he was closely associated with the curriculum design and development of the university's postgraduate department of journalism and mass communication. He guided a of newspapers and magazines such as the *Times of India*, *DNA*, *Mid-Day*, *Bombay* and *Gentleman*. For the past eight years, she has been a free-lance columnist for the media website MxMIndia.com, critiquing journals, websites and news channels. Currently, she is Consulting Editor, MxMIndia.com.

She also writes on politics, and social and gender issues for *Mid-Day*, the *Asian Age*, scroll.in, thewire.in, *DailyO* and various other websites and newspapers. In 1997, she co-wrote and edited *India 50: The making of a nation* with Ayaz Memon, to commemorate 50 years of India's independence.

Amar Chandel was Associate Editor and Leader Writer with over three decades of experience in the *Tribune*, Chandigarh. He held various positions in the newspaper, including as Magazine Editor of its weekly publications, *Saturday Extra* and *Spectrum*. He was also in charge of 'Middles' in the Opinion Page. He left the *Tribune* in 2011 to pursue his other interests. He is the author of *Perfect health in 20 weeks* (2010).

Raj Chengappa is a former Editor-in-Chief, the *Tribune*, Chandigarh. Before joining the *Tribune*, he was Managing Editor of *India Today* and concurrently Editor of the Indian edition of *Scientific American* and *India Today Aspire*. He has returned to *India Today* as the Group Editorial Director (Publishing). He is often a discussant in India Today Television debates.

Earlier, he pioneered *India Today*'s Top Colleges Survey, which has become a benchmark for academic excellence, apart from digitising the magazine library services and starting its Internet edition. He covered the 2008–2009 Sri Lankan Civil War, the 2003 Iraq War, the 2001 Afghanistan War and the 1999 Kargil War.

He won the Prem Bhatia Award for Political Analysis and Reporting in 1998 and the Statesman Award for Rural Reporting in 1987. Chengappa was a Nieman Fellow at Harvard University, a Henry Stimson Fellow for International Security at Washington, D.C., and a Harry Britain Fellow partly at Oxford University.

He is the author of the bestseller on India's nuclear weapons, *Weapons of peace: The secret story of India's quest to be a nuclear power* (2000).

Neerja Chowdhury is a well-known political commentator in both print and electronic media. She is a recipient of the Chameli Devi Jain Award for the Best Woman Journalist in 1981. Over the years, she has created a niche for herself in the realm of political reporting. She was the Political Editor of the *Indian Express*, the *Economic Times* and the *New Indian Express*. Her weekly column 'Power Play' in the late 1980s, in Op-Ed

Page, the *Indian Express*, was very popular among readers. It reflected her attention to detail, incisive analyses and a thorough grasp of the dynamics and functioning of various political parties.

As a Civil Rights Correspondent of the *Statesman* (1982–1987), Neerja highlighted the problems and sufferings of the marginalised, the oppressed and the underprivileged sections of society. She got the People's Union of Civil Liberties' Human Rights Award in recognition of her services to society. Later, she began writing on Indian politics. She was awarded the Prem Bhatia Award for Political Analysis and Reporting.

Currently, she is a columnist of many newspapers, including the *Times of India* and the *Economic Times*. She participates in television discussions and visits SIMC to train budding journalists on political reporting.

H.K. Dua is an eminent Editor, political commentator and parliamentarian. A former Member of Parliament (Nominated), Rajya Sabha, and currently Adviser, Observer Research Foundation, New Delhi, he actively participated in parliamentary proceedings and debates. He was Member, Standing Committee of Parliament, External Affairs; and Consultative Committee of Parliament, Home Affairs. He was Editor, *Hindustan Times* (1987–1994); Editor-in-Chief, the *Indian Express* (1994–1996) and the *Tribune* (2003–2009); and Editorial Adviser, the *Times of India* (1997–1998).

He was President, Editors Guild of India and India–Philippines Parliamentary Group. He was Member, Jury of the Jawaharlal Nehru Award for International Understanding, Parliamentary Delegation to the UN and National Security Advisory Board. Before becoming India's Ambassador to Denmark, he was Media Adviser to Prime Ministers Atal Bihari Vajpayee and H.D. Deve Gowda. He has been a member of several parliamentary committees on Personnel, Public Grievances, Law and Justice, Ethics, External Affairs, Home, Defence, Salaries and Allowances of MPs, House Committee and Health and Family Welfare.

He received many awards for his distinguished service to journalism. Some of these are the Padma Bhushan, the G.K. Reddy Award, the B.D. Goenka Award, the Durga Rattan Award, the Freedom of Information Award and the Lokmanya Bal Gangadhar Tilak Award.

Gahana Gopal C. is a Junior Research Fellow at Symbiosis Institute of Technology, SIU. She has completed her graduation in chemical engineering from St. Michael College of Engineering and Technology under Anna University, Chennai. She has done her master's in computer-aided process design (Chemical Engineering) from Government Engineering College, Calicut.

Currently, she is pursuing her PhD under the Faculty of Engineering, SIU. She has published a few research papers in the areas of biodiesel and waste management and has attended several workshops.

Shashikala Gurpur is Dean, Faculty of Law, SIU, and Director, Symbiosis Law School, Pune. She has an outstanding career with wide range of experience in teaching, research and industry. She is a former Member of the Law Commission of India.

She has 24 years of experience in postgraduate teaching and research. She has been associated with many law schools and universities in curriculum development and enrichment. Currently she is Member of the Curriculum Development Committee, Bar Council of India, and the Academic Council of National Judicial Academy, Bhopal.

Shashikala Gurpur's areas of specialisation are international law, human rights jurisprudence, legal education and legal research, innovation law, comparative law and global justice. She is on the editorial board of *LexisNexis Butterworths*; *Journal of the IPR* by CSIR; *Law and Policy Journal*, Dublin, Ireland; and *Polish Law Review*. She has authored two books, 66 articles and six book chapters. She was listed among notable Kannada authors in 1995 and 2007.

She has guided 12 PhD students.

Vinaya Hegde is a specialist in editing copy, rewriting, headline writing, caption writing, designing layout and bringing out the edition. She started her career with the *Indian Express*, Chennai, and later shifted to the same newspaper in Bengaluru. She learnt the ropes under the benign tutelage of C.P. Seshadri (fondly called 'Master' by all journos of his time), the de facto Resident Editor of the Chennai edition of the *Indian Express*.

After a decade as a full-time Copy Editor with the Chennai and Bengaluru editions of the *Indian Express* and dabbling in Web journalism with the Zee group, she opted to freelance and continues to do so.

Ruchi Jaggi is Director, SIMC. She is also Member, Academic Council, SIU. A postgraduate in mass communication from Panjab University, Chandigarh, she has been teaching undergraduate and postgraduate courses for almost a decade now. She currently teaches communication theories, culture studies and research methodology.

She is a dedicated academic, scholar and researcher. Her papers have been published in reputed research journals and books. Her research interests include media representations, popular culture analysis, gender studies, television studies and emerging discourses of identity on new media. She was recently awarded PhD for her thesis on 'Gender Portrayals on Children's Television in India' by the Department of Communication Studies, Savitribai Phule Pune University.

She has been participating in academic conferences nationally and internationally. She had recently presented her research work at the International Association of Media and Communication's annual conference at Leicester, United Kingdom, where she also chaired a session in the 'Gender and Communication' section.

Hari Jaisingh, a former Editor of the *Tribune*, has worked in key positions for some of India's leading newspapers over four decades. He is also a former Editor of Observer News Service and Resident Editor of the *Indian Express*, Ahmedabad and Mumbai, where he started a series of daily supplements such as Business Express, Science Express, Education Express, Express Sport and Express Weekend as part of the newspaper. This is considered a pioneering effort in Indian journalism.

A former Assistant Editor of the *Tribune* he has also contributed articles to the *Morning Telegraph* and the *Guardian*, London. A champion of press freedom, he is committed to public causes and human rights and is a crusader against corruption.

He has authored many books. Some of them are: *No, my Lord! A window on India's realpolitik* (2005); *Kashmir: A tale of shame* (1996); *Between dream and reality: The Indian paradox* (1992); *India after Indira: The turbulent years* (1989); and *India and the non-aligned world* (1982).

He has been associated with bodies such as the Press Council of India, the Editors Guild of India, the Namedia Foundation and the Indian National Commission for Cooperation with UNESCO. He has been a senator of various universities. He is currently Editor, *Power Politics*, New Delhi.

Kamlendra Kanwar is a senior journalist and political commentator. He was Senior Associate Editor, the *Tribune*, Chandigarh; Editor (Tamil Nadu), the *New Indian Express*, Chennai; Editor (Gujarat), the *Times of India*, Ahmedabad; and Resident Editor, the *Indian Express*, Hyderabad, Mumbai and Delhi. In the early days of his career, he served in the *New Straits Times* in Kuala Lumpur, the *Statesman* and United News of India, New Delhi.

He is the author of *Icons of Gujarat industry* and *Trailblazers of Gujarat*. He was Director, Nissa Group's 24-hour English news channel at Ahmedabad. Currently, he contributes Edit Page articles to various newspapers.

Hiranmay Karlekar is Consultant Editor of the *Pioneer*, New Delhi. A Nieman Fellow at Harvard (Class of 1967), Karlekar, in his career as a journalist spanning five-and-a-half decades, has been Editor of *Hindustan Times*, Deputy Editor of the *Indian Express* and Assistant Editor of the *Statesman* and the *Hindustan Standard*. Karlekar started his journalistic career with *Anandabazar Patrika* as a Staff Reporter in 1963. He was also Associate Editor of *Aajkaal*, Kolkata.

He has been a member of the Press Council of India, General Secretary of the Editors Guild of India; Member, Board of Directors, Press Trust of India; and the Editors Guild's nominee in the Central Press Accreditation Committee, Government of India. He was also a Member of the Animal Welfare Board of India.

Karlekar's publications include two Bengali Novels, *Bhabisyater ateet* (1994) and *Mehrunnisa* (1995), the latter based on Bangladesh's liberation war during which he played a role that brought him the 'Friends of Bangladesh Liberation War Award' in 2012. He has authored four books in English—*In the mirror of Mandal: Social justice, caste, class and the individual*; *Bangladesh: The next Afghanistan?*; *Savage humans and stray dogs: A study in aggression* and *Endgame in Afghanistan: For whom the dice rolls*.

He edited—and contributed chapters to—*Independent India: The first fifty years* (1998), an anthology of essays published to mark 50 years of India's independence.

Charu Sudan Kasturi is Assistant Editor with the *Telegraph* in New Delhi. He has earlier worked with *Hindustan Times*. He writes on international relations and politics. He closely follows the rapid evolution of the digital medium. His work has appeared across formats—on radio, television, print and online. His articles have appeared in the California-based online publication *Ozy*, in *Foreign Policy* and in New York City's popular publication, *City Limits*. He has appeared on All India Radio, Lok Sabha TV and Rajya Sabha TV for panel discussions.

He has a master's degree in journalism from Columbia University, a master's in physics from IIT Delhi and a degree in physics from St. Stephen's College, Delhi.

He has taught digital journalism at SIMC. He is the recipient of major international awards, including the Pulitzer Fellowship and the New York Foreign Press Association Award.

Sneha Kumari is a Junior Research Fellow at SIU. She has completed her graduation in agriculture with an Indian Council of Agriculture Research fellowship and her master's in agribusiness management under the Indian Council of Agriculture Research merit.

Currently, she is pursuing her PhD from SIU. She has published research papers in the areas of agriculture, sustainability, technology and climate change. She has also attended several national and international conferences.

Ramesh Menon is an author, journalist, educator, film-maker and corporate trainer. A recipient of the Ramnath Goenka Award for Excellence in Journalism, he began his career with the *Times of India* as a reporter. He was Associate Editor, *India Today*; Executive Producer, Business India Television and TV Today; Roving Editor at rediff.com; and columnist with *Daily News and Analysis*.

He is the author of *Modi demystified* (2014), *Carbon footprint: Exciting ways of reducing it for a better world* (2014), *Night sparkle*, a coffee table book on the best lighthouses of India (2013), and *Whatever the odds* (2011). He has been involved in the making of over 20 documentary films, and many of them have been shown at film festivals.

A former Managing Editor, *India Legal*, New Delhi, he is currently an adjunct professor at SIMC, Pune.

Dileep Padgaonkar, a distinguished Editor and political commentator, who was closely associated with this book project, passed away in Pune on 25 November 2016, following a cardiac arrest.

Born on 1 May 1944, he graduated in political science from Fergusson College, Pune, obtained a diploma in direction and scriptwriting from the Institute of Higher Cinematographic Studies in France and received a doctoral degree in Indian Aesthetics and Cinema from the University of Paris (Sorbonne) in June 1968.

He served as the Paris correspondent of the *Times of India*. He was its Editor from 1988 to 1994 and Consulting Editor until his demise. He joined the editorial board of a leading international news portal, the *Huffington Post*, which launched the *World Post*, an online publication with 10 editions around the world.

For eight years (1978–1986), he worked as an international civil servant in UNESCO in Bangkok and Paris. He was also Editor of the Sharjah-based daily, the *Gulf Today*. In 1994, he became Chairman of Asia-Pacific Communications Associates (APCA), a multimedia organisation active in news and current affairs on TV and in print journalism. He was the founding Editor of *Biblio: A Review of Books*. He authored a book, *Under her spell: Roberto Rossellini in India*.

Padgaonkar was a member of several bodies, including the Indo-French Forum, the Nehru Memorial Museum and Library, the South Asia Free Media Association, the Prince Claus Fund of the Netherlands, the Minorities Commission and the Observer Research Foundation. In April 2002, President Jacques Chirac awarded him the *Legion d'Honneur*, France's highest civilian distinction, for his services to journalism He also received the Dinanath Mangeshkar Award in 2016.

Padgaonkar was the Government of India's Chief Interlocutor for Jammu and Kashmir. As the R.K. Laxman Chair Professor, Faculty of Media, Communication and Design, SIU, he was associated with many initiatives aimed at honing the skills of student journalists. He was also guiding the curriculum structure and design of various courses of the Symbiosis School of Liberal Arts, Pune.

Sushobhan Patankar is Assistant Professor at SIMC, Pune. A postgraduate in Communication Studies from Savitribai Phule Pune University, he has 12 years of experience in the television industry. He had worked with IBN7 Hindi (News) as Deputy Bureau Chief, Mumbai, where he covered politics, business and sports, and at CNN-IBN as the Correspondent of the Pune Bureau. Sushobhan was a freelance news reporter with ESPN Star Sports (2002–2005), for their news shows *Sportsline* and *Sportscentre*. Earlier, he had a stint with Star Plus for a talent show.

At IBN7, he has done stories on the General and Railway Budget, the RBI credit policy and the Centre's economic policies. He has also covered the 2009 Lok Sabha and Assembly elections and produced documentaries on the power plants in the Konkan region and the Lavasa project near Pune. At SIMC, he teaches television news (basics and advanced), current affairs, newsroom management, investigative journalism and sports journalism.

In 2015, he visited Germany under a doctoral student exchange programme between the Savitribai Phule Pune University and Eberhard Karls University of Tuebingen, Germany.

Yogesh Patil is Professor and Head, Research and Publications, at Symbiosis Centre for Research and Innovation (SCRI), SIU, Pune. He is a PhD in environmental sciences from Savitribai Phule Pune University and has over 16 years of postgraduate teaching and research experience in environmental science, management and technology. His research areas of interest include waste management, bioremediation, sustainability, climate change and industrial ecology.

He has published 50 research papers in journals of national and international repute. He has published two edited books, namely, *Applied bioremediation—active and passive approaches* (Croatia) and *Reconsidering the impact of climate change on global water supply, use, and management* (IGI Global, USA). He has edited three special issues of an Elsevier journal. He has undertaken research/consultancy projects funded by UGC, Sweden's International Foundation for Science (IFS) and Organisation for the Prohibition of Chemical Weapons (which won the 2013 Nobel Peace Prize), The Netherlands, the World Bank and the Pune Municipal Corporation.

He is a recipient of fellowships from the Department of Science and Technology, Government of India, and the Council for Scientific and Industrial Research, the Best PhD Research Award and the UGC Post Doctoral Fellowship. He is a reviewer and editorial board member of several journals indexed in Scopus and SCI.

Gagan Prakash is a photojournalist. An Assistant Professor at SIMC, he teaches photojournalism, cinematography, digital photography, advanced photography, lighting and editing and visual communication to postgraduate students (journalism and audio visual). He was recently awarded the PhD degree by SIU for his thesis on journalistic ethics.

He has had stints with the *Times of India* (Mangaluru) and *Khaleej Times* (Dubai) as a photojournalist. He has produced documentaries and conducted exhibitions in photojournalism. Currently, he is working on a book on photography and film history.

S.Y. Quraishi is a former Chief Election Commissioner of India. A former member of the Indian Administrative Service (Haryana cadre, 1971 Batch), he held top positions in the Government of Haryana and Government of India. He is an alumnus of St. Stephen's College, University of Delhi. He did MA in history and PhD in social marketing.

Currently Distinguished Fellow at Ashoka University, Quraishi is known for his proactive role in electoral reforms. He played a notable role in checking paid news. He is known for many innovative strategies for voter education and participation. He also founded India International Institute for Democracy and Election Management, which has already trained election managers from 75 countries in five years.

Quraishi has been active in championing the cause of electoral reforms even after his retirement. He has authored *An undocumented wonder: The making of the great Indian election* (2014). He is also the author of *Social marketing for social change*, *Old Delhi—living traditions*, and two important research papers, 'Islam, Muslims and family planning in India' and 'Islam and AIDS'.

Uttam Sen joined the *Statesman*, Kolkata, after being selected for the *Times of India*'s trainee journalist scheme. He acquired his basic skills at the desk of the *Statesman*. He also worked briefly as Chief Subeditor at the *Economic Times*, Kolkata, following which he was Assistant Editor and Leader Writer, *Deccan Herald*, Bengaluru. He covered political crises in Nepal and Bangladesh, a disarmament conference in Geneva and the Commonwealth Heads of Government Meeting (CHOGM) at Edinburgh. He went to Rangoon (Yangon) to interview Aung San Suu Kyi. He jointly wrote a monograph on South Asia for the Mahbub-ul-Haq award at the Regional Centre for Strategic Studies in Colombo. He has made regular contributions to *Mainstream*, New Delhi.

He did his PhD on federalism from Calcutta University while working for the *Statesman*. He has visited the USA on International Visitors Programmes on Government and Regional Security. He did honours in political science from Presidency College, Kolkata, and MA in sociology from Delhi School of Economics where he was a recipient of an advanced centre fellowship. He has made presentations at the National Institute of Advanced Studies, Bengaluru, Manipal Institute of Communications, the University of Mumbai, the India International Centre, Delhi, on subjects ranging from human development and political communication to current affairs.

Uttam Sengupta is a Consulting Editor, *National Herald*. As Associate Editor of the *Tribune*, Chandigarh, he was in charge of newsroom coordination and special features for news pages.

Earlier, he was Deputy Editor in *Outlook*, New Delhi; State Editor, *Dainik Bhaskar*; Resident Editor, the *Telegraph*, Calcutta; Resident Editor, the *Times of India*, Patna, Lucknow and Calcutta; and Principal Correspondent, *India Today*, Calcutta.

Manju Singh is a social scientist, researcher and trainer. A PhD in economics, she has done research projects funded by the Indian Council of Social Science Research, the Ford Foundation, the Global Network of Government Innovators at Ash, and the Institute for Democratic Governance and Innovation at Harvard University's John F. Kennedy School of Government.

She has led various evaluation studies funded by the Planning Commission, the Government of India's Department of Science and Industrial Research and various state governments. A keen project planner, strategist and implementer of social engineering projects, she was awarded Sir Ratan Tata Fellowship in 2011–2012 to do research at Asia Research Centre, London School of Economics and Political Science.

A former Professor and Head, PhD Programme and Research Projects, Symbiosis Institute of Research and Innovation, SIU, she is currently Director, Faculty of Arts and Law, Manipal University, Jaipur, Rajasthan.

Soli Jehangir Sorabjee is a former Attorney General of India (1989–1990; and 1998–2004). A distinguished jurist and constitutional expert, he was designated as a Senior Advocate, Supreme Court of India, in 1971. He practices mainly in the field of constitutional and administrative law as also in civil and commercial law. He was a member of the National Commission to Review the Working of the Constitution. He has done pioneering work on All-India Police Reforms.

Sorabjee has appeared and argued several cases of constitutional importance in different High Courts and the Supreme Court of India, particularly important cases relating to the freedom of speech and expression, freedom of the press, independence of the judiciary and judicial review and protection of human rights. He has authored several books, notably, *The law of the press censorship in India; The Emergency, censorship and the press in India; Monographs on equality in the United States and India;* and *Protection of human rights in emergencies.* He has edited a book on *Law & justice: An anthology of legal essays.* He has been writing for newspapers and participating in television discussions on contemporary issues of constitutional importance.

Over the decades, Sorabjee has received many national and international awards. He was awarded the Padma Vibhushan, India's second highest civilian award, in 2002.

Daya Kishan Thussu is Professor of International Communication and Co-Director of India Media Centre at the University of Westminster in London. He is the author or editor of 18 books, including *International communication—continuity and change*, third edition (forthcoming); *News as entertainment: The rise of global infotainment* (SAGE, 2007) and *Communicating India's soft power: Buddha to Bollywood* (SAGE, 2016). Dr Thussu is also Managing Editor of *Global Media and Communication*, a journal published by SAGE Publications.

Abhay Vaidya has more than 30 years of experience as a journalist. He has worked as Foreign Correspondent of the *Times of India* at Washington, D.C.; Resident Editor, *Daily News and Analysis*, Pune; and Assistant Resident Editor, the *Times of India*.

For some time, he edited *The golden sparrow on Saturday*, a Pune-based weekly. He was an adjunct faculty at SIMC and worked for the R.K. Laxman Chair Initiatives.

He has recently taken over as Resident Editor, *Hindustan Times*, Pune. He is the author of the recently released book *Who killed Osho?*

Pooja Valecha is Assistant Professor at SIMC, Pune. She is an alumnus of Mudra Institute of Communications (MICA), Ahmedabad, from where she acquired her postgraduate diploma in communications management. She has a graduate degree in psychology and economics.

She started her career in media management with the *Indian Express*, Mumbai. She has eight years of industry experience in various facets of the media business—management, consulting, marketing and planning. Her last position was Associate General Manager with Vizeum Media Services (Dentsu Aegis Network), where she was acclaimed the Campaign Agency of the Year and awarded the EMVIES along with a host of other industry awards and credits.

She has worked on multiple media brands of the media and entertainment industry such as Fox Star Studios, MTV, Nickelodeon, Sonic, ETV Network, Bloomberg TV India, Only Much Louder, Tata Sky, Zee Entertainment Enterprises Ltd, Zee International, Star India Pvt. Ltd and Cable & Satellite Broadcasting Association of Asia (CASBAA). She has also worked with non-media brands such as Essar Corporate, Essar Steel, HDFC Credila Education Loans, AMW Trucks, Equinox Reality, IMS Learning Resources, D'Oleo (Figaro Olive Oils) and SREI Infrastructure Finance Pvt Ltd.

B.G. Verghese was a distinguished Editor. He started his career in journalism with the *Times of India*. He was later Editor of *Hindustan Times* (1969–1975) and the *Indian Express* (1982–1986). He was a Visiting Professor of New Delhi's Centre for Policy Research (1986–2014). He was Information Adviser to Prime Minister Indira Gandhi (1966–1969), a Gandhi Peace Foundation Fellow and Information Consultant to the Defence Minister (2001). He was a recipient of the Magsaysay Award, Assam's Sankaradeva Award and the Upendra Nath Brahma Soldier of Humanity Award. He was a Fellow of Hyderabad's Administrative Staff College of India and Chairman, Commonwealth Human Rights Initiative, New Delhi. He authored several books, namely, *Design for tomorrow*; *Waters of hope*; *Harnessing the Eastern Himalayan rivers*; *Winning the future*; *India's northeast resurgent*; *Reorienting India*; and *Rage, reconciliation and security*. His memoirs, *First draft: Witness to the making of modern India* (2010), was followed by *Post haste-quintessential India* (2014).

Index